A TASTE FOR DIVERSIONS

Sport in Georgian England

Dennis Brailsford

The Lutterworth Press
Cambridge

To Eileen

The Lutterworth Press
P. O. Box 60
Cambridge
CB1 2NT

e mail: publishing@lutterworth.com
web site: http://www.lutterworth.com

British Library Cataloguing in Publication Data:
A catalogue record is available from the British Library

ISBN 0 7188 2981 6

Printed by
Bell & Bain Ltd, Glasgow

Contents

Illustrations

Preface

This book is the product of a long-held feeling that the early creative stages of our modern sport had never been fully explored, that extensive consideration seldom went beyond the Victorian days. This suspicion was strengthened over the years by spasmodic searches for contemporary material and particularly as a result of sustained perusal of the complete volumes of the *Sporting Magazine* and *Bell's Life* in London, to both of which I was fortunate to have full and free access in the University of Birmingham Library. Although other projects intervened, the hope always remained that it would be possible to present an overview of this early modern period.

It proved a longer journey than expected, not least in reducing a mass of material to digestible proportions, yet much still remains to be explored in the period. That even this present survey was achieved owes much to many. First of all, from the University of Birmingham itself, the cooperation and friendship over many years of Charles Jenkins, and the facilities of the university library, most recently to Christine Penny, the university archivist, and the photographic unit for help with illustrations (which, incidentally, concentrate on less usual sporting scenes from the period.) I am indebted also to the City of Birmingham Library with its excellent collection of West Midlands material and, especially over the last decade, to the Dorset County Library and the Dorset County Museum. My thanks go also to Adrian Brink and a succession of his commissioning editors at the Lutterworth Press for their continuing efforts and support. Most of all though, and inevitably, I am indebted to my wife, whose patience, photographic advice, diligent proof-reading and occasional exasperation were essential for the production of the book.

Preston
Weymouth
Dorset
March 1998

Abbreviations

BLL	*Bell's Life in London*
CRO	County Record Office
SM	*Sporting Magazine*
VCH	*Victoria County History*

Introduction

It saw solid squires riding furiously to hounds, it felt and heard the colourful excitements of the race ground and took its ease in the pastoral calm of the cricket field, but there was much more to it than the provision of comfortable scenes for nostalgic prints. The debt owed by modern sport to the English eighteenth century has never been fully acknowledged, yet this was its most creative period, more formative than any that followed and to which so much attention has been paid. From the start the age was badly served when Joseph Strutt's *Sports and Pastimes of the People of England* quite under-valued the sports of his own day, informative as he was on the more distant past.[1] In turn, the first full modern study, Malcolmson's survey of popular recreation between 1700 and 1850, was wholly excellent on its own terms, but folk pursuits were acknowledged to be under pressure in those years and subsequent general histories, if they did dare venture into pre-industrial sport, could still give only modest space to the period.[2] Positive pointers did begin to appear with studies on the commercialisation of leisure and its role in what used to have the convenient shorthand title of the Industrial Revolution. A recent widening interest in the history of popular culture has opened up further new avenues for sporting consideration, with extended original studies on, for instance, poachers, inns and crowds, to name but three, but there is still no overall review of the sport of this all-important formative era.[3]

Definitions of sport are never easy and seldom stable. This age's concepts were imprecise and impermanent. The *Sporting Magazine*, for instance, in its early years in the 1790s saw everything from bat-fowling to bell ringing as within its brief and was even prepared to give sporting status to adultery in its reporting of court cases. Four decades later the same magazine was concentrating on horse racing, coursing, hunting, shooting and fishing, abetting in that appropriation of the word solely to the field sports of a gentry readership. In this present exploration a fairly eclectic view is taken,[4] embracing a whole spectrum of pursuits from traditional play to newer and more organised activities, often catering for spectators as well as for players. It is a mix of the old and the new that characterised the whole sporting experience of England at this time – and it is essentially the *English* experience and not the *British* that is the subject of this study. In contemporary statements it is invariably the 'Englishness' of sport that is being celebrated.[5]   Quite apart from the task of giving consideration to the other countries in the British Isles, there is difficulty enough in ensuring that England itself is being fully covered, so dominant is London and the south east in so much of its sporting activity. By way of counterbalance any regional emphases here tend towards the West Midlands, Wessex and the West Country.

While it might seem idiosyncratic to set chronological bounds that are identified by reigns and a royal family, nevertheless kings and princes do often have their significances in this age's sport and the period they delimit does in any event have its own integrity. The first George, for instance, while remaining Hanoverian at heart, did go to Newmarket with his racing manager, Tregonwell Frampton, and an interpreter (who needed to understand both German and broad Dorset.) George II was more inclined to sponsor musicians such as Handel than games players but his son, Frederick, Prince of Wales, no respecter of family habits and opinions and one of royalty's lost white hopes, took up cricket and tennis with enthusiasm and his death may even have been the result of an old sports injury. The younger brother, William Augustus, notorious as 'Butcher' Cumberland from his slaughter of the Scots clansmen at Culloden, crops up repeatedly but seldom creditably in the sporting annals of the day. Later still there was a new trio of young princes looking for fresh amusement – two future kings and the father of a future queen – who were to show various and fluctuating sporting enthusiasms for the whole of their lives, all of them at home on the cricket field, on the racecourse and at the prizefight.

The shape and nature of sport during this era, reflecting royal involvements to some extent but not dependent upon them, suggests the approach taken here. Up to the early 1780s sport developed in a steady and largely undramatic fashion, with just a few highlights around the mid-century, and a survey of the various styles of sporting experience of those years lays the foundations for the next phase, the period of great innovation and expansion, which lasted into the second decade of the new century. These thirty or more years of great sporting richness provide the main (but not exclusive) focus for the examination of its most significant themes – the constraints of status, time and place, the patrons, players and spectators and important structural elements, clubs, rules and arbitration. Thereafter the last twenty Georgian years appear almost as a coda, with an old order of play fading fast and a new still in its infancy, a process which shows itself variously in the individual sports.

Throughout the period the material context of games and sports was subject to rapid and accelerating change. There was growing prosperity but also growing squalor as the extremes of society were pulled further apart. Wealth accumulated but it accumulated unevenly. Land became more profitable from better farming methods and improvements in wool processing. Industrial production surged ahead, many master craftsmen flourished, helping to give a new and firmer identity to a growing middle class, and a new body of major manufacturers emerged, soon to be hardly distinguishable from those wealthy by inheritance. The social consequences of such far-reaching change and rapid urban growth produced forbidding problems of overcrowding, dirt, disease and disorder, problems which were only beginning to be challenged to any effect as the period closed.

For the first three-quarters of the eighteenth century the national mood embraced both fear and complacency – a sense of satisfaction at the apparent success of the Glorious Revolution in securing what seemed to be an equitable balance of political and judicial powers and a fear that this might be upset by Stuart pretenders, bent on dictatorship and Catholicism. Sportsmen could argue that its almost reverential respect for institutions and practices inherited from the past was a potential protection of any surviving traditional play,[6] while Tory squires, frozen out of national government during the long years of Whig administrations, could prove to be allies of country play, disposed to reinforce their local standing by support and patronage of sports and even sometimes, on the racecourse and the cricket field, by active participation. On the other hand this was an age which prided itself on its rationality, freed from former passions and excesses, where 'enthusiasm' was a pejorative word,[7] and there was likely to be little intellectual credit given to the zests of athletic contest.

It was an environment in which, under the first two Georges, sport pursued the even tenor of its way, tolerated rather than encouraged, and not unduly interfered with. There was for over twenty years a time of peace. It was when the country was drawn into international conflict in the 1740s and 1750s that there was, and by no means for the last time in the period, a burst of new sporting activity. Cricket was prospering under the first generation of aristocratic players and patrons, pugilism had its covered emporia and Jem Broughton's rules, while Parliament itself legislated to control horse racing, hardly in the immediate interests of the majority of spectators but to the sport's long-term benefit. By the time the country entered the last quarter of the century the national mood had become deeply pessimistic and much of its sport had the same subdued air about it. Government based upon bribery and corruption was all the more unpopular because of its failures and particularly those in North America where General Burgoyne (later to have some sporting significance himself) surrendered to the colonists at Saratoga in 1777 and Cornwallis at Yorktown four years later. Even a compliant House of Commons reacted, passing Edmund Burke's Bill abolishing sinecures. Among the posts to disappear were those of Keepers of the Stag, Buck and Fox Hounds and the Rangers of St James's Park and Hyde Park, to no perceptible detriment to either the royal hunting or the populace's playgrounds.

Confidence returned by the 1780s bringing a new vitality that was by no means confined to high matters of church and state, and went far beyond London, taking, for instance, the new classic horse races to Doncaster and Epsom and not to racing's capital, Newmarket. The Price of Wales and the young royal dukes encouraged by example a whole sporting revival, but one for which the climate was already prepared. The fop was losing currency and the new man of the day was a more physical being. Fencing academies were enjoying a new popularity and dress itself was less showy and more functional. It was almost as if men were putting themselves into a more warlike posture well before war actually came.

The handful of years on either side of 1790 were brimful of sporting excitements. The country's sport took on a whole new appearance. As well as the turf classics there was the founding of the Marylebone Cricket Club, the pugilistic championship at its best, sailing and rowing on the Thames and an almost overnight resuscitation of archery once the Prince took an interest. It was a burst of activity which repeated itself in more frantic fashion in the most perilous of the war years just after the turn of the century. There was then much that had become usual but also much that was far from commonplace. Contrast and contradiction were among the hallmarks of the day, hardly better symbolised than by two neighbouring events in 1804 when the glamorous Alicia Thornton rode a match against Mr Flint before a record crowd at York Races – and the British and Foreign Bible Society came into being.

During the last twenty five Georgian years that followed, sport certainly grew in quantity but changed only marginally in style. The post-war decade was a difficult one with high prices, unrest and large scale repression. Sport underwent its own growing difficulties of dishonesty, disorder, and distrust, none of them ever far below the surface through the whole of the period but now surfacing much more visibly and calling for urgent action. Whether the action would be positive or negative was still an open question as the period closed. Some of the older sports were at their coarsest as the Victorian age began but there were too the first glimmerings of something new that was evenly balanced, not pursued for stake money, and entered into solely for the athletic satisfaction which it promised.

Effectively this is the earliest age in which there can be any prospect of making a comprehensive examination of the country's sport, and certainly the first to offer the possibility, from the late 1780s onwards, of identifying any year on year change. First it was the existence of an extensive weekly and a growing daily press that made sporting information available. Increasingly, substantial provincial newspapers appeared[8] and by the 1770s there was already almost complete press coverage of the country, with nearly 150 newspapers being published outside London. Certainly the reporting of sport was often spasmodic, uneven and incomplete and most newspapers were still haphazard in lay-out, but they contain what is still a substantially untapped amount of information.[9]

Race meetings were the most consistently reported sporting events in both London and provincial papers. Later in the century, in The Times and its predecessors racing monopolised the 'Sporting Intelligence' and, within its racing, news from Newmarket always dominated. It was almost inevitable that the first regular specialist sporting publication should centre on this, the most sophisticated of the age's sports. The Racing Calendar was founded by John Cheney at Arundel in 1727, became an annual publication and was securely in the hands of the Weatherby brothers by the 1770s. The subsequent appearance of a more general sporting press coincided, not unexpectedly, with the growth of fashionable interest in sport in the later 1780s. First to appear was The World in 1787, its founder and editor being the redoubtable Captain Topham, a man of parts, playwright, beau, socialite and sportsman, whose liason with the noted actress, Mrs Wells, produced three children before she went mad and he gave up his publishing to retire to his broad Yorkshire acres in 1791.[10] This left the way open for the appearance of the

The comprehensive nature of the Sporting Magazine's intentions was declared on its earliest title pages

Sporting Magazine. In the 'Address to the Public' at the head of the first issue in October 1792 it expressed 'astonishment' that among all the magazines in circulation there was not one 'expressly calculated for the sportsman.' It promised to report racing, archery, cricket and other 'respectable' sport, which it did indeed do with some fidelity during the first thirty or so years of its existence, padding its sports reporting out with stage criticism, the spicier court cases, some excruciating verse supplied by readers and, under the title 'The Feast of Wit,' some usually impenetrable attempts at humour.

The efforts of Evangelicals and Methodists were helping the spread of literacy but reading, once learnt, could not be confined to the religious tracts they promoted. Newspapers began to appear on Sundays, as well as on weekdays, in spite of numerous complaints and questions in the House of Commons. Indeed, the first newspaper with sporting leanings, *Bell's Weekly Messenger*, appeared as a Sunday publication in 1796,[11] and within a few years was selling 6,000 copies weekly. *The Weekly Dispatch*, again with a sporting emphasis, appeared in 1801 and by 1814 Pierce Egan, the doyen of sporting journalism, was making his distinctive contributions to it. It is at about this time that the newspaper begins to take over from the magazine as sport's prime historical record, a movement that was completed by the late 1820s when Egan had merged his own journal with Bell's to produce *Bell's Life in London*, that massive resource of sporting detail over the next half century.[12]

There is much that later historians owe to these early editors and sports journalists, so long as their work is treated with some caution, with an awareness that apparent corroborations of events may just be borrowings, that many factors could influence the inclusion or omission of events and that they did look to a literate and 'respectable' readership and will be inclined to understate plebian pursuits except by way of curiosity at best or condemnation at worst. There is, though, more to be laid on the doorstep of the early sporting journalist than an occasional bias. From the beginning he was setting a writing style, raising expectations, creating scenes that were larger than life and heroes who were superhuman. Pierce Egan was to take its slang, its hyperbole and its extravagances to the heights, feeding them into the broader literary culture, but it did not have to wait on his pen for the tone to be set. By 1808 the *Sporting Magazine* had become quite accustomed to exciting the imagination, spilling the blood and painting the bruises in graphic colours. Here were just two early rounds of one celebrated fight:

'6. Some obstinate rallying ... Gregson was hit about at pleasure. Gully received a tremendous blow to the right side of his head at the close of this round.

7. Gully rallied his man ... and hit him about six blows on the head with great ease, and he also stopped those of Gregson, whose left eye was closed, his nose broken, and his face hideously disfigured; Gregson was at length hit off his legs.'[13]

The point is that even with men in this apparently hopeless state and with Gregson seeming near to death's door, the fight still went on for over twenty more rounds! It was all part of the new world of play, the creating of sporting gods, the reality and the fiction each feeding off and strengthening the other. It is a world of both fact and fantasy that the historian of sport has to move in. Much remains to be uncovered still, but much of that fact is now to hand and its availability makes feasible an exploration of the vigorous and varied sporting lives of our Georgian predecessors in the hope that future historians will be able to evaluate the significances of this most creative of periods from a much more solid factual base than has so far existed. An author who is too close to the subject matter may well fall short of doing so, but others may be able to see woods where he can only recognise trees.

Notes

1. He wrote of people 'resorting to such games and recreations as promoted idleness and dissipation,' football 'but little practised, 'horse races degraded by gambling and foot races set up solely for betting.' Joseph Strutt, *The Sports and Pastimes of the People of England*, 1801, Bath 1969 reprint of J.Charles Fox's 1903 edition, pp xxiii, 94, lii, 66, 55.

2. R.W. Malcolmson, *Popular Recreations in English Society*, Cambridge, 1973. Among more general histories see Thomas S.Hendricks, *Disputed Pleasures: Sport and Society in Preindustrial England*, New York, 1991, written predominantly from a sociological viewpoint; Derek Birley, *Sport and the Making of Britain*, Manchester and New York, 1993, principally on upper class sport with good use of literary references and, in particular, Richard Holt, *Sport and the British: A Modern History*, Oxford, 1989.

3. J.H. Plumb, *The Commercialisation of Leisure in Eighteenth-century England*, Reading, 1973; Neil McKendrick, John Brewer and J.H. Plumb, *The Birth of a Consumer Society: The Commercialisation of Eighteenth Century England*, 1982; Hugh Cunningham, *Leisure in the Industrial Revolution*, 1980; J.M. Golby and A.W. Purdue, *The Civilisation of the Crowd: Popular Culture in England 1750-1900*, 1984; P.B. Munsche, *Gentlemen and Poachers: the English Game Laws 1671-1831*, Cambridge, 1981; Peter Clarke, *The English Alehouse: A Social History 1200-1830*, London and New York, 1983; Mark Harrison, *Crowds and History: Mass Phenomena in English Towns 1700-1833*, Cambridge, 1988; Stephen Deuchar, *Sporting Art in Eighteenth Century England*, New Haven, Connecticut, and London, 1988. Among well refer-

enced relevant sporting texts are Wray Vamplew, *"The Turf": A Social and Economic History of Horse Racing*, 1976 (and early chapters of his *Pay up and Play the Game*, Cambridge, 1988); James Walvin, *The People's Game: A Social History of British Football*, 1975; Eric Dunning and Kenneth Sheard, *Barbarians, Gentlemen and Players: A Sociological Study of the Development of Rugby Football*, Oxford, 1979. Notable essays relevant to the period include Allen Guttmann, 'English Sports Spectators: The Restoration to the Early Nineteenth Century,' *Journal of Sport History*, vol. 12, no. 2, Summer 1985, pp 103-125; Wray Vamplew, 'Sport and Industrialisation: An Economic Interpretation of the Changes in Popular Sport in Nineteenth Century England,' and Derek Birley, 'Bonaparte and the Squire: Chauvinism, Virility and Sport in the Period of the French Wars,' in J.A. Mangan, *ed.*, *Pleasure, Profit and Proselytism: British Culture and Sport at Home and Abroad 1700-1914*, 1988, pp 1-20, 21-41; Douglas A. Reid, 'Beasts and brutes: popular blood sports c.1780-1860,' in Richard Holt, *ed.*, *Sport and the Working Class in Modern Britain*, Manchester and New York, 1990, pp 12-28.

4. Though without following the frequent continental practice of including card and table games, well illustrated in *e.g.*, Alessandra Rizzi, *Ludus/ludere: Giocare in Italia alla fine del medio evo*, Treviso and Rome, 1995, with its heavy concerns over gambling; Jean-Michel Mehl, 'Jeux, Sports et Divertisements au Moyen Age et   La Renaissance: Rapport Introductif,' in *Actes du 116e Congrés National des Sociétés Savantes*, Chambery, 1991, and other papers in this collection.

5. While this period's sporting experience hardly supports Linda Colley's central theme of 'Britishness' in her *Britons: Forging the Nation 1707-1837*, New Haven, Connecticut, 1992, that work very well illustrates some of its aspects and particularly the enhanced role of women in sport.

5. See *e.g.* M. Dorothy George, *London Life in the Eighteenth Century*, 1925; 1966 edition, *passim*.

6. Kingston footballers in 1790, charged with riotous behaviour, defended themselves on the grounds that they were celebrating the anniversary of an ancient Saxon victory over the Danes! Asa Briggs, *The Age of Improvement 1783-1867*, London and New York, 1959; 1979 edition, p 9.

7. N. Bailey, *An Universal Etymological English Dictionary*, 2nd edition, 1724.

8. Among the many areas being served by local journals even before 1750 were Ipswich, Gloucester, Worcester, Nottingham, Northampton and Suffolk.

9. Many newspaper references here, especially from the midland counties, derive from Malcolmson and others, particularly from the South East, are indebted to the too seldom acknowledged John Goulstone in his cyclostyled journals, the *Sports Quarterly Magazine* and *Sports History*, and in *The Summer Solstice Games: A Study of Early English Fertility Religion*, Bexleyheath, Kent, 1985.

10. John Ford, *Prizefighting: The Age of Regency Boximania*, Newton Abbot, 1971, pp 167-170.

11. See *e.g.*, Mary Ransome, *ed.*, *Wiltshire Returns to the Bishop's Visitation Queries 1783*, Wiltshire Record Society XXVII, 1971, p 248.

12. J.C. Reid, *Bucks and Bruisers: Pierce Egan and Regency England*, 1971, p 17.

13. *SM*, April 1808, p 76.

FOUNDATIONS

1.
The Course and the Combat

There have been conspicuously different summaries of the nature of eighteenth century sport. Norman Wymer, in his outdated but still interesting *Sport in England*, was one jump ahead of even Norbert Elias in seeing it as reflecting the general civilising process. For him it was 'The Golden Age,' claiming that

Throughout the Georgian era we notice a gradual refinement taking place in people's play, at once in complete accord with the aesthetic merit of the new architecture, with the superb standard of craftsmanship so rapidly developing, and with sobering, though somewhat gay, influence of the mannerly Beau Nash.[1]

J.H. Plumb, by contrast, found that

The amusements of all classes were streaked with blood and cruelty. Cock-fighting and bear- and bull-baiting were little more than shambles; prize-fighting was carried on in the savagest manner; blood sports were popular and widespread ... The slaughter of animals was the principal pastime of the nation.[2]

Both views could find some justification, facing as they did in different directions. Wymer's eyes were fixed mainly on ball games, especially cricket, on other broadly acceptable sports and newer forms of play. On the other hand, the animal sports offered much to support Plumb's verdict and the various forms of man-to-man competition, though less wholesale in their destructiveness, may be ranked alongside them. Another of their usual features was continuity, inheritance from the past being a more usual element than refinement in the present, though within the animal sports themselves there was the most systematised and regulated of all the period's sports as well as the crudest and most barbarous.

At the boorish extreme was cock-throwing. This had several variants on the basic theme of throwing missiles at a captive cockerel which was either tied to a stake or a heavy log by tether or placed in an earthenware pot. It was recorded over virtually the whole of the country though when Strutt described a version of it in 1801 he considered it to be only surviving fitfully in the last quarter of the century.[3] It had remained closely associated with particular days in the calendar, unlike other once ritualistic sports like football or bowling which had long since loosened such ties. Shrove Tuesday was much its main occasion though in the south-west Good Friday, Easter Monday and Tuesday and even Whitsuntide were all variously favoured. As with other dubious traditional practices it had acquired several 'justifications' – revenge for the cock's crowing as a signal for the denial of Christ, or it was the stand-in for Pontius Pilate, but a more practical explanation arises from the habit of killing birds for one last feast before Lent (it was 'the usual day for cock killing,' according to one diarist) and the temptation to make a game out of it.[4]

Attempts at suppression had a long history, dating from at least the Commonwealth years. It faced sustained and widespread attacks from the middle of the eighteenth century, with half a dozen critical articles in the Gentleman's Magazine between 1750 and 1762, complaints in provincial newspapers and many local prohibitions.[5] The bans appear to have been comparatively effective, unusually so in an age of sketchy policing. There are few records of actual prosecutions though fines of 3s. 4d. were imposed on offenders at Norwich in 1753 and a few years later Londoners were warned that constables would be carrying press warrants to direct offenders into the army to serve against the French in Canada. Outside the towns the situation is less clear and certainly cock-throwing would persist locally and spasmodically into the next century. The only sign of county-wide interest comes from Essex where justices meeting in Quarter Sessions issued bans against cock-throwing and similar disorders every year between 1758 and 1761.[6]

Cock-throwing was a trivial enough episode in the whole scheme of sporting history but it is well documented and its abatement may throw some light on wider issues. It was not just predictability that made it a soft target. It was small scale. It would never attract such crowds as a bull-bait, still less a prize-fight, and they would be both entirely plebeian and consist predominantly of youngsters. Some London parents actually gave their children money for the cock-throwing. It would, though, probably be too cynical to ascribe the opposition purely to opportunism. Objections on the grounds of cruelty played some part, if only at the extremes of ill treatment of wounded birds. Essentially though it was the perceived *unfairness* of cock-throwing that was a main factor in its early suppression. For many who could usually accept the pain or death of an animal in sport the fact that here the bird had neither means of defending itself nor of escape was objectionable. Much the same arguments would put bull-baiting next on the list of suspect sports – and preserve cock-fighting, fox-hunting and hare coursing for much longer. The description of cock-throwing as 'unmanly' by John Wood, the architect of Bath, must be one of the earliest uses of the term, which was to feature so prominently in the ultimate authentication of modern sport.[7]

There was, too, the ever present fear of commotion and disturbance. Shrove Tuesday was a traditional occasion for boisterous merrymaking and any element of it that could be curtailed was vulnerable. There may even have been some incipient fear also that, like other traditional pastimes, cock-throwing was showing embryonic signs of systematisation and organisation. A common worry was not only about what popular sports might *be* but also about what they might be *becoming*. Attacks on popular play were not so much signs of its weakness but a fear as to its strength and of its emergence in new forms. Cock-throwing might seem the unlikeliest of candidates for promotion into any sort of ordered sport, but some signs were there. Originally the birds had been provided by subscription from the players, making it a form of sweepstake, but later the basis often became entrepreneurial, the owner of the cock typically charging twopence for three throws. A successful competitor might then himself turn promoter if the bird was still in a passable state when he caught it – and some of the cocks even seem to have been trained for their role and showed considerable skills in evasion![8] It is a slight enough hint at the commercialisation of a popular sport, but does have the authentic ring of small-scale eighteenth century recreational capitalism.

The timing of the mid-century burst of action against cock-throwing also has its wider interest. Attacks on popular recreations (and on the blood sports in particular) did tend to come in discernible waves and be inspired by some or other movement for moral reform. Here concerted action by magistrates does coincide closely with the revival in 1757 of the Societies for the Reformation of Manners which had been active earlier in the century but had lapsed for the last twenty years. So far as recreation was concerned these societies always tended to narrow their attentions on to some specific and recognisable ill. It was usually Sabbath breaking, but in this case it may well have been cock-throwing that became one of their targets, though so far there is only the concurrence of dates to support this view.[9] Controversy is often one of our main sources of information in the history of popular recreation. Cock-throwing was occasional, widely criticised, and a matter for both comment and recorded formal action. It could well be that it was the one animal sport that was in decline by the 1770s. Bull baiting, by contrast, was frequent, widely tolerated, taken for granted and not greatly remarked upon. Bailey's early eighteenth century dictionary had defined 'bull' simply as 'a beast well known,' and left it at that. Information from this period on baiting the animal often makes the same assumption. There is, of course, an abundance of general description of the practice,[10] the rudiments of which were starkly simple. The bull was tethered to a stout stake at the end of a strong rope some fifteen feet long, giving it a circle of some thirty feet diameter within which to move. The spectators formed a ring outside this circle – a practice carried over into boxing contests – and the dog owners set their animals (often bulldogs, held back by the ears) to attack the bull in turn. The usual rationale had been produced to defend what people enjoyed doing and watching. Baiting was claimed to make the meat more tender. So persuasive was this argument that it was common for baiting to be a local requirement before a bull was slaughtered with the butcher liable to a fine if he failed to do so. The frequent closeness of the bull stake to the butchers' shambles reflects this requirement.[11] However, the sponsoring of formal baits by municipal authorities themselves, widespread in the earlier part of the century, gradually diminished, either from growing distaste or as part of the general decline in their provision for popular recreation.

Bull baits came in various styles. Where it was seen as little more than a required element in the slaughtering process it could doubtless be a perfunctory and little regulated affair. At the other end of the scale, baiting could be more organised and the animals might even demonstrate a measure of specialisation. Just as there were cockerels apparently trained to avoid the missiles thrown at them, stags which later earned individual reputations on the hunting field and dogs bred specially to engage the bull, so there were bulls which would ensure a good bait, and were kept as long as possible for that purpose. They could become well enough known to figure in advertisements for future baits, as the bull 'Fury' was in parts of Lancashire. Sometimes an untried bull was preferred and could win praise, though not necessarily preservation, if it performed well. The baiting itself could be organised in a series of bouts, first bait, second bait, and so on, in a form of knock-out competition with the dogs withdrawing progressively from the fray. At other times it seems that all dogs had their chance at each round of baiting, the prize going to the best performer.[12]

Baiting took place on many occasions and in many locations. Apart from those specialised venues where there was a permanent bull stake it could happen in fields, on commons or waste land, or in inn yards. Bull rings were quite common, especially in the West Midlands where, apart from Birmingham's own, there are still three in the immediate vicinity, at Kidderminster, Halesowen and Nuneaton. It could take place at almost any festival or holiday in the year, national or local, or as part of any one-off celebration from the squire's coming of age to the opening of a new road.[13] Some accounts, especially from country areas, give the impression that a bait was a rare treat but in many towns it was part of the weekly round. In London the regular Monday and Thursday baitings at the notorious Hockley Hole ended in the 1750s but they continued at Spitalfields.[14] *Sunday* baitings were reduced, in the face of sabbatarian pressures, though they had not altogether disappeared as one bizarre incident in October 1771 shows, when a bull being baited escaped and fled through the open door of the church during service time and settled quietly in the mayor's pew! Some more orthodox links between the church and baiting did still remain, particularly at parish wakes. At Stone in Staffordshire, for example, the feast of St Michael and All Angels was celebrated with bull-baiting, bear-baiting, dog-fighting and cock-fighting into the early years of the next century, doubtless seen as an appropriately combative gesture to the leader of the celestial armies![15]

Support for bull-baiting was narrowing, however. There were increasing demands that it should be fair, in so far as this notion was applicable. Crude practices from the earlier part of the century like fixing a pair of great oxen horns over the stumps of a bull's own, or goading it with hot irons or fireworks, seem to have finally ended with the disappearance of Hockley Hole when the Fleet Ditch was drained in 1756 and even advocates of the sport were now likely to protest if a bull was maimed or unfit for baiting. The country squire, increasingly tinged with a metropolitan politeness from his visits to London and Bath, was distancing himself from the more boisterous pastimes of the masses and less inclined to give a bull for baiting, though the extent of the withdrawal of the gentry classes can easily be exaggerated. Where they were traditional, occasional and had a measure of symbolic ritual about them, baits could still have widespread support. They were, for example, often embedded in the traditional programme of the parish wake. At Beverley, in Yorkshire, it was customary for the mayor to provide a bull annually and aspiring burgesses would sometimes have a bull ring fixed to the pavement outside their door in anticipation, a hint that they were ready for office, while the practice of providing a *bear* for baiting on the day of the mayor's election at Liverpool was still, in the 1760s, attracting 'the most elegant ladies and gentlemen in the town.'[16]

Bear-baiting did still go on elsewhere, though with a declining frequency which probably owed more to the cost of bears than the sensitivities of the participants. Actual suppressions of bull-baiting were rare before the mid-1770s, that by the Birmingham magistrates in 1772 being the most notable,[17] and in spite of some opposition it is almost certain that bull-baiting was, numerically, on the increase in line with population growth and particularly of urban expansion. It needed capital to obtain a bull for baiting and as private and civic patronage declined, innkeepers and other promoters were moving in, a process which was to characterise so much of popular recreation in the coming decades. A growing demand for sporting enter-tainment was met by those with an eye to profiting from it, and with the growing success that is confirmed by the criticisms they aroused. Equally, though, bull-baiting had already begun its translation from the churchyard, the town square and the market place to the back alley, the urban waste and the inn yard, away from more scrupulous eyes.

Other practices involving the baiting or tormenting of animals disappeared or diminished – whipping a blindfold bear or baiting a leopard or a mad ass in the old Hockley Hole days[18] – though still hardly any creature was reliably safe from exploitation. **Bull-running**, a specialised form of baiting where the bull was chivvied through the barricaded streets of the town, persisted as very much a minority sport confined principally to Tutbury, where its hold was precarious and soon to be broken, and to Stamford, where it was to endure stubbornly far into the next century. Sometimes it was sheep which were harried. In the Eton College annual ram hunt the beast was set off with a blow or two from a club and then chased and beaten round the town, eventually to death. The boy Duke of Cumberland played a leading role in 1730, early showing those propensities which were to win him his title of 'Butcher.' A gentler version, though with the same outcome for the animal, took place at Kidlington, Oxfordshire on Trinity Monday, where a fat lamb was provided and

> the young women of the town, having their thumbs tied behind them, run after it and she that, with her mouth, takes and holds the lamb is declared "Lady of the Lamb."

After other amusements, she presides next day at the feast where her prize is eaten.[19] Badger baiting was common, usually with captive boxed badgers which were enticed out by threatening dogs, the dog that could bring the animal out most often in a given time being the winner of the prize or wager. Publicans would also provide merrymakers with a ram or a pig,

> well soaped, with the tail, and the horns, and the ears, respectively cut off. He that catches the tup is to have him, but if he be not taken he returns to the landlord.

This was Norfolk in 1765. Sometimes it would be a bird that was presented for goose-riding – its neck was greased and it was hung by the legs from a convenient branch while the contestants tried to drag it down as they rode beneath it.[20]

The cruder animal sports reached their greatest intensity in the capital city itself. Their continuing frequency there through to the last quarter of the eighteenth century may be judged from the later memories of the reformer, Francis Place, remembering his youth:

> There were scarcely any houses on the eastern side of Tottenham Court Road; there and in the Long Fields were several large ponds; the amusements here were duck-hunting and badger-baiting; great cruelty was constantly practised and the most abominable scenes used to take place. It is almost impossible for any person to believe the atrocities of low life at that time, which were not as now confined to the worst paid and most ignorant of the populace.[21]

The identification of the class issues raised by the sporting exploitation of animals is a valid one, but in a wider reaching sense. Even though voices like Hogarth's were raised from time to time,[22] objections to animal sports did not predominantly rely on arguments of cruelty. John Wesley reprinted with approval a letter sent to him in 1756 attacking cruel sports 'for the pain given to every Christian, every human heart, by these savage diversions,' these 'irrational sports,' but it is, whatever the intention, the pain and damage to the Christian rather than that to the animal that comes through the more strongly, 'the concomitant and the consequent vices of these savage routs.'[23] This indeed was the keynote of such early opposition as had emerged. The greater concern was over the offence they gave to good order, their attraction to lazy, noisy, blasphemous and possibly dangerous crowds. Given this emphasis, attitudes towards animal sports inevitably took on a class bias, and did so earlier and usually more sharply than happened with other popular play activities. Animal sports pursued by the leisured classes could not be seen as possible hindrances to steady labour or any hazard to the public peace. Those that excited and distracted the common people certainly could. By the 1770s a confused and often contradictory rationale was being created to justify those blood sports which could be approved and to condemn those that could not. Animal baiting might face growing opposition for its basic unfairness, its predetermined outcome, but even here there were gradations, from the outright condemnation of cock-throwing to the less stringent attitude towards bull-baiting. An even firmer distinction was drawn between cock-fighting, pursued by all classes and sponsored by the gentry, and dog-fighting, essentially (at least at this stage) a plebeian pursuit, and always suspect. It could bring together the '250 dog-fighters, bullies, chimney

Greyhounds, whose ownership was limited by Game Laws, in pursuit.

sweepers and sharpers' tackled by the Holborn constables in the fields behind Bedford House in 1766, as well as similar crowds elsewhere, particularly in Birmingham and the West Midlands, where it was noted with distaste by local historians.[24]

The ancient sport of *cock-fighting* was another matter. As bowls had done in previous centuries, it drew in all ranks of society, even to the same event, 'so that an hostler in his apron often wins several guineas from a lord,' according to a foreign visitor in the 1760s.[25] It was common all over the country, and at several levels of sophistication. At the rougher end of the sport there were the random 'shake-bag' contests at the local tavern, so called because the cock was just tipped out of its owner's sack, without ceremony, to fight whatever other bird turned up. At the other extreme were the highly formalised, heavily staked pre-arranged contests, spread over several days, between gentlemen who would often describe themselves as the representatives of their respective counties. It could still even be a schoolboys' sport, especially in its time-honoured associations with Shrove Tuesday.[26] Where cocking was on a knock-out basis its most organised form, the Welsh Main, demanded 16 or 32 contestants and produced just one winner. Such competitions continued to be fought through the whole of cocking's history but in the second half of the eighteenth century more emphasis among the gentry began to be given to team competitions, a series of one-off fights, with an identical stake for each individual fight and an overall stake for the side gaining most victories. Typical of many hundreds of such contests reported was that for '10 gs. a battle, and 200 gs. the main,' between the Gentlemen of the East and West Ridings at York in 1773.[27]

Cock-fighting had already developed a complex set of rules and practices. The conditions under which victory was awarded were carefully defined –

for instance, if both birds should be killed, it was the one that survived the longer which was the winner. They extended to such detailed stipulations as allowing cocks to be 'tasted,' that is, licked by the opposition to make sure that they had not been treated with some harmful substance.[28] The general rules of cocking would then be backed up by specific Articles of Agreement where any significant money was involved. Such Articles, a regular feature of all stake money sports through into the earlier nineteenth century, were essentially contracts between the two contending parties, setting out the particular terms (times, place, and so on) for the intended match. They had become so regularised here that a model form of 'an Article for a Cock-Match' appeared annually in the *Racing Calendar*, leaving only the names and the amounts of the wagers to be filled in.[29]

Its appearance there reflects the strong links between the turf and the cockpit. Race meetings were a favourite occasion for major cock matches. In 1773 alone the *Racing Calendar* reported them at Newmarket, Guildford, Newcastle, Nantwich, Pontefract, Canterbury, Bedford, Spalding and York, a list which was doubtless incomplete. Race towns would usually have at least one pit and they were widespread elsewhere. Birmingham's version of Vauxhall at Duddeston Hall boasted a pit from the 1740s as did commercial pleasure gardens in the bigger cities, and there were inevitably well-known ones in London, including the Cockpit Royal in Hyde Park, one in Gray's Inn Walk, and another in Jenny's Whim Tea Gardens. Even where there was no specialised cockpit other venues could readily be pressed into service. Fives courts housed cock-fights and at the more perfunctory level of the sport almost any barn, farmyard or inn room could be used.[30]

It was cock-fighting's association with horse racing that had much to do with one of the century's most significant advances in the organisation of sport, namely the development of inter-county competition. Blandford, for example, had a new pit built in 1755. Within months, alongside its races, it was housing a match between the Gentlemen of Dorset and the Gentlemen of Wiltshire. Whether such county cocking matches actually pre-dated county cricket matches is not easy to determine but what is certain is that through the whole of the century the cocks fought many more county contests than did the cricketers. It was one of the many instances where the future of sport was moulded from the practices of a bloody ancestry. Among the cocking counties engaged in matches in the early 1770s alone were Surrey, Sussex, Staffordshire, Kent, Northumberland and Durham, and looking back over the previous decades at least half the English shires can be found competing in the cockpit. The development of county competition, in sports dominated by the local ruling classes, was a readily explicable consequence of contemporary local government arrangements. Outside the corporate towns, the only administrative body was that comprising the county magistrates, meeting, as the law required, three times a year in their Quarter Sessions. Such meetings ensured the regular coming together of the like minded, and gave a county base for any sporting expression to which they were disposed. There was an added spice to matches made, not just at random, but against colleagues – and rivals – in the next county. Significantly, the Dorset Sessions were not tied to Dorchester, the county town, and the justices often held their summer meeting at Blandford.[31]

In face of its influential support and its popularity across the classes opposition to cock-fighting was muted and largely ineffective. All the circumstances suggest that it was growing rather than diminishing throughout the whole of the century. Its importance in the overall development of sport has been consistently understated. Possibly from a proper distaste for its barbarous practises, historians have given it little consideration, yet it constituted what must have been the most common experience of organised competition that contemporaries grew up with. Fundamentally flawed as it might be by later ethical judgements, it did introduce would-be contestants to practices which they would apply to less reprehensible pursuits. There was the precision as to the terms of a match, the notion of competition between equal teams, the barring of interference by spectators with the competitors, and the idea of equality of opportunity by matching birds of similar weights. Its claims to be actually mounting county competitions might appear superficial, the representatives being entirely self-selected, but there is much evidence of enthusiasm among spectators, many of whom would give their firmest geographical allegiance to their county and were ready to lend support to all manner of county competitions, creating eventually an organisational pattern that still in many sports has the county at its base.

Equal competition might be allowed to gamecocks but it was certainly denied to fellow human beings in the hunting sports. The Game Laws were fierce and always threatening to become fiercer, making shooting essentially a sport for the landed gentry. Whether for pot or pleasure, game was the monopoly of the well born and the wealthy. A prosecution of 1751 can spell it out – the offender was 'not the son and heir of an esquire or person of higher degree' and did not possess either a £100 freehold or the £150 leasehold property qualification. For some of the qualified the shooting of game was beginning to take on features of organised sport, and for some larger landowners even becoming commercialised. There was investment in rearing birds and 'vast wastes' in Yorkshire were being rented 'for the purpose of shooting Moor Game.' In what was second in time to only the Jockey Club as a quasi-national sporting body, the Game Association had a brief existence in the 1750s and 1760s, being replaced afterwards by protective county associations – in Hampshire in 1769 and Devon in 1773, for instance. Records show many cases of illegal fishing, setting snares and keeping guns for poaching and while most offences would be prompted by hunger or profit, in some cases sport itself must have been the driving force. Keeping greyhounds, for instance, and using them to chase hares was for pleasure if the size of the fines imposed is anything to go by – ten to twenty pounds – clearly implying that the offenders were persons of some substance.[32]

Coursing, a competition between two dogs chasing a released hare, had a long history, with rules dating back before Shakespeare, who knew it well. Since the hare was classed as game the sport also enjoyed the social exclusivity of the Game Laws. By the last quarter of the eighteenth century it was just starting to take off as a more systematised pursuit and it is possible that it, too, was seeing county competition by the mid-1770s. When the Gentlemen of Wiltshire met those of Norfolk on Salisbury Plain in 1780 it was described as an 'annual coursing meeting,' though sporting events did have this habit of calling themselves 'annual' by their second year at the latest. A more significant date in its history was that of the founding of the influential Swaffham Coursing Society in 1776.[33] The other animal chase, hunting in various forms, was likewise in transition in the third quarter of the century. The stag, the approved prey since the elimination of the wild boar centuries before, was becoming a rarity in the wild, except in a few protected areas such as Cranborne Chase. Packs of staghounds had been reduced to some half dozen and most of these had resorted to chasing carted animals. Many other dog packs had gradually been shifting their original interest from the hare to the fox, as giving a much more satisfying chase, although it took some time to overcome the inbuilt prejudice against hunting an animal that was vermin as against one classed as game.[34] By the 1770s attitudes were changing rapidly and William Beckford was about to lay the foundations of the sport's literature with his *Thoughts upon Hare and Fox Hunting.*

The one country-wide recreation in which all classes did have some share of interest was horse racing, the nearest the eighteenth century came to having a national sport. Its practices were relatively consistent wherever it occurred and it already had features familiar to the modern racegoer – a more or less regular schedule of meetings, from spring through to autumn, a rudimentary daily card of races, known odds, jockeys in their owners' colours, published results, and the organised breeding and trading of racehorses. Among all that would still be familiar, however, were characteristics which belonged securely to its own age.[35]

Newmarket racing, as a prime example, was sharply different from that which took place elsewhere. Founded as a hunting lodge by James I, Newmarket had become the unchallenged centre for upper class horse racing. The court circle and the aristocracy stabled their horses there permanently and established a unique concentration of races. Typically, by the 1770s, there would be seven racing weeks a year – three in spring, a July meeting, and three more in the autumn. This racing still consisted almost entirely of two-horse challenges though the movement towards sweepstakes and other races with more than two starters had been given impetus after the town tradesmen had provided two plates of £50 as prizes in 1744. Newmarket racing was unique, too, in not being at all a spectator sport, except for the owners and their hangers-on. It took place on various courses, marked only by stakes, over the open heath. The only role there for the lower orders was as servant, groom or jockey. Watching on foot was almost impossible and it was common for sportsmen to gallop alongside the racing horses, a habit fraught with danger when it happened at local meetings. Socially, too, Newmarket was exclusive, and by gender as well as class. Ladies were not catered for, a fact noted by Daniel Defoe, who followed Pepys in taking a jaundiced view of the place, and there were no facilities for any other spectators.[36]

On all the other racegrounds both the social and sporting scenes were very different. First of all, they were essentially once a year events – only York and Epsom had two meetings in the early 1770s. A few managed to extend their races over a full week, but typically meetings lasted two or three days. Single day meetings were also a rarity, only five in 1773 for example. Races took place on open ground, often common land, which could not be enclosed, and so there was a free sight of the racing for all, though those who wanted a better view could usually pay for it, by one means or another. At Ascot, for instance, a £2 subscription to the race fund carried with it the right to build a private viewing gallery and many courses had their temporary 'grandstands,' usually insubstantial structures with a repeated tendency to collapse. Where the races had a high commercial and social significance there could, though, already be more impressive permanent accommodation. At York, with municipal sponsorship, Carr's grandstand was built around 1750, along with a new road to the course, and further buildings were added in 1768. Epsom and Ascot both had grandstands from which prize-fights were sometimes viewed after the races and the Stamford cricketers met regularly 'at the stand on the Horse Race Ground.'[37]

The local race meeting was the social event of the summer for all classes. Gentry, even at the smaller country events, filled the town's inns and passed their evenings at their assemblies and the race ball. Grander meetings like Ascot could even boast nightly balls and public breakfasts. For the rest of the population, thronging around the raceground and the town, it was a festive coming together, one of their few chances of an assured holiday, and the racing itself was only part of the fun. There were the stalls for food and drink, the gambling tables, the sideshows, the ever-open taverns, the strolling players and the local whores, reinforced for the occasion by a troupe of travelling Jezebels. There would, too, be other sport as well as racing, cudgel play in Wessex, wrestling in the north and the far west country, and cock-fighting virtually everywhere. Little wonder that the races would draw folk in from miles around. James Clegg, the kindly dissenting minister at Chapel en le Frith in Derbyshire's Peak District, regularly deplored their attraction to his congregation, who would go off not just to Buxton and Tideswell Races, five or six miles away, but also to Stockport, twelve miles distant, and still further to Manchester Races, which attracted 'many' in 1736, including the workmen roofing his house.[38]

Racing was in a sound state as the eighteenth century moved into its final quarter. Newmarket had taken firm control of its own affairs. It had gone into decline in the 1730s after the death of the remarkable but disreputable Tregonwell Frampton who for over a quarter of a century, as the royal 'Keeper of the Running Horses,' had been looked upon as the crown's representative there. Meanwhile the sport had been spreading rapidly elsewhere. Meetings had multiplied and, in consequence, prize money became more and more thinly spread. Whatever the dominant motive – the concern for racing standards or the opposition to the growth of holiday opportunities – parliament produced the 1740 Act (13 Geo II c 19) designed 'to restrain and prevent the excessive increase in horse races' which had become conducive to idleness among 'the meaner sort' of subjects and was 'prejudicial to the breeding of strong and useful horses.' The remedy was to make illegal matches for less than £50, except at Newmarket and Black Hambleton, Yorkshire.[39] By the 1770s Hambleton had sunk virtually out of sight, to a one day meeting with just a single race for the king's prize of 100 guineas. By contrast Newmarket had gone from strength to strength. It rarely used the exemption granted by the act.[40] Matches were regularly made for 300 guineas or more and 1,000 guineas was not uncommon. A major factor in Newmarket's progress was its improved organisation following the establishment of the Jockey Club to manage its affairs. From 1752 the *Racing Calendar* was published annually, uniquely giving the sport a standing record of its events. In 1762 the first official list of racing colours appeared. At its head was the ubiquitous Duke of Cumberland, whose early death and the dispersal of his immense stud in 1765 was a temporary setback for Newmarket, leaving, as perhaps his only unsullied legacy, a yearling called Eclipse.[41] By the end of the 1760s Sir Charles Bunbury, at the age of 28, had become steward of the Jockey Club, was soon to be recognised as its permanent president, and a golden age of racing innovation was about to begin.

Progress was not confined to Newmarket and some of it has to be put down to the 1740 Act. The price that had to be paid was the loss of the many small scale events which had sprung up, like the racing at Kilmington Common in Devon, tagged to the annual fair, or the slightly superior Lavington Races in Wiltshire with its 15 and 19 guinea prizes for horses and a 5 guinea prize for ponies and boasting also, 'for the ladies,' a ball every night over the three days. The improvements that took place in the middle half of the century can be well illustrated by comparing the Blandford meeting of 1737 with that of 1773. At the first, three days in May, there was just one race each day, run in heats, with modest purses of 30, 20 and 10 guineas respectively. Racehorses, as such, only competed on the first day. The racing on the second day was for ponies ('galloways') and on the third for hunters, and it was still thought necessary to quote the rules in notices of the meeting – 'Jostling, crossing, or whipping is debarred.' The 1773 meeting had a much more worldly air about it. Again a three-day event but now in July, it was well placed to attract itinerant horses, coming immediately after Winchester and immediately before Stockbridge and Exeter, all well within hacking distance. The prizes were also much more attractive, including a sweepstake which had raised 110 guineas and three races for £50 purses, each for different ages, and there were two matches for wagers of 100 and 200 guineas respectively. By the standards of the day the fields were very good with half a dozen or so horses in each race.[42]

While the fortunes of all provincial meetings tended to fluctuate, in the overall racing scene Blandford's progress was not untypical. As at Blandford, the usual pattern in the early 1770s was for there to be no more than two races a day at most, and frequently only one, but run in heats. If the same horse won the first two heats that was the end of the contest, but if there were different winners it would go to a third or even, exceptionally, a fourth race. It was a means of compensating for the relatively small number of horses at many meetings and naturally called for stamina as much as speed in the horses, especially as courses could be up to four-mile circuits. Horses might well run twelve miles one day and then be called upon to race again the next. Racing in heats was never the fashion at Newmarket, where there was no shortage of horses and the concentration, in any event, on matches. There were though increasing links between the two and quite a number of Newmarket owners raced their horses at other meetings, particularly in the gap between July and Autumn, and often following well defined regional circuits.[43] These interactions between major and minor race meetings were important in producing the wider spread of common practices. Owners from Newmarket or Epsom would expect the same rules to apply in the country and local stewards would always be likely to listen to the opinions of these more metropolitan racing men. Even provincially based horses would sometimes make ambitious tours and the only racing that was relatively self contained was that in the far north where distances could be forbidding. The compensation lay in the importance of York which could attract influential owners from both Newmarket and Epsom, and where the social and cultural tone of its meetings may be judged from a comment by Thomas Gray that he had heard from a friend of three richly dressed men discussing his poetry there, 'and then they bought me' – hardly a common topic of racecourse conversation or bookstall fare in most later times![44]

Some of the low level horse racing proscribed by the 1740 did manage to survive fitfully for a few years but most meetings disappeared quickly. The strongest opposition to change came from Londoners, who did not fancy a trek to Egham, Epsom or Barnet for their racing entertainment. The annual August races at that tough London sporting ground, Tothill Fields, Westminster, proved especially resistant and were only finally put down at the expense of a full scale riot in 1749.[45] Some racing of dubious legality did continue in country areas, if not on any scale. It had sometimes been a feature of wakes or other traditional festivities and there is the possibility that some race meetings were themselves transmutations of earlier wakes celebrations. Their timings through the spring and summer months, their similar duration and the overall scene they presented all invite such a hypothesis though the evidence is as yet virtually non-existent.[46] Where racing was associated with traditional festivals it seems often to have been tolerated and could even occasionally be safely advertised. Among the sports promised at a 1770s scouring of the Uffington White Horse on the Chiltern Downs there was to be a race, the best of three two-mile heats, for horses 'that never run for anything' as well as a similar race for ponies. It may be significant that this was both an event which occurred only every four years and was always noted as attracting the local gentry as well as the working population. More usually races at communal festivals and fairs featured the humble donkey and these were extremely common, typically for the half guinea prize promised at the Yattenden Revel in 1773.[47] Certainly the 1740 statute reinforced the elitism of actual horse racing, but meetings did continue to provide what for most was the only large scale entertainment on offer and only a small minority of the population had no racing within reach. And as they liked their racing, so the sport needed them. Without the pennies of the humble, innkeepers and tradesmen would not be putting their guineas into the race fund and without the prospects of large crowds and good takings there would be no hiring out of booths and stalls.

Racing had grown, therefore, within this framework of government intervention. Cricket was growing without any expression of government interest at all, while pugilism, by contrast, developed and eventually flourished in the face of its own illegality. It was taking all styles to make the eighteenth century sporting world. Already, in those sports where man was pitted against man (and occasionally woman against woman) there were nationally known sporting heroes. **Pedestrianism** had emerged from its long but largely unrecorded earlier history, of which we have only occasional glimpses – Fitzstephen's reports of track and field events in medieval London, Henry VIII's claims to be the first pan-athlete, the strictures of foot races as 'exercises of profaneness' by such as the Reverend Hinde in the Puritan heyday and Pepys' accounts of the innocent contests between the ladies of his household on a bowling green for small wagers. By his day, though, athletes were beginning to at least partially emerge from anonymity and he also records a celebrated race between Lee, the Duke of Richmond's footman, and 'a tyler, a famous runner.' [48] In the eighteenth century the materialisation of the athletic hero from the chrysalis was complete, with published feats and public renown.

One was Levi Whitehead, 'without doubt the greatest pedestrian ever known in England,' according to an obituary, and the winner of many races in the north. He was said to have covered four miles over Bramham Moor in 19 minutes, regularly walked four miles in an hour even in his nineties, and died aged 100 in 1787. By the 1770s another noted athlete, Foster Powell, was already famous both as marathon walker and short-distance runner, the two recognisable branches of the sport. In the nature of things the two were differently set up and organised. The long distance event was invariably a lone challenge for a wager, and usually with much side betting. The London to York return trip was such a favourite that its record times were becoming as well known as, say, those for the 1500 metres in the twentieth century. These events aroused enormous interest and large crowds would turn out to greet the performer. Other well-known runners of the period included Reed of Hampshire who was reported as running 10 miles in an hour at the Artillery Ground in 1774 and Andrew Smith, 'a famous runner,' who inflicted one of his few defeats on Foster Powell at Barham Downs near Canterbury in 1776.[49] Races over the shorter distances were mounted in many different settings. Their long associations with seasonal festivals, with parish wakes and fairs still continued. They were sometimes adjuncts to other sporting spectacles, a growing number were products of the publican's search for profit and some even, in London, could be part of actual athletics meetings, thoroughly commercial, in enclosed grounds and with paying spectators.

Seasonal festivities often had something of an athletic flavour. Running and jumping contests were quite common at Whitsuntide and even more so at Easter, when they could be found from Carlisle and Berwick in the far north to Exeter and Liskeard in the distant south-west. The competition was usually for traditional prizes, typically the shirt for men and the shift or smock for women. Races featured at such local feasts as those at Castle Howard, Didsbury, Eccles, Pangbourne and even in towns like Birmingham with its St Phillip's wake, and also took place at numerous and widespread fairs, including those at Hayes, Chesham, Boughton Green in Northampton-shire, Toller Down in Dorset and many others.[50] To set against this style of athletics, essentially arising out of and remaining close to communal recrea-tion was that which was geared to paying spectators. The advent of the enclosed playing area, with payment for entrance, dates from around the 1730s in cricket, pugilism and athletics alike, all apparently centred on London. Events for 'running footmen' were being advertised at Belsize Park from 1731 and the ground there was certainly enclosed by 1743, when sixpence was being charged to see the Whitsuntide foot races. By the 1740s the Artillery Ground in Finsbury, more noted as a cricket venue, was also housing athletic events – it was here that Thomas Calile, 'a lamplighter,' ran 21 miles in two hours in 1740. There must too have been the expectation of profit behind the advertising in 1746 of a foot race between 'two of the most noted runners' in Suffolk at Beccles Racecourse, 'where the ground will be roped.' The same motive also inspired the occasional innkeeper to put on athletic events, sometimes on his own field. In addition, as well as enjoying a separate existence in their own right, foot races were often additional attractions at all manner of other events – before a backsword contest, at the local races, or at cricket matches, or indeed at almost any recreational event, traditional or commercial.[51]

Where races took place in the more rustic settings the distances run are rarely quoted. Where distances do appear there is already a familiarity about many of them – 220 yards, 440 yards, half mile and mile.[52] Like the horses, the human racers were often required to run in heats, and particularly so where the prize was on the generous side or where the competitors were women. There were already record times for some distances though these have to be approached with obvious caution. Apart from a dubious four-minute mile, there were such alleged feats as four miles in 19 minutes over rough ground claimed for Levi Whitehead, 15 miles in one hour 20 minutes, 21 miles in two hours, and so on. However, what was perhaps the most interesting feature about athletics in the 1770s was that it was flourishing and making progress at a time which for most sports was a relatively quiet decade of consolidation before the dramatic developments that were to come. In athletics there was positive growth. Its events remained uncomplicated, walking and running, with virtually no mention either of recognisable field events or of the esoteric wagers that were later to become fashionable, but their frequency and the interest they aroused was markedly increasing. This applied to women's races just as much as men's and so-called 'smock races,' where the prize might actually be anything from a tea kettle to a petticoat, are recorded in every year of the decade and from most parts of the country. One factor in this early acceleration may well be put down simply to the comparative ease with which athletic competitions could be arranged, allowing them to react more quickly to changing circumstances and expectations than could sports with more complex organisations. A similar precocity was, after all, to make pedestrianism the first sport to profit from the workers' free Saturday afternoon in the next century[53] and it is just possible that in the early 1770s it was already responding to the first stirrings of the sporting enthusiasms that would fuel the energetic years to come.

While athletics made steady progress from at least the 1730s onwards the combat sports continued to be in the various stages of transition which marked their history through most of the century. Popular old forms of man to man fighting, with or without weapons, remained common at wakes and seasonal celebrations, though with considerable regional differences. As the century moved into its last quarter polite society was beginning to rediscover its own mode of swordplay in the fencing academies, but pugilism, after its first epoch of distinction in its legitimate mid-century years, was in the doldrums.

Wrestling was widespread, in several forms and numerous settings. It persisted in many of the surviving midsummer celebrations, its most traditional occasion, but did occur at other seasonal feasts, even, at Hornchurch in Essex, at Christmas for the customary prize of a boar's head. In many counties it was a feature of parish wakes – in Devonshire, Wiltshire, Oxfordshire, Norfolk and Westmoreland, for example. It took place at fairs, could mark the local mayor-making (as at Kendal) or be part of any one-off local celebration.[54] Occasionally it drew large crowds, 10,000 in Berkshire in 1737, and those reported at Devonshire matches. These were certainly exceptional, but while it fell well short of being a major spectator sport publicans found it worthwhile to act as sponsors, particularly it seems, where they grafted their own commercial interests on to some traditional festivity. In the early 1770s, for instance, wrestling featured in the Yattendon Revel – organised from the Royal Oak – and in the midsummer sports at Stow-on-the-Wold, where the King's Arms was crowning the day with a ball in the evening.[55]

Competitions usually took the form of Knock-outs, for a single prize. Sometimes there would be several prizes offered for the best performances 'as shall be agreed by the gentlemen present,' and there were some team contests, usually six a side, even occasionally with sides seen as represent-

Cudgel-playing, particularly popular in the West Country. The ornate hat, a common prize, is hoisted on a pole behind the temporary stage.

ing counties. In London wrestling of any note was largely confined to migrant workers but there was a team match reported from Highgate in 1744, involving the 'gamesters of London' and a team of countrymen. Again there was publican sponsorship, from the Mitre Inn. There is some evidence of gentry interest as spectators, occasionally as judges and spasmodically as providers, though not as performers. The sport's lone protagonist on any scale was that remarkable and single-minded sponsor from early in the century, Sir Thomas Parkyns, who not only wrote a treatise on wrestling and promoted the sport generously during his lifetime, but also left a bequest to provide an annual prize for the wrestlers of his native Nottinghamshire. In spite of the thinness of its gentry backing wrestling does have all the appearance of a healthy, if possibly increasingly regionalised sport.[56]

The same applied to the combat sports with weapons, all of which tended to be orientated towards the south-west of the country. **Cudgelling, singlestick** and **backsword** all appeared frequently and **sword and dagger** contests were still surviving, either free standing or as additional attractions at some west country race meetings or as part, for instance, of the summer sports at Stow. By the 1770s it was competition with various wooden weapons which had become much the more common. In singlestick play the fighters had a stick of between three and eight feet in length, depending on local usage. The shorter staff was held in one hand only, the player's other arm being tied to his side. Players with the longer staff used both hands. Cudgelling contests were in essence less hazardous versions of the old sword and dagger play, and possibly sometimes even went under that title. Here players had a 'shield stick' in the left hand, with a wicker-work guard to protect the hand itself, and the right arm wielded the cudgel. In both forms of contest the bout ended when a blow to the head produced a trickle of blood an inch long, and the art was to achieve this with as light a blow as possible.[57] The publican again was early in the field – in the late 1730s, within the space of only a few months, the *Sherborne Mercury* was advertising numerous local inn-based events in these combat sports. There was also some upper class sponsorship, the most conspicuous subscription being that by the users of the Hot-well, Bristol, which was said to have attracted no fewer than seventy players in 1753![58]

For the gentleman of the day, though, any personal excursion into the combat sports had to be within the ambit of mannerly behaviour. The sword ceased to be an essential part of male attire but a new enthusiasm arose for play with the foils, as an art in its own right, as a means to social poise and grace of movement, and an aid to modest physical well-being. Numerous fencing masters, most of them from France and Ireland, had gravitated to London and other cities. It was, though, an Italian family, the Angelos, from their Carlisle House in Soho Square, who became society's leaders in the new fashion for swordplay. The dynasty was later to have its place also in the history of that other form of man-to-man combat – with the fists – though at this time, given prize-fighting's current reputation, nothing could have seemed less likely.[59]

Pugilism had a dual history, combining elements from both wrestling and cudgel play. Its early home as a recognisable sport was on the stages of the great London fairs such as Southwark (where Samuel Johnson's uncle was said to have had a booth) in the first quarter of the century. Fights that began there with cudgels then continued as fist contests after first blood was drawn and the cudgels discarded, leaving incidentally a legacy of betting on 'first blood' throughout the whole of prize-fighting's history, in another example of the transfer of practices from one sport to another. It was natural that, in the absence of rules, wrestling holds should be included in the ensuing tussle. More regularity was brought into the sport with the opening of specialist venues, the first in the Oxford Road by James Figg who not only mounted fights but also established what was to become another pugilistic tradition by offering instruction to gentlemen. The social thrust of the new sport was indeed emphasised from the start in the high admission charges – John Byrom from Lancashire had to pay 2s. 6d. to see a contest there in 1725. Slack's amphitheatre followed and then, most conspicuously and with noble support, Jem Broughton's.[60]

Broughton, the best boxer of his day, was an important figure in both the history of pugilism and the history of sporting rule-making. He was directly responsible for bringing forward rules for the ring that were to be the basis for boxing for the whole of its bareknuckle existence. These rules, 'approved by the gentlemen, and agreed by the pugilists' on August 18, 1743, were no doubt a codification of existing good practice and were concerned more with the organisation of fights than with the fighting practices themselves. They were formulated solely for his own amphitheatre, but appear to have been quickly accepted for all fights of any importance, wherever they took

Figg's business card, advertising his training services as well as his amphitheatre.

place. They provide a novel example of rule making by *ex cathedra* pronouncement rather than through the stage by stage evolution which happened in horse racing and cricket. So far as the contest itself was concerned they were minimal – no blows below the waist, rounds to end when a man was floored and a half minute pause before he was brought up to the 'scratch', the yard mark which divided the two fighters at the start of a round. Minimal as they were, they were enough to bring some order into what could have been, and was often in danger of becoming, a very disorderly sport.

The years of approval and prosperity for pugilism came to an abrupt end on April 10, 1750. Broughton had been encouraged by noble supporters, led by the inevitable Duke of Cumberland, to open his own amphitheatre for the sport. It was here that an apparently routine fight against his old rival Jack Slack ended with Broughton temporarily blinded by a desperate chance blow from an obviously well beaten opponent. What made that single blow so crucial to the whole history of the ring was the fact that the Duke of Cumberland lost heavily on his man's defeat. He was said to have just laid a bet of £1,000 at odds of ten to one on Broughton and the loss was too much for his temper to bear. Within weeks the amphitheatre was closed, though quite how is difficult to trace. The old boxing histories talked of parliamentary action, but the records of neither house show any evidence of this. However, a royal duke, especially one who had saved the country from the return of the Stuarts, had many channels of influence and boxing already offered ample opportunities for legal intervention if the motive was there – as a duel, an affray, a disturbance of the peace and even a riotous assembly. The consequence was that in the 1770s, pugilism was existing at best on the frontiers of the law. It had lingered fitfully at public venues in the capital during the 1760s, at Maylebone Basin, where 3,000 were said to have watched a fight in 1760, and at The Hollow, Islington, in 1768 and even briefly indoors at the Tennis Court early in the decade. When, however, the high constable put a stop to a fight at Sampson's Riding School in Islington in 1773, after contests had been successfully mounted there for several months, public boxing of any consequence in London came to an end. Henceforth fighters and their followers had to trek to more distant fields, or for lesser fights to the rougher and relatively unpoliced edges of the city. Such venues, in the third quarter of the century, included the Long Fields to the east of Tottenham Court Road, Moorfields, Tothill Fields, Stepney Fields and, more distantly, Kennington Common (now the site of the Oval cricket ground), Mill Hill, Blackheath and Hounslow Heath, then a notorious haunt of highwaymen and now housing Heathrow Airport. None the less, the number of fights increased though the quality of the boxing was, according to several long-term observers, well below either that of the old amphitheatre performers or that of the later champions. Lacking the firm hand of Broughton and with few influential supporters, the honesty of contests was often in question. No less a sporting character than Denis O'Kelly, the owner of Eclipse, gave a £100 bribe to Bill Darts to throw a fight in 1771 and fighters themselves would claim that they could make more by losing a fight than by winning it.

Among the favoured venues for fights were race grounds. Contests there could be pre-arranged or set up for a purse collected at the end of the day's racing. Epsom had housed fights from the early days and they were being recorded at Ascot Heath and Maidenhead. The public house, too, had begun its long association with the ring. The Crown Inn at Staines would become a popular boxing centre in the later 1770s, following upon others closer to London, such as the White Lion, Putney, a decade earlier. Several contests of would-be significance took place around Staines, but these inn-based fights were even more likely than most to be of dubious reliability. Nevertheless, the level of betting on them – between £500 and £600 on the match between Harry Sellars and Peter Corcoran in 1776 – suggests the return of a modicum of gentry support. Boxing, though, remained precarious, and more on account of its frequently rigged fights than its illegality. There were few fighters of any great repute in the mid-1770s, the best of them probably Stephen 'Death' Oliver (soubriquets were already part of the trade), a lightweight who had to rely on agility more than strength and was praised for his 'scientific' method.

In spite of its doubtful current quality boxing did enjoy a popular underlay of support even if it still appears to have been fairly limited geographically. London apart, there were certainly already strong pugilistic traditions in Birmingham, Norwich and Bristol, and while there is little record as yet of fights at the local, everyday level, the number of fighters who graduated to the national ring indicates that there must have been many such local contests. Some of the great annual fairs like Lansdowne near Bristol, a long-standing nursery of young boxers,[61] undoubtedly continued their old traditions of pick-up fighting – such gatherings were too well known to need much publicity, which the fragile legal status of pugilism would in any case have discouraged. Yet in spite of the occasional notable fight and local popularity it would have been difficult, in 1775, to predict any very prosperous future for the sport.

Of all the sports surveyed here pugilism's unique feature is its comparative novelty. Boxing apart, the combat and racing sports all had a continuously recognisable ancestry from at least the previous century, all making just modest refinements in their practices during the first sixty years of the Georgian era. Charles II would have had no difficulty in recognising them. It was in pugilism that there was major change, the discarding of the weapons and the imposition of a set rythmn that depended on the clear completion of one set of actions in a fall and a pause before the next began. While horse racing had started an unconscious revolution in the organisation of the sport through the foundation of the Jockey Club, Charles would have seen little change in the actual horse racing itself, which used to draw him so regularly to Newmarket. It might be argued that the sports dealt with here, incorporating chase and conflict, are closer to humanity's primeval soul and more ingrained than those involving corporate activity through a team or the intervention of secondary objects in the conflict such as sticks and balls and that, as such, changes in their forms are likely to be the slower. In any event one of the great features of the second Georgian sporting phase was its innovative nature as new sports and new practices in older ones tumbled over each other to make their appearance. It is in some of the ball sports and in other novel activities that the first three-quarters of the eighteenth century affords a preview of what was to come in the decades that would follow.

Notes

1. Norman Wymer, *Sport in England: A History of Two Thousand Years of Games and Pastimes*, 1949, p 125.
2. J. H. Plumb, *The First Four Georges*, 1956, p 15.
3. In his version the bird was in a special pot suspended across the street about twelve feet from the ground. Strutt, *Sports and Pastimes*, p 207. For details of local variants see *e.g.* Francis W. Steer, ed., *The Memoirs of James Spershot*, Chichester Papers, 30, 1962, p 14; A. R. Wright, *British Calendar Customs*, 3 vols., Folk Law Society, 1936-40, I, pp 66/7; Dennis Brailsford, *Sport and Society: Elizabeth to Ann*, London and Toronto, 1969, pp 202/3.
4. Wright, *British Calendar Customs*, I, pp 66/7, 112, 163; Walter Rye, *ed, The Journal of Thomas Isham, of Lamport, in the County of Northampton, 1671-1673*, Norwich, 1875, pp 27, 85, quoted in Malcolmson, *Popular Recreations*, p 48.
5. There were bans from the Bristol magistrates just before the Restoration but they were side-stepped by throwing at hens and geese instead! John Latimer, *The Annals of Bristol in the Seventeenth Century*, Bristol, 1900, p.292. The criticisms (from *e.g.* Oxford, Birmingham and Sheffield) and prohibitions at London, Reading, Bristol, Northampton, Newbury, Wakefield, Nottingham, Sheffield and Norwich are well documented in Malcolmson, *Popular Recreations*, p 120.
6. *Norwich Mercury*, 10 March 1753; *Public Advertiser*, 7 February 1758, 17 February 1768; Malcolmson, *Popular Recreations*, p 120.
7. George, *London Life in the Eighteenth Century*, p 30; John Wood, A Description of Bath, 1765; Bath 1969 reprint, p 87.

8. Reid, 'Beasts and brutes,' Holt, ed., *Sport and the Working Class*, pp 22/3; Cunningham, *Leisure in the Industrial Revolution*, p 51; Malcolmson, *Popular Recreations*, p 48.

9. See W. B. Whitaker, *The Eighteenth Century English Sunday*, 1940, p 121 and passim.

10. See particularly Henri Misson, *M. Misson's Memoirs and Observations in His Travels over England with some Account of Scotland and Ireland*, ed., John Ozell, 1719, pp 24-27; Nicholas Blundell, *The Great Diurnal of Nicholas Blundell of Little Crosby, Lancashire*, ed., J. J. Bagley, 2 vols., Record Society of Lancashire and Cheshire, 1968-70, I, p 35; II, p xvi. See Malcolmson, *Popular Recreations*, pp 63/4.

11. Malcolmson, *Popular Recreations*, p 45 (Darlington, Skipton and Alnwick were among the many towns where baiting was obligatory); A. Lindsay Clegg, *A History of Dorchester, Dorset*, undated, plan of Dorchester, facing p 16.

12. T. F. Thistleton Dyer, *British Popular Customs: Present and Past*, 1875/6, p 370; Blundell, *Diurnal*, II, pp 25-27.

13. For examples see *Weekly Worcester Journal*, 17 November 1732; *Gloucester Journal*, 9 November 1736; Malcolmson, *Popular Recreations*, passim.

14. Boulton, *Amusements of Old London*, I, pp 10, 32.

15. F. M. Eden, *The State of the Poor*, 1797, quoted in George, *London Life in the Eighteenth Century*, p 295; Whitaker, *Eighteenth Century Sunday*, p 140; Wright, *Calendar Customs*, III, p 166.

16. Reid, 'Beasts and brutes,' Holt, ed., *Sport and the Working Class*, pp 13/14; *Hull Advertiser*, 1 November, 1817; Thomas Troughton, *The History of Liverpool*, Liverpool, 1810, pp 92-4.

17. Victorian County History (henceforth VCH) *Warwickshire VII*. 1924, p 221.

18. Boulton, *Amusements of Old London*, I, pp 9-13.

19. H. C. Maxwell Lyte, *A History of Eton College 1440-1875*, 1875, pp 302/3; Wright, *Calendar Customs*, I, p 273.

20. Malcolmson, *Popular Recreations*, pp 46/7, 73.

21. *Parliamentary Papers (Commons), Report on Education, 1835*, Evidence of Francis Place, pp 836/7.

22. See J. B. Nichols, *Anecdotes of William Hogarth*, 1833, pp 64/5.

23. *Journal of John Wesley*, ed. N. Curnock, 8 vols., 1909, IV, p 176.

24. *Daily Gazetteer*, 10 June 1766; J. A. Langford, *A Century of Birmingham Life: a chronicle of local events, 1741-1841*, 2 vols., 1868, I, p 257; VCH, *Warwickshire VII*, p 221.

25. *London in 1710. From the Travels of Zacharias Conrad von Uffenbach*, ed. and translation W. H. Quarrell and Margaret Mare, 1934, p 49.

26. At Wimborne Grammar School it still took place under the auspices of the master who not only excused the boy with the winning bird from whippings during Lent but also allowed him to place his hat on the rump of a friend to save him from the lash! See 'Extracts from the Diary of John Richards, Esq., of Warmwell, in Dorsetshire, 1679-1702,' *Retrospective Review*, I, 1835, p 205; M. B. Weinstock, *Old Dorset*, Newton Abbot, 1967, p 142.

27. *Racing Calendar 1773*, 'Cocking in 1773,' p xxiii.

28. A reminder, incidentally, as Jean-Michel Mehl has shown in France that the history of cheating can throw its own lights on the history of sport. See Mehl, 'Rapport Introductive,' *Jeux, Sports et Divertissements*, p 16 for further refer-

ences.

29. *Racing Calendar 1773*, p xxiii.

30. ibid., passim.; Langford, *A Century of Birmingham Life*, I, p 257; Boulton, Amusements of Old London, I, pp 75, 177 and *passim*; John Armitage, 'The History of Ball Games,' in Lord Aberdare, *ed.*, *Rackets, Squash Rackets, Fives and Badminton*, London, undated, pp 39/40.

31. Cecil N. Cullinford, *A History of Dorset*, Letchworth, 1980, p 77; F. E. Lanning, 'Horse Racing in Dorset,' *Dorset Year Book 1988*, ed. F. M. Langford, p 13; Bernard G. Cox, *The Book of Blandford Forum*, Buckingham, 1984, p 107. Further research into the relationship between the timing of Quarter Sessions and race meetings could well be illuminating.

32. Munsche, *Gentlemen and Poachers*, pp 44/5, 36, 57-59; *Shropshire Records: A full List and Partial Abstract of the Contents of the Quarter Sessions Rolls: 1690-1800, ed.*, Lancelot J. Lee, Shropshire County Council, undated, pp 11, 63, 79, 88 and *passim*. See also Harry Hopkins, *The Long Affray: The Poaching Wars in Britain 1760-1814*, 1985.

33. Munsche, *Gentlemen and Poachers*, p 33.

34. See *e.g.* William Somerville's long poem 'The Chace' (1735) with its derogatory views – in Miltonic blank verse – on hunting foxes.

35. The most satisfactory account of the sport, particularly from the nineteenth century onwards, is from Vamplew in *"The Turf": A Social and Economic History of Horse Racing*. Apart from the quite invaluable annual *Racing Calendar*, useful pre-Victorian information can be found also in John Tyrrel, *Racecourses on the Flat*, Marlborough, 1989, and Richard Onslow, *Headquarters: A History of Newmarket and its Racing*, Cambridge, 1983.

36. *Racing Calendar 1773*, passim.; Daniel Defoe, *A Tour through the Whole Island of Great Britain, 1724-26*, 1971 edition, pp 98/9; Pepys, *Diary*, March 1868.

37. *Racing Calendar 1773*, passim.; Dorothy Laird, *Royal Ascot*, 1976, p 25; VCH, *A History of York*, ed., P. M. Tillott, 1961, pp 232, 248; Dennis Brailsford, *Bareknuckles: A Social History of Prize-Fighting*, Cambridge, 1988, pp 16/17; *Stamford Mercury*, 20 June 1771.

38. Laird, *Royal Ascot*, p 25; *The Diary of James Clegg of Chapel en le Frith 1708-1755, ed.* Vanessa S. Doe, 3 vols., Derbyshire Record Society, 1978-81, II, p 495; III, p 774; I, p 259; II, p 372.

39. 13 Geo II c.19. The act even laid down a scale of weights for ages but this was withdrawn in a 1745 act (18 Geo II c.34) largely devoted to card playing.

40. The few matches made for nominal stakes of 25 guineas were usually between horses thought to have very uneven chances of winning and the real money was in the side betting at odds.

41. Laird, *Royal Ascot*, p 22; SM, May 1795, p 63.

42. *Sherborne Mercury*, 26 July, 1737; 22 August, 1738; 31 May, 1737; *Racing Calendar 1773*, pp 57-58. For other minor pre-1740 Dorset meetings see *e.g.*, 24 May 1737 ('Ridgeway'), 2 August 1737 (Pulham).

43. See *e.g. Racing Calendar 1773*, p 71 and *passim*. One extensive tour took Pauper from Newmarket to Stamford, Grantham, Worcester, Hereford, Abingdon and Epsom.

44. *ibid., passim.*; Thomas Grey, *Poems, Letters and Essays*, 1912 edition, p 202.

45. *Ipswich Journal*, 26 August 1749. The Tothill Fields incident has tended to

be taken as typifying plebeian race disorder but the intended races here would obviously have contravened the recent legislation.

46. The one possible example is from Burrough Hill, Leicestershire, where Whit Monday sports were replaced by horse racing. J.Nichols, *The History and Antiquities of the County of Leicestershire*, 2 vols., 1798, II, p 524.

47. *Reading Mercury*, quoted in Goulstone, *Summer Solstice Games*, p.17.

48. William Fitzstephen, 'Description of the City of London 1170-1183,' *English Historical Documents: 1042-1189*, ed. David Douglas, 1968, pp 960/1; William Hinde, in *The Journal of Nicholas Assheton of Downham*, Chetham Society, 1848, p 18n.; Pepys, *Diary*, 14 April 1667; 30 July 1663.

49. *Times*, 21 December 1787; *Northampton Mercury*, 18 June 1770; *SM.*, October 1792, pp 13-14. See also Geoffrey Murray, *The Gentle Art of Walking*, 1939, pp 30-32.

50. Wright, *British Calendar Customs*, I, p 106; Goulstone, *Summer Solstice Games*, pp 22, 32; Malcolmson, *Popular Recreations*, pp 21/2; *Sports History*, 7, 1985, p 9; *Western Flying Post*, 17 May 1756.

51. *Daily Advertiser*, 5 June 1731; Goulstone, *Summer Solstice Games*, p 22; *SM*, October 1792, p 13; *Ipswich Journal*, quoted in *Sports History*, 1, 1982, p 7. For innkeepers and foot races see *e.g. Kentish Weekly Post*, 17 June 1738; 4 June 1743; *Reading Mercury*, 4 July 1757; *Bath Journal*, 1 October 1759.

52. Distances are quoted in *e.g. Kentish Gazette*, 20 May 1750; *Reading Mercury*, 4 July 1757; *Kentish Post*, 18, 28 July 1773, all references deriving from Goulstone. For timings, see *e.g. SM*, October 1792, pp 8, 13-15; June 1795, pp 147/8.

53. Dennis Brailsford, *Sport, Time and Society*, London and New York, 1991, p 107.

54. *Bell's Life in London* (henceforth BLL) 11 January 1852; Goulstone, *Summer Solstice Games*, pp 107n, 28, 91 and *passim.*; *Gloucester Journal*, 9 November 1736.

55. *Northampton Mercury*, 18 June 1770; Malcolmson, *Popular Recreations*, p 43; Goulstone, *Summer Solstice Games*, pp 107n, 14, 17, 30 and *passim*.

56. *Gloucester Journal*, 5 May 1741; *Daily Advertiser*, 2 July 1744; Sir Thomas Parkyns, *The Inn-Play: or, Cornish-Hugg Wrestler*, 3rd edition, 1727.

57. Recalled by the Dorset poet William Barnes in Hone's Year Book 1832, reprinted in Theo Brown, *ed., Some Dorset Folklore by William Barnes*, St Peter Port, C.I., 1969, pp 10/11; 'Dorset Folk and Dorset,' *The Leisure Hour*, 1883, pp 240/1.

58. *Sherborne Mercury*, 7 June, 27 September 1737; 25 July, 8 August, 12 September 1738.

59. Trevor Hearl, 'Polite Accomplishments: A Forgotten Heritage in British Physical Education,' David McNair and Nicholas A. Parry, *eds., Readings in the History of Physical Education*, Hamburg, 1981, pp 59-78.

60. John Byrom, *The Private Journal and Literary Remains of John Byrom*, I, part 1, Chetham Society, 1854, p 117. For the early history of pugilism see anon, *Pancratia*, pp 39-63; Henry Downes Miles, *Pugilistica: The History of British Boxing*, 3 volumes, Edinburgh, 1906, pp 30, 39-45; *Brailsford, Bareknuckles*, pp 1-20.

61. See Pierce Egan, *Boxiana: or, Sketches of Modern Pugilism*, 3 vols., 1821, III, pp 470-473.

2.
Balls, Bowls and Beginnings

Most eighteenth century opinion would have regarded it as a small leap from the combat sports to football, and, indeed, many would have asked why it had not been included among them. Most public attention was drawn to the annual mass contests that took place up and down the country under that name, the sprawling mauls that had little regard for property, life or limb. Yet football was not so much a single game as a whole broad species of competitive team play with little in common beyond the use of a ball of some sort which was kicked, thrown or scrummaged towards one of two set goals. There was hurling and camping, both basically handling and throwing games. There was the kicking game, which could run the gamut from impromptu street play to set matches on delimited pitches between evenly numbered sides. Even within each style of play there was great scope for variety and for differences in its occasions and frequency.

Hurling, for instance, in its west country form, had been played in relatively organised fashion for the past two centuries and so far as is known was much as reported by Sir Richard Carew in 1602. His unusually detailed account described a small ball contest between two equal teams of fifteen to twenty a side. Its rules were quite sophisticated. The game began with the ball thrown in the air at the centre of the playing space, there was only single man-to-man marking, tackling, and no forward passes. It was then a long-distance, cross-country encounter with goals – some parish landmarks or great house – three or four miles apart, though it may have become more contained in those eighteenth century revels where it occurred. Even in Carew's day there were variations with a more hectic version in Western Cornwall played with uncontrolled numbers and fewer rules.[1]

There are somewhat more continuous records of the 'camping' or 'camp-ball' game whose original heartland was East Anglia. While it is sometimes hard to distinguish camping from other forms of football (the terms tend to be used loosely) it was capable of being a formalised game with a small ball, and regulated numbers. The existence of many topographical references to 'camping closes' in the eastern counties reinforces the view that it was often played within a circumscribed space. Again, though, too much generalisation is dangerous. Like hurling, camping took on several styles, including 'kicking camp' with a larger ball, an inflated bladder encased in leather, and also 'savage camp', so called because the players wore heavy boots. Diversity was the hallmark of eighteenth century football. In addition – and more so than any other game – football was imbued with cultural and social implications which could go far deeper than the play itself, as well as being played on its own account, for its own sake, with neither thought for, nor dependency on, any ancient custom. Annual mass contests did usually derive from distant rites, particularly from fertility festivals involving a struggle for some symbolic aid to fruitfulness in the coming year. Where justification was looked for they had usually been blessed with some Christian overlay, as with the Haxey Hood game, or some alleged historical precedent, as at Kingston-on-Thames. There was little basic variety in the play itself. Essentially it was a free-for-all scrimmage, punctuated by occasional breaks with the ball by some individual or group. The ball was usually a stuffed leather case and the goals were local landmarks of many sorts, from church porches to inns, or even just some broader home territory. There were occasional minimal gestures in the direction of rules, a caution perhaps against hurting a man who had been knocked down, but it was accepted that the football day would bring disorder, fighting, bloodshed, broken limbs, and the occasional death. Some places where the play was deep rooted, such as Kendal and Dorking, even had their set tariff of fines for damage caused by the players.[2]

Many customary footballing sites are suggested by old field names. In addition to the East Anglian 'camping closes', there are the 'football garths', 'football closes', and 'football fields' over much of the country. While these have to be treated with caution, given their dependence on oral transmission and susceptibility to corruption, there are indications that the game did continue to be commonly played and particularly that it was widely known. In Bolton youngsters were playing in the streets in their clogs, at Bedford the noise of footballers often disturbed Moravian worshippers, and football was reported as a popular recreation in places like Bletchley, Waterbeach in Cambridgeshire and Shifford in Berkshire, where it was mentioned as a main sport in 1759. None the less, the hard evidence of the game for much of the earlier Georgian period is hard to come by. Much has to be derived from inference and from the strong impression of the sport's essential continuity. Football made no great impact on any of our usual sources of information. It was rarely sponsored, either privately or by public bodies, so does not appear in financial accounts. There is little sign of any external contributions to the game after the 1720s, when a Cambridgeshire rector was paying his customary 2s. 6d. to the Shrovetide footballers and Addison was at a match sponsored by his Worcestershire host.[3] It was not a spectator sport and attracted no advertising in its own right. Where it was advertised it was either as an adjunct to other sporting events[4] or occasionally for less playful purposes. In 1740 a match of 'Five Hundred Man a side' in East Anglia was publicised by the town crier, but the real object of the thousand strong crowd was to pull down mills at a time of food shortages and high prices. Similarly in 1765 two days of football at West Haddon were advertised, promising valuable prizes to 'all Gentlemen Gamesters' but the real objective again was to pull down enclosure fences and four years later it was enclosures at Holland Fen in Lincolnshire that prompted three more such 'matches' over the land in question, though perhaps more as a token protest than with intent to do direct damage. They were rare examples of the linking of sport with popular political and economic causes. What they may also suggest is that the holding of large-scale football games was common enough for them to be called without arising undue suspicion.[5]

Another reason, in fact, for the thinness of the evidence is the absence of any significant intervention by the authorities between the middle of the century and the 1790s. There were attempts at suppression at Louth in 1745 and 1754, at Worcester in 1743 and at Derby in 1747, another instance of the attempted repressions that ran alongside the sporting enthusiasms of the mid-century years. Thereafter there seems to have been little action against footballers for the next forty years. While this could mean that the game had lost its following, the other explanation is the more likely – that local magistrates and burgesses had become acquiescent. Football, in fact, seems to have been taken for granted. Big communal games were no more than an annual nuisance and the lesser play could be left to itself. The greater threats to the game were coming not from the law, but from changes in land use and urbanisation. The loss of playing space is known to date back to at least the mid-seventeenth century and Tudor enclosures may well have started the erosion even earlier.[6] Agricultural improvements tempted landlords to plough up more of their pastures and the traditional 'rights' of villages to use land for football and other sports were increasingly hard to prove in the courts without written evidence. The nature of the conflict had been well illustrated in the celebrated and well recorded Great Tey case in 1728 where the villagers won a verdict against a landlord who ploughed up and sowed a traditional November 5th bonfire and footballing site. By some means or other, however, these particular playing rights had been lost by the end of the century.[7] Doubtless games playing practices did sometimes lapse of their own accord, local fashions and local populations would change, or the people lose the strength of purpose or the means to carry their cause forward. While playing space was gradually being diminished there was a growing popular demand for leisure and recreation, adding to the pressure for newer forms of sporting entertainment. The history of football – the outstanding example of the continuing energy of traditional forms of play – would show that this could happen without destroying the old. Football, in the middle Georgian years, whatever its local form, constituted a common and virtually national playing experience that had within it its own vigour, drive, and elemental appeal.

If what was to become the nation's winter game was still largely unrecorded, its summer game was already well publicised and uniquely developed. Apart from being, as Richard Holt succinctly put it, 'the first team game in which the upper classes were expected to exert themselves without the aid of a horse,'[8] it had other novel features. Cricket involved all social classes and both sexes as both players and spectators. It could be everything from an inherited customary recreation to a highly organised aristocratic encounter for very high stakes. It could be business for innkeepers and professional players and a pleasant pastime for spectators, paying or otherwise.

The game enjoyed an initial period of prosperity in the middle of the century but faded with the loss of its important early sponsors such as the Duke of Richmond, Lord John Sackville and Frederick, Prince of Wales, whose early death, described by such contemporaries as Horace Walpole as deriving from a tennis injury, was subsequently appropriated to cricket. It could well have been neither.[9] There was broader disagreement over the state of the game itself. Reports that cricket was giving way to golf in 1767 and a reference to 'the expiring game of cricket' in 1771 are hardly supported by the numerous accounts of matches that begin to come through in the 1770s. Nearer the mark is the 1769 assertion, doubtless with Hambledon in mind, that 'Nothing can exceed the vogue that Cricket is in in some parts of Surrey and Hampshire,' or the evidence of its popularity in complaints about the Artillery Ground and its crowds in 1774.[10]

Whatever the conflict in contemporary judgements of cricket it soon became clear in retrospect that this was the beginning of another prosperous phase for the game. Reviewing John Nyren's *Young Cricketer's Tutor* when it first appeared in 1833, the Rev. John Mitford stressed its great progress in the 1770s.[11] The Hambledon Club was not solely responsible for this quickening of the sport's development and was, of course, far from being the birthplace of cricket, but it did play an important role. Founded in the late 1760s, it rose rapidly to prominence as gentlemen amateurs tapped both the skills of professional players and the interests of spectators over a wide area of Southern England. County matches had been growing steadily in number from the start of the Georgian period although under whatever banner teams took the field the big games were still mounted by the wealthy aristocrats whose predecessors had made the game conspicuous earlier in the century. In the 1770s they included the Duke of Dorset, Lord Tankerville and Sir Thomas Mann. There was now, though, a growing tendency, reflected in the Hambledon Club itself, for groups of individuals from the upper classes to come together jointly to sponsor the game.

With up to £1,000 sometimes at stake there had to be regulation sufficient to define the terms of the wager and cricket had had its embryonic rules since at least 1727, with a 1744 revision only months after Broughton had set out his pugilistic code. In a dynamic game, law revision was frequent, there were local meetings to settle rules (one at Norwich just after the 1744 review, for example) and a further recasting of the code in 1774. As in boxing, the general rules would be supplemented by specific contracts – Articles of Agreement – defining the terms of the individual match. As to the play itself, the wickets still had just two stumps and a single bail, while the bat was still likely to be curved or cudgel-shaped. Bowling was still underarm, though the ball was now pitched and not rolled along the ground, and teams were usually eleven a side.

More rustic forms of bat and ball play also continued to exist and the dividing line between cricket and stool-ball, with an upturned stool as the original wicket, is sometimes hard to draw. It has been suggested that the 'stoball,' to which there are several Gloucestershire references in the late seventeenth century, was in fact a form of cricket, but close identification is elusive. 'Stool and ball' itself was still flourishing, particularly as a Shrovetide and Lenten game in parts of the country,[12] while between the grand matches for high stakes and these elements of customary bat and ball play a whole variety of formal cricket matches were now taking place.

Villages and county towns in the south eastern heartland of the game fielded their regular teams, there were many local matches in London (some like that between Battersea and Clapham being described as 'annual'), and games between different occupational groups. While the most heavily wagered matches were supported by the money of the wealthy both they and many humbler games depended on that inevitable sporting entrepreneur, the innkeeper, acting as the facilitator for the gentry or on his own account. With such rare exceptions as the Artillery Ground, where admission had to be paid for, profit had to come from other sources, most commonly from the monopoly provision of food and drink, but sometimes also from the hire of equipment or, for bigger games, special seating when grandstands might be erected.[13]

There are uncertainties over the geographical spread of cricket, with the game in places lapsing after its first occurrence and subject to revival later. Through to the end of the Napoleonic Wars the majority of references to matches continue to be from the south-east, but by the time the wars began the game was also known and played over a considerably wider area. It was well established in parts of East Anglia and had extended into at least the south of Lincolnshire. There were strong pockets of play in the industrialising midlands where Nottingham, Leicester, Coventry and Birmingham had clubs, while Sheffield was unlikely to have been its most northerly regular outpost. Since the game was well enough known to be played in Northumberland on ice it is reasonable to suppose that it was also played there on grass.[14]

The unique sight that cricket could offer was that of men of widely divergent origins and background competing directly against each other. The different classes might bet with each other in the cockpit, jostle and rub shoulders with each other at a prizefight and even ride against each other on the racecourse, but on the cricket field alone was there actual face-to-face and man-to-man opposition. It was, by and large, conducive to good order. Where cricket was a rough and ready game played by the urban underclass it could and did give offence, with several cases of action by London magistrates against play in the less salubrious London locations. In the industrial areas too, where the upper class influence appears to have been weaker, matches were likely to be more robust and disputatious than elsewhere, but while there were bound to be many disagreements in what was already both a complex game and a rapidly developing one, these seldom led to public disorder. In earlier days the Duke of Richmond's team had been set upon by the crowd after the duke's late arrival meant that the game could not be finished, Brentwood players had been attacked by a mob of bargemen in an away game at Ware and crowd interference at the Kent v England match in 1744 had meant that 'it was with difficulty that the match was played out.[15] What is perhaps the more remarkable though is not the occasional violence attending cricket matches but the fact that disorders seem to have been no more pronounced or frequent than they were in several later ages, and this in spite of the volatile nature of eighteenth century crowds, the dominance of betting on all aspects of the play and the virtual absence of policing. This contributed to the general tolerance of the game and made its prospects for the future more promising than most. Public comment on cricket, while by no means wholly uncritical, would make it the only large scale sport with a substantial plebeian element to win any measure at all of positive approval.

Other small ball games were attracting little attention. Bowling enjoyed mixed fortunes. The number of active bowlers was probably increasing but the social parameters of its appeal were narrowing. In London new venues had appeared on the edges of the expanding city, many of them in the voguish tea gardens, one of which actually inherited the once famous greens in the gardens of Marylebone Manor House where Pepys and Pope had been regular players.[16] These may have made up for the earlier losses of bowling places when those in and about the centre of the city had been built over as their leases fell in. A few of the famous did still play, including Sir John Vanbrugh and Charles James Fox, but as the greens moved to the periphery bowling was losing its upper class following. The green at Regent's Park Manor House was soon to close (in 1777) after 'persons of rank had ceased to play upon it owing to its having fallen into disrepute,' while one of the later and most popular of the new gardens, Bagnigge Wells, opened in 1759, had relegated skittles and bowling to one corner.[17]

Neither of the factors that affected the fortunes of bowling in London had quite the same force in the provinces. In most towns and cities land was still under less pressure and the impression is that not only did ancient greens like those at Chesterfield, Southampton and Bedford survive but that new ones came into use and the sport still had its notable local enthusiasts, from John Dalton in Manchester to Josiah Wedgwood in the Potteries. The innkeeper had long ago seen the opportunities for profit from bowls and skittles and could often find space for an alley if not for a green. Even where skittle alleys were unpopular with magistrates, as at Birmingham in the 1770s, greens themselves appear to have been tolerated. The bowling sports did take several forms and had many different settings. They still featured in some wakes and revels, but were as likely to reflect a promoter's eye to business as be survivals from any traditional folk origins – the sporting entrepreneur was always ready to use seasonal emphases as stimulants, but not as restrictions![18] Skittles and ninepins had been common Easter and Lenten games and some vestiges of this seasonal stress may certainly have remained. More certain is the persistence of local variants such as the half-bowl game in Hertfordshire, where it was known as 'rolly-polly.' In Strutt's description it was complicated to play, the targets being fifteen small conical pins. There was probably also a miniature version of this since Birmingham licensees were also under threat if they kept 'Roly-poly' tables. It was a far cry from yet another style of bowling, that played on the greens of great houses where lawns of slow-growing camomile were kept trim by skilful scything and endless broom work.[19]

Handball and **racquet** play had as long a history as bowling and skittles and had taken forms virtually as diverse. While their Victorian historian's assertion that all racquet games were once played with the hand and had a common origin is doubtless correct, they had been separated out into dis-

The inviting north wall of Martock church's tower is now largely hidden by by heating apparatus, but the mid-eighteenth century measures to hinder youths from climbing the buttresses to retrieve fives balls from the roof are still readily identifiable.

tinct forms for at least two centuries,[20] but in spite of their long history none of the games apart from Real Tennis was much systematised before the last quarter of the eighteenth century. Competitive handball play against a wall had been a recognised game as fives for over a century – it had its place in Johnson's Dictionary as 'a kind of play with a ball.' In some parts of the country it was a long standing common pursuit and there was commercial provision for play in the capital. It has left both written and physical evidence of its early history in the south west, where the smooth stone walls of many a church tower provided sites for play and where repairing damage caused by fives players is itemised in churchwardens' accounts. At Mere in Wiltshire four shillings had to be spent in 1705 'for mending ye fives place window' and at Martock in south-east Somerset, the future heartland of the organised game, the problems were so persistent that eventually, to prevent players from climbing up to the roof to retrieve balls, the deep climbing footholes were filled in and the favourite buttress chamfered at the corners, rounded to make climbing difficult. The results are still plainly visible and this was certainly one part of the country where fives playing entered the last quarter of the eighteenth century as a thriving popular game.[21]

Meanwhile, fives courts were advertising for custom in London and may have existed commercially elsewhere – it was said to be one of the commonest games in Birmingham at this time. The Fives Court in London's St Martin's Lane (later to play its part in the history of pugilism) was a going concern by the 1740s when its owner publicised his new tennis court in Holborn. Fives playing, too, was relatively cheap at 2d a game, compared with the 1s. 0d. charge for tennis at the new court. At the other extreme 'handball' still persisted as part of seasonal play, common between Shrove Tuesday and Easter, it was said, in Yorkshire, Lincolnshire, Suffolk and other counties. Occasionally it could still have some ritual significance. At Keswick, on Easter Tuesday, girls played handball in a form of competition to decide who should host the evening's celebrations, 'at what house the merry night is to be.' Handball play was sometimes promised at fairs and markets, but it is much easier to imagine play against Josiah Wedgwood's factory walls, which attracted a fine of two shillings if it happened where there were windows.[22]

The racquet games were much less widely played. The most sophisticated of them, **real tennis**, with its architecturally complex courts, had never been more than a minority sport and had gone out of fashion after the passing of Charles II and the loss of its royal support. Pressure on space may also have contributed to the quite rapid reduction of London's courts from fourteen in the Stuart heyday to a mere two. That at Hampton Court had been restored by William III, but this seems to have been part and parcel of his general renovation of the palace rather than any sign of interest in the game itself, whose historians have described it as moribund during the eighteenth century. However, to set against this, a proprietor could see profit in building a new court and charge high fees for its use.[23] More plebeian forms of racquet play had certainly advanced very little. That between equal teams, played outside over a central cord or net, known since Elizabethan days, seems to have gone out of use. Beating a ball against a wall doubtless had a long history of informal competition but its systematisation into the game of racquets was yet to happen. The most common form of racquet or board play was probably the shuttlecock and battledore which was still one of the seasonal games particularly associated with Shrovetide, usually as a recreation for women or children. At Leicester Shrove Tuesday was actually known as 'Shuttlecock Day' and among places where it was common was the West Riding of Yorkshire – at Morley, near Leeds, 'the highways of the village were occupied by hundreds of children and grown-up women playing the game of battledore and shuttle-feather.'[24]

In general, the small ball individual games were waiting to be invented. They would not have to wait very long. The foundations for sporting expansion were already firmly laid, with new competitive recreations waiting in the wings and the old apparently fading into the background of the passing years, but rarely wholly forgotten. The continuing history of the already established major sports forms an important element in this study, but alongside them were many lesser pursuits, all contributing to the general sporting scene, all in their varying states of readiness by the middle of the Georgian years.

Attempts to be comprehensive, though, even in these earlier stages, are bound to fall short. Too much is spontaneous, fleeting and elusive. Even among known games there are likely to be many scantily recorded. To take, at this time, billiards as an example. Bailey's dictionary described it just as 'a Game,' Boswell added that it was 'a pretty game,' which he resisted because it would take up too much of his time, and Strutt was to dismiss it not because it was unpopular but because it was so well known that there was 'no enlargement necessary.' Then there is the enormous diversity of play itself nowhere more so than among children's games. A list of the pursuits of just one school, Eton College, is as forbiddingly extensive as it is frequently impenetrable:

> Shirking Walls, Scrambling Walls, Bally Cally, Battledores, Peg-top, Peg in the ring, Goals, Hopscotch, Heading, Conquering Lobs, Hoops, Marbles, Trap ball, Steal baggage, Puss in the Corner, Cut Gallows, Kites, Cloyster and Flying Gigs, Tops, Humming Tops, Hunt the Hare, Hunt the dark lanthorn, Chuck, Sinks, Starecaps, Hurtlecap.[25]

Such a catalogue typifies the sporting state of England in the later eighteenth century, in that its play came in all shapes and sizes and under innumerable titles. Much traditional folk recreation still remained, some still punctuating the year with the rhythms of the past, some increasingly mutating into the quasi-commercial. There were young people's competitive activities, some of which, such as swimming, were yet to grow into sports in any modern sense. There were, too, many sports that existed in a minor key, some like golf, skating and sailing with the potential for growth and others, like prison bars or cudgel play, gradually being left behind as moods and tastes changed.

Chasing games, for instance, had always been a regular element in folk play. They had sometimes been ordered into various forms of hare and hounds or roughly formulated into team pursuits such as barley break, a relatively mild form of team tag which, since it usually involved both sexes, gave obvious opportunities for pairing between them.[26] In tougher form as prison bars (or prisoners' base – the names of folk games are multifarious) it was confined to men. Strutt recalls 'a grand match at base' that he saw around 1770 in the neighbouring fields behind the British Museum, played between 'twelve gentlemen of Cheshire' and twelve from Derbyshire 'for a considerable sum of money' and providing 'much entertainment' for the crowd. Could there possibly be any ancestral connection with baseball in the version he also describes from Essex, played on a marked ground, with the bases thirty yards apart?[27] Essentially the game was too limited and offered too little scope for refinement to ever become a serious spectator sport. There were slightly more possibilities in converting tug o' war contests from customary expressions of local rivalries (like that traditionally between two wards of the town at Ludlow) into occasional competitions at athletics meetings.[28]

Many stick and ball games were being played. Variations on stoolball were common. There was trap-ball, played at Bury St Edmunds on holidays not only by women, but by old women as well, and 'kittycat and backstick' in Northumberland, all forms of striking a ball or other missile with some short stick, developed in the northern counties into the formal game of knurr and spell.[29] Among the stick and ball games that did have a future were two that were still, so far as England was concerned, the province of émigrés – the Irish form of hurling and golf from Scotland, where Strutt acknowledged it to be widely popular. There had been a few early initiatives south of the border. In the 1750s there was play at Molesey Hurst on the

Thames, near Hampton Court and one of the capital's all-purpose recreation spaces, while the Blackheath club was probably even earlier. It was said to have originated, as many Scots clubs had done, from a single competition – here a silver cup – in 1767, but it seems as yet to have had no imitators anywhere else, either in the capital or the country.[30]

The **Water Sports** were poised for expansion. Swimming was rarely competitive in any formal fashion though doubtless boys raced against each other in the country's rivers and some schools, such as Eton, had their recognised bathing places. The popularity of swimming with London young-sters is evident from a 1764 account of their activities in the Thames at Chelsea and in the ponds on Hampstead Heath. Two years later the Bow Street magistrates were threatening the frequent Sunday bathers in St James's Park, presumably grown men as well as boys. The fear of water had cer-tainly gradually diminished and medical authorities were beginning to give bathing some cautious approval.[31] Swimming seems to have been a fairly common skill – Samuel Johnson, for instance, was taught as a boy by his father – and bathing started to attract commercial provision. This ranged from hiring out discrete bathing huts by the side of a river advertised as an additional attraction by a Norwich inn, to a fully fledged sea water bath at Wivenhoe, which was actually eight miles from the coast. The distance was argued in its favour, the seaside itself was still looked on with suspicion and the discovery of real sea bathing still lay some years ahead.[32]

Rowing was a business long before it became a sport, a fact which in the future was to have considerable implications for the whole concept of amateurism. For Londoners the Thames was the city's great highway and for its watermen speed was a necessity as they competed to reach prospective travellers arriving on the banks. From 1717 their rivalries were acknowledged in the annual race for the rich Coat and Badge bequeathed by the comic actor, Thomas Doggett.[33] Other competitive rowing also took place. London appren-tices were in the habit of hiring cutters and rowing up to Richmond or Kew, competing against each other for wagers. Because they inevitably did this on their one free day – Sunday – they not only aroused the displeasure of sabbatarians but also provoked criticism of boat hirers by watermen, whose own Sunday working was restricted by law. Sunday rowing on the Thames for pleasure alone was also common, as was punting further up-river – there was even a punting match reported at Shepperton in 1758.[34]

Most of the evidence for rowing during the first three quarters of the eighteenth century comes from London and the Thames but from the rapid spread of rowing and sailing regattas over the whole country within a few decades it seems safe to assume that boating in several forms was wide-spread and poised to become competitive. There had for many years been occasional sailing matches on the Thames, but again regular sailing races still lay in the future. The water was more likely to be put to full sporting use when it was frozen over. Sliding and skating were popular pastimes with Londoners and again as Sunday amusements provoked critical comment. Skating had already also begun to be competitive, particularly and most suitably on the Fens – a report from 1763, for example, spoke of a 15 mile race for ten guineas a side, won in 46 minutes. Many more races and challenges would follow in the cold winters to come.[35]

Individual sports can have their own distinctive histories, not always sharing in the general recreational current. **Archery** was one such. When it was compulsory as military training it was often the bane of governments by being used as a sport, shooting at small targets over short distances, or not being practised at all. The last few flights of arrows were shot in anger early in the Civil War and from the Restoration onwards archery became simply a recreation. The return of the monarchy itself had been celebrated by 'a splendid and glorious show' of four hundred bowmen in Hyde Park, and archery had continued to have a limited vogue. The Finsbury Archers, based on the Artillery Ground, together with the Honorable Artillery Company, kept up the tradition, having many permanent marks set up in the fields that were still adjacent to the ground. These 'marks' were used as targets by the marksmen as they moved from field to field, giving targets at various ranges. They were not popular with the landowners and they began to be removed during the first half of the century, the start of a running battle that continued for several decades until the last marks were removed. Meanwhile, shooting at butts began to win some slight measure of support, but this was another sport that was awaiting its time.[36]

One final minor activity which was already thriving was **bell-ringing** and not just as a pleasant recreation or a musical experience but as a competitive sport, noted by foreign visitors such as Henri Misson as unique to the English. Its popularity may well have arisen by way of reaction against the limitations placed on ringing church bells in the Commonwealth years and it was a well reported pursuit through the eighteenth century, and one to which – unusually – there could be little objection. It was a regular attraction at fairs while matches between parish teams were both frequent and fiercely contested. Hats were the common prizes. A typical advertisement from Berkshire had four teams competing, subscribing a guinea a man, and there were also prizes of gloves and ribands for the second and third teams.[37] Bell ringers could be a regular, well organised body like the 'Sherwood Company of Change-Ringers' from the village on the edge of Nottingham who were in the habit of making an annual whitsuntide tour, much after the manner of cycling clubs a century or more later. In 1770 it took them to Burton-on-Trent, where the bells were 'in very bad Order,' and to All Saints Church in Derby. Competition could be keen enough to land contesting parties in court. A team of Sherborne ringers took the organisers of a match at Mudford to Taunton Assizes in 1737 and successfully gained possession of the 'six Prize-Shirts' they had won there – and wagers over times for ringing set peals would soon be commonplace.[38]

Where exactly competitive bell-ringing (which appears to have had no pre-Restoration history) should be placed on the scale of progression from communal folk play to modern sport is just one of the complexities that the sport of mid-1770s England presents. In general terms, the first three-quarters of the eighteenth century had seen another phase in that long transmutation of play from forms rooted in medieval chivalry and Renaissance manners on the one hand and rustic ritual on the other into sport that was organised, regulated, largely self-contained and often commercialised. At no stage was this gradual change of emphasis coordinated or consistent – after all, the Tudor tourney had most of the elements usually associated with modernity in sport – and during the eighteenth century there was no neat straight-line development. Innovation and progression were there, and often significantly so, but the apparently permanent and unchanging could be at least as important as the new. There have, in fact, subsequently been two significant if apparently contradictory underestimates of the make-up of the country's sporting experience from the later years of the eighteenth century through to at least the 1820s and possibly for a further decade beyond that. On the one hand there can be little doubt that, in sheer quantity of events, the coarser and traditional sports, and particularly the blood sports, outnumbered those in the newly developed forms of play. There were fifty cock-fights or bull-baits to one cricket match or horse race. At the same time, while commercialism would lie somewhere near the heart of most of the newer sporting activities it was, as will become increasingly evident, virtually as often, an actual support to traditional festivals, sports and celebrations.

When change did occur the process of transition itself was usually undirected, often uneasy, and sometimes contradictory. Indeed paradox and progress were seldom far apart. There was both regional diversity and the beginnings of centralisation. In terms of class participation, there was both increasing separation and increasing interaction, while no single social class behaved always in total unison.

In a society so firmly based on property ownership class differentiation in sport was inescapable, but in only a few pursuits were the barriers of rank insurmountable, such as those protected by the game laws. The crudest sports in notorious venues might become pre-eminently the preserve of the most economically and culturally impoverished, but even here there were individual exceptions. The roughest of pick-up prize-fights could often find a gentleman present who could be called upon to arbitrate and there were others like J. J. Brayfield who attended sports of every kind, including regular badger baits and was also, according to his obituary, 'constant at Newgate executions.'[39] At the other end of the scale total isolation on the basis of wealth or position was unusual. Even where there was no mutual participation there was enough common ground for cross-fertilisation, the sports of one class borrowing the habits and practices of another, and sometimes modifying a game's affiliations in the process. Cricket provides the obvious example, growing out of and influenced by its origins as rustic folk play and developed in the context of the gaming habits and regulatory needs of the wealthy, but at the same time still providing the one game where they and the plebs might compete directly against each other. In sports spectating the togetherness could lie anywhere between nearly total and the practically non-existent. The cockpit might have Cheney's Rules and Orders with their demands for social stratification,[40] but both illustration and comment point to a high level of social mixing in the crowds. In pugilism the immediate circumstances of the individual fight would determine where on the scale of mutuality the crowd found itself – from the separation produced by the racecourse grandstand or the effectively enclosed site, with paid entrance, to the rough and tumble crowding together of the pick-up fight or that hounded from one intended venue to another. Among the major sports of the day the racecourse was likely to demonstrate the most regular separation of the classes, sometimes through the exclusivity of the grandstand, more often by the gentlefolk's presence in their carriages, but even so there was a genuine sense of sharing in the same event, the local comments of all groups invariably referring to 'our races.' It may be argued that such impressions of togetherness were, over the whole sporting scene, largely illusory, but what is believed to be happening often has at least as much historical significance as what actually is.

One real contribution to the coexistence between the sporting classes lay in the readiness of the gentry to make use of commercial facilities for their play, going to Smith at the Artillery Ground, or to Broughton at his emporium while they could, and having generally some minor local business-man – a stable proprietor or the like – as the clerk, and effectively the manager, of their race meeting. The motives of matchmakers may have been no more elevated than laziness, a disdain for the details of arrangement and a smack of ostentation in wanting to put on a conspicuous show, but by taking the route they did, throwing their contests open to spectators and not coralling them behind high walls in their own parks they were helping to produce a sporting culture with the capacity to expand and to take in an ever widening sector of the country's recreation. Generalisations about the sporting experience and expectations of any social class do, though, have to have their reservations. It is all too tempting to think of the eighteenth century aristocratic and landed classes as endlessly playing cricket, running their horses at Newmarket and sponsoring pugilists and pedestrians. There might be an imposing catalogue of the nobility among the subscribers to the *Racing Calendar*, but this had rapidly become an essential contemporary equivalent of the coffee table book for any country house and opening it would show that only a minority of the titled actually raced their own horses, even on their own local circuits. It is even questionable whether sport was of immediate interest to a majority in the upper classes, particularly before fox hunting became widely popular. There were certainly those like the Earl of Chesterfield who had little but contempt for sport of any sort and aspiring socialites like Boswell who could spare it no time.[41] The casual and spasmodic nature of much reporting of sporting events in both the national and provincial presses indicates that editors did not always put it high on the priorities of their readership. Equally, though, it would be a mistake to follow the common practice of dismissing the literate and rising middle classes from all sporting consideration. They did have their own way to make. They were more likely than most to lean towards the frowning dissenting religions and be devotees of the Protestant work ethic, but they were far from completely shunning all sport. Merchants were known to sponsor pugilists and pedestrians, lawyers to play cricket, and large numbers across the commercial classes to be involved in horse racing, particularly at the local level, and whether for pleasure or profit. The minor capitalist had, indeed, already come to see sport itself as offering enough opportunities for good new business to overcome any suspicions of its dangers that his class attitudes might have housed.

The sporting experience of the working masses doubtless showed the greatest diversity of all, both in terms of inclination and opportunity. At one extreme was that underclass which clustered around the coarser sports, crudely carried on in known disreputable venues, but there was also extensive rural poverty, revealed in poor law records, with large numbers of 'the ragged poor' (as one Wiltshire vicar was about to describe them) who could have had little chance of enjoyments of any sort. The 'respectable' working man was hardly as yet being celebrated as such but there were already many who had grown out of throwing at cocks and a small but increasing minority that was subscribing to beliefs which actively rejected most of what was on offer by way of sporting entertainment. The various sects were all alert to the sporting sins of their members but differed in the fierceness of their treatment of offenders. The Bedford Independents would demand public repentance for 'foolish conduct in going to cock-fighting' or to 'nine pinns and quoits,' while the gentle James Clegg reluctantly accepted that his flock would sometimes fall short of perfection and be tempted away by fairs, wakes and race meetings. Wholesale conversion to new ways was never easily come by and many must have lived uneasily between the old habits they had abjured and the new life that they sought. Evangelicalism was a growing force both within and without the Established Church, but the growing sin of 'backsliding' came with it.[42]

A more tangible factor making for diversity in popular recreation was that of geography. The continuing diversity found in both town and country contrasts with that more acknowledged sporting theme of centralisation and unification, the tendency to produce rules of play which, however limited their original intention, came to have wider and wider application. This was a London based movement, whether its progenitors happened to be there at Broughton's emporium, at Hambledon, or racing at Newmarket. Nor did it come about through conscious proselytising but as a matter of practical convenience, first to the originators themselves and then to others in the sporting world as they applied the rules elsewhere, quickly in the prize ring, fairly readily on the cricket field, and somewhat more gradually on the turf. The phenomenon of London itself, much the largest urban centre in the land, with nearly 700,000 and over 10% of the total population by 1750, had much to do with both this centralising process and the early appearance of new sporting provision. For pugilists it was already necessary to come to the capital to win any national status. The best jockeys gravitated to Newmarket and cricketers seeking the most profitable employment were attracted to sponsors who invariably had London associations.

London's rapidly expanding population had its own more and more demanding sporting needs, putting its capacity to satisfy them under steady pressure and making for innovation. Much of the people's play could still be accommodated in the great open spaces of the royal parks, where everything was to be found from foot races and prize-fights to the sight of regional games by immigrant workers or ice skating in winter. There were too those other open spaces, often rough and litter strewn and tinged with various degrees of ill-repute. Some, like Tothill Fields and the Long Fields still remained, but they had gradually been reduced – Lincoln's Inn Fields by its enclosure by Act of Parliament in 1735, because 'many wicked and disorderly persons have frequently met therein using unlawful sports and games,' and the notorious Hockley Hole by culvetting the Fleet Ditch twenty years later.[43] Londoners persisted in their search for recreation. Like most new urban populations – and only a minority of its inhabitants were more than two generations away from their country roots – their first attempt was to preserve their old rural play, but crowding and lack of space presented growing problems as more and more nearby villages were swallowed up by the capital's continuous growth.

There were, though, other diversions. The quarterly hanging day at Tyburn was one such, effectively a holiday for most Londoners. They sought competitive entertainment, however, and many had a modicum of money to spare for it. There were few sporting venues where they would actually have to pay for entrance, apart from the cockpits, the Artillery Ground and the short-lived Bellsize Park and the boxing arenas, but once drawn to many sports, they would often find a single provider of food, drink, and other enticements. The commercialisation of sport, mainly through catering, gathered pace throughout the century and the hand of the innkeeper was everywhere, both promoting organised sports and in the underpinning of wakes and other customary celebrations, putting them on a new economic footing. It could be by resuscitating what was weakening or by exploitation of what was still enduring – what it did often mean was some modification in what was on the programme, for example the introduction of relatively organised competitive activities such as foot races, cricket matches, bowling and skittles.

Other changes of significance were also under way. As corporate interest in sport had diminished in the towns – except where there was an economic thrust to support its races – the county orientation of sporting competition had strengthened. The club, too, had begun to make its appearance as the first permanent sporting institution, a stabilising element in the organisation of play but also a powerful means of influencing its social contexts. It may have begun at Newmarket to avoid any return of royal dictatorship there but it had the potential – which it would eventually use in many sports – to limit and control participation and to prevent open democratisation. Among the players themselves, the status of the professional was also changing. Less often was he the permanent retainer of his sponsor and more often the paid man on a match fee, while more broadly the tie of a man to his native place, basic to the old customary contests, was beginning to loosen.

All in all the first three-quarters of the eighteenth century saw a flourishing and varied sporting life. While still suffused by the folk traditions of the past it was already taking on features out of which a distinctly novel and more systematic mode of competitive play would emerge – already cricket was beating this pathway strongly. At the same time, the continued existence of the old, and the pressure on it of new habits, new assumptions and changing environments was producing tensions which, with an expanding population, seemed bound to increase rather than diminish. The sporting future might have been hard to predict in the 1770s. It was not the most optimistic of decades, the thoughts of inevitable progress that were to flourish in the next century had as yet put down few firm roots. The most that might have been ventured was a trust among the literate classes that the cruder and more socially damaging sports would be reduced and a hope and expectation among the people at large that their play would go on uninterrupted by the changes they began to experience all around them. From our standpoint, and with our realisation that play never exists in a social, economic and political vacuum, it is clear that the momentous shifts in the national life over the next forty years could never have left sport unaltered or unscathed.

Notes

1. Richard Carew, *A Survey of Cornwall*, 1602, pp 73-75. Doubtless it was the rougher style of game watched in Hyde Park by Oliver Cromwell in 1654 and said to have involved no fewer than 150 Cornishmen, Robert S. Paul, *The Lord Protector: Religion and Politics in the Life of Oliver Cromwell*, 1955, p 24. See also *Hamilton's Papers*, Camden Society, p 171, quoted in supplementary material in Strutt, *Sports and Pastimes*, p 93; Percy M. Young, *A History of British Football*, 1968, p 38.
2. *Kendal Book of Record 1575*, ed., R. S. Ferguson, Kendal, 1892, p 103; J. L. André, 'Miscellaneous Antiquities of Dorking,' *Surrey Archaeological Collections IV*, Surrey Archaeological Society, 1899, p 15. There was not always even the need for a ball at all – at the Wrekin Wakes in Shropshire there was a mass struggle for possession of the Wrekin hill itself, *Shropshire Folklore: A Sheaf of Gleanings*, ed., Charlotte S. Burne, 1833, pp 262/3.
3. H. G. Tebbutt, *ed., The Minutes of the First Independent Church (now Bunyan Meeting) at Bedford 1656-1766*, Publications of the Bedfordshire Historical Record Society, vol. 55, 1976; William K Clay, *A History of the Parish of Waterbeach in the County of Cambridge*, Publications of the Cambridge Antiquarian Society, vi, 1861, p 60n. See Malcolmson, *Popular Recreations*, pp 38/9; Young, *History of British Football*, pp 56/7, 53, 48.
4. *e.g.* during the Eton v England cricket matches at Newmarket in 1751 and as part of a 'country wake' at Hendon, *Norwich Mercury*, 6 July 1751; J. G. W. Davies, 'Cambridge University,' in E. W. Swanton, ed., *The World of Cricket*, 1966, p 173; *General Advertiser*, 28 August 1752.
5. Goulstone, *Summer Solstice Games*, pp 101, 32; Walvin, *The People's Game*, p 24; Malcolmson, *Popular Recreations*, p 40; W. Marrat, *The History of Lin-*

colnshire, 3 vols., Boston, 1814, I, pp 138-146.

6. R. W. Goulding, *Louth Old Corporation Records*, Louth, 1891, p 54; John Noake, *Worcester in Olden Times*, 1849, p 197; *Derby Mercury*, 27 February 1747; Malcolmson, *Popular Recreations*, p 139. The camping close at Milton, near Cambridge, became part of the rectory land in 1653, William K. Clay, *A History of the Parish of Milton in the County of Cambridge*, Transactions of the Cambridge Antiquarian Society, xi, 1869, p 25.

7. Fully documented in Malcolmson, *Popular Recreations*, pp 112-114.

8. Holt, *Sport and the British*, p 24.

9. Horace Walpole, *Memoirs of George II, in Works*, 1798, vii, pp 61/2. See also William Chafin, *Anecdotes and History of Cranborne Chase*, 1818, ed., Desmond Hawkins, Wimborne, 1991, p 95.

10. *Whitehall Evening Post*, 11 August 1767; 20 July 1769; Rowland Bowen, *Cricket: A History of its Growth and Development throughout the World*, 1970, p 55; *Morning Chronicle*, 23 August 1774. Many newspaper references to early cricket derive from George B. Buckley, *Fresh Light on Eighteenth Century Cricket, Birmingham*, undated (Preface 1935) and *Fresh Light on Pre-Victorian Cricket*, Birmingham, 1937, and from Goulstone, *Sports History*, 1-10, where contributions can be presumed to be his own unless another author is quoted.

11. *Gentleman's Magazine*, July and September, 1833. Also reviewed by Leigh Hunt, *London Journal*, 21 May 1834.

12. 'Stoball as a 17th Century Form of Cricket,' *Sports History*, 1, 1982, pp 19-21; Wright, *British Calendar Customs*, I, p 40; Malcolmson, *Popular Recreations*, pp 42, 38/9. See also Strutt, *Sports and Pastimes*, p 101.

13. See *Morning Chronicle*, 17 July 1779; *Public Advertiser*, 10 September 1773; *Kentish Gazette*, 5 August 1780; Buckley, *Eighteenth Century Cricket and Pre-Victorian Cricket*, passim. See also, e.g., 'Cricket in Ashford, Kent,' *Sports History*, 9, 1986, pp 17-19.

14. *Stamford Mercury*, 20 July 1771; 'Warwickshire Cricket Notes 1760-1850,' *Sports History*, 7, 1985, pp 13-23.

15. *Fog's Weekly Journal*, 28 August 1731; *St James Evening Post*, 18 August 1737; *Daily Advertiser*, 30 June 1744. For magistrates' threats against disorderly cricket see *Public Advertiser*, 3 August 1764; *Whitehall Evening Post*, 3 August 1764; *Lloyds Evening Post*, 17 August 1767.

16. Among those with greens in the 1770s were the Belvedere Tea Gardens, Dobney's in the Pentonville Road, the Black Queen Coffee House and Cooper's Gardens.

17. Boulton, *Amusements of Old London*, I, pp 57, 68, 53; George T. Burrows, *All About Bowls*, undated, p 11; Alfred H. Haynes, *The Story of Bowls*, 1972, p 17.

18. Burrows, *All About Bowls*, p 12. For bowls at festivals see *e.g.*, Yattenden (1773) and Reading (1775), Goulstone, *Summer Solstice Games*, pp 17, 54.

19. Wright, *British Calendar Customs*, I, pp 34, 106, 163; Strutt, *Sports and Pastimes*, p 221; Langford, *Century of Birmingham Life*, pp 257/8

20. John Armitage, 'History of Ball Games,' in Aberdare, *ed.*, *Rackets*, p 23. Richard Mulcaster had noted that handball was played with a soft ball, racquet play with a harder one and that both could be played 'with an other, or against a wall alone,' *Positions: Wherein Those Primitive Circumstances be examined which are Necesessarie For the Training up of children either for skill in their books or health in their bodie*, 1581, *ed.*, R. H. Quick, 1888, pp 104/5.

21. *Somerset and Dorset Notes and Queries*, 17, 1923, pp 75-77. For similar prob-

lems near Bath see B. M. Willmott, *An English Community: Batheaston with S. Catherine*, Bath, 1969, pp 51, 65.

22. William Hutton, *History of Birmingham*, 1789, p 130; *Daily Advertiser*, 28 October, 1742; Wright, *British Calendar Customs*, I, pp 34-37; Goulstone, *Summer Solstice Games*, p 54.

23. In Aberdare, *ed.*, *Rackets*, p 22 and passim.; Julian Marshall, *The Annals of Tennis*, 1878, p 78; Lord Aberdare, *The Story of Tennis*, 1959, *passim*.

24. *Nichol's Progresses of Queen Elizabeth*, quoted in Aberdare, *ed.*, *Rackets*, p 22; Dorothy Osborne, *Letters of Dorothy Osborne to Sir William Temple, ed.*, E. A. Parry, 1914, p 62; Wright, *British Calendar Customs*, I, p 28; William Smith, *Morley: Ancient and Modern*, 1886, p 142.

25. Lyte, *History of Eton College*, p 321.

26. Wright, *British Calendar Customs*, I, pp 9/10. See also Dyer, *British Popular Customs*, pp 16, 380 and *passim*.

27. Strutt, *Sports and Pastimes*, p 68.

28. Wright, *British Calendar Customs*, I, p 29.

29. Dyer, *British Popular Customs*, p 86; Wright, *British Calendar Customs*, pp 34-37, 110. See also Holt, *Sport and the British*, p 68.

30. Strutt, *Sports and Pastimes*, p 97; Sir Guy Campbell, 'The Early History of British Golf,' B. Darwin et al., *A History of Golf in Britain*, 1952, pp 50 ff.; Robert Browning, *A History of Golf: The Royal and Ancient Game*, 1955, pp 39, 45; Geoffrey Cousins, *Golf in Britain: A Social History from the beginnings to the present day*, 1975, pp 13/14. Garrick was among those who played with Scottish friends at Molesey.

31. Robert Burton had described cold bathing as 'a severe method of Cure,' *The Anatomy of Melancholy*, 1621; 1932 edition, 3 vols., II, p 33. See also *e.g.* William Cullen, M.D., *First Lines in the Practice of Physic, 1776-84*, 1796 Edinburgh edition, II, p 249.

32. James Clifford, *Young Samuel Johnson*, 1955, p 29; *Norwich Mercury*, 10 May 1746; *Ipswich Journal*, 25 April 1761 – Wivenhoe avoided the 'noxious inhalations' of the seaside and was kept free 'from all contagious Disorders.'

33. With Jem Broughton, in 1720, its most famous winner, Hylton Cleaver, *A History of Rowing*, 1957, p 24.

34. *ibid*, p 22; George, *London Life in the Eighteenth Century*, p 272; Whitaker, *Eighteenth Century Sunday*, p 131.

35. *Public Advertiser*, 12 January, 1760; *British Magazine*, II, p 4, quoted in *Sports History*, 4, 1983, p 3.

36. Strutt, *Sports and Pastimes*, pp 56-58.

37. Misson, *Memoirs*, p 306; *Northampton Mercury*, 30 September 1765, 6 October 1776; *Chelmsford Chronicle*, 19 May 1775; *Reading Mercury*, 16 May 1768.

38. *Northampton Mercury*, 18 June 1770; *Sherborne Mercury*, 5 April 1737.

39. *SM*, March 1821, p 283.

40. For Cheney's directions see Roger Longrigg, *The English Squire and His Sport*, 1977, p 174.

41. Deuchar argues in fact for the emergence of a distinctive sporting class from about the 1730s onwards, *Sporting Art in Eighteenth Century England*, p 10.

42. See *e.g.* Tebbutt, *ed.*, *Minutes of the First Independent Church*, Bedfordshire Historical Record Society, vol. 55, 1976; *Digest of the Minutes of the Methodist Conference*, Halifax, 1827.

THEMES

3.

The Status of Sport

The *Sporting Magazine*, in its first issue and after setting out its prospectus, roundly asserted that the need for 'recreation and exercise' was 'self-evident.' The preface to boxing's *Pancratia* made the same claim that 'human nature' was 'so constituted as to require both bodily and mental recreation.' The best physical exercise, the magazine argued, would be had from 'athletic rural sports' and the mental refreshment would come from the gambling involved.[1] These, though, were very partial views. Medical opinion was cautious over the degree of exercise needed for health. Dr John Armstrong's 1744 poem, *The Art of Preserving Health*, berated the 'athletic fool' and William Cullen's *First Lines in the Practice of Physic* from twenty years later would only sanction moderate exercise that was neither 'heating not fatiguing to the body.' Even the *Sporting Magazine* itself could offer little more. It dealt with the specialised training of jockeys, pugilists and pedestrians, but its one significant excursion into the general promotion of health was by way of an extended extract from Churchill's *General Guide to Health*, which advocated nothing more vigorous than horse riding.[2]

In practice, the broad proposition that physical exertion was beneficial was gradually gaining ground through the eighteenth century – and was it perhaps by way of cautions that both Armstrong and Cullen had new editions in 1796? What was much slower to find general acceptance was the proposition that sport provided the best means of taking that exercise. Apart from those who subscribed to Richard Baxter's old Puritan view that all the exercise needed could be found in useful tasks, without the need for play, one of sport's great disadvantages in the eyes of many was its seemingly unbreakable connection with gambling. There were sportsmen like William Wyndham who never wagered, and the admirable 'Yoicks' who claimed 'to need not the excitement of betting to raise my spirits and interest my heart,'[3] but for many others gambling, as well as being morally dubious of itself, provided the principal door through which many other ills could enter. William Law's *Serious Call to a Devout and Holy Life*, which was significant both directly and also through its profound influence on the Wesleys, had insisted that a gentleman could not 'live in *idleness* and *indulgence*, in *sports* and *gaming*.' It was a message to be preached to all classes, condemning everything from the 'savage diversions' of the animal sports to attendance at wakes. Sport was under suspicion for the evil company it attracted and the time that it wasted. It did not require religious fervour for many to share much the same views as to its worth.[4]

How widespread such wholly critical views were, even among the literate classes, is hard to estimate. There is the suggestion that for much of the eighteenth century the sporting world was seen as a world apart, and that, for instance, the low aesthetic status afforded by the cultured to sporting art reflected the low esteem granted to sporting activities themselves.[5] It is an analysis which manages to be at once both pertinent and over-simplified. Certainly a sporting class may be recognisable but as well as those who loved all sports and those who loved none there was an increasing number whose sporting tastes were quite selective. It is generally acknowledged that attitudes towards sport became more complex towards 1800, as sport developed its own greater complexity and as national needs changed. The arguments now were more searching than at any time since the great Puritan controversies of the past. They took on, though, a different flavour. The debate was based as much on rational morality as on the spiritual and had new dimensions of social class, public order and commercialism. Most conspicuously, with the concept of sport itself still only half-formed, much argument tended to concentrate on just one of its aspects – that of the time it consumed. A firm notion of what might constitute legitimate and accept-able sport, should time be found for it, would take most of the nineteenth century to emerge. It was here, in this period, that the first tentative and uncertain moves towards formulation began, and they began not with any comprehensive philosophical enquiry into the nature of sport itself but in a whole mesh of partial arguments, reflecting a wide range of value judge-ments and usually directed to a single element in the age's sporting life. Accordingly any valid appreciation of the status of sport in these years has, in the main, to come from comment on the particular rather than on the general.

The period saw, for instance, the start of the decisive movement against blood sports that was to lead to the 1835 Cruelty to Animals Act. There had been a very muted strain of concern about animal fighting and baiting from Puritan days[6] and there was a critical article in *The Craftsman* in 1738 but expressions of general concern, such as Humphry Primatt's influential *Dissertation on the Duty of Mercy and the Sin of Cruelty to Brute Animals* (1776) only became more frequent towards the end of the century when the 'savage and diabolical cruelty of man towards animals' as Soam Jenyns called it became a common theme. 'Every act that sanctions cruelty to animals must tend to destroy the morals of a people, and consequently every social duty,' claimed the *Manchester Mercury* in 1800, at one of those times when moral issues were in the air and Parliament saw the first bill against bull baiting.[7] Thereafter critical opinion strengthened as the move-ment for reform gradually gathered pace with the formation of both local and national societies against animal cruelty, out of which the Royal Society for the Prevention of Cruelty to Animals emerged as the leading force.[8]

The innovative nature of attempts at reform was underlined when Lord Erskine introduced such a bill in the House of Lords in 1810 and opponents argued that it was 'a novel proposition' to legislate for animals.[9] The notion that the human and animal kingdoms were completely separate from each other was of course still immovable, but it was increasingly being tempered by the argument that animals had been created not for man's pleasure but on account of their usefulness to him, and that he had a primary responsibility of care for them. They were not for exploitation at his own whim and pleasure. Within this context conflicts of opinion became specific to the individual sport. Disputes over cock-throwing were effectively over. Even the *Sporting Magazine*, tolerant in its early years of much that it later came to oppose, was hostile from the start.[10] The focus of attention moved to bull-baiting. Even before the central debate began, the old butchery argument in favour of baiting was being disputed. Bulls killed in 'high fever' after being harassed and goaded by dogs, it was alleged, produced poor meat without natural juices. On the other side there were attempts to defend it as a sport, in that both dogs and bulls could show their own skills and the outcome could be uncertain. Between 1800 and 1802, there were, in addition to press criticisms, no less than three tracts published specifically attacking bull-baiting,[11] the Societies for the Suppression of Vice were on the march and baitings were one of their targets. They had certainly put a stop to London's commercial badger-baiting, even if the activity did continue elsewhere, often to highly critical comment as 'an amusement for the rabble' at the expense of an 'inoffensive animal.' The Societies, usually realistic in choosing susceptible vices to attack, may have found bull-baiting too large scale a problem for them to tackle on a broad front, but criticism continued.[12] By the new century the *Sporting Magazine*, previously largely supportive of baiting,[13] was taking an ambivalent stance. An orderly traditional bait, supported by the upper classes and possibly with an element of charity towards the poor was one thing while an unruly and unregulated commercial affair catering for the idle masses was another.[14] Both, however, had been preceded by a bitter anti-baiting poem which had described all that was worst in the practice, where the spectators were 'the village rabble,' 'vile and base,' 'rough boobies' who far from being hardened by such events were made 'fitter far for mutiny than war.'[15]

Bull-baiting was thus provoking already the question that is still relevant – whether a sport that has as its fundamental element a practice which is found to be morally reprehensible can ever be so sanitised and regulated as to justify its survival. It is the same basic question whether it applies to the chasing and killing by dogs of stags and foxes, attempts to beat a man into unconsciousness, or the baiting of bulls. Another question already opened up by the debate was over the extent to which any sport involving animals could be classed as other than cruel. A.M. Young, fellow of Trinity College, Cambridge, in his *Essay on Humanity to Animals*, included fishing among the cruel sports, particularly where live bait was used, and by 1814 the *Sporting Magazine* itself was accepting substantial contributions such as that 'On the Cruelty of English Amusements,' questioning fishing and shooting as well as the fighting and baiting sports, although the writer had to conclude that it would need 'more than human aid' to achieve such wholesale change.[16] Certainly the traditional exploitative view of animals could still find the sort

Pigeon Shooting. Handicapping the birds ensured that they would fly low and be easier targets.

of expression that took place in attempts to make a viable sport out of pigeon shooting. At first the birds were released with their legs tied together, but the marksmen were unable to bring any of them down. At length it was found that the birds made feasible targets if they had their pinions clipped before being released. For one critic it was 'the most contemptible of all cruelties,' but it became a frequent sport towards the end of the period. At least pigeons were now also being put to more peaceable use with the founding of the Columbarian Society which was organising homing sweepstakes among its members by the 1790s.[17]

These, though, bull-baiting apart, are marginal manifestations of current attitudes towards the exploitation of animals in the name of sporting entertainment. It was in relation to the major established sports of horse racing, hunting and cocking, supported as all were by the ruling classes, that the more complex debates took place, debates which went beyond questions of animal cruelty. In horse racing, for example, the issue of cruelty made only occasional and minor intrusions into the arguments. In neither of two discussions of its pros and cons, reported in 1804 and 1806, was cruelty mentioned though, admittedly, neither were pleasure, enjoyment, excitement or even recreation – the arguments were economic and social. Some voices were raised as the new century became more sensitive. 'In nine cases out of ten there is cruelty,' wrote one critic in 1808, 'and generally a dreadful degree of it.' Another in 1814 condemned owners who demanded that their jockeys use the spur and the whip without regard, and a third in the same year claimed that such methods were not only heartless but also ineffective, contrasting the natural efforts of competing horses, 'spontaneously exerting every effort, unaided by the whip or spur,' with the sight of one 'torn and mangled' by its rider in a futile effort to make it go beyond its capabilities.[18] These were though by no means the final or most telling value judgements so far as the reputation of the turf was concerned.

Fox hunting's status went from strength to strength during the second half of the Georgian era. It had the assurance of the sporting press, if any doubts remained, that 'Fox-hunting is now become the amusement of gentlemen, and gentlemen have not any reason to be ashamed of it.' Great chases and grand hunt balls were reported with approbation and the sport continued to grow in prestige among the classes who supported it.[19] Hunts, however, were far from universally welcome. A stag released for Lord Derby's staghounds, one of the few such packs remaining, was found shot through the head, presumably by a disgruntled farmer who had suffered damage from the hunt, an incident which gave rise to the newspaper caution that gentlemen 'should be careful not to injure the property of inferior persons.' What gentlemen were coming to consider as *their* own property was the fox itself. For the hunter it became virtually a protected species – that is until he killed it himself. The law counted for little and the destruction of the animal by others could have drastic consequences. When Sussex farmers killed seven cubs it was noted that in some places this would be 'deemed little short of high treason' by sportsmen.[20]

A sport which was directed solely at the chasing and killing of an animal, however pestilential, could hardly escape all criticism. Even if the objective was acceptable, the usual question arose as to its moral effects. It could, in the usual phrase of the day, 'produce a habit of cruelty' and even its followers could sometimes acknowledge its 'trivial incidents of less pleasing effect,' though these were

> but the shades requisite to give due effect to the light in a picture – the passages between the grand apartments in a palace – the contrasts and reliefs in an ornamental landscape – that infusion of bitters, without having tasted which we should never find the sweets!

What did pass almost unremarked was the cruelty to the horses if the chase was long and hard. It was the endurance of the riders which was celebrated. Of the 70 hunters who set off with the Lexden Hounds in Essex in April 1809 only two were reported to be in at the death, after a run estimated at over forty miles. It was only by way of postscript that it was noted that one horse was found dead in its stable the next morning and another 'famous young horse' was much feared for. Hunting was, though, a fortunate sport in that the fox could have few friends and its pursuers, as both landowners and justices, were too powerful to be seriously threatened.[21]

The animal fighting sports could be more exposed. Most comment on dog fighting was prompted by its appearance as an element in the misbehaviour of some particular rabble. If it was reported without disfavour it was usually because many of the gentlemen amateurs were present (as in a 1795 instance) and there was heavy betting. It even had some passing popularity among the sporting class during those first hectic years of the new century and appeared as part of the cockpit's entertainments in the 1820s For most of the period though it was on a small scale, confined to the rougher classes and aroused little comment.[22] Cock-fighting was another matter. After bull-baiting it was to be the next of the animal sports to come under pressure from reformers. There are some signs before the 1830s of the serious opposition to come but they tend to be limited and, indeed, its eventual suppression came somewhat out of the blue. Criticisms of the actual fighting were answered by the argument that, as with dogs, it was 'natural' for the animals to fight each other. At the more sophisticated end of the sport it was also possible to claim that the contests were made as fair as possible by having contestants of equal weights, even if this was done to promote closer and more exciting fights. In practice, the fact that cocking was popular across the social classes, all of whom could participate, and the fact too that it enjoyed strong gentry support, made it immune as yet from serious attack. Where criticism found occasional expression in action this tended to take the form of pressure on innkeepers for mounting fights – a London raid on the cockpit behind the Cock Inn, St Giles in 1806 for example.[23] Among the arguments in its defence were those familiar in other fighting sports in that it helped to satisfy man's 'pugnacious desires.' One irate farmer, when his sport was under attack, was prepared to admit that it might be 'Cruel, unmanly, and even wicked,' but, he asked, what else was the gamecock made for, if not for fighting?[24]

New attitudes towards man's relationship with animals did have some influence on the status of sports that made use of them. They were, though, not the only factor and seldom even the main one. The animal sports were deeply ingrained in the national culture and highly resistant, while opposition to them was, for the most part and for most of the period, diffused and ill-defined. For some it would not be so much the sports themselves as any perceived unfairness in their practice, such as the chase of a wounded stag by the royal hunt in 1814.[25] For many others it was the setting that was decisive. Both the bull ring and the cockpit demonstrated a continuous round of barbarous and bloodthirsty behaviour, but one was an open attraction to the idling and uncontrolled masses while the other was usually contained, on a smaller scale, and had its own rough and ready internal discipline. The more rowdy and unordered the context, the more the animal sports were considered demeaning. The many elements that could become involved will be well illustrated in the contrasting fates of the two major inherited bull runs, where the validity and strength of tradition, the degree of cruelty and disorder, and the nature of the local community, all played parts in determining their standing.

What proved significant also was time as well as place. Towards the end of the period, there was a rising consciousness of the need for change over a broad front, a growing belief that the country was 'throwing off the shackles of ignorance,' and that the cruder sports had outlived their time. When the first substantial history of boxing was produced in 1812 it made great play of the distinction between pugilism and animal baiting. It was 'our duty as well as moral advantage, to refrain from all acts of wanton cruelty to the brute creation,' gory descriptions were given of bull-baits, and even cock-fighting was condemned as a barbarous diversion. In the pages of the *Sporting Magazine* itself, by 1814, bull baits were likely to be ascribed to 'gothic darkness,' or seen as 'disgraceful remnants of feudal tyranny.'[26] The consequences of these shifts in opinion are hard to over-estimate since, although they were mainly prompted by the animal sports, their effects did not stop there. It was often difficult to discriminate between the circumstances and the crowd behaviour at bull baitings and the like and the same apparent scene on many other popular sporting occasions. The approbrium prompted by animal sports readily spilled over and added to existing suspicions of much in the people's recreation, reinforcing the well rehearsed accusations of time-wasting, money-wasting, disorder and criminality.

Even though they disturbed only one day a year, the mass football games found few articulate friends. The claims of national utility in the promotion of hardness and valour, so often raised on behalf of pugilism and other combative sports, were rarely voiced in their favour. It was exceptional that an observer of the Derby game should note that the 'power and spirit' of the players would fit them well for military service, a view echoed by the visiting Frenchman, if with less unqualified enthusiasm, that if the English called this 'playing,' it would be impossible to say what they would call 'fighting.'[27] All the inherited objections to the annual contests – their unruliness, the settling of old scores and the general suspension of law that people assumed they granted – were now being given a new dimension. Property had always been at some risk and the new consumerism meant that there was more property to damage. The growing importance of travel and transport meant that blocking the roads, even for a single day, gave another cause for complaint,[28] while there was little contemporary awareness of the positive social benefits which later historians have perceived in these mass struggles, the sense of community which they promoted, their assertion of local identity and cohesion and the opportunity they could offer to gain individual status. If this was noted it was with surprise and scarcely with approbation. William Hutton, the Birmingham Quaker, wrote of the Derby game that he had 'known a foot-ball hero chaired through the streets like a successful member,' although he was no more than a butcher's apprentice. The best that he could find to say otherwise was that it was a 'coarse sport.'[29] Football's persistence through the whole Georgian age, here and elsewhere, is persuasive evidence of its local high regard among the mass of the population and, although it seldom provoked comment outside the communal contest, there could be the occasional kind word for it – 'many a time have I had my shins broken in playing at football' but it still (in 1807) remains a sport that 'has charms for me.'[30] It seems generally to have been dismissed as an informal activity, largely for the young, and allowable so long as it did not unduly disturb the peace.

The same could not be said of pugilism which provoked a wealth of comment. Its critics and defenders vied with each other in their claims and counter-claims. For its opponents the objections were obvious enough. It was a misuse of human strength and a perverse form of behaviour, it brought together large and apparently uncontrollable crowds, and – inevitably – it promoted idleness, gambling and criminality. It also happened to be illegal, the only major sport that was a disturbance of the peace in the eyes of the law as well as in the minds of its critics.

The Times (originally as the *Daily Universal Register*) was early on the attack as pugilism began its revival in the late 1780s, voicing the opposition that it was to keep up intermittently for the rest of the period. It looked forward to the Johnson and Ward fight with scathing comment on 'the prospect of two fellow creatures prostituting the spirit, strength and agility that nature had bestowed them, in exertions to destroy each other.' Opposition, however, did not prevent the newspaper from reporting arrangements for fights or the fights themselves in some detail, a favoured stance later, condemning in its leaders events which the back page reported fully. It could occasionally appear more tolerant, but always with the impression of some reluctance, as when it acknowledged, in 1787, that 'as a *fashionable* sport it demands our notice,' or suggesting that a hall might be set aside for boxing matches, charging a guinea for entrance to ensure an orderly crowd.[31] But most of its comments continued to be derisory. It was 'the blackguard exercise of boxing' in 1795 and 'this brutal practice' in 1802.[32] *The Times*, though, was far from being a lone press critic. Provincial newspapers could be equally censorious. The *Northampton Mercury*, for example, was describing prize-fights in 1791 as 'dreadful catastrophes' and castigating them as 'so disgraceful, so dangerous and so increasing an evil.' Typically the comment comes from those first highly active years of sporting expansion, when even *The Times* was having to grant that 'Bruising is likely to continue quite the rage,' and the growth itself was provoking complaints. There was Edward Barry's protest that 'the established order, the good decorum of society, have been, of late, much disturbed, and nearly set at defiance' by the mounting of fights in what were usually peaceful country areas. County magistrates, from Bedfordshire and Sussex, for example, were echoing the same criticisms.[33] Even the sporting press, the natural ally of the prize ring, began to find space for some critical comment as the years passed. At first it was merely a matter of questioning the quality of the physical development promoted by boxing and wrestling.[34] By 1808 it had gone so far as to present arguments for and against the sport. The charges were those of cruelty to the fighters and degradation to the spectators, whose delight at the sight of blood was 'the strongest indication of a depraved, cowardly, and cruel mind.' It was also, inevitably, 'productive of idleness, riot and immorality amongst thousands of the lower classes of our countrymen.' A more measured critique, just as the period sport's better days were drawing to a close, indicates how much some opinion had moved and is particularly significant because it identifies those elements in bareknuckle fighting which, many years ahead, would lead to its eventual abandonment:

two men, erect in all the pride of strength and manhood, are put under a course of regimen, and brought to the utmost pitch of bodily perfection, to qualify them to deal their deadly blows, and sustain their antagonist's with more effect; are pitted against each other for an insignificant prize, and in a few minutes scarce a feature of the human face divine can be discerned, till, by repeated blows, all sense is completely fled; and the vanquished remains a pitiful spectacle, unable, without surgical assistance, to be conveyed from the scene of combat. He who wishes for a reform in our amusements, cannot connive at boxing, however fair and honourably conducted, particularly if they proceed to incite and compel a man to continue to fight against his inclination, which, if he refuses, then branding him with the approbrious name of a coward, to exasperate him to persevere, till very likely a broken limb closes the disgraceful combat.[35]

However, defenders of the ring were always on hand. Pugilism would bring both physical and moral benefits to the boxers themselves, bracing the sinews, opening the chest, imparting 'a firm and vigorous tone to the whole body' and 'forming an erect and graceful carriage,' as well as exercising the 'mental facilities.' The combat itself taught honour, equity, courage, strength and dexterity and, not unexpectedly, the spectators, by example, would become suffused with these same qualities, learning valuable character lessons from the sport. The ring also had its own literature to defend it. The 'J.B.' who penned the peculiar would-be philosophical introduction to *Pancratia* commended boxing 'as an exercise to inspire fortitude and intrepidity,' but only if pursued for these particular ends. If it was viewed 'merely in the light of yielding gratification as a public spectacle, or furnishing an opportunity for gambling speculation, all its native deformity is exposed.' The irony is that after all the ethical/historical high flying of this preface the book itself descends immediately into over three hundred pages describing fights where spectacle and gambling are dominant features and chicanery and fixing their frequent accompaniments.[36] Boxing was, though, becoming a subject for serious discussion. In 1806 Dr Bardsley was arguing, before the Philosophical Society of Manchester, that 'the exercise of the pugilistic school' should be clearly distinguished from animal baiting, and suggesting that both public schools and 'large manufactures' might 'introduce the system of boxing, and the laws of honour by which it is regulated.' Even more glowing support came in the debate on prizefighting at Jeremy Bentham's Society for Mutual Improvement in 1820 where 'Mr M' waxed lyrical over pugilists as 'actors on the stage of valour' and 'playing a glorious part.'[37] Influential support came also from John Lawrence in his work on animals in general and horses in particular, though he was nearer to the ideal than the real in claims that the practices of the ring, the presence of umpires, the handshakes, and 'the general solicitude and caution of the spectators' ensured 'that perfect equity takes place between the contending parties.'[38]

The great aids to the reputation of pugilism, though, were neither scientific nor philosophical. They were nationalism and war. If royal patronage first brought the sport into fashion it was national need which did much to keep it there. It is more than coincidental that the great age of the bare-fist ring coincided almost exactly with the war years. What remained afterwards was to live on ever-fading memories of past glory. With Britain facing the might of Continental Europe, any means of claiming national superiority was welcome, and pugilism could readily be made to fill the bill. Comparisons with means of settling disputes in other countries were common, and always to their disadvantage. Foreign practices gave 'striking proof of the incompetency of savage and cruel amusements to create a courageous and warlike disposition.' Boxing, by contrast, was distinguished by honour, equity, courage, strength and dexterity. It teaches discipline and bravery, sets fine examples and is, in short, a most excellent training for service on the battlefield.[39] During the brief and uneasy peace following the Treaty of Amiens the government was being warned that it was policy, 'if not its duty,' to 'encourage those exercises which are best calculated to promote national spirit' and not have 'effeminacy nurtured and encouraged by the law of the realm.'[40]

Thus the paradox persisted. Pugilism, an illegal sport, continued to have a far higher status (however far this fell short of universal approval) than sports such as bull baiting, against which there was no legal impediment. Such was its standing in 1815 that its acknowledged master of ceremonies, the former champion John Jackson, was called upon to organise a pugilistic display for the allied monarchs visiting London to arrange the peace, an honour surpassed, if anything, by his commission to supply uniformed ushers from the pugilistic fraternity to keep order in Westminster Abbey at George IV's coronation.[41] Boxing's golden age was fading out as it had begun, with the highest possible seal of approval.

Pedestrianism was to share many of the characteristics of pugilism and much of its growing ill-repute. Until the 1820s it avoided most of the controversy surrounding the ring – it was legal, did no perceptible damage to participants, gave rise to few crowd problems and could even be commended to gentlemen, some of whose recent 'wonderful feats' in the sport were being applauded in 1801, but with the caution that careful preparation and training were needed.[42] The occasional disputes in the sport were usually settled without much rancour and it was not yet marred by the regular fixing of matches that was later to become commonplace. Again, while contests could attract large crowds these often took place either in enclosed grounds such as Lords or on venues such as Scarborough sands or racecourses, where they were unlikely to cause great inconvenience. Indeed, the only serious criticism of a specific athletic event came in 1815 when George Wilson set out to walk 1,000 miles at 50 miles a day on Blackheath, and without any significant gentry backing. Crowds gathered, victualling booths and other stalls were set up and the heath took on all the appearance of a fairground. Eventually the magistrates had all the liquor stands removed and arrested Wilson himself 'as creating a public nuisance.'[43]

One impediment to the sport's good repute lay in dress – or its absence.

It was a diminishing problem, but the sight of naked athletes could still provoke cries of disgust. Informal contests such as that between two coffee house waiters who ran 'quite naked' round St James' Park for a guinea wager at 7.00 a.m. on a November morning can have disturbed very few and when Foster Powell ran a trial for his four minute mile wager 'entirely naked' it was in the relative seclusion of Molesey Hurst. It was where there was public display that criticism and police interference was likely – nude men running for a pair of breeches given by a Chelsea tavern keeper and watched by a large crowd of both sexes ('no clothing could hide the shame of such a transaction') or a man running through the City 'in a perfect state of nudity' for a ten guinea wager and taken into custody as he passed the Mansion House![44] It was not, though, a major issue for the sport nor one that much harmed its contemporary standing.

The two great summer sports, cricket and horse racing, prompted differing reactions, largely favourable to the one and more qualified towards the other. Horse racing flourished through the period but had to do so in face of some repeated questioning. As well as those sporadic complaints about horses being hard ridden there were, for instance, frequent and fierce comments on the make-up and behaviour of its crowds. They were a sign of 'idleness in manufacturers and labourers' and gave special opportunities for crime and immorality. Pickpockets, whores, swindlers and thieves were all drawn to the honeypot of the race meeting.[45] The betting also attracted much criticism, both on its own account and because of the deceits and crimes which it invited. Corrupt practices were frequently reported in the sporting press, but usually by way of cautions to the unwary rather than as condemnations of the sport itself. Failure of horses to start and rigged races were among the most frequent complaints, while the chicaneries of 'grooms, jockeys, helpers, hangers-on, and the long list of collateral *harpies*' were common topics.[46]

Although its vices attracted more attention than its virtues the turf's standing was secure. It enjoyed the crown's patronage and investment, direct aristocratic involvement, the sponsorship of the gentry locally and wide support from the population. Racing was virtually a national institution, 'the proper amusement of the most exalted ranks of society,' according to John Lawrence. For all its admitted faults it could still, to the end of the period, be seen as belonging to an inherited right ordering of things, a frequent subject of discussion but this usually centres on its practices – the racing of younger horses, the value of local meetings, and so on – rather than its worth. Even evangelical opposition, with its particular distrust of large and boisterous gatherings, was relatively slow to turn on horse racing though its influence was beginning to be felt by the 1820s as was the threat to the right ordering of society seen by many in the rise of professional racing men like the pugilist John Gully, risen 'from the *sod* of boxing' to have become 'one of the principle betters on the most distinguished racing courses.'[47]

A sport could, however, be shot through with gambling and still enjoy high regard. Cricket, seldom played without a wager, was the one large-scale game, capable of attracting large crowds, which was not merely accepted but had its virtues more prominently voiced than its vices. It was 'the true old game of English cricket' in 1776 and 'the noble game of cricket' in 1815, frequently attracting favourable epithets right through to the end of the age. Its values were manifold. It required 'the utmost exertion of strength and agility,' was 'animated by a noble spirit of emulation' and above all it was 'manly,' the coming hallmark of all approvable sports.[48] The prominence of the aristocracy in the establishing of the game, and as players and patrons, gave cricket a standing and publicity which no other enjoyed. The mix of lords and commoners on the field conveyed a sense of social harmony, however superficial this might be. The sight of dukes, earls and honourables disporting themselves energetically gave the plebeian spectators the opportunity to admire – or to envy. As for the polite world, it found cricket acceptable because it came as near as any confrontational game could be to meeting the demands of the age. It had rules which constrained behaviour, it was a non-contact game with no built-in cruelty, and yet it called for toughness as well as skill. Much, indeed, was made of this hardiness. The fact that batsmen had to face a hard ball hurled at them, and the courage displayed in doing so, had come to illustrate an admired national characteristic, imbuing the game with the same patriotic overtones as pugilism. It was an *English* game, and lauded as such as the Reverend M. Cotton, its early poet, claimed, 'No nation e'er boasted so noble a game.'[49]

Cricket could strike another chord. It could successfully tap the mood of romantic rural nostalgia that had been strengthening through the latter half of the eighteenth century and was there in the period's poetry and painting. Migrants from the countryside often tried to translate their old recreations into their new and usually more constricted settings. Cricket was a country pursuit which could, more conveniently than most, be transferred into the towns, even if pressure on land pushed many grounds (and notably Lord's) further and further out.[50] The idyll could, of course, never be unsullied. While the irregularities and the spectator problems associated with the game would fall well short of those associated with, say, the ring and the turf, they did raise some doubts. One of the most persistent was over the continuous betting that the game involved, its statistical basis allowing constant opportunities for new wagers on individual and team scores, numbers of scoring strokes or balls bowled and so on, as well as on the final result. Other censure was prompted by, for instance, disorder among spectators, or playing games on unsuitable occasions, such as working days or on Sundays.[51] For a time even the radicalism of the 1780s may have had some impact on cricket. The mix of peers and plebs was not an infallible guarantee of concord between the classes and the sight of a ploughman bowling out a lord can hardly have failed to arouse in some minds thoughts of the same pattern of events in another and more serious context. Even the Hambledon Club, for all its elitist membership, always had more than a touch of irreverence about it. Its customary fifth toast at its dinners, to the ladies, was 'to the immortal memory of Madge,' current slang for the female genitalia, and among the guests at the last dinner was none other than Tom Paine, while Henry Botham, its honorary secretary, was known to have radical leanings.[52] However, Hambledon faded, the national mood changed and cricket, far from being a potential threat to the country's stability, became almost an assurance of its health and well-being. By 1815, in the new days of peace, it could typically present a scene suffused with sweetness and light, as at Boston where, for the first game with Spalding in 1815, 'the bells rung the whole day; the ground was attended by a numerous and genteel company, and the evening was spent in perfect harmony.'[53]

Cricket's comparative respectability raises interesting questions. How, at a time when any recreation which drew in the crowds was likely to be viewed with suspicion, could cricket come through comparatively unscathed? The experience of other sports which escaped the age's worst calumnies may well help towards an answer. These included rowing and sailing, swimming and skating, backsword, cudgels, singlestick and wrestling, all of which enjoyed comparatively unsullied reputations and even a measure of positive approval. They obviously fell into two categories. They involved either the application of competition to some commonplace physical activity, creating new sports which had no inherited problems of social disruption or were accepted as traditional, part of a wholesome rustic past, sharing in the pastoral idyll.

Of the newly popular sporting activities only rowing and sailing lent themselves readily and regularly to gambling and some matches were certainly made for money wagers. However, from the start, prizes and trophies appear to have played a much more prominent role as rewards for success than they did in almost any other sport apart from archery, which very deliberately distanced itself from betting. Similarly, it was struggling for the prize that was more important than any gambling in the 'ancient, manly and innocent' sports of the countryside, wrestling and the combat contests. As a lower class sport (according to Strutt) wrestling was probably under-reported for most of the period but where it took place in organised fashion it was well celebrated. In Norfolk in 1806 it drew 'a large concourse of spectators' and prompted rejoicing that such rural sports were again becoming common, contributing much 'to the spirit, manliness, and character of the English people.'[54] Swordplay, cudgels and singlesticks were linked with wrestling as means to 'improve the inhabitants in courage and activity, and prevent all the drunkenness and ill-effects of nine-pin grounds and cock-pits.' Singlestick contests attracted comment which verged on the lyrical – they were 'so productive of intrepidity and confidence' that through such sports 'were formed those heroes who carried triumphant the British standard o'er the vine cover'd hills and gay vallies (*sic*) of France.'[55]

There is, though, amid all the praises, often more than a hint of desperation in comments on the rural sports. Too often they were being corrupted in the interests of the amusing or the spectacular, by way of sack races, grinning matches, or eating hot pudding competitions. There was J.J. Brayfield arguing in favour of government encouragement for 'public sports and games, such as may allure their minds to virtue, and innure their bodies to strength and activity.' The message occurs with growing frequency. Popular recreation was moving in undesirable directions and into the wrong hands. At root there was the feeling that was to become almost endemic in sport – that the profit motive was damaging and that this lay behind the corruption of the old country pursuits. The implication is, though, that sport, including popular play, *could* be beneficial, that it might well be of value to the state, and that it might, ideally at least, have the potential to achieve the clean orderliness and symmetry of Stubbs' repesentations of it, free of Hogarth's disturbing crowds and chaotic scenes.[56]

Sport, though, even in its approvable rustic forms, was to be hedged in with cautions, with regulation and 'certain restrictions,' with an eye on social control. There was, even so, a whole set of circumstances which could work not only in favour of simple rural activities such as singlestick play or wrestling but could also benefit the reputation of the one inherited rural sport which had achieved a degree of sophistication, a sport which had long ago shown how hitting a missile with a stick could be developed into a complex game with an attractive competitive edge. It appeared to maintain the endangered qualities of rustic play, yet in forms which new tastes could accept. It was pastoral without being provoking. While often gentry led, it was not socially exclusive and the very fact that it already had 'laws' and not mere 'rules' gave it at least a symbolic distinction. It was traditional, it was 'manly', *and* it was very English.

The good standing of cricket was particularly important at a time when so much of even the flourishing sport of the day was open to question. So, too, was the easy acceptance of new competitive ventures such as rowing and sailing. The one gave an assurance of continuity to the country's sporting experience, the other showed a readiness, even an eagerness, to move into new forms of organised competition that could hope to be free of the more damaging contaminations of the past. It was in the coalescence of these two themes that the future of English sport could be rooted, growing, in all its major aspects, out of traditional forms of competitive play but refining and reorganising them, at once both innovating and conserving. The often confused and clouded vision of sport that was characteristic of this period, with its areas of doubt, uncertainty, and occasional disgust, did at least hold the possibilities of a future emergence into wholesale respectability.

Notes

1. *SM*, October 1792, 'Address to the Public,' p iii; *SM*, pp iv/v; *Pancratia*, p 'B'.
2. John Armstrong, M.D., *The Art of Preserving Health*, 1744, 1796 edition, p.100; Cullen, *Practice of Physic*, p 249; *SM*, February 1810, 'On the Necessity of Exercise,' pp 222-22.
3. Richard Baxter, *A Christian Directory or a Summ of Practical Theologie and Cases of Conscience*, 1677, 2nd edition 1678, Part II, 'Directions about Sports and Recreations, and against excess and sin therein,' pp 387 ff.; *SM*, October

1807, 'The Comforts of Sports and Games,' pp 22/3.

4. William Law, *A Serious Call to a Devout and Holy Life, adapted to the State and Condition of all Orders of Christians*, in *Works*, 9 vols., 1762; Brokenhurst, Hampshire reprint, 1893, iv, p 17.

5. Deuchar, *Sporting Art in Eighteenth Century England*, p 10.

6. *e.g.* 'I think it utterly unlawful for any man to take pleasure in the pain and torture of any creature, or . . . to make a recreation of their brutish cruelty which they practise one upon another.' William Hinde (1641), quoted in F.R. Raines, ed., *The Journal of Nicholas Assheton of Downham*, Chetham Society. 1848, p 287.n.9

7. Soam Jenyns, 'On Cruelty to Inferior Animals,' from *Disquisitions on Several Subjects*, 1792, reprinted *Annual Register* 1792, p 166; Malcolmson, *Popular Recreations*, pp 136, 124: *Manchester Mercury*, 15 April 1800. See also *SM*, February 1802, p 268; February 1808, p 195. Both this bull-baiting bill and one two years earlier failed. (*Parliamentary History*, XXXV, pp 202-214; XXXVI, pp 829-854; *Cobbett's Parliamentary Debates*, XIV, pp 851/2, 989-990; 1029-1041; 1071; XVI, p 726.)

8. The first at Liverpool in 1809 and later the one specifically anti-blood sports society, the strong South Staffordshire Association for the Suppression of Bull-baiting (1824.) Malcolmson, *Popular Recreations*, pp 172/3; Holt, *Sport and the British*, p 24.

9. *SM*, May 1810, p 73.

10. It reported with approval how an Ipswich reformer had persuaded youths to aim at an earthenware pot instead of their usual tethered bird and when the pot was broken it turned out to contain an owl, which promptly flew away. (June, 1795, pp 157/8.)

11. *SM*, August 1795, p 252; Reid, 'Beasts and brutes,' in Holt, ed., *Sport and the Working Class*, p 16; Malcolmson, *Popular Recreations*, p 124, n.35.

12. Whitaker, *Eighteenth Century Sunday*, p 194; *SM*, April 1805, p 19.

13. *e.g.*, *SM*, April 1795, p 55.

14. It clearly approved of the efforts of the young men of Windsor to claim their traditional right to use an ancient grant from the crown to mount a bull bait, which was supported on the day by several of the nobility, most of the officers of the Staffordshire Militia and some Eton scholars. *SM.*, October 1806, p 43; December 1806, p 160. See also the enthusiastic report of the St Thomas day bait at Wokingham, *SM*, October, 1808, p 120.

15. *SM*, April 1808, p 52. For other references to bull baiting see e.g. July 1795, p 223; October 1801, p 38; February 1802, pp 267/8; March 1805, p 350; April 1805, p 20; January 1815, p 206.

16. *SM*, October 1804, pp 30/1; October 1814, p 28.

17. Sportsmen were also noting that they could fly from Newmarket to London in less than three hours! *SM*, January 1807, p 206; January 1808, p 272; May 1793, p 121.

18. *SM*, May 1804, p 387; October 1806, p 48; January 1808, p 195; October 1814, p 30. Similar complaints began to be made in the 1820s over the new trotting races, *e.g.*, *SM*, July 1820, p 173. At another level was this little cautionary poem found on the cover of the 1821 census return for a Dorset village!

The cruel Sportsman whips his Horse,

To gain a paltry prize;

And those encourage dangerous sports,
Who ought to be more wise.

Let all good boys make haste to School,
And go there clean and neat;
Nor ever near the Race-Course come,
Where people game and cheat.

(Dorset CRO PE/HOR: 0VI. I am indebted to Ann Smith for this reference.)

19. February 1787; *SM*, October 1793, p 27.

20. *Times*, 10 January 1787. An Essex farm worker who took cubs which he had discovered to his churchwarden who paid 'the customary sum' for their destruction but was driven out of the county by a neighbouring cleric under threats of the press gang. *SM*, May 1812, p 83.

21. 'Yoicks,' 'The Comforts of Sports and Games,' *SM*, October 1807, p 23; October 1809, p 9.

22. But see *SM*, August 1795, p 236; October 1803, p 43, for instances of heavy financial involvement.

23. Sixty spectators who had each paid sixpence entrance were taken into custody but all appeared 'to get their living honestly' and were released. *SM*, January 1806, p 212.

24. *SM*, April 1811, p 39.

25. *SM*, May 1814, p 59.

26. *Pancratia*, pp 13-19; *SM*, October 1814, p 28.

27. *Derby Mercury*, 9 February 1815; Football Association, *The History of the Football Association*, 1953, p 7.

28. e.g. the Kingston-on-Thames game was criticised as a 'great nuisance' to 'persons travelling through the town' and the Stamford bull run faced a similar charge. Malcolmson, *Popular Recreations*, pp 140, 127, 85; *Stamford Mercury*, 10 October 1788.

29. William Hutton, *The History of Derby*, 1791, p 219. Some newspaper reports speak of gentry support for each side but another local opinion saw the game as 'disgraceful to humanity and civilisation.' See Malcolmson, *Popular Recreations*, pp 141-144; Birley, 'Napoleon and the Squire,' Mangan, *ed*, *Pleasure, Profit and Proselytism*, p 23.

30. 'Yoicks' on 'The Comforts of Sports and Games.' *SM*, October 1807, pp 22/3.

31. *Times*, 20, 21, 23 December 1787. See also *SM*, June 1795, p 137.

32. *Times*, 26 November 1801; 21 October 1802; 27 November 1801. This last was in course of criticism of the Berkshire JPs for failing to stop the Belcher v Burke fight, for once unfairly as they had tried beforehand to prevent the bout and the fighters and their seconds faced criminal charges after it.

33. *Northampton Mercury*, 11 June 1791; *Times*, 21 December 1787; Edward Barry, *A Letter on the Practice of Boxing*, 1789, p 7; Malcolmson, *Popular Recreations*, p 145; *SM*, October 1804, p 46.

34. Forming strong upper bodies that were, it was alleged, weak below the waist, *SM*, July 1798, p 211.

35. *SM*, November 1808, pp 63/4; October 1814, p 30.

36. *SM*, November 1808, pp 63/4; September 1806, p 261; *Pancratia*, p 23. 'J.B.' was almost certainly Jonathan Badcock who later, as 'John Bee,' produced the *Annals of Sporting and Fancy Gazette* in the 1820s, while the book itself was

almost certainly the work of Bill Oxberry, comic actor, dramatist, theatre manager and part-time sports reporter.

37. *SM*, September 1808, p 263; . Egan, *Boxiana*, III, pp 583-584, 589-597 in a full report of the debate. See also Dennis Brailsford, 'Morals and Maulers: the Ethics of Early Pugilism,' *Journal of Sport History*, Vol 12, No 2, Summer 1985, pp 137-142.

38. John Lawrence, *A Philosophical and Practical Treatise on Horses, and on the Moral Duties of Man towards the Brute Creation*, 2 vols., 1796-8, II, p 29

39. *Pancratia*, pp 25/6.

40. *SM*, September 1806, p 261 It had been a time of even greater contention than usual over the desirability of pugilism – see e.g. *SM*, February 1802, p 268; *Pancratia*, pp 175-80; 307-310; Miles, *Pugilistica*, I, p 111; *SM*, February 1802, pp 269-272; October 1805, p 39.

41. Miles, *Pugilistica*, I, pp 100; 270; DNB.

42. *SM*, December 1801, p 158.

43. *SM*, September 1815, p 246.

44. *SM*, November 1792, p 203; *Times*, 21 December 1787; *SM*, September 1798, p 302; 'Nudity in English Athletics,' *Sports History*, 7, 1985, pp 9/10.

45. *SM*, July 1793, p 238; *SM*, April 1793, p 53; May 1795, p 108. – when every lodger at the principal inn at Chester Races was robbed of his watch, cash and bills.

46. *Times*, 16 April 1787; *SM*, September 1797, p 304, commenting on Lord Grosvenor's reasons for withdrawing from the turf, having lost £300,000 in 30 years.

47. Lawrence, *Treatise on Horses*, II, p 23 (he added the note that its expense would keep the lower orders 'to their proper place as spectators'); *SM*, June 1813, p 141.

48. *Whitehall Evening Post*, 11 August 1776; *Stamford News*, 23 June 1815; *Morning Chronicle*, 23 August 1774; *Ipswich Journal*, 10 May 1745.

49. Quoted in Pierce Egan's *Book of Sports and Mirror of Life*, 1832, p 338; Malcolmson, *Popular Recreations*, p 41.

50. *Public Advertiser*, 2 September 1757. See also Malcolmson, *Popular Recreations*, pp 160/1.

51. See e.g. *Morning Chronicle*, 17 July 1799; *Northampton Mercury*, 11 August 1787; *Stamford Mercury*, 21 September 1787; *Times*, 28 September 1789.

52. Bowen, *Cricket: A History*, p 63. See also Buckley, *Eighteenth Century Cricket*, p 218; Birley, 'Napoleon and the Squire,' Mangan, ed., *Pleasure, Profit and Proselytism*, p 23.

53. 'A History of Cricket in Lincolnshire 1770-1850,' *Sports History*, 8, 1986, p. 12.

54. Strutt, *Sports and Pastimes*, p 62; *SM*, June 1806, p 107.

55. *SM*, April 1813, p 29; December 1809, p 97.

56. *SM*, April 1813, pp 29/30; June 1806, p 147.

4.
A Time to Play

Cohesive and all-embracing views on the nature and worth of contemporary sport were hard to come by but there was one topic on which opinion was more clearly defined, where much consideration of sport and recreation actually began – and often ended. This was on the availability of sport's prior necessity, namely leisure. Comments on the desirability of free time, its extent and its legitimate occasions, were frequent, often precise, and nearly always restrictive, a theme now well documented.[1] It was a debate to which the common people contributed by their behaviour rather than their words and on which the wealthiest also tended to be silent, content in their own freedom to take their pleasures when they wished and only beginning to feel any need for circumspection about how they did so late in the period.[2] The sporting aristocracy might complain occasionally about the unruly behaviour of the plebs but for the most part they were quite content with the present state of affairs and, the game laws apart, saw few reasons to interfere with others. It was indeed one of their number, the Honourable William Wyndham, Pitt's Minister of War and Macaulay's 'first gentleman of the age,' who led the opposition to all attempts to limit popular recreations and who defended animal sports with the same unwavering determination as he employed in attacking the slave trade.

The lead in attacks on working class leisure came from economists and employers, moralists and clerics. The profitable use of man's limited time on earth had been a central thrust of the earlier Puritan message. It had served well, both spiritually and economically, in the initial stages of capitalist development and it could be conveniently adapted to the mercantile needs of the new age. Here again, in economic terms, the time of the gentleman could be exempted – it was the time of the working man that had value and should not be squandered.'[3] *Leisure* was not a commodity to be made freely available. It was allowable only to the few. What the rest had was *idleness*, and much was made of it. Servants and workmen had long been warned that 'A frequent Taste for Diversions is apt to grow upon the Palate, and give too strong a Relish for them.' Sober hard work was the well beaten road to prosperity and a whole clutch of clerics was repeating warnings against indolence – Edward Whitehead in Bolton, Josiah Tucker at Bristol, and Robert Drew among the Societies for the Reformation of Manners.[4]

The defenders of law and order agreed. Idleness was the main prop of crime and commotion. Henry Zouch, writing on policing in 1786, deplored the opportunities for 'the common people' to be drawn together in numbers and censured their 'unlawful pastimes,' their 'vulgar amusements,'[5] and Lord Chief Justice Ellenborough condemned prize-fights for drawing 'industrious people away from the subject of their industry.'[6] It was the employers, though, who produced the most telling and detailed complaints and it was from them that the strongest attacks on popular holiday habits could be expected. There was the Lincolnshire estate manager who could not get his hay mown because two local feasts and the assizes were in the offing, and Josiah Wedgwood in 1772 castigating his potters for keeping 'wake after wake in summer when it is their own good will and pleasure.' Voices raised in the other direction were rarely heard, though Robert Southey was claiming in 1808 that 'the want of holidays breaks down and brutalizes the labouring class' and their very rarity means that 'they are uniformly abused.'[7]

The conflict, at heart, was between the changed demands of many employers and the inherited expectations of the employed. More and more folk found their old rhythms of labour and leisure disrupted as they were drawn into industry from the land and the village crafts. The enormous acceleration in economic activity in the second half of the eighteenth century pointed to large scale social upheaval though change was far from universal. England was still to be a predominantly agricultural country well into the nineteenth century and as to its towns, such was their diversity that none could confidently be described as 'typical.' Employments might change dramatically – or be little altered at all. Where there was population movement, and all indications are that this was more common than changes in the nature of employments, there were likely to be problems of varying intensity. No change in life-style could be completed within a single generation. New urban dwellers brought with them their old habits and their old expectations of both work and play. The difficulties of reconciling the one with the differing requirements of employers and the other with urban living conditions were at the crux of many conflicts during the whole long period of industrialisation.[8]

Changes in methods of production always tended to put leisure under pressure. It happened early on the land itself. New farming techniques not only reduced the demand for labour and made movement elsewhere often as much a matter of necessity as of choice, but also modified much in the very nature of the agricultural round. Better cultivation, crop rotation and winter fodder undermined the possible force of any mystic annual ceremony to ensure fertility or propitiate the gods. The old festivals tied to the agricultural calendar had strong roots but some of their essential meaning had been lost. They, and the holidays that went with them, were increasingly at risk,[9] making agricultural workers the first large group to find their leisure being hemmed in, just as they were to be the last to benefit from the eventual reductions in working hours nearly two centuries later. As agriculture became more highly capitalised the yeoman farmer was often forced to become a hired hand and so lose control of such free time as he has enjoyed. His hours were set for him, his leisure dependent on local conditions and the goodwill of his employer. It did not, of course, bring all rural amusements to a stop, mean that all the seasonal rhythms were displaced, nor the recreational opportunities that went with them. Free time, however, became much more exposed to external pressures, and it meant also that the once common mixed occupations – miners who were part-time fishermen and craftsmen of all sorts who were part-time farmers and the like – were all much reduced.[10]

The population movement that was taking place was not new. What was new was the pace of it, prompted by the employment changes, though by no means all of these arose directly from industrialisation. The new service industries and domestic labour, for instance, also played their parts. The doubling of London's population during the eighteenth century to little short of a million was at its fastest during the last quarter and it has been estimated that by this time one adult in every six in the country had some experience of London life, which in itself must have acted as a powerful solvent of old rural traditions.[11] More widely, the population balance of the country as a whole was changing. By 1815 the two long standing provincial capitals, Bristol in the west and Norwich in the east, had been overtaken in size not only by Liverpool and Manchester, both with populations topping 100,000, but were now rivalled also by Birmingham, Leeds and Sheffield. Such urban growth could bring its own leisure conflicts as it spread over neighbouring villages. Moreover, improvements in living standards were not only shared unevenly between the classes but also within the working classes themselves. The agricultural worker in the south and west, where the lack of alternative employment kept farm wages uniformly low might appear to have less and less money to spare for even the occasional sporting jaunt,[12] though only towards the end of the period does there begin to be much evidence of geographical shifts in spectator provision.

Did the gains outweigh the losses for the many affected by these economic and social changes? Was the loss of an integrated existence, moving in tune with the seasonal rhythms and enjoying some flexibility and choice in working hours, compensated for by the gains in income, intensity and excitement that came with industrial and urban life? What is clear is that the call of free time was still strong and, according to critics, often heeded, even when the factory system spread and tightened its demands as water power gave way to steam, as factories became concentrated in the expanding towns and there was a tendency to increase shift lengths to twelve hours. Even so, the majority of manufacturers were still outside the factory system, operating in small craft workshops and often inclined to labour no longer than their immediate needs demanded. In the later seventeenth century framework knitters had been said 'seldom to work on Mondays and Tuesdays, but to spend most of their time at the ale-house or ninepins,' and little had changed. The Birmingham metal shops, even in the early nineteenth century, were often silent on Mondays and Tuesdays and then, towards the end of the week, would be working from as early as 4.00 a.m., or even 3.00 a.m., not finishing until 8.00 p.m. at night, in order to make up their weekly quota. Even so the men would still look to their recreation, taking three or four hours off in the middle of the day, time for the skittles, dog fighting or the alehouse.[13]

The early experience of the industrial towns underlines the continuing importance of the *annual* holiday sequence. Race meetings and parish wakes were still notable highlights in the yearly calendar and, for all their harassment and diminution, the annual festivities were still insisted upon, sometimes even as occasions for the promotion of newer forms of sport. The leisure scheme, like sport itself, was in a state of long transition. The spasmodic and often uncertain freedoms that punctuated the working year were in growing competition with the notion of some assured if extremely constrained liberty within the working week. The eventual transmutation of leisure time from being largely periodic to being predominantly weekly was to be a major factor in the growth of modern sport in England. On average, workers enjoyed nine or ten free days a year, but there were wide variations both in their extent and in the circumstances under which they were taken. By the end of the Napoleonic Wars agricultural workers, in spite of the growing pressures on them, could still benefit from the varying demands of the farming year, with a few weeks of relative relaxation after the spring sowing and after harvesting, while factory hands, much the minority of the work force, often had to make up for lost time by adding it to their already long weekly hours. *Official* holidays remained extensive – the Bank of England observed 47 in 1761 and there were still above 40 in 1815.[14] Most of these meant nothing to the labourer in the factory or the field, but he could still have his annual local celebrations – wakes, fairs, and race weeks. How many of these survived and the extent to which he could enjoy them was very much a matter of geographical chance and the conditions of his particular employment.

The most widely assured holidays, so far as sporting possibilities went, were at Easter and Whitsuntide. Easter week was said to have been, from 'time immemorial,' a 'season of mirth and festivity' and Whit Monday 'a universal festival in the humble ranks of life throughout the kingdom.' The role of these holidays has been well described, presenting a picture of communal merry-making, incorporating what were usually traditional forms of play.[15] Easter in London, for instance, saw the usual Sunday outings writ large and the entertainments were tailored to local tastes – the 'middling classes' eating, drinking and playing games at Greenwich or enjoying themselves at the many tea gardens. There was the annual Easter Fair at Tothill Fields, where no great refinement could be expected,[16] while another customary event near the capital was the so-called Epping Easter Hunt, more farce than actual hunt, and usually reported as such.[17] There are few signs of formal sport in most Easter celebrations. Where there is competition it is usually old-style, informal, and comparatively light-hearted, typically including such activities as bell-ringing, quoits, and, above all, cocking. There was some customary football playing, but little organised competition or commercial exploitation.[18] Presumably – and the same would apply to Sundays – tavern keepers could be sure of good trade on the holidays without mounting additional attractions. Whitsuntide offered recreation in similar style. If there was somewhat greater emphasis on organised sports this owed much to the many fairs that fell in and around the holiday.[19] Essentially it, too, remained a popular ancestral celebration, more attuned to the sporting amusements of the past than to the newer forms of competition, the most assured of all the annual playtimes for the population as a whole, and often looked down upon with unusually benign amusement by the literate classes. It was the time for country cousins to come to visit relatives in town, their open mouthed astonishment at what urban life had to offer causing Whit Sunday to become known as 'gaping Sunday' in some parts. It was no occasion for more serious sportsmen or women.[20]

Other annual festivals, where they still held recreational significance, also tended towards preservation rather than innovation. In winter they were, so far as sport was concerned, limited by both climate and habit. November 5th had its bonfires but there was little by way of sport beyond the occasional bull-bait and a belief in some parts that, as at Christmas, the game laws were briefly suspended. Christmas itself was the longest festive season of the year, running from December 24th to Twelfth Night, though it rarely brought a holiday of that length and its pleasures were social rather than sporting. Its main contribution to sporting life was in the communal footballing.[21] Cock-fighting was virtually universal at Shrovetide,[22] but at the more plebeian level, becoming less usual, and without large-scale matches, while the old summer festivals – May Day, Rogation-tide, Ascension Day and Midsummer Day itself – had all lost much of their force by the end of the period. If May Day was still actively observed it was mainly spent in dancing, bell-ringing and chasing games.[23] Rogation-tide races were still being run in Sussex in 1772 and in Northumberland as late as 1822, but the trend towards the disappearance of these summer festivals is exemplified in the Mayor of Carlisle's refusal in 1814 to donate his usual prize for the annual Ascension Day race while the sports associated with Midsummer's Day had all but ceased by the end of the eighteenth century.[24]

Generally speaking, the traditional feasts of the old religious and agricultural calendar had little impact on the development of newer forms of sport. The earlier concentration of much of the research on these inherited festivals has contributed to the undervaluing of the sporting changes that were taking place through the eighteenth century, but essentially taking place on other occasions. The old holidays form less a part of the history of modern sport than of the history of folk play. The weakening of their sporting relevance, however, prompted a balancing response from an age which set high store by its recreation and leisure. While national holidays tended to diminish, the evidence suggests that local festivities and particularly fairs and wakes, continued to be significant, certainly so to judge from the increasing number of criticisms they prompted and the attempts made at containment and suppression.

Fairs, many of them protected by ancient charters, often served valid economic ends. Some were predominantly commercial events, but it was a feature of the times that wherever a large crowd gathered, whether for a bargain or a hanging, there would be some entertainment on hand.[25] Although the information is patchy the sports fairs offered almost certainly changed materially between the middle of the eighteenth century and the early years of the nineteenth. The earlier competitive entertainment consisted typically of flat racing, the combat sports and bell ringing.[26] Later trends in the entertainment they offered show a coarsening, an unremitting quest for sheer amusement with, for example, fewer of the once ubiquitous morris dancers and the bell ringers largely taking their skills elsewhere. Smock races for women survived for most of the period, but the common athletic event became the sack race, while donkey races gave an opportunity for gambling, and were always as likely to provide hilarity as pure competition. Laughter at the expense of others arising from contests such as eating hot porridge with a fork had become very much the order of the day.[27] The hand of the innkeeper begins to be sensed behind the sporting provision, the combat sports assume a more organised air and prizes both at London fairs and in the country could be attractive enough to bring in competitors from a distance.[28]

Wakes had much in common with fairs as providers of popular recreation. They had a long and sometimes uncertain history, but Malcolmson noted 206 in the 290 parishes in Northamptonshire alone in the earlier eighteenth century and while they were gradually reducing from that time forward they were still persisting into the last of the Georgian years. The wake, feast or revel – the title varied locally – usually began with a religious service on the Sunday morning following the saint's day of the church's dedication. Afterwards there would be dancing, merrymaking and sports, eating and much drinking, all of it traditionally contributing to the church's coffers and usually for some special purpose such as repairing the bells.[29] By the eighteenth century, however, the religious element had much diminished, and, where the local tradition was strong, the celebrations had often extended themselves considerably.[30] Such expansion added to the opposition they already provoked by their sabbath violations, and some parishes did put off their sports and diversions, deferring them until Monday, but nearly a hundred years later the Lord's Day Observance Society still found it necessary to give practical advice on how to put a stop to the Sunday feasting and merrymaking.[31]

There can be little doubt that wakes were usually an occasion for behaviour that was less than restrained.[32] Robert Raikes, in 1787, described the scenes on feast Sunday at Painswick in Gloucestershire – 'drunkenness and every species of clamour, riot and disorder filled the town.' He was making the case for his new Sunday schools, which had brought 'peace and tranquillity' to the Sabbath, much to the satisfaction of the more sober citizens who filled the church and expressed their relief in a much better collection than usual, amounting to £57.[33] Clearly many wakes provided no setting for formally organised play and where it did exist at such feasts and revels there are invariably signs of commercial sponsorship.[34]

Many country wakes did doubtlesss preserve much of their original bucolic innocence. At Longford Budville, in Somerset, after the morning service the villagers danced in a ring around the church, gathered in another ring on the local common, where they gave a great shout 'to drive the devil out of the parish,' and then returned to the village for their sports of wrestling and cudgel playing. Like many others this wake was eventually discontinued 'on account of the drinking, &c. which went with it.'[35] As essentially backward-looking events they were always vulnerable to accusations of primitiveness and barbarism. Where wakes often displayed a particular tenacity was in urban settings, where they might have been thought to be especially unsuitable but where they were, at the same time, more susceptible to commercial sponsorship. Here, too, it can be more than usually difficult to identify what a 'wake' or 'revel' actually was, whether it had some authentic relationship with the local patronal festival or whether it was the creative invention of some profit-making entrepreneur.

The wakes of the industrial north-west were certainly genuine and often did more than merely survive. Clegg's journals show the frequency and attraction of wakes in the mid-eighteenth century on the edge of the newly industrialising areas of Lancashire, where factory owners had accepted that one lengthy break in production was preferable to occasional idle days. Monday was always the greatest revelling day with sports on offer that were essentially traditional and unreconstructed – bull-baiting, dog-fighting, duck hunting with dogs, and such competitions as climbing the greasy pole.[36] By contrast, in London and in the south-east generally, the term 'wake' was much less used, and parish feasts are harder to recognise as such. Where a 'country wake' was advertised it was almost certainly a contrived entertainment put on for nostalgic Londoners.[37] A good deal of light on annual local festivals in and around the capital is shed by the full reports available of the 1810 entertainments at Plaistow, variously described as 'Rustic Sports,' even as a 'Fair,' and adding to the complications by occurring in Whit Week. The complaints against them were lodged by Methodists, Quakers and some Anglicans, stating that they had formerly been patronised by the villagers alone, but that in the past two years they had begun to draw in vast numbers of outsiders (who 'were almost all Irish people'.) The roads were blocked and the place subjected to unbearable rowdyism, with jack-ass races, sack races, a smock race and other sports. Mr Justice Heath agreed that while the sports might be a nuisance, that was not the charge – they were neither a riot nor a breach of the peace and the jury was directed to a not guilty verdict.[38] Wake or not, the Plaistow case was an early example of the classic conflict that was frequently to be repeated – religious activists leading an attack on old-style popular recreation, aggravations caused by population growth and urban expansion which brought the rough and the respectable too close to each other for comfort.

Pressures on wakes were continuous from the eighteenth century onwards and are well described by Malcolmson. Sometimes it was legal action, at others the decision of influential citizens and at least once a consequence of the devil's appearance in the shape of a large dog and so ending a Palm Sunday wake![39] One of the few positive alternatives for reform rather than outright suppression came in a project in 1811 to replace wakes with annual sports which would be more contained, well regulated, and better timed in the year – in June, which would cause least interference with farming. Competitors would be confined to the parish and the sports would last for just Monday and Tuesday, but would hope to have the impression of a festive week by concluding with a prize-giving on the following Saturday. Given the strength of the people's leisure preference all through the period – a parliamentary committee in 1812 reported that 'it is very well known that they will not go further than necessity prompts them, many of them'[40] – it is doubtful whether they would take the impression that they were having a week's festivities on the strength of just two allotted days. There were, though, some strong indications that wakes were often transmuted rather than simply suppressed. Their relationship to the annual *sports* that begin to be quite common is still obscure, but their programmes are usually very similar to those of the wakes and particularly where the latter were enjoying some form of sponsorship.[41]

In spite of the gradual reduction of parish wakes particularly during the second half of the period this by no means meant any inevitable reduction of popular sporting opportunities as a whole. Ever since the middle ages sports had been escaping from specific feast days, finding their own occasions and paying less deference to traditional holidays. Each moved into its own favoured times and settled on its own broad season. This applied to activities both old and new, but the evidence from the well reported spectator sports, is a fairly certain indicator of contemporary leisure opportunities, showing when spectators were most able to take time off for play. The three sports with a considerable popular following – horse racing, cricket and pugilism – all had vested interests of one sort or another in attracting as many spectators as possible and so it may be supposed that they would find the best times to do so.

There was, of course, one day of the week when leisure was assured, legitimate, almost total and already established as the great playing day over much of Europe. In England, however, a restrictive attitude towards Sunday behaviour was one of the continuing legacies of Puritanism. So far as sport was concerned the law did technically allow 'legal' games to churchgoers, within their own parish. It was an allowance open to endless different interpretations, was impossible to police and for much of the eighteenth century the mass of the people were said to be spending Sunday much as they pleased,[42] though much of the reported Sabbath play seems to have been casual, marginal, and particularly involving the young. The variety of Sunday recreations in mid-century London show in two contrasting pictures, – one from 1764 is a sunny scene of apparently undisturbed sport and play, with rowing on the river, swimming at Chelsea and in the Hampstead Heath ponds, and footmen in Hyde Park, 'wrestling, cudgel-playing and jumping.' Another though, two years later is of up to 250 'dog-fighters, bullies, chimney-sweepers and sharpers' in the fields behind Bedford House with others 'playing and betting at unlawful games, bathing, running races naked, etc.'[43]

In the last quarter of the eighteenth century attitudes towards the general use of the Sabbath became more restrictive. Its first notable sign was the Sunday Observance Act of 1781 (21 Geo III c. 39) which banned the Sunday opening of any place of public amusement or entertainment for which admission was charged. Its avowed targets were the 'promenades,' rightly seen as no more than places for picking up prostitutes. Its other object was political, to prevent the opening of public rooms for sceptical and possibly seditious debates. It held no sporting intentions, though these were to be discovered a century later. [44] At the time, more immediate consequences for Sunday recreation were likely to flow from George III's 1787 proclamation *For the Encouragement of Piety and Virtue, and for the preventing and punishing of Vice, Profaneness and Immorality.* Sunday behaviour in particular was to become more circumspect – all his subjects, 'of what Degree or Quality whatsoever,' were banned from playing dice, cards, 'or any game whatsoever,' in public or in private. It was not easy for all the loyal subjects to take too seriously an edict which would have emptied the courts of the king's two predecessors and which appeared just as his own three sons, among the least of their peccadillos, began to sponsor an illegal major sport, but there was some sympathy, if only from local justices, for stricter control of taverns, and particularly on Sundays.[45] However, F.M. Eden, writing in 1797, remarked that the only change in people's Sunday behaviour during the course of the century had been that, instead of attending bear-baitings, bull-baitings and cock-matches, they now 'spend their Sunday evenings at skittle-grounds and ale-houses.' [46] Even so large scale Sabbath disorder remained hard to put down in some rougher urban areas, as the Rector of Bethnal Green complained in 1814 when crowds gathered in the field by his church during service time to 'fight dogs, hunt ducks, gamble, (and) enter into subscriptions to fee drovers for a bullock.'[47] More peaceably, thousands of Londoners made Sunday their excursion day, escaping to the leafier villages on the edges of the city, the slightly better off had their assorted transport and as for the poorer trippers

Through clouds of dust, with weary steps and slow,
They pant to Hackney, Islington, or Bow.'[48]

Formal fights had no place on the Sabbath and had made little attempt to find any. Two pugilist contests did take place on a Sunday morning in Hyde Park in 1804, the spectators including 'some gentlemen of the fist.' The second bout was between fighters of some repute who fought 36 hard rounds, but this is the only reliable record of a Sunday prizefight and the date is significant – it was one more of the unusual episodes that marked the start of the nineteenth century.[49] There certainly was some Sunday fighting, usually part of the weekend's customary quarrelling and brawling. Two such combatants in Norwich found themselves in the stocks, prompting the wry observation that their fighting happened 'at the very hour in which two members of the British Senate were engaged in an *affair of honour*,'[50] underlining the much greater scope for the rich to spend Sunday as they wished, even if that extended to killing each other.

They did not, though, choose to spend it in organised sport. Although they might not be unduly concerned over the fragile reputation of much of their play, gentry sponsors, so long as they were not inconvenienced by doing so, saw no particular need to risk unnecessary additional offence by disporting themselves on the Sabbath. Their horse racing had no history of Sunday meetings[51] and cricket matches never appear to have been actually arranged for Sundays, though it is possible that they did occasionally run over in order to finish and for most of the period there was certainly, after service times, the informal play on village greens recalled by Mary Mitford. The game's commercial sponsors, predominantly tavern keepers, were always wary of possible harrassment by magistrates for their Sunday provision and had, in any event, no need of sport on what was much their busiest day of the week.

The avoidance of organised sport on Sundays had important if totally unforeseen long term consequences for the future shape of sport. Play was to first become organised on any scale in the single European land where the one free day available for it was, even among the Protestant countries, the most strictly curtailed. This meant that it had to find other occasions. It did so eventually through early Saturday closing, giving free time that could be constrained and controlled – the tight time dimensions within which many games grew into modern adulthood. For the moment, however, the lack of regular legitimised free time raises the question of when the sport which sought to attract spectators actually *did* take place. If events did succeed in drawing in considerable numbers from the working as well as the more leisured classes they throw some light on what free time actually existed over the long decades when so little of it might appear to have been formally sanctioned.

It was very rare for sporting crowds to be brought together out of unalloyed and uncommercial goodwill. Contests might arise from the stakes and wagers of the upper classes but they were invariably managed on the ground by those who were far from disinterested in the custom they could attract. Matches would be arranged with at least one eye on potential profit, though how this profit might be achieved varied somewhat from sport to sport. Innkeepers such as George Smith at the Artillery Ground and his successors, most notably, of course, Thomas Lord, with his own grounds, wanted as much custom as they could attract and the gentlemen players were, for the most part, by no means averse from showing off their skills to the populace, even if the crowds did prove an occasional nuisance. After an incident in 1744, when an important match was concluded only 'with difficulty,' Smith had been persuaded to raise his entrance charges from 2d. to 6d. The result was disastrous for him. The customers stayed away. By next season the entrance fee had slipped quietly back to its old level. The spectators had proved their necessity, and Thomas Lord's answer to any similar potential crowd problems was to be his high perimeter fence. At all levels of the game, even though admission charges were not usually feasible, similar commercial interests applied through the victualling rights.[52]

Pugilism, on the face of it, had no apparent need of crowds, at least so far as its wealthy backers were concerned and they indeed, like the cricketers, were occasionally incommoded by 'the rabble' attracted to big fights. For the pugilists themselves, though, crowds and profits were of considerable importance. The organising and control of fights on the ground was almost entirely in their hands and any gate money that could be collected was due to the actual fighters. Pugilists past and present also had the established right to draw up their waggons to serve, at a fee, as temporary grandstands. More widely, the greater the enthusiasm and excitement they could generate in the actual fights, the higher the profile they could give to their sport, the more the pugilists could hope to benefit from their legal sparring exhibitions in London and the provinces, or as teachers of their art. In short, they had every incentive to involve as many people as possible in their sport. The economics of horse racing were more varied and more complex. Their most common feature was the race fund out of which prizes were provided. It would derive from subscriptions raised locally and the site fees charged for stalls and booths on the course, these at reduced rates for subscribers. Clearly the size of the anticipated crowd would dictate the fees that could be demanded and so again there was every incentive to attract as many spectators as possible.

In all three sports, therefore, there were strong motives to identify the leisure time to which they were most suited – and all the evidence suggests that they were successful. Hard information on crowd sizes is always difficult to come by before the much later advent of the mechanical turnstile and most of the evidence derives from possibly over-enthusiastic reporters. Even so, and allowing for exaggeration, some contemporary sporting crowds were certainly very large – they would need to be multiplied by at least ten to give some present day equivalent. As might be expected the London area provided some of the largest, and from a variety of events. Three thousand would cram into the Fives Court for sparring exhibitions, cricket at Lords frequently drew several thousands, ten thousand was a common figure quoted for even relatively undistinguished fights towards the end of the period when the largest sporting crowds of the year were flocking to Epsom for the Derby meeting.[53] What is more surprising is that similar crowds could come together elsewhere in the country, with five figure attendances reported from the provinces for all three major sports.[54] Whatever the precise reliability of the figures, they do tend to be confirmed by both the advertisements from promoters and the equally regular complaints from employers – and large crowds were not an uncommon phenomenon in other contexts, to judge from the presumably dependable testimony of John Wesley and other preachers.

The purest evidence of a sport's response to its followers' free time might be expected to come from pugilism. Prize-fights were self-contained, one-off, one day events, technically illegal certainly, but having no apparent inbuilt constraints as to which day of the week they occupied. The popular fighting days were, predictably, at the start of the week, when work was slack. Within this expected pattern, though, they present an intriguing puzzle. Of some 60 fights involving named pugilists between 1788 (when the sport became fashionable from its royal backing) and 1804, 27 were fought on Mondays, 9 on Tuesdays, and then a falling away through the rest of the week, all in correspondence with known patterns of labour, and with Monday always having been the favourite fighting day. From 1805, however, there is a remarkable change. Between that year and 1820, the halcyon days of the ring, out of 131 significant fights nearly half now took place on *Tuesday*, with Monday a poor second, having just 20 in all.[55] Tuesday was clearly settled upon as *the* fighting day and, what is more, it remained so for the rest of the sport's bareknuckle history. The comparative suddenness of the change points to contemporary events and to the conflict between moral revival and sporting enterprise which marked these particular early years of the nineteenth century. The activities of the Society for the Prevention of Vice were reflected in the increased interference by the law officers in fights around London. Usually safe venues such as Willesden Green were harried and sporting crowds began to be chivvied from one site to another.[56] At a time when more great pugilists were active than at any other in the sport's history, neither they nor their supporters were to be denied. The first expedient was to move further away from the capital and try a different day. Shepperton Common, on Saturday 27 April 1805, had the unique sight of contests fought by three of the ring's great all-time heroes – Tom Belcher, Henry Pierce (the 'Game Chicken') and Dutch Sam. The experiment was repeated three months later, on Saturday 20 July, this time at Virginia Water, and with the attraction now of another future champion in John Gully. These venues, though, were still close to London, still attracted the rowdier fight followers and in any event Saturday, the settling day for many, was one of the least convenient days of the week. Eventually, in October that year, when Gully fought again, it was at Hailsham, deep in the Sussex countryside, convenient for Brighton but well removed from the capital – and it was on a Tuesday. The advantages of the new arrangement were quickly appreciated. The sporting gentry avoided offence to sabbatarian sensitivities from overnight travel. Better off artisans, who could afford to lose two or three days labour, were not excluded, and 'the company was of the better order, and not molested by the rabbles who frequent the fights nearer town.'[57] So far as the bigger fights were concerned Tuesday would henceforth be their most favoured day, and the countryside their favoured venue.

Cricket also made use of the slackness at the start of the week. With the length of matches often uncertain, the most reliable evidence of playing days in cricket comes from the days on which games actually *started*, the day on which, weather permitting, play was assured, and which would presumably be the day of the week most likely to be available to both players and spectators and it is quite clear that this was Monday. An examination of 566 matches in the eighteenth century from Buckley shows more than twice as many starting then as on any other day. The only variation in the pattern comes in the new century when Thursday begins gradually to emerge as the second favourite starting day, largely because some of the bigger teams were getting into the habit of fitting two games into the week. Saturday was always the least popular day for starting games.[58] It was also unpopular as a racing day. Here, though, other factors operated unrelated to the working week. Newmarket apart, as so often, horses had to be walked from one course to another if the races were not to be purely local affairs and so there had to be at least two or three days between one meeting and the next. With Sunday racing out of the question, the weekend was the obvious time for this travelling. Taking a typical year in the middle of the period (1787) the peak days for racing were clearly those in the middle of the week. Out of 66 meetings, 48 had Wednesday racing, 41 on Thursdays and 34 on Tuesdays (many, of course, had two-day or three-day meetings) but the other days saw very little racing. The avoidance particularly of Monday (when racing took place at only eight meetings) allowed as long an interval as possible between meetings to bring in visiting horses and also meant that the raceground preparations did not take place on Sundays.[59] The unique feature of the race meeting, however, was that it belonged to the annual rather than the weekly scheme of work and leisure. The races took on, in their own right, the nature of a holiday.[60]

Confirmation of this pattern of leisure possibilities came later from Mark Harrison, tackling the question of free time from the other side of the coin. Starting with the assumption that 'non-working hours' were Sunday, Monday and from 12 p.m. to 2 p.m. and 6 p.m. to 6 a.m. from Tuesday to Saturday inclusive, he found that the considerable majority of crowd references took place *outside* what could be, and some cases actually were, described as 'working hours.'[61] In particular he reinforced the emphasis on Mondays as potentially or actually free days. Certainly where sporting events had to accommodate themselves to the weekly labour pattern it was virtually inevitable that they would fit into the early part of the week. *St Monday* and *Holy Tuesday* had long been the workers' sardonic responses to the disappearance of the old saints' days from the holiday calendar and they even prompted a rare plea for Sunday recreation as a means of keeping men from spending the day in the ale-house with the consequence 'that Saint Monday, Holy Tuesday, and oftentimes more days that should be devoted to work, are wasted on the skittle-ground.'[62]

To what extent sport was responsible for the 'loose and wandering habits' complained of in the new factory workers is uncertain.[63] There is little earlier evidence of the regular and almost weekly sporting entertainment of the sort that the pedestrian grounds of the northwest were offering towards the middle of the nineteenth century. The great recreational events of the new industrial areas were annual and not weekly. Race meetings flourished, large-scale cock-fighting took place at most of them, and pugilism at many – ten(!) bouts of fisticuffs and a wrestling match between two 'gentlemen,' were reported after the second day of Lancaster's races in 1813.[64] Apart from these crowd-pulling annual events, however, the early overall picture of the sporting life of the new industrial areas is hard to draw with firmness, with just occasional glimpses of, for example, a bowling match for 50 guineas a side, a fox turned out on Cheadle Heath near Stockport, another giving a five hour chase to the Leeds Harriers and, more distantly, the huge foot racing crowds on Scarborough sands.[65] Boxing was certainly almost everywhere, whether of the local free-for-all variety or according to Broughton's rules,[66] but to achieve any national fame, northern performers such as Gregson the boxer or Wood the runner had to make their way to London. There the press was so heavily weighted towards the capital and the Home Counties that it was inclined to report only the more bizarre activities from the northern outposts – such as a race between a bull and an ass, both ridden, at New Mills – or to take a patronising view of its sporting standards. Of a boxing match near Stockport it was reported that 'little science could be expected in so remote a country.'[67]

Not only was there this identifiable wakes 'season' in the north west, but each individual sport began more regularly to acknowledge its own annual calendar. The cricket season, with the exception of those specialist grounds which had no need to recognise the demands of agriculture, normally only started after the first hay crop had been taken off the field, and so was later in the year the further north the game was played. High summer, before the harvest, provided the opportunity for many county race meetings over much of the country, while along the south coast the early harvesting there produced a string of August race meetings, still identifiable through the twentieth century. Everywhere, after harvesting, the summer sports would pick up again, often going through to late October or even early November. In so far as they needed to do so the sporting seasons meshed in well with the country gentleman's yearly round. His parliamentary duties in London would occupy the early months between the end of his fox-hunting and the Craven Meeting at Newmarket at the beginning of April, effectively the start of the national racing season. The Newmarket spring season ran up to the July Meeting, early in the month, and then took its three month summer break, during which the country races were at their most numerous. Newmarket rounded its season off with the two Autumn meetings in October and then it was back to the estates, the fox-hunting and the coursing.[68]

Prize fighting, of course, took place in various settings but at its highest levels, where it was dependent upon the stakes and wagers of the wealthy it usually avoided the summer months, when the sponsors were enjoying their country pleasures. Where big fights fall outside the usual December to March pattern they can often be associated with some other attraction – racing at Newmarket, for example, hunting in Leicestershire, or the Prince of Wales holding court at Brighton. The one developing sport which had no readily discernible season was pedestrianism, which floated somewhat untethered between monied sponsorship and popular spectator sport. A cursory examination of pedestrian events in the 1790s, based largely on the *Sporting Magazine*, shows them taking place in all months of the year with an understandable but not particularly marked preference for the period between March and June. At quite the other extreme was the one sport in which the season had been precisely defined from the middle ages – hunting was traditionally sanctioned between the Feast of the Nativity on September 8th and the Purification of our Lady on February 2nd,[69] but to judge from just the experience of the king's stag hunting in 1787, the date for the ending of the season had become somewhat adjustable. There are, in fact, so many examples of fox-hunting continuing well into March that it was perhaps the farcical Epping Easter Hunt which had become the practical end of the season.[70] Coursing, too, followed much the same winter pattern.

The prospect of known seasons for play figured now both in the gloomy anticipations of employers and the rising expectations of spectators. Holidays, and the sports associated with them, were certainly under growing pressure but the overall conclusion is that they at least held their own. The strengthening and virtual acceptance of the alternative leisure calendar, represented typically by St Monday observance, made holidays all the harder to target and helped to hold what was still a balance between the expansion of free time and the restrictive inclinations of the commercial, political and moral establishment. Given the periodic opportunities most could find to extend their playing times and the tendency, wherever possible, to work for less than a full week, the total span of leisure – even if it was often uncertain and locally very variable – was still relatively liberal. The expansiveness of leisure, moreover, was not confined only to the number of sporting days that could be wrung from the working round but also in the comprehensive use that was made of them.

The intermingling of one sport with another is a repeated theme of the age – the prize-fighting and cocking at race meetings, foot races at cricket matches, bull-baiting and prize-fighting partnering each other, and so on. Neither players, sponsors or spectators were exclusively specialised and many took their interests into a variety of sporting directions. Among performers there was a distinguished line of pan-athletes from Jem Broughton to John Jackson. There was Noah Mann, the cricketer, always ready to take on foot racing challengers at the end of play, Grindlay, the runner, prepared to try fist-fighting, and many a pugilist who fancied himself as an athlete. Versatility was always welcome. The more entertainment that could be provided and the longer it could be extended the better pleased the promoters would be as the crowd grew hungrier and thirstier. As for the spectators, once time had been taken off from work it had usually to be for a full day. There was little thought at this time of the *half-day* holiday which had once characterised many saints' days and was to become in turn a salient feature in the emergence of later Victorian popular sport. Only a handful of events, such as the sparring at the Fives Court and the evening boating races on the river, could be grafted on to the working day. Diversity and enlargement were constant themes. On the country racecourses, for example, with limited fields, the actual racing could sometimes be the least of the entertainment, with many other attractions from the gambling tables to the jugglers.[71] Race days were unhurried. A starting time would be quoted for the first race but even that was not taken too seriously and thereafter it was usually a matter of chance. Racing in heats meant, of course, that not even the number of contests could be predicted. While there was always much to keep the spectators amused between the races, the time was not, judging from a comment made on the 1805 Bickley Races, always best spent. Here the organisers had arranged 'foot matches, running in sacks, and the various round of rustic revelry' between the heats and were much praised in the *Sporting Magazine* for promoting the spirit of competition and giving 'a dignified intercourse' to the proceedings. However, it does not seem to have been much repeated and more spectacular and esoteric entertainment was coming into fashion, with the crowds at Yorkshire race meetings gazing up in wonder as Mr Sadler in his famous balloon soared into the sky above them.[72]

The race meeting, with its fairground atmosphere, was a prime candidate for providing a full day's entertainment. Cricket was also doing so as play became more skilled, innings lasted longer and morning starts became common, usually at 10.00 a.m. but sometimes, by the turn of the century, as early as 9.30 a.m.[73] The common practice in club matches was to end play at sunset. The fact that many games were played in late summer meant that there was much variability and the highly staked aristocratic contests, risking neither darkness nor a late dinner, usually laid down an earlier close of play time, typically between six and seven thirty. There had also been a long history of combining foot races with cricket, stretching back at least to 1744 when there was a well advertised smock race at the Southwark v High Kent match, but the practice seems to have diminished as the game itself came to take up the whole day.[74] Prize-fighting, once it had been expelled from its indoor arenas, often filled a day on its own account. The model programme, inherited from its legal days, was to have at least three contests, a main bout, which always came first, followed by two or more 'bye-battles' though this was not readily achievable without powerful patronage. Otherwise, with fights seldom timed to begin much before noon, the probability of police intervention and the early fall of winter darkness, it was unusual to manage more than one fight. But while the sport itself might occupy only a fraction of the day it is hard to escape the impression that the contest with the authorities to find a site and the trek to reach it often generated as much excitement as the fight itself. There would usually be little time at the venue itself to set up other diversions beyond the bookmakers' stands and the portable gambling tables such as the old champion Tom Johnson hawked around in his fading years. Occasionally fights could have a more settled air about them, but the tents regularly set up at Molesey Hurst in the later days, with their refreshment marquee, were a rarity. However, if pugilism could not provide a vehicle for other sports it could often extend the day's entertainment elsewhere. Rough and ready fights were got up at fairs and wakes and more serious contests often followed a day's horse racing. At Epsom in particular there were always willing pugs on hand looking for a pick-up fight. Ascot was another favourite venue, and other courses such as Egham occasionally saw contests of some note.[75] The racecourse grandstand would provide one style of audience. London bull-baiting crowds could provide another, with fisticuffs providing a postscript to their entertainment – the regular Tuesday baits at Tothill Fields in 1810 were being accompanied by the amusements 'usual on such occasions,' concluding 'with a boxing match.'[76] In extending the entertainment they provided, these newer organised sports were doing no more than what had long been a habit in traditional folk celebration, providing a *day* of pleasures, not to be confined within a morning, an afternoon, or a few set hours. The lengthy and varied programmes of events at wakes and feasts invariably imply not only early starts but also that they will be running until well into the evening. Notions of time were still generally vague, as likely to be set by the sun as by the clock. Precise scheduling was not usually expected and where it was promised, as it was at Tonbridge Fair in 1809, it could even be versified, after a fashion, and not taken unduly seriously:

At half-five
A neddy race for a Gloucester cheese from the Chequer sign-post,
The winner of it is to be the one that comes in hindmost.
No gentleman permitted to ride his own ass.
At six
To split your sides with laughing, two new shoes, worth two dollars,
Will be grinned for by three smilers thro' three horse collars ...'[77]

It was all part of the aim to keep the merry pot always on the boil, and for as long as possible. If the time-table here was kept to it would be at odds with current practice. Soon, though, time-tables of all sorts would come to be taken more seriously. When it happened, as labour and leisure came to be more exactly measured, the expansiveness of sport which this period could still celebrate would itself be lost, constrained within defined limits, more highly skilled and more equally competitive, but with what still remained here of easy innocence and relaxed indulgence belonging to a lost past.

Notes

N.B. The research on the incidence of sporting events as indicators of leisure time was first published as 'Sporting Days in Eighteenth Century England,' *Journal of Sport History*, vol.9, no.3, Winter 1982, pp 41-54 and a version of part of this chapter was presented at the Eleventh International Economic History Congress, Milan, 1994, for which see Ian Blanchard, *ed., Labour and Leisure in Historical Perspective, Thirteenth to Twentieth Centuries*, Stuttgart, 1994, pp 101-110.

1. See Malcolmson, *Popular Recreations*, pp 89-100 and particularly p 90, n.5.
2. See praise for the Duke of Dorset, *Whitehall Evening Post*, 8 July 1783.
3. *Gentleman's Magazine*, XIII, 1743, p 486.
4. *The Servants Calling; With some Advice to the Apprentice*, 1725, pp 80/1; Joseph Stott, *A Sequel to the Friendly Advice to the Poor of Manchester*, Manchester, 1756, pp 19/20, both quoted extensively in Malcolmson, *Popular Recreations*, pp 93/4.
5. Henry Douch, *Hints Respecting the Public Police*, 1786, pp 6/7.

6. *Pancratia*, p 180.

7. Malcomson, *Popular Recreations*, p 100; Katherine E. Farrar, *ed.*, *Letters of Josiah Wedgwood 1762-1780*, 2 vols., II, p 14.

8. See Harrison, *Crowds and History*, p 42; J. M. Golby and A. W. Purdue, *Popular Culture 1750-1900*, ch.1 'The "old" popular culture.'

9. See Vamplew, 'Sport and Industrialisation,' Mangan, ed., *Pleasure, Profit and Proselytism*, p 9.

10. John Denson, *A Peasant's Voice to Landowners, on the Best means of Benefiting Agricultural Labourers, and of Reducing Poor's Rates*, Cambridge, 1813, p 17; *Collections Towards a Parochial History of Berkshire*, 1783, in Nichols' *Bibliotheca Topographica Britannica*, 10 vols., IV, p 55.

11. E.A. Wigley, 'A Simple Model of London's Importance in Changing English Society and Economy 1650-1750,' *Past and Present*, 37, July 1967, pp 24, 50.

12. E. H. Hunt, *British Labour History 1815-1914*, 1981, p 34. See Plaistow court case, *SM*, August-October, 1810.

13. E. P. Thompson, 'Time, Work-Discipline and Industrial Capitalism,' *Past and Present*, 38, 1967, pp 72/3; Douglas A. Reid, 'The Decline of Saint Monday 1766-1876,' *Past and Present*, 71, 1976, pp 77-79.

14. M. A. Bienefeld, *Working Hours in British History*, 1972, p 34. J. A. R. Pimlott, *The Englishman's Holiday: A Social History*, 1947, Hassocks edition, 1976, p 81; *Times*, 1787, passim.

15. *Manchester Chronicle*, 1841; William Hone, *Every-Day Book 1827*, col. 666, both quoted in Malcolmson, *Popular Recreations*, pp 29, 31. See also in particular, ch.2, 'The Holiday Calendar.'

16. See *SM*, April 1813, pp 20/21.

17. See *SM*, April 1805, p 55; April 1811, p 2, for Epping Hunt reports.

18. William Whellan, *The History and Topography of the Counties of Cumberland and Westmoreland*, Pontefract, 1860, p 479; Clarkson, *History and Antiquities of Richmond*, p 294, *Times*, 1787, passim. See Goulstone, *Summer Solstice Games*, p 36 for an example from Sandgate of the intermingling of new and old.

19. *SM*, July 1795, p 223; see also e.g. John Beresford, ed., *The Diary of a Country Parson: The Reverend James Woodforde*, 5 vols., Oxford, 1824-31, 5 June 1786, 12 May 1788.

20. See Maidenhead Whitsuntide Sports advertisement, *SM*, May 1797, pp 87/8.

21. W. H. Chaloner, ed., *The Autobiography of Samuel Bamford, Vol.1, Early Days*, 1967, pp 159/60; *Stamford Mercury*, 10 November 1809; Malcolmson, *Popular Recreations*, pp 26-28; Wright, *British Calendar Customs*, III, p 260.

22. Edward Peacock, *ed.*, *John Mackinnon's Account of Massingham in the County of Lincoln*, Hertford, 1881, p 10; Malcolmson, *Popular Recreations*, pp 28-29.

23. Denson, *Peasant's Voice*, pp 17/18; For May Day celebrations see Malcolmson, *Popular Recreations*, pp 30/31; Thistleton Dyer, *British Popular Customs*, pp 223-273; Wright, *British Calendar Customs*, I, pp 76-120.

24. Goulstone, *Summer Solstice Games*, pp 19, 23; *SM*, May 1814, p 94. At Carlisle the citizens elected their own mayor for the day, provided their own prize and enjoyed the day's sport 'with greatest hilarity and good humour.' (*SM*, May 1814, p 94)

25. Malcolmson found few specifically 'pleasure' fairs, *Popular Recreations*, p 22.

26. For examples see *Kentish Post*, 20 July 1751; *Northampton Mercury*, 30 September 1765, 20 July 1761; Malcolmson, P*opular Recreations*, p 24; Goulstone, *Summer Solstice Games*, p 32 and *passim*.

27. See *e.g. Sports History*, 4, 1984, p 19 (Anstey); *SM*, June 1811, p 115 (Harlesden Green).

28. See *e.g. SM*, July 1814, p 183; May 1808, p 98; July 1808, p 148. For fuller discussion of fairs and their activities see *e.g.* Mark Judd, 'The oddest combination of town and country: popular culture and the London Fairs 1800-60,' Walton and Walvin, *eds.*, *Leisure in Britain*; Brailsford, *Bareknuckles*, p 3. For suppressions see e.g. *Essex Quarter Sessions Order Book*, 20 April 1762, A. F. J. Brown, *English History from Essex Sources 1750-1900*, Essex Record Office Publications, no 18, 1952, p 167; *Chelmsford Chronicle*, 8 June 1787.

29. Malcolmson, *Popular Recreations*, p 17. See *e.g. Gloucester Chronicle*, 15 January 1790; Brailsford, *Sport and Society*, pp 111-114 and *passim*.

30. John Brand, *Observations on Popular Antiquities*, Newcastle upon Tyne, 1777, revised Henry Ellis, 2 vols., 1813, ch. 30; Strutt, *Sports and Pastimes*, pp 288/9; Malcolmson, *Popular Recreations*, p 53.

31. *Gentleman's Magazine*, October 1738, p 523; Lord's Day Observance Society, *Quarterly Publication*, no. 10, January 1846; no. 12, October 1848.

32. See Samuel Fisher, 'An Answer to Dr John Gaudin,' in *The Testimony of Truth Exalted*, 1679, p 23, quoted in Christopher Hill, *Society and Puritanism in Pre-Revolutionary England*, 1964, p 196.

33. *Times*, 4 January 1787.

34. See advertisements from *Reading Mercury*, Goulstone, *Summer Solstice Games*, p 17; *Salisbury Journal*, 2 July 1781; *Reading Mercury*, 18 June 1781; *Canterbury Journal*, 12 July 1785; George Burton, *Chronology of Stamford*, Stamford, 1846, p 175.

35. *Somerset and Dorset Notes and Queries*, xx, pp 245/6.

36. Robert Poole, 'Oldham Wakes,' Walton and Walvin, *eds.*, *Leisure in Britain*, p 72.

37. *General Advertiser*, 28 August 1752.

38. *SM*, July 1810, p 167. 192; August 1810, pp 209-214; September 1810, p 268; October 1810, pp 17-24; Egan, *Book of Sports*, p 257/8.

39. Malcolmson. *Popular Recreations*, p 147; K. T. Meady, *Nottinghamshire: Extracts from the County Records of the Eighteenth Century*, Nottingham, 1947, p 147. Goulstone, *Summer Solstice Games*, p 89.

40. *SM*, January 1811, pp 141-142; Reid, 'Decline of Saint Monday,' *Past and Present*, no 71, May 1976, p 78.

41. See *e.g.* Goulstone, *Summer Solstice Games*, pp 62, 28, 48, 30, 32.

42. Brailsford, *Sport, Time and Society*, pp 31-46. See also John Wigley, *The Rise and Fall of the Victorian Sunday*, Manchester, 1980, pp 18-25; Whitaker, *Eighteenth Century Sunday*; Dennis Brailsford, 'Religion and Sport in Eighteenth Century England: "For the Encouragement of Piety and Virtue, and for the Preventing or Punishing of Vice, Profaneness and Immorality,"' *British Journal of Sports History*, vol. 1, no. 2, September 1984; Malcolmson, *Popular Recreations*, p 162 and passim.

43. Whitaker, *Eighteenth Century Sunday*, pp 105/6, 131; *Daily Gazetteer*, 10, 21 June 1766. See also Joan Varley, 'An Archdiaconal Visitation of Stow,' *Reports and Papers of the Lincoln Architectural and Archaeological Society*, New

Series, III, 1948, p 160

44. See Wigley, *Victorian Sunday*, pp 26, 206.

45. *Times*, 12 April, 2, 28 July, 7 September, 9 October, 13 November 1787. For the full text see 29 June 1797.

46. Eden, State of the Poor, quoted in George, *London Life in the Eighteenth Century*, p 295. See also J. L. and Barbara Hammond, *The Town Labourer (1760-1832)*, 2 vols , 1917; 1949 edition , II, p 65.

47. *Report of the Police of the Metropolis*, 1816, p 151.

48. See *SM*, May 1808, p 100; April 1805, p 39; May 1806, p 86; December 1801, p 114.

49. *SM*, November 1804, p 100. See also Brailsford, *Bareknuckles*, p 54 and there is also a dubious report of a Sunday contest between two well-known fighters in *Pancratia*, p 72.

50. *Times*, 18 October 1787; *SM*, February 1800, p 254. *SM*, November 1804, p 100.

51. There was even criticism of travel to Newmarket for Monday starts, see e.g., Hammonds, *Town Labourer*, I, p 64.

52. *Daily Advertiser*, 30 June 1744; *Penny London Morning Advertiser*, 6 July 1744; *Daily Advertiser*, 28 September 1744; *Times*, 1787.

53. See *e.g.*, *SM*, January 1811, p 195.

54. See *e.g.* Bowen, *Cricket: A History*, p 265; *SM*, June 1805, p 165; April 1813, p 24.

55. Based on fights recorded in *Pancratia* and Miles, *Pugilistica*.

56. *SM*, July 1804, p 195; April 1805 p 50.

57. *SM*, July 1805, p 213; October 1805, p 38.

58. For a full analysis see Brailsford, 'Sporting Days,' *Journal of Sport History*, vol.9, no.3, Winter 1982, p 50. For the difficulties in identifying playing days see *Nottingham Journal*, 13 October 1792 – Bingham v Newark began on Saturday morning and 'was not concluded till Monday at noon.' Over 300 runs were scored and the light would fail early. Did this imply Sunday play?

59. Based on races reported in the *Times*. Analysis of meetings in 1797 from the *Racing Calendar* gives a virtually identical distribution.

60. They became so embedded as to feature later in negotiations over the introduction of the Saturday half day. See *e.g.* Roy A. Church, *Economic and Social Change in a Midland Town: Victorian Nottingham 1815-1900*, 1966, p 375.

61. Harrison, *Crowds and History*, pp 44 ff, 102.

62. *SM*, May 1809. p 1809, p 180; January 1820, p 100.

63. See E. P. Thompson, *The Making of the Working Class*, Harmondsworth, 1968, p 394.

64. *SM*, June 1805, p 165; July 1813, p 156; July 1809, p 196. North-eastern meetings in the first decade of the nineteenth century included Chester, Lancaster, Nantwich, Newton, Ormskirk, Penrith, Preston, Skipton and, of course, Manchester.

65. *SM*, June 1806, p 111; February 1805, p 236; March 1807, p 302; July 1803, p 222; June 1813, p 140.

66. See e.g. Robert Poole, 'Oldham Wakes,' Walton and Walvin, *eds.*, *Leisure in Britain*, p 85.

67. *SM*, November 1794, p 105; November 1805, p 87.

68. *Racing Calendar 1797*. There were few meetings, and none of any signifi-

cance, outside the Newmarket season.

69. For hunting seasons see Brailsford, *British Sport: A Social History*, Cambridge, 1992, p 7.

70. *Times*, 3 April, 10, 15 May 1787. For racing earlier in the year see e.g. *SM*, March 1807, p 302; April 1809, p 7; February 1811, p 327.

71. *SM*, October 1814, p 42; October 1822, p 84.

72. *SM*, November 1805, p 84; August 1814, p 227; September 1814, p 275.

73. Under special circumstances there could be very early starts – completing a game before the assizes sat or before the day's racing began, for example. See the well detailed article 'Cricket: Hours of Play,' *Sports History*, 6, 1985, pp 3-5.

74. *SM*, June 1797, p 147; *Penny London Morning Advertiser*, 11 June 1744.

75. *Pancratia*, pp 60, 63; SM, August 1805, pp 295/6.

76. *Pancratia*, p 341.

77. *Kentish Notebook 1899*, quoted in *Sports History*, 4, 1984, p 19.

5.
Patrons and Promoters

Many traditional sporting events relied on little more than folk memory for their maintenance. Much other play, however, and an ever increasing proportion, depended on some outside agency, upon patronage or profit seeking. The form that this took could hardly fail to have considerable consequences for the nature and style of the sports themselves. The importance of patronage, and particularly of aristocratic patronage, in the growth of competitive sport in the eighteenth century has always been recognised. This became less prominent in its last years as the club began to replace the individual in the promotion, a change in stress which would seem in accord with both the lessening of official patronage of public offices and the widespread weakening of the traditional support given to inherited recreational activities, already extensively documented by Malcolmson.[1] As Perkin and others have emphasised though, 'patronage brings us very close to the inner structure of the old society,'[2] and any overall decline in sporting patronage was unlikely. It was less the principle of privileged benefaction that came under attack as its use in such central national institutions as parliament, the church, the army and the law. There was still scope and welcome for sponsorship in sport and recreation, and often the expectation that it would be forthcoming. Moreover, as sponsorship was all-pervading in society at large, it could, in sport, be expected to take on many other forms beyond the staking of conspicuous cricket matches or prestigious prize-fights. Where patronage has been examined in this broader sense – in a regional study in Scotland – it was shown to be widespread and often critical to an activity's success or failure.[3] Likewise In England, throughout the Georgian age, overall sporting sponsorship, far from being in decline, was becoming more diverse, operating in more and more different directions and from more and more varied sources.

This is not to underestimate the significance of that patronage which came from the most elevated levels of society, starting, as already indicated, with the crown itself. The first two Georges may have done little more than sanction their King's Plates to favoured racecourses[4] but the sons of George II were of another stamp. The first, Frederick, Prince of Wales, was an ardent cricketer in the game's first important phase – in one month, June 1737, he was leading teams in two 'great matches,' one against Lord Sackville and the other against Sir William Gage.[5] His younger brother, the Duke of Cumberland, had his finger in virtually every sporting pie from boating, through cricket and horse racing to pugilism, but he proved a fickle sponsor, regularly backed the wrong man and produced horses that ran better for other people than they ever had for him. There was something of the same inconstancy in the enthusiasm shown later by the three sons of George III though the rapid revival of the pugilism in the later 1780s undoubtedly owed very much to their support. Where the Prince of Wales and his brothers went, others would follow, and many would remain with the sport after the Prince himself saw a man killed in the ring and vowed never to watch boxing again. He did, though, retain some sympathy with the sport, taking on a pugilist, Tom Tring, as sedan chairman, and, much later, having a corps of pugilists as ushers at his coronation. His brothers, too, remained linked with the ring and the long-term support of the Duke of Clarence, the future William IV, was particularly valuable, ensuring, for some twenty years at the start of the nineteenth century, that fights on the edge of his estate at Bushey Park would take place undisturbed.[6]

There were no legal barriers, thin as they might prove, to royal support of horse racing, where the practice of providing regular prizes for selected meetings became well established. In 1797, for example, there were some nineteen of these 'Royal Plates' awarded to English courses, as well as those to meetings in other parts of the kingdom. The princes' direct involvement in the turf, though, came to an abrupt halt in 1792 when, on the same day, both the Prince of Wales, out of extravagance, and the Duke of York, out of sympathy, sold their impressive strings of horses.[7] None of the family, though, completely deserted the sport. All were reported at race meetings from time to time, as well as continuing to head the list of subscribers to the *Racing Calendar*. The brothers, York and Clarence were, for instance, the stewards together at Egham in 1808, and the Prince, as George IV, regularly attended Ascot.[8]

The royal encouragement of cricket was also spasmodic. The princes must have shown an astonishingly early appreciation of the game, prompting their father, George III, to present a silver cup to the players on Richmond Green because the boys had been 'much pleased' by a cricket match there – and this was in 1770 when their ages ranged between three and eight.[9] The Prince of Wales played the game in his teens. His brother, York, was said to have been a batsman and made matches from time to time,[10] while the Prince himself seems to have been something of a bowler, though it is never easy to recognise where reporting ends and sycophancy begins. He was playing again in 1804, after a gap of fifteen years[11] but his support for cricket was as inconstant as his patronage of the turf and later there were complaints that both the Brighton players and the game generally missed his 'fostering influence.'[12]

Royal patronage of sport might be intermittent and unpredictable but it could produce rapid and dramatic results. Nowhere did this show more clearly than in archery, which had enjoyed only a tenuous existence earlier in the century. A Mr Waring and a few friends founded the Toxophilite Society in 1780. It had just twenty-four members when it began to use the Artillery Ground in 1784 but three years later the Prince of Wales, always attracted by the unusual and the exotic, agreed to become its patron, giving it the right to have 'Royal' in its title. The consequences were both immediate and impressive. Within twelve months not only had the Society's own membership shot up to 168, but other archery societies, most of them socially exclusive, had sprung up over the whole of the country.[13] This, apart from the longer term encouragement given to swimming by the king's successful sea dipping, was the most conspicuous example of the direct influence exerted by royal patronage, itself virtually creating – or at least re-creating – a sport. What, indeed, was as important as the individual backing which happened to be given to this or that particular form of play was the notion that sport was socially acceptable at the highest levels. What was fitting for members of the royal family was fitting, too, for many other potential patrons, of whatever rank. Patronage of old ceremonies and celebrations might well be on the decline, particularly where such occasions seemed primitive, disorderly, cruel or time-wasting, but there was much scope remaining for sporting and recreational patronage, and the royal example was there to commend it.

In one dimension there were sound pragmatic reasons for backing competitive play. It could smooth the relationships between lords and commoners, landlord and tenant, employer and employed. This was periodically recognised by correspondents to the *Sporting Magazine*, and directly pointed out by that contemporary recorder of popular customs, John Brand, who noted that people appeared to need 'their proper Intervals of Relaxation' and it was 'of the highest political Utility to encourage innocent Sports and Games among them.'[14] But to ascribe all sponsorship to the bread and circuses principle would be too facile, too simple and too cynical. There were often other motives at work as well – the love of display, perhaps, the keenness for a good local gamble, the wish to back a favourite performer, or even just a passion for sport itself.

Within a single sport like horse racing there could be both complexity and contradiction. Newmarket was entirely devoted to the self indulgence of the wealthy and well connected. The only immediate element of patronage about Newmarket lay in the employment that the racing generated. Provincial meetings, on the other hand, as a result of the high thresholds set for prize money in the 1740 Act and the cost of suitable horses, would not have survived without the sponsorship of the better off. Without backing, the local sport would almost inevitably have been limited to the ass and donkey races which innkeepers and other promoters of local events resorted to. There was little danger that this would be allowed to happen. In virtually every county there would be at least one landowner with an interest in the sport and in encouraging the local meeting, though the fluctuations in patronage over the years was one factor behind the constant changes in the racing map through the eighteenth and most of the nineteenth centuries. Financial support could take several forms. The least that would be looked for was a contribution to the race fund. Acting as steward for the meeting usually involved contributing at least a half share towards the Stewards' Cup. Many courses could expect to benefit further and have a race sponsored directly by a local magnate. At the turn of the century these included Preston (by the Earl of Derby), Lewes (the Duke of Richmond), Bedford (the Duke of Bedford), Carlisle (the Earl of Carlisle), Derby (the Duke of Devonshire)

The first page of the list of subscribers to the Racing Calendar *in the 1770s reads like a nominal roll of the peerage.*

L . I S T

OF THE

S U B S C R I B E R S.

HIS Royal Highnefs the Duke of Cumberland
His Grace the Duke of Cleveland
His Grace the Duke of Richmond
His Grace the Duke of Grafton, 2 fets
His Grace the Duke of Beaufort
His Grace the Duke of Devonfhire
His Grace the Duke of Portland
His Grace the Duke of Bridgwater
His Grace the Duke of Northumberland
Her Grace the Dutchefs of Northumberland
His Grace the Duke of Argyle
His Grace the Duke of Buccleugh
His Grace the Duke of Gordon
His Grace the Duke of Leinfter

Right Honourable the Earl of Thanet
Right Honourable the Earl of Sandwich
Right Honourable the Earl of Carlifle
Right Honourable the Earl of Abingdon, 2 fets
Right Honourable the Earl of Scarbrough
Right Honourable the Earl of Pomfret
Right Honourable the Earl of Orford
Right Honourable the Earl of Gower
Right Honourable the Earl of Fitzwilliam
Right Honourable the Earl of Errol
Right Honourable the Earl of Haddington
Right Honourable the Earl of Aberdeen
Right Honourable the Earl of Portmore
Right Honourable the Earl of Deloraine
Right Honourable the Earl of Cork
Right Honourable the Earl of Donnegal
Right Honourable the Earl of Cafllehaven

and Lambourne (Lord Craven). Lord Grosvenor gave a gold cup at Chester and the Earl of Exeter, at the very time when he was trying to suppress the town's bull-running, was giving a fifty pound purse as a race prize at Stamford's annual meeting. As individual patrons of races the few commoners were in a considerable minority though in the latter part of the period local members of parliament sometimes contributed prizes.[15]

Such contributions might well seem to be obligatory, coming with the territory, but there is also the simpler explanation. Many of these patrons did actually *like* horse racing and appear to have enjoyed their local meeting for its racing's sake, apart from the social opportunities it offered as one of the yearly occasions for allowable ostentation and the assertion of rank. Much the same motives could persuade some to bring a Newmarket horse to the country meetings – showing it off to neighbours and seeing it win, which it was always likely to do against local opposition. This itself could be varied. Provincial owners generally were a broad social group, including the larger farmers, military men, and a range of the gentry. There were few county meetings that could not boast at least a baronet or a knight or two among its active participants and some went considerably higher up the ranks. When Exeter was advertising a sweepstake in 1804, for instance, its 14 subscribers included Lord Lisle, Lord Graves, two honourables and four baronets, and this was an exaggeration of the normal picture, not an aberration.[16]

Occasionally the local grandee would be called upon to find a site for the races, though they were often held on some open and usually common land. The royal control of Ascot and the crown's sponsorship of races there was an outstanding exception, as also was the development of Goodwood under the Dukes of Richmond in the first years of the new century, although there were some other examples on a less grand scale.[17] The patronage of the turf by the gentry classes, however, can never be solely reckoned in material terms. Their mere presence on the racecourse added tone and status to any meeting. The 'quality' of the attendance and the number of lavish equipages on the race ground was all-important. The support of the wealthy assured success, their absence was a threat to the meeting's future. Comments could be scathing – at Reading in 1796 the company 'barely exceeded the show of a *field preacher's* congregation,' with 'no sportsman of the least celebrity on the grounds.' Even Goodwood could not thrive in the Duke's absence in 1807, and even in the sporting press the quality of the company regularly attracted at least as much attention as the quality of the racing.[18]

There were few changes in the patronage of horse racing during these years, the main ones being, as will be seen, the increased role assumed by women and the increased support from tradesmen in general, later to be added to by that from railway companies in particular. Historically, though, while the horse sports had always been an upper class preserve, patronage of cricket was both relatively recent and also shifting its emphasis. Cricket, a popular folk game, achieved system and sophistication by being taken up by the landed classes. During the eighteenth century a relatively small number of aristocrats were the main force behind its growth. In its middle years they gave the game its laws – not mere rules – and were challenging each other in highly staked matches. After the hiatus following the loss of three of the first great wave of patrons, revival came in another form, still firmly based in the upper classes but centred on that premature idiosyncrasy, the Hambledon Club. As often with football clubs generations later, it originated from the enthusiasms of men who had enjoyed playing the game at school, in this case Westminster. Members of the Club, however, never felt themselves tied exclusively to it and many matches were still contests between great magnates, and this no matter what names the teams might be playing under. Nevertheless club based matches were increasing[19] and the process was strengthened not only by the founding of the premier London clubs, first the White Conduit and then the MCC, but also by the increasing numbers of local cricket associations. Matches set up by wealthy patrons continued into the nineteenth century,[20] but were becoming rare and, indeed, the aristocratic monopoly of control over the game, even in its upper reaches, was relatively short-lived. The membership list of the White Conduit Club in 1784 shows the titled very heavily outnumbered by the mere gentlemen,[21] a trend which was repeated in what was virtually its successor, the MCC. Other changes were also taking place in the nature of cricket patronage. It was in tune with what was happening in other master and servant relationships that permanent duty and dependency were rapidly giving way to time-limited contractual arrangements. After Aylward had scored 167 in 1777, when centuries were still rare, Sir Horace Mann recruited him as bailiff and gave him charge of the catering at his home matches. Such retainer relationships, however, became less and less common, with the Hambledon

Club already having a detailed system of specific single payments for services. By the start of the nineteenth century the cricket professional seldom had any alternative but to operate on a match fee basis.[22]

With horse racing it can safely be said that an absence of patronage meant, with a few notable exceptions, the absence of any races. In cricket this was certainly not the case, though how far down the line the game did depend upon some upper class support is hard to know. Some great land-owners gave encouragement without apparently being personally involved. The Earl of Buckinghamshire, for instance, mounted a match on his Blickling Park estate for the local players to take on Norwich, and the hand of the Earl of Exeter can be seen again in support of the 'Noblemen and Gentle-men' of the Stamford Club.[23] Many local clubs did make it clear that they were for gentlemen only – in their advertisements for members, in other public notices, or merely by the size of their membership fees – but there must have been many teams which had little or no dependence on upper class support and were accessible to the future professionals who learned their cricket there. Expansion, too, took place under many auspices once peace had returned and through to the end of the period.[24] In short, not only was the high patronage which had made it a formal game being diluted and broadened but cricket continued to exist, to thrive, and even to expand at levels where patronage was likely to be minimal.

The success enjoyed by pugilism from the later 1780s through to the 1820s has rightly been ascribed to the interest and involvement of supporters from the powerful classes, many of whom, incidentally, also patronised other sports. As with cricket, the original aristocratic backing did change and quite important fights came to be fought not for stakes but for prize money raised collectively by the enthusiasts[25] and the single individual backer became even less important during the brief effective life of the Pugilistic Club after 1813.

No sporting performer depended more completely on a patron than the pugilist. Without one he would have no fights of any consequence. As to the motives of the patrons gambling played its part but staking a man could bring its own great attractions for some – the sweaty excitement of the fight, the dramatic show, the directly reflected glory of having the champion alongside, all so much more immediate in its impact that parading a winning racehorse, though the picture of a victorious John Gully being driven back to town in Lord Barrymore's barouche has to be set against the frequent examples of stark neglect when a fighter was defeated.[26] Occasionally pugilistic patronage could be long term – Mr Bradyl's staking of Humphries for example, or the Prince of Wales employing Tring as a sedan chairman, but what became more usual was for the pugilist to be taken on essentially as a minder, and certainly the behaviour of some of the more objectionable sponsors made an attendant bully boy essential.[27]

By the 1820s the age of the great individual patron, heavily staking major events from his own pocket, was effectively over. What did continue was widespread patronage of other play, taking many forms and involving many different sports. How complex gentry patronage and participation could become is well illustrated in pedestrianism, which was more actively cross-class than any other individual sport. While the majority of running or walking races were purely professional events, locally organised and for relatively small stakes of less than £100, there were others where wider interests can be assumed from the amount of the stakes, the size of the betting involved, or even from a fashionable location.[28] Matches were also still occasionally made between backers to run 'their man' – a duke and a baronet staked 1,000 guineas a side on such a contest in 1793[29] and, as with cricket, there were aristocrats and gentlemen who were personally prepared to exert themselves. Gentlemen pedestrians might on occasions try to keep their matches private, as Beauclerk and Harbord did when they ran at Lords in 1805 – vainly in this case as half the fashionable ladies in London turned up – but their contests usually became public entertainment.[30]

To set against the decline in sponsorship of both customary celebrations and major sporting events has to be set a whole diverse range of minor sporting benefactions which ran all through the period and which, if anything, appeared to be on the increase rather than in decline. It could be the gold laced cap given by Captain Wells for a skating race between the Gentlemen of March and those of Croyland at Whittlesea, the £20 cup given by Sir Charles Morgan, Bart., for competition between Brixham fishing smacks, or Mr George Rose's prizes for cutter racing on Southampton Water in 1804.[31] It could reach into almost any game or sport, backing racket players in the King's Bench Prison or the staking of the professional performers in the billiard rooms at Brighton,[32] and included many sponsored one-off celebrations from a coming of age to the opening of a new road.[33] It might, too, be just the long-term tolerance shown by Lord Egremont in allowing his farm workers to play bowls and cricket on his lawns. The old pattern of sponsorship of servant by master also still persisted. There was the Warwickshire gentleman backing one of his gamekeepers 'for a large sum of money' in a foot race in 1787 and Allardyce Barclay sponsoring his groom (unsuccessfully as it happened) in the same sport.[34] In pugilism, Sir P.W. Franklin backed his servant, Code, in a remarkably highly staked fight at 500 guineas a side in his park in Wiltshire in 1808, and two years later Colonel Hare, with three other 'provincial gamesters,' was putting together a 100 guinea purse for a fight by one of his workmen.[35] In addition to such individual sponsorships corporate action by the gentry contributed to any number of sports. They regularly raised purses for prizefights at the end of a day's horse racing. The putting in hand of prize money for the next year's meeting was a usual feature of the race dinner, and by the beginning of the nineteenth century any successful event, from singlesticks and cudgels to wrestling, rustic sports and rowing, was likely to be concluded with a resolve (not alas always sustained) to make it an annual event and with contributions sought to that end. Sponsorship money collected could be large or small, the few guineas dropped into a hat for a pick-up fight or the 18 guineas mustered by the gentlemen of St John's parish, Horsley Down, for a boat race on the Thames. They could, too, defend a sport from attack as 'the indefatigable exertions of the gentlemen of the turf' did in saving Epsom Downs from the threat of enclosure.[36]

The interest and involvement of the titled, the landed and the wealthy certainly gave a material impetus to many sports during this period. Their very presence helped to give organised play a higher profile and make it more and more a subject of comment. Among the sponsors there certainly were some eminent public figures. The cricketing Duke of Dorset, as ambassador-extraordinary and plenipotentiary, was in effect the government's spy in France during the critical decade of the 1780s. His attempts to introduce cricket there may have borne little fruit and the cause of his return may have been an injudicious affair of the heart,[37] but he was undoubtedly of valuable service to the state. Other sporting sponsors distinguished themselves by their support of liberal causes. Sir John Sebright, who opened his park for the much harried Gully v Gregson fight, was a respected Member of Parliament for Hertfordshire for a quarter of a century. He was said to be 'free from most of the prejudices of the country squire,' spoke out in the Commons against injustices in the Game Laws, supported all the Reform Bills, built and endowed a local school and was an acknowledged authority on animal breeding and behaviour.[38] As the Honourable Edward Harbord, Lord Suffield had competed in some notable foot races at Lords in his youth and was an M.P. from 1806 until he succeeded to the title in 1821. As a progressive reformer in the Lords he pressed constantly for the complete abolition of the slave trade while in his own neighbourhood he was a popular figure, a good landlord – and founder of Norfolk Cricket Club. Most distinguished of all doubtless was the Honourable William Wyndham, passionate defender of all popular sports, one time War and Colonial Secretary, supporter of Cobbett in starting the *Political Review* and a consistent and powerful advocate of such worthy causes as the anti-slavery movement.[39] There were, too, other sporting members on the benches of the House of Commons whose political contributions may not have been particularly distinguished but who appear to have led comparatively blameless lives. There was Paul Methuen, M.P. for Wiltshire, a crack shot and a noted pedestrian,[40] and General Tarleton who represented Liverpool for 22 years, another of the age's wide ranging sports enthusiasts. He umpired the Johnson v Perrins fight in 1788 and was regularly reported as among the distinguished amateurs present at contests. He survived a cricket injury In July 1788 and spoke in the House with 'earnestness and some power,' though his lack of knowledge of industry and his own love of pleasure made him, in the words of his biographer, 'no very efficient representative of an important commercial town like Liverpool.'[41] There was, too, Harvey Christian Coombe, an enthusiastic backer of pugilists and a frequent umpire at fights, who was four times elected for the City of London. Typical, too, of the better sort of early nineteenth century sportsman was Sir John Shelley, who would always remind the House of Commons of the pitiful state of the agricultural labourer whenever the Game Laws came up for discussion. He was the breeder of

The Death of Lord Barrymore

two Derby winners, the first Phantom in 1811. He was an active cricketer, a tennis player and an excellent shot, and the company he kept went well beyond the sporting world, including as it did such friends as Sydney Smith and Canning.[42]

Such worthies have, though, to be set against the considerable and often more noticed sporting names on the age's roll of dishonour. Early among their number was Dennis O'Kelly, most famed as the owner of Eclipse, but distinguished for a whole career of slippery dealings spotted with occasional suspicions of downright villainy. He was a major patron of prize-fighting during its least reliable decade, the 1770s, and contributed significantly to that unreliability.[43] In unpleasantness if not in dishonesty he was soon surpassed. In the two decades around 1800 wealth probably multiplied as fast as it has ever done and at the same time its employment was at its least tramelled. Arrogance, self-centredness, extravagance and brutality could all too easily take over and it is hardly surprising that the sporting villains of the piece tended to outnumber the virtuous, so much so that only a few of the more outrageous qualify for mention here. Among the most objectionable was the 7th Earl Barrymore, one of the group of courtiers who sponsored the revival of pugilism in the 1780s and employer of the pugilist, Hooper who, finding himself hopelessly overmatched against the champion, Ben

Brain, managed to keep his opponent out of reach until darkness fell, explaining that, 'If I can't win your Lordship's money, I takes care not to lose it.' Hooper's fidelity appeared to be rewarded when an annuity was settled on him, but the frantic life-style to which he was introduced had within a few years so reduced him to such an offensive alcoholic ruin that he was discarded by the family and he died a pauper in 1797.[44] As a cricketer Barrymore was simply described in the press as 'a bad player.' As an owner he had some success on the turf, but he usually lost any winnings, and more, in the card room after dinner. He would rashly take on the best whist players and often went down heavily – to the extent of 2,800 guineas on one night. It was acknowledged that he needed his minder, seldom appearing 'without a *theatrical* or *pugilistic* companion' whether on the raceground, 'in the chace, at the *election*, the *debating society*, the billiard room, or the *bacchanalian institution*.' Brighton was shocked by his behaviour and it was hard to muster convincing grief when he met with a death that matched his erratic life, accidentally shooting himself with his own loaded rifle as he raced back in his jolting coach for the evening's pleasures after a day's duty with his Berkshire militia.[45]

Thomas Pitt, second Baron Camelford, was, if anything, even more in need of his own pug for protection, but though he took Bill Richmond into his employ his own immediate resort was to the duelling pistol rather than to any protector – indeed he has the rare distinction of being described as 'naval commander and duellist' in the Dictionary of National Biography! He, too, was an inconstant pugilistic patron, leaving his man, Bourke, unhelped in Reading jail after his defeat by Belcher. He had a stormy naval career, followed by riotous years in London. By 1798 the *Sporting Magazine* was already predicting 'some fatal catastrophe' in his future and exactly this happened some six years later when he fought one duel too many against an expert shot, Mr Best, who tried vainly to make up the quarrel before the pistols were fired.[46]

One of the great sporting oddities, at a time when they were particularly plentiful, was George Hanger, who succeeded to the family title as fourth Baron Coleraine while in business as a coal merchant. Previously he had been a guards officer, served in North America with the Hessians, married a gipsy girl, and lived for a year in the house of the horse dealer, Richard Tattersall, before being taken up by the Prince of Wales as equerry and boon companion. Eventually the prince tired of Hanger's particular style of cavorting and pleasure seeking and one of the regular royal economy drives saw him out of employment, in debt, and in the King's Bench prison. He published several books, which were almost as bizarre as his life, itself the subject of one of them. In the heyday of pugilism's revival he was one more of its sponsors, patronising Watson from Bristol – another opponent of Barrymore's Hooper – and being one of the organisers of the purse for the Jackson v Fewtrell match. He was a regular attender at prize-fights to the end of his long life.[47]

Two characters at opposite ends of the financial scale in their sponsorship were the ninth Duke of Hamilton and Counsellor Michael Lade. Hamilton did make his appearances in the House of Lords but was said to be better as a pugilists' bottle holder than as a parliamentary speaker. One of the ring's strongest supporters in the years immediately following its revival, it was Hamilton who put up the 500 guinea stake for Ben Brain's fight against Tom Johnson, and had the Ward v Mendoza put off, to suit his convenience, to the 1790 Doncaster Races. Among 'the first sporting characters in the country' his name would appear immediately after that of the Prince of Wales and his interests also extended to cricket, cocking and dog fighting. His behaviour and general demeanour, though, were such that even the sporting press found it hard to stomach. The association with persons of the theatre by Hamilton and other like minded peers was bad enough and his deep involvement with the ring, his close connections with 'members of the Mendozian academy,' also prompted criticism. And this was just the least of it. He was accused, under a thinly veiled anonymity, of animal-like behaviour, no better than that of his favourite dog, 'both equally eminent in affairs of gallantry . . . they range through all the kennels of copulation.'[48]

Great wealth was, of course, a remarkable sustainer of repugnant behaviour. There was, though, the example of Michael Lade to demonstrate that it was not an essential. Lade was certainly one of the most disliked and despised figures in the late eighteenth century sporting world. A lawyer, he kept a stud at Cannon Park, near Kingsclere in Hampshire, but he was not wealthy enough to support it properly and just one of his many disagreeable qualities was his meanness. His horses were seldom in the best of condition, and he usually confined them to relatively local meetings to spare expense. Even so, his racing groom, Scott, had to go to court to recoup the wages that were owed to him. His turf winnings were reported to be 'very, very, inadequate' compared with his outlay and efforts, and in spite of a few successes in his two forays to Newmarket in 1797 and 1798. After his death in 1799 his horses looked wretched on their way to auction and many went for only two or three guineas each. Personally he was equally unattractive, 'seldom seen in company upon the race track or elsewhere . . . cynically rigid and innately parsimonious.' He had married a titled wife who had brought him some £5,000 a year, but she was mentally incapacitated. By way of compensation he kept ladies in Pall Mall and Turnham Green, though he was 'a total stranger to the powers of attraction and we may safely presume that *his amours* were regulated much more (on the part of the ladies) by interest than *affection*.' In short, 'he *lived* without regard, so he *died* without *regret*.'[49]

Whether a man like Lade who pursued his sport for his own personal and mean-spirited ends deserves the title of 'patron' is of course extremely doubtful. His example does lead into areas of even wider doubt and the blurring of lines. In particular there could increasingly be a merging of patronage with commercial exploitation, as happened outstandingly in one sporting enterprise in 1815. This was George Wilson's attempt to walk a thousand miles in twenty days, backed initially by patrons to the tune of 100 guineas. He was to perform on Blackheath and the landlord of the Hare and Hounds inn there stepped in smartly, by way of promotion, with an offer of free accommodation and £20 on successful completion. With large crowds gathering on the heath the publican was soon reaping good rewards from his investment, but the noise they made at all hours interfered with Wilson's sleep. Patronage once more took over when a 'disinterested' gentleman offered him quieter accommodation elsewhere. Likewise, when he faced a Sunday ban on the heath Lord Gwydir allowed him to walk in his private park. Eventually, though, it was all to no purpose. Local residents' complaints about the 'very tumultuous assemblage of people' by night and day caused the justices to end the attempt after fifteen days. Even then, sponsorship and profit-taking still went on side by side. A subscription fund was set up to reward Wilson for his efforts, while he himself not only rushed into print with a booklet of memoirs but also appeared in the London theatres in athletic gear, demonstrating his walking style.[50]

Here was one of the many routes into the commercial exploitation of sport – by attachment to an already arranged contest. Entrepreneurs might take over traditional wakes or festivals, or even create new ones on largely traditional lines. There was the frequent managing of arrangements and provisions for others' cricket or cocking matches and soon the novelty of setting up of sporting events to directly increase a sponsor's business. Promoters came in all shapes and sizes. There was the publican on the Great West Road whose hand-written notice promised bull and badger baiting, wrestling and singing (!) contests at his Whitsun sports. There were, too, such large-scale commercial enterprises as that initiated by the proprietors of Ranelagh Gardens in 1775 when they mounted, on the Thames, what is usually regarded as the country's first regatta.[51] In spite of the enormous interest which this generated, sustained commercial promotion did not begin until ten years later. The Vauxhall Gardens had been a focal point of the capital's entertainment through the eighteenth century, fondly recalled by Wordsworth for their

wilderness of lamps
Dimming the stars, and fireworks magical
And gorgeous ladies, under splendid domes,
Floating in dance, or warbling high in air
The songs of spirits.[52]

In the 1780s the Vauxhall management took on a sharper edge, doubled the entrance charge from one shilling to two and among the new attractions were boat races on the Thames, which flowed along their northern boundary. The first of the annual races for a 'Silver Cup and Cover' was sailed in 1785, between boats owned by gentlemen and entered in their names. A further race followed two years later, a rowing contest for a new boat between professional watermen who (as in the long standing Doggett's Coat and Badge race) had just completed their apprenticeships. The expectation that this would be 'the best match ever seen on the river' seems to have been fulfilled and soon there was virtually a sponsorship war on the

Astley mounted sporting events like these pony races in his amphitheatre, as well as sponsoring racing on the Thames and being an excellent sailor himself.

Thames.[53] Astley's Equestrian Amphitheatre, the prime entertainment rival of the pleasure gardens, and prompted also by Astley's personal enthusiasm, began its own race for watermen, in 1790. This continued as an annual event until well into the next century, with the advantage of taking place on the king's birthday when many would take a holiday. Not to be outdone, the Vauxhall proprietors responded in 1793 with a cup to be competed for by winners of their previous races, with the added attraction of the Duke of York's band, in full uniform. They went one better still in 1805, having a boat with a band on board preceding the sailing boats as they raced. The irony of it was that by this time the Vauxhall race had been won five times by, of all people, Mr Astley![54]

Shooting contests became popular vehicles for sponsorship when war was at its height – at Ranelagh and Bermondsey Spa within a few weeks of each other in 1801. The commercial gardens, both in London and some other places were also direct providers of facilities for sport, though generally in a minor, marginal fashion. There were some exceptions. Copenhagen House was a long standing sporting venue, famous for fives playing but catering at times for other interests, including cricket matches, which were also played quite frequently in Montpellier Gardens, Walworth. Peerless Pool in Clerkenwell (its name still preserved in Peerless Street) was transformed from a duck hunting pond to provide two stretches of water, one for swimming and one stocked with carp and tench for angling.[55] Elsewhere the sporting entertainment still often had a traditional flavour, reflecting the continuing appeal of the long familiar alongside the new.[56]

There were the many others who looked to profit from sport, from saddlers, horse dealers, and equipment manufacturers to the makers, printers and sellers of sporting prints. On the other hand the aims of sporting promotion could occasionally be unconnected, even indirectly, with finance. There was the recruiting festival organised in 1779, where there was an ox roast, free beer, gold laced hats for cudgelling, and prizes for racing. Forty thousand Londoners turned up for the event, though few of them took the king's shilling willingly and most of the recruiting was done by press gangs. The enterprise does not appear to have been repeated, probably because the able-bodied had become wary of the gods bearing gifts. Another sponsored event, the sailing race for a £50 cup given by the Contractors of the Lottery, may well have provided an opportunity to sell tickets to the crowds but it seems likely that it was primarily another early exercise in favourable image building.[57]

Sports promoters came in as many varieties as patrons. The profits that could be made from sport were many sided, but the most frequent source of income went to the providers of facilities and victualling. There were the owners of the few enclosed sporting grounds who could not only charge for admission to their cricket matches and pedestrian contests but also then had a captive crowd to cater for. There were also the hirers of boats on the Thames who did particularly good business on Sundays from the cutter racing by apprentices.[58] The one constant provider, though, the one long established specialist in exploiting the people's zest for play, was of course the tavern keeper. He was the sports promoter *par excellence* whose hand was evident, and not just in the newer sports but also in apparently traditional celebrations. Publicans had been early in the field. In 1722 the landlord of the Red Lion, Barton Street, Gloucester, was advertising jumping, dancing, bowling and wrestling at Barton Feast and some ten years later the Melksham innkeepers were earning the disapproval of local landowners by organising a 'petty horse race.' Some old midsummer day's sports had fairly obviously been sustained for some years by tavern keepers after the calendar reform of 1752.[59] This appropriation of traditional celebrations can often be deduced not only from monopoly control of the victualling and provision of the venue often also from the introduction of more 'modern' events such as organised races or cudgelling competitions. As well as exploiting existing special occasions the innkeeper was also always alert to those everyday -recreations, such as bowls, skittles and ninepins, which he was well placed to provide for, and was often also mounting individual sporting events in both older and newer styles. In the 1780s he could still sponsor the occasional bull bait,[60] though this was increasingly frowned upon by licensing authorities. On the other hand, cock fighting continued to be provided extensively by innkeepers and most of the organised highly staked cocking matches in the period were housed in taverns. At the other end of the scale, with the minor 'shake-bag' contests, the publican would himself be promoter, provider and manager. When, on the other hand, the gentlemen had their county matches he might appear to be no more than the supplier of facilities, but he still had a major financial interest in the event, from entrance charges and from his provision of food and drink. Most of the advertising of forthcoming matches clearly originates from the innkeeper and, with a favoured hostelry, his opportunities for profit could be quite frequent and doubtless substantial.[61]

The publican had his greater or lesser part to play in all the major sports. His inn was the common administrative centre. Arrangements for boxing matches of any standing were made in the tavern, horses had to be entered for races in one of the town's prominent inns, and the inn was the most frequent meeting place for cricket clubs. Each sport presented its own opportunities for the publican to exploit. He did usually have to distance himself from the actual mounting of prize-fights, though in the late 1770s the Crown Inn at Staines was well known as an important boxing centre while later in the century the Swan yard at Ingatestone in Essex was also housing notable fights and even the decisive third fight between Humphries and Mendoza managed to take place in a large inn yard at Doncaster.[62] There is no sign of this direct tavern involvement with fights of any substance after the turn of the century when even the mounting of sparring exhibitions in public houses became a risky business.[63] However, the publican's part in the sport's promotion increased rather than lessened as its procedures became more complex and protracted.

At the top of the tree were those taverns being run by pugilists themselves, and quite often taken on even before their ring careers were over. By 1815 there were at least a dozen such in London, and some of these were at the heart of the ring's affairs. There was the Coach and Horses, adjacent to the Fives Court in St Martin's Lane, which had a succession of pugilistic landlords, starting with Bill Richmond in the early years of the new century. There was Jem Belcher's Jolly Brewers in Wardour Street, and the one that was becoming the most famous of all, his brother Tom's Castle Inn in Holborn.[64] Many other public houses could also become involved. There would be the preliminary negotiations, then a more formal meeting to sign the articles setting the terms for the fight, and at least one meeting for handing over the stake money. Then there would be crowds in the likely taverns to discover the intended location, more later to await the result, and finally the joy or sadness when the stake money was handed over. Such rituals became more elaborate, and offering ever more prospects of profit, by the end of the period. The London arrangements could well be copied on a more modest scale in the provinces where, from the success of pugilists' tours giving sparring exhibitions, magistrates could be more relaxed (or less alert) than they were in the capital. The other adventitious opportunity presented to some publicans came from the trade presented by the swarming crowds making their way to forthcoming fights. The exploitation of the fight followers by innkeepers by weakening the beer, crowding the bedrooms, and inflating the prices for both had already become part of the ring's mythology. The scene at Woburn on the eve of Gregson's battle with Gully was typical:

When Monday night arrived hundreds had flocked into the town and all were eagerly enquiring for beds. Nothing could be obtained of this kind, for the night's lodging, under 30s. a head, and to sit or lie in the chairs of the public rooms the usual price of a bed was extorted. In one room at Woburn fifteen gentlemen laid on the floor, and were happy to pay for this hard fare, and hundreds reposed in their carriages.'

To make sure that nobody got away without paying the landlord usually took possession of the boots of the travellers, who in this case had other hazards to face before the fight finally came off in Sir John Sebright's park – a long cat and mouse chase over the countryside, harassed by the Dunstable volunteers with colours flying and bayonets fixed, so that the 'peasantry were shaking with fear, supposing the French had landed.' So advantageous was a major prize-fight for local trade that by the 1820s Mr Hewlings of the Swan Inn, Chichester, was prepared to pay £200 for the second Spring v Langam fight to be brought to the town.[65]

The publican's role in cricket was less dramatic but often more sustained. It was similar to that which he played in cock-fighting, though usually with the prospect of larger crowds. At the centre of the sport, first at the Artillery Ground and then at Lords, the tavern was, so far as the proprietor was concerned, at least as important as the cricket field. George Smith, at the Artillery Ground, had been essentially an innkeeper, with two victualling outlets to cater for spectators. He later became a landlord in Wiltshire, with no mention there of cricket. Thomas Lord was a notable cricketer himself and gave more priority to the game, but, for him and his successors the sale of liquor remained a conspicuous part of the ground's provision, a tradition still preserved in the Tavern and its new stand. Many other innkeepers had suitable, if less notable playing areas attached to their promises or available close by,[66] and their role could lie anywhere on the scale between active promotion (and even participation), encouragement, the provision of a pitch, or merely of refreshment. What is clear is that he was an important element in the support of the game, and that the game was, in turn, an important source of income to him. As with cocking, many advertisements for matches bear his imprint. Quite frequently, particularly in the eighteenth century, matches were the result of straightforward direct promotion by the publican, who might offer prizes for games played by his local team, an offer sometimes even open to all comers.[67] Occasionally it was effectively the landlord's own team, as seen very noticeably in the cricket activity reported from Coventry in the late 1780s, when at least three publicans there were all involved enough to act as their teams' umpires.[68] Moreover the inn itself could serve the game in many ways. Prospective new members would be invited to attend there. It was where matches could be made and challengers answered, and where the innkeeper was often empowered to make and take deposits on stake money. The inn did have its occasional rivals – the Norwich players in the early days met at a coffee house and those at Stamford based themselves at the racecourse grandstand – but wherever the game was played the tavern was much its most usual home. In the Birmingham area, for instance, there was first the Bell in Smallbrook Street, later the Shake-speare Inn, and shortly the Bull's Head, Mosely, not far from the existing Edgbaston ground.[69]

All the inn's cricketing functions could be expected to bring in money, but the publican's main consideration, with little opportunity to profit from gate money, was the victualling of players and spectators. A single county such as Kent can provide many examples of his stress on this provision – at for instance, Maidstone's Union Flag and Ashford's Red Lion where on at least one occasion the provision on the ground was in the hands of Sarah Tonbridge, the commercial precursor, perhaps, of the long line of tea mak-ers on which the sustenance of club cricketers would come to depend.[70] There were sometimes various levels of provision. At a match at Bishopsbourne during race week (where there was a grandstand with a one shilling entrance charge) the first sitting was at five shillings a head for the gentlemen and the cricketers, followed by an Ordinary at 1/6 each for the rest.[71] From the mid 1790s the role of the tavern and the innkeeper does become less noticeable, possibly, though far from certainly, as a result of an actual decline in cricket playing itself. There was certainly an increase in the number of specialised grounds, such as Prince's at Brighton, the Hull Cricket Ground, or Cockerell's New Ground at Warminster, and there was also a tendency to refer to venues just as 'the Cricket Field,' implying that its prime sporting function was well established, whether attached to the tav-ern or not. The most that can be safely ventured is that, given the innkeeper's persistently successful exploitation of sporting opportunities of all sorts, it is most unlikely that his financial interest in cricket was much reduced during these years.

What was not in decline was the profit being generated by race meetings. During its race week all the publicans in the town could expect extra business, from letting out accommodation, serving meals and selling more drink. If, as many did, they wanted to benefit directly by trading on the course itself they would usually have to subscribe to the race fund or find themselves paying the much higher rentals charged to outsiders. There were several methods of applying this protectionism and the charges indicate that trading on the course was a sound commercial proposition. Furthermore competi-tors were often obliged to stable their horse in the town during the meeting, while for the town's major coaching inns there were more lucrative opportunities. One would be the usual administrative centre for the meeting and where entries had to be made – the Cross Keys Inn, Castle Street, Warwick, and the Antelope at Sherborne, for example – and there was usually an established hierarchy of entertainments provided by the leading hostelries. At both Sherborne and Dorchester (with inns with identical names) the dinner on the first night was at the Antelope and on the second at the King's Arms while at Bromsgrove it was the Cross Keys, as the one major establishment, which provided both the management and the entertainment.[72]

Although race meetings were usually mounted on the initiatives of the local gentry there are some important instances of publican involvement which went beyond this servicing.[73] Catterick Races owed much to Tom Ferguson, landlord of the George and Dragon adjacent to the race ground, who would drive flocks of sheep round the course if the inclement North Yorkshire climate should bring unseasonable snow and threaten the forthcoming races. Mr Ferguson was, indeed, a prosperous business man who kept up to fifty post horses at his inn for the busy Great North Road traffic and also bred racehorses as a sideline, with such success that his Antonio won the disputed St Leger in 1819 and was sold afterwards for 1,000 guineas.[74]

Making money out of sport has often been seen as undesirable. When so much of it was seen to be going into the pockets of publicans this was even more the case. Throughout the period there was general disapproval of the tavern, save with its customers. It came from social commentators such as Henry Zouch and from bodies such as the Society for Bettering the Condition and Increasing the Comforts of the Poor in its reports, between 1798 and 1808. Clerical condemnation came from all quarters – they were 'the continual nurseries for sin,' for one vicar and 'the bane of the nation' for another.[75] The attacks, moreover, were not by any means confined to the drinking habits which the inns encouraged and nourished but were directed with equal vigour at the recreations they provided, whether they came under the guise of old festivals or whether they belonged to those broader facilities for amusement which the tavern had for long been making available – its playing cards, its shuffle board, its skittle and ninepin grounds, its quoits, its lottery and its betting lists. They were readily ranked by the Essex magistrates along with 'other public places of Entertainment' as generators of 'depravity and dissipation of manners' among the 'lower ranks of people.'[76]

William Blake was one of the few contemporaries to sense the positive contribution of the inn, particularly to the life of the poorer classes, noting how it had moved into the space left empty by traditional providers of popular recreation such as the church, and commending it for doing so:

Dear Mother, dear Mother, the Church is cold,
But the Ale-house is healthy and pleasant and warm;
Besides I can tell where I am used well,
Such usage in heaven will never do well.[77]

Opposition to the public house's recreational role was easy enough to voice and was itself clear evidence of the innkeeper's success. Effective action was much harder to secure, and not merely because the inn was so deeply embedded in the life of the community. In the first place, licensed houses were widely different one from another, ranging from the large coaching inns and well appointed city taverns, with their prosperous clientele, to the back street alehouse, crude, rough, and often unruly. It was not easy to differentiate in law or practice between them, between the wholly respectable and the downright disreputable, and attempts at control were not helped by the uncertainty of most policing arrangements, and particularly by the fact that constables were still often innkeepers themselves.[78] Moreover, the inn was essential, not merely as a provider of food and drink, but also as an indispensable link in the country's transport system, becoming all the more important as the new turnpike roads brought about a rapid increase in coach traffic. The great age of the coaching inn was also the great age of the inn's entertainment and recreational role – at no time before or since did it make such a dominating contribution to the country's sporting life. It is likely, too, that in no other period did the inn enjoy such a large share of the profits that could be derived from sport as it did in this age when patronage and commercial promotion travelled so thoroughly alongside each other in its development.

Notes

1. A persistent theme in Malcolmson, *Popular Recreations*. See *e.g.* pp 67-69.
2. Harold Perkin, *The Origins of Modern English Society 1780-1880*, London and Toronto, 1969, p 49.
3. N. L. Tranter, 'The Patronage of Organised Sport in Central Scotland, 1820-1900,' *Journal of Sport History*, vol. 16, no.3, winter 1989, pp 229 ff.
4. For example, Nottingham was one of the King's Plate meetings in 1727, Tyrell, *Racecourses*, p 134.
5. *Sherborne Mercury*, 21, 28 June 1737. For the prince's death see *e.g.* Walpole, *Memoirs of George II*, in *Works*, VIII, pp 61/2; Chafin, Cranbourne Chase, p 95.
6. That is at Molesey Hurst, Coombe Wood or Coombe Warren. *Pancratia*, pp 51, 69, 81; pp 84/5. Miles, *Pugilistica*, I, pp 84/5, 100; Brailsford, *Bareknuckles*, pp 26, 79 and *passim*.; Ford, *Prizefighting*, pp 95/6.
7. *Racing Calendar 1797*, p 67; *SM*, December 1792, pp 153-156.
8. *SM*, August 1808, p 208 and *passim*.
9. *General Evening Post*, 17 August 1770.
10. He lost to Colonel Tarleton at Brighton in 1789. John Ford, *Cricket: A Social History 1700-1835*, Newton Abbot, 1972, p 148.
11. See *Kentish Gazette*, 13 August 1790; *Sussex Weekly Advertiser*, 10 September 1794.
12. Birley, 'Bonaparte and the Squire,' Mangan, *ed.*, *Pleasure, Profit and Proselytism*, p 36.
13. Robert P. Elmer, *Archery*, Philadelphia, 1926, pp 104, 88; George Hansard, *The Book of Archery*, 1841, p 269; Henricks, *Disputed Pleasures*, pp 140/1.
14. Brand, *Popular Antiquities*, pp v-vi, in Malcolmson, *Popular Recreations*, p 71.
15. The local MPs sponsored a race at Stockbridge and at Durham the members for both the county and the borough each supported one. *Racing Calendar* 1797, passim.
16. *Western Flying Post*, 9 July 1804 .
17. *e.g.* Pontefract was revived by Lord Darlington in 1801, Newcastle-under-Lyne was laid out by local gentry in 1788 and the Duke of Portland promised patronage for a new racecourse at Mansfield in 1830. See Tyrrel, *Racecourses*, pp 66, 134, 164; D.I. Benning, 'The development of physical recreation in the Staffordshire Potteries,' M.Ed degree dissertation, University of Liverpool, 1979: *SM*, December 1830, p 169.

18. The duke had just been appointed Lord Lieutenant of Ireland. See *SM*, September 1796, p 302; May 1807, p 98.

19. See in particular John Nyren's classic *The Cricketers of my Time*, 1833 edition in E. V. Lucas, ed., *The Hambledon Men*, 1907. See also e.g. Ford, *Cricket*, pp 20, 57-60 and *passim*.

20. *e.g.* Harry Mellish's challenge to Lord Frederick Beauclerk for 1,000 guineas. *SM*, June 1807, pp 146/7.

21. Finch MSS., Leicester CRO, in *Sports History*, 2, 1982, pp 13-15.

22. Buckley, *Eighteenth Century Cricket*, p 110. Ford, *Cricket: A Social History*, pp 94/5; Christoper Brookes, *English Cricket: The Game and its Players through the Ages*, 1978, pp 58-61, 79.

23. *Norwich Mercury*, 1 September 1787; *Sports History*, 8, 1986, p 18; SM, June 1919, p 144.

24. Mary Russell Mitford, *Our Village: Sketches of Rural Character and Scenery*, 5 vols., 1824-32, I, p 148, and *passim*.; Ford, *Cricket: A Social History*, p 28; *Drakard's Stamford News*, 23 June 1815. Among many new (or revived) post-war places of play were Lichfield (*Lichfield Mercury*, 8 July, 8 August 1817), Bristol (*Felix Farley's Bristol Journal*, 21 August 1819) and Penzance (*Falmouth Packet*, 5 September 1829 'after an interval of ten years.')

25. *e.g.* Tom Belcher's 1804 fight against young John Ward in 1804 was for a 50 guinea purse. *Pancratia*, pp 202-204. Multi-sport enthusiasts included the Duke of Hamilton, Sir Charles Lennox (who became the third Duke of Richmond) and Lord Barrymore, involved in racing, pugilism and cricket, while William Wyndham, Sir Watkin Williams Wynn, Dennis O'Kelly and Mr Bullock were among ring followers who raced their own horses.

26. Miles, *Pugilistica*, pp 189, 214, 141; *Pancratia*, pp 315, 186, 148.

27. Ford, *Prizefighting*, p 76 (with more examples of long term sponsorship); *Pancratia*, p 83. See also Miles, *Pugilistica*, p 103n.; *SM*, August 1795, p 249.

28. For example, the £5,000 wagered on Beal v Harmsworth at Knavesmire, York or Hopcroft performing at Lords with 'great sums depending.' *SM*, March 1796; September 1811, p 290.p 337. See also Jones v Edwards at Newmarket for £1,000 a side. *SM*, July 1809, p 198.

29. An odd contest involving four steps forward and one back! *SM*, March 1793, p 369.

30. *SM*, June 1805, p 167.

31. *SM*, October 1795, p 23; September 1809, p 260; August 1804, p 266.

32. *SM*, September 1796, p 310 (when billiards was described as being 'the morning rage at Brighton'); October 1804, p 44. See also November 1797, p 100.

33. *Hampshire Chronicle*, 18 July 1744; *SM*, July 1809, p 196; May 1811, p 99. See also Goulstone, *Summer Solstice Games*, p 32.

34. *SM*, November 1804, p 100; *Times*, 9 October 1787; *SM*, May 1813, p 85.

35. *SM*, December 1808, p 149; May 1810, p 80.

36. *SM*, September 1797, p 328; May 1813, p 91.

37. *Times*, 9 September, 17 December 1789.

38. *Pancratia*, pp 308-311; Miles, *Pugilistica*, I, p 187; Munsche, *Gentlemen and Poachers*, p 167; *DNB*.

39. *SM*, November 1804, p 98; June 1805, p 167; *DNB*.

40. *Sports History*, 5, 1984, p 8.

41. Miles, *Pugilistica*, I, p 61; *Times*, 8 July 1788; *DNB*.

42. Munsche, *Gentlemen and Poachers*, p 165; *Sports History*, 5, 1984, pp 9/10.

43. He was, for instance, said to have paid Bill Darts 100 guineas to 'play cross,' *Daily Advertiser*, 17 May 1771.

44. Ford, *Prizefighting*, p 72; Miles, *Pugilistica*, I, pp 67/8. 'Fighting for the dark' became a common tactic in the ring's less reputable later days.

45. Ford, *Cricket: A Social History*, p 148; *SM*, January 1793, p 206; April 1793, p 8; May 1793, p 85. The three Barrymore brothers earned the nicknames Hellgate, Cripplegate and Newgate – to which the Prince of Wales ungallantly added that their sister should be Billingsgate, after the old fish market!

46. *SM*, June 1798, p 151; March 1804, p 300; *DNB*. See also *SM*, December 1803, p 160.

47. Ford, *Prizefighting*, pp 74/5.

48. *Times*, 12 July 1787; Miles, *Pugilistica*, I, p 68; *SM*, August 1795, p 249. See *Pancratia*, pp 100, 104, 121 and passim.

49. *SM*, September 1794, p 64; December 1799, p 107; January 1800, pp 163-5.

50. *Memoirs of the Life and Exploits of G. Wilson, the Celebrated Pedestrian*, 1815; *SM*, September 1815, pp 244-246. At the age of 56 he was still active, though the report that he covered 90 miles in 4 hours on Newcastle raceground (*SM*, April 1822, p 51) is doubtless more than somewhat exaggerated.

51. *SM*, July 1795, p 223; Boulton, *Amusements of Old London*, I, p 242.

52. Wordsworth, *The Prelude*, Book 7. 53. *Times*, 2, 6, 12 July 1787.

54. *SM*, June 1806, p 112; June 1807, p 107; July 1805, p 200; July 1804, p 21; Times, 11 July 1793; *SM*, July 1805, p 115. Individual promotions followed from *e.g.* a Millbank innkeeper and Mr Cliffe of the Waterman's Arms, for 'young aquatic amateurs' and 'private gentlemen' respectively. *SM*, August 1808, p 195; September 1809, p 260

55. *SM*, August 1801, p 259; September 1809, p 260; *Morning Herald*, 28 September 1798; *Morning Post*, 9 July 1808; Buckley, *Pre-Victorian Cricket*, pp 343, 51; Boulton, *Amusements of Old London*, I, p 65.

56. Boulton, *Amusements of Old London*, I, pp 64, 53, 69, 55 and passim.

57. ibid., II, pp 235/6; *SM*, November 1795, pp 78/9; July 1807, p 160.

58. *Report of the Police of the Metropolis*, 1816, p 212; George, *London Life in the Eighteenth Century*, p 272. See also Whitaker, *Eighteenth Century Sunday*, pp 152, 163.

59. *Gloucester Journal*, 17 September 1722. For innkeepers involvement in old midsummer day sports see *Kentish Journal*, 2 July 1781; Goulstone, *Summer Solstice Games*, pp 16, 83. For the inn's general involvement in recreation see Clarke, *The English Alehouse*.

60. At *e.g.* the White Hart, Maldon, and the Bull, Purley. *Chelmsford Chronicle*, 31 December 1794, 23 June 1786.

61. Within a few months in 1787, for example, inns were housing at least four well advertised matches over a limited area in the midlands. *Aris's Birmingham Gazette* 12 February, 19 March, 21 May, 23 July. See also *SM*, June 1795, p 163.

62. Miles, *Pugilistica*, I, p 46; Brailsford, *Bareknuckles*, p 16; *Pancratia*, pp 81-84, 96.

63. Jem Belcher was arrested for exhibiting at the Pea Hen Inn, Grays Inn Road in 1801 and some years later a Southwark innkeeper was raided for putting on displays by minor pugilists. *Pancratia*, p 140; *SM*, January 1808, p 208.

64. For pugilistic innkeepers see Ford, *Prizefighting*, pp 52-54.

65. *Morning Chronicle*, quoted in Miles, *Pugilistica*, I, p 187; Ford, *Prizefighting*, p 91. (The two boxers, Spring and Langan, each received half the money.)

66. *Kentish Gazette*, 9 August 1793; Buckley, *Eighteenth Century Cricket*, p 167.

67. Among such offers was, for example, one by the landlord of the Red Lion, Smitham Bottom, Croydon of half a guinea a man to the winners and 5s. 3d. to the losers in any challenge to the local team. *Daily Advertiser*, 12 May 1768. Buckley, *Eighteenth Century Cricket*, pp 70-71,103, 205-206, 89-90, 96.

68. *Coventry Mercury*, 24 September, 8 October 1787

69. *Ipswich Journal*, 10 May 1745; Sports History, 8, 1986, p 18; 7, 1985, p 13. (The Stamford Club did also meet at The Bull, in the town.) See also Buckley, *Eighteenth Century Cricket*, p 38; *Pre-Victorian Cricket*, pp 42, 44.

70. See 'Cricket in Bexley 1746-c1860,' *Sports History*, 6, 1986, pp 18-21.

71. For examples see 'Cricket at Ashford, Kent 1743-1842' and 'Early nineteenth century cricket in Thanet,' *Sports History*, no.9, 1986, pp 18-21.

72. Handbill, Sherborne Museum; *Aris's Birmingham Gazette*, July 1787; Tyrrel, *Racecourses*, p 136.

73. Yarmouth Races had actually been founded by a syndicate of landlords in 1715 and the publican's interest there remained strong – in 1810 entries were being made with Mr John Buck at the Three Wrestlers Inn. Tyrrel, *Racecourses*, pp 140/1.

74. *ibid.*, p 38; *SM*, October 1819, p 3.

75. J. Benson, *Life of the Rev John William de la Flechere*, quoted in Brian Harrison, *Drink and the Victorians: The Temperance Question in England 1815-1872*, p 91; Ransome, *ed., Wiltshire Returns*, p 28. For further references to contemporary criticisms of public houses see Malcolmson, *Popular Recreations*, p 98, n 41.

76. *Chelmsford Chronicle*, 27 July 1787.

77. 'The Little Vagabond,' from *Songs of Experience.*

78. George, *London Life in the Eighteenth Century*, p 349.

6.
Players and Spectators

Two indisputably notable sportsmen who were also indisputably members of the patronising classes have so far made no more than passing appearances here. In their different ways – and they were different to the extent that they became implacable enemies – they personify significant changes that were taking place in the playing of games. Their attitudes towards play had little benevolence in them. They present their paradoxes. In their serious and unwavering application to sport they are ahead of their times, while in their devotion to gambling and their equally unwavering resistance to change they set themselves firmly in the early part of the nineteenth century and by the time of their deaths, well into Victoria's reign, both had begun to appear very much as relics from the past.

Lord Frederick Beauclerk, born in 1775, fourth son of the Duke of St Albans, and so descended from Nell Gwynne, found his way into the church by way of Eton and Cambridge. His tenure of the family living as Vicar of St Albans made no particular moral demands on his sporting life, which was singularly devoid of charity. As cricketer and matchmaker in a career that stretched over thirty years he boasted that he could make over £600 per annum from stake money alone, and early demonstrated his readiness to take money from anybody in a youthful athletic challenge, beating a fish-monger in a 120 yard race.[1] He went about the business of winning his bets with such single mindedness that the paid men were soon taking pleasure in thwarting him, by any number of means.[2] Gentlemen could be equally antagonised. Towards the end of Beauclerk's career Mr John Willes introduced his new style of round arm bowling, to the confusion and anger of most batsmen, including Beauclerk, who could well have been behind the no-balling of Willes in 1822, which so exasperated the bowler that he flung down the ball in disgust and gave up the game completely.[3] There is no doubting Beauclerk's great ability as a cricketer and he had some remarkable figures as both batsman and bowler.[4] Indeed, much of the opposition that he provoked could well have stemmed from the fact that he was skilled enough to have made virtually as much as he did from the game without resorting to bullying and sharp practice.

Only slightly less offensive was his lifelong rival, George Osbaldeston, whose shortcomings included aggressiveness, arrogance, snobbery, profligacy and bad judgement, the last of which, on the turf alone, cost him at least £200,000 of his vast inherited wealth. Born in 1787 and heir to 10,000 Yorkshire acres, by the time he became of age in 1808 he had already been thrown out of Eton, fallen out of favour with his Oxford college, raised his first pack of hounds, and embarked on his permanent feud with Beauclerk.[5] Intensely irritated by the fact that so many less wealthy men he considered beneath him had titles while he had none, and equally ill disposed towards parsons who interfered with his hunting, he found the ideal enemy in the noble clergyman. In 1806, while still at Oxford, he had made a two-a-side cricket match with him for 50 guineas, which, in spite of his own illness, Osbaldeston won through the bowling strategy of his wily partner, Lambert.[6] However, the unforgiving Beauclerk certainly blackballed Osbaldeston's attempts to rejoin MCC after he had resigned in a fit of anger and exasperation, and could well have influenced the eventual banning of Lambert from Lords.[7] This did little to sweeten Osbaldeston's always fiery temper or his disdain for much of the rest of humanity. Even with the benefit of his own autobiography to state his case he still comes down the ages as an egotistic wastrel who did virtually nothing to aid the country's war efforts and for whom even the courtesy title of 'The Squire' was soon itself a hollow sham as his patrimony was frittered away.

Again, though, as with Beauclerk, he was a games player of considerable distinction, a pan-athlete of unusual range, never quite as perfect as he thought he was in any of his activities but a very good performer in most. The fulsome dedication from Pierce Egan in his *Book of Sports* is near the mark so far as the width of Osbaldeston's sporting enterprise is concerned – 'a cricketer of the very first class, either with the Bat or the Ball,' completely 'at home' as a sculler, 'conspicuous in the Annals of Trotting,' a crack shot, an expert breeder of hounds, a 'mighty Hunter,' and as a rider on the racecourse noted for his excellence.[8] More realistically, his performances were often typified more by self confidence, energy and enthusiasm than by skill, as in his tearaway fast bowling, or achieved by means which some considered unsporting, as in his use of the latest firearms innovations in some of his prodigious shooting feats.[9] He lingered on into the middle years of the century, an amusing and rather pathetic survivor from a bygone age, adding little to his repute, still giving his support to pugilism in some of its worst years, refereeing both the match in which McKay met his death at the hands of Sandy Byrne (and much criticised by the judge for making no appearance at Byrne's trial for manslaughter) and also the farcical encounter between Bendigo and Caunt in 1845, when his decision in favour of the former defied all justice.[10]

What Beauclerk and Osbaldeston demonstrate is not, of course, the professionalism that has making money as its prime necessity, but the play became central to their life style, dominating it with the intensity of a paid employment. They did so out of their free choice, with specialist dedication, and at a time when such an approach was being reflected in the growth, in both numbers and in individual status, of the actual paid professional sportsman for whom play was also a living. There were differences in style from one sport to another, but there are some discernible common factors. Paid cricketers began to appear more often, usually in ones or twos, in matches at many levels and no longer in just the great contests. The popularity of pugilism prompted more and more to try to make a trade out of it, while on the racegrounds both the growing keenness of competition and the move to lighter horses, and hence to lighter jockeys, meant that the professional rider became much more common, whether from preference or from necessity. The professionals did usually begin their careers as amateurs, though some were born into their sport, such as the boxing descendants of Slack in the Belcher line. Newmarket families were already beginning the selective breeding of lightweights for the stables, with, for instance, the Day family, already setting up a dynasty of racing trainers, riders, and eventually owners. There were nascent cricketing families like the Smalls and the Nyrens. The great majority of the first generations of professionals, though, moved into their sport from other occupations, some activities having their own favoured route. The greater weighting of craftsmen was to be found among the cricketers, few of whom came from urban backgrounds. Pugilists, by contrast, were rarely countrymen and included a remarkable concentration of former butchers, including Sam Martin, Bob Watson, Jem Belcher and John Gully, all of these incidentally hailing from the notable nursery of boxing in and around Bristol. Professional sportsmen as a whole tended to be drawn predominantly from the south east, where the spectator sports were most developed. Provincial fighters (and to a somewhat lesser extent provincial pedestrians) still had to make their way to the capital to secure tangible rewards and only on the turf were there substantial possibilities of a good income from sport elsewhere. By and large, though, the profits to be had were unremarkable. A few achieved wider distinction, Gully being the most conspicuous example. Jockeys, partly because they might have a long career in the saddle, had the best chance of achieving financial security, but hosting a comfortable public house like Tom Cribb's Union Arms in the Haymarket usually marked the summit of the ambitions of even the best paid fighting men.

The professional sportsman's customary payment came from his patron or backer, and usually by way of a one-off payment agreed in advance and/ or a reward after victory. Sometimes cricketers or jockeys could appear to be virtually open to hire for an individual event,[11] but usually the professional in all sports had some longer term arrangement with one or more of his paymasters. The security of some permanent employment was still available to a few but for the great majority it had, well before the end of the period, become a limited contractual relationship of greater or less precision. The well organised Hambledon Club set a pattern that was to persist with little change in its underlying attitudes until the second half of the twentieth century, a system of hiring players that owed more to the factory owner than to any pastoral paternalism. Its professionals were paid at set daily rates (with fines for lateness) and while the wages were better than most craftsmen could earn, they did not constitute a full-time income even for the best of players.[12]

The Hambledon cricketers were a diverse group, mostly countrymen and with some craftsmen among them. Their variety is well illustrated in the lives and deaths of just two of them, Noah Mann and John Small. Mann, a short, swarthy, gypsy-like character, kept an inn at North Chapel, near

Petworth in Sussex, some twenty miles from Hambledon. He was an excellent horseman, specialising in picking up handkerchiefs at full gallop, and thought nothing of riding to and from matches. Always hatless – he said that he had no complexion to protect – he was a fine all-rounder on the cricket field. Noted as a 'severe hitter' he batted and bowled left handed, swinging the ball, it was said, 'the whole way.' In addition he was fast in the field and an accurate thrower, specialising in covering both slip and long stop. Nor was his prowess confined to cricket and horsemanship. At the end of a day's play he would often make impromptu running matches, claiming that so long as he was alongside his opponent at the half way stage he was sure to win.[13] The accomplished professional cricketer's year could be a full one but his end was both early and in tune with his free-wheeling life style. It came in 1790, 'a victim of his own intemperance' according to an obituary notice. After a day out shooting with his cronies, and carousing with them afterwards, he fell asleep in front of his own alehouse fire and was burned to death.[14]

Wisden takes no note of poor Noah. On the other hand it does remember one of his contemporaries, namely 'Small, John, sen. (Hants and All-England) b April 19, 1737, d Dec 31, 1826.' He certainly was a remarkable man, even more varied than Mann in his talents. After a day's play he was more likely to be entertaining the gentlemen with his fine violin playing than collapsing into a drunken stupor. As a cricketer, where Mann was dashing and cavalier, Small was cautious and controlled, 'considered the surest batsman of his day.' Typically, in one England v Hambledon match he was on the field for the whole of the three days, batting through his side's innings. What he did share with Mann – and, indeed, with many professionals of every sort – was an all-round sporting interest, in his case particularly in shooting and skating. While his main full time employment was as a gamekeeper on the Beckford estate at Greatham, he had begun life as a craftsman and he also turned his hand to making cricket bats and balls, which came to be much in demand.[15] He enjoyed a long and active life, continuing to play into his seventies and known personally by Pierce Egan who held him up as an example of temperance, a man of 'encouraging cheerfulness and equanimity of temper' and 'enjoying to the last, health of body, peace of mind, and the rational amusements of life.'[16]

The example of John Small is a reminder that professional players were by no means all hewers of wood or drawers of water, that they could occupy every social niche below that of gentleman, where the line could rarely be crossed. Small was an enthusiastic follower of the local hunt for many years – but he did so on foot. A number of other cricketers had very long careers[17] and as their numbers grew matches were often dominated by the paid men.[18] The influence of the professional on the sport, and the possibilities of a lengthy career, were features which cricket shared with the turf, though the evidence from horse racing is less clear cut. Although racing was the most comprehensively reported of all sports neither

Weatherby's nor the *Sporting Magazine* consistently provided the names of jockeys in their Racing Calendars and we know much more about the horses than we do about their riders. The paid rider had certainly, in most cases, become something more than the horse's travelling groom by the end of the eighteenth century. While the man who walked his master's horse from course to course through the summer on the often long provincial circuits had to be a jack of all the equine trades as well as a competent rider, the best of the jockeys were not to be wasted in such time consuming tasks. When spring came round many had to go into strict training routines to bring down their weight and this could be a drastic process, involving the loss of over twenty pounds in a week to ten days. The dress was heavy – several waistcoats, coats and pairs of breeches for sweating – the diet sparse, the drink largely wine diluted with water, and the exercise severe, fifteen miles or so of brisk walking a day.[19]

Many were based where the employment was most regular, at Newmarket, Epsom or, later, at Doncaster and already there were notable racing families – the Singletons, with John, senior, winning the first St Leger before going to France as trainer for the Duc d'Orleans, and his son, another John, in his turn becoming a successful jockey. There were the Chiffneys, father and son, and the remarkable Day dynasty of jockey/trainer/owners.[20] The first professional jockey, in fact, to achieve national fame – and national ill-fame – was Samuel Chiffney who, with an annual retainer of 200 guineas from the Prince of Wales, was the best paid professional sportsman of the day.[21] He was certainly a very skilful jockey who had perfected the knack of saving a horse for a final acceleration to the winning post, a knack which contributed to suspicions over his honesty, in that it could be difficult to say whether he was driving a horse hard or not. If he could manage a horse so well to win its races, could he also ride it to lose, to give it better odds in its next race? There were suggestions that he had done this on the Prince's horses at York in 1791[22] and the same complaints were made at Newmarket a few months later, in the notorious Escape affair. The horse had failed to win as favourite one day, but romped home at 5 to 1 a day later, when Chiffney had 20 guineas on it. The consequences were far reaching, with the jockey warned off, the Prince turning his back on Newmarket, and the Jockey Club flexing its muscles. The Prince settled a generous annuity on Chiffney but the jockey still fell on hard times and died, in debt, in the Fleet Prison in 1805, his annuity mortgaged and wrangled over in the King's Bench.[23]

As Chiffney left the riding scene, his place at its head was taken by Frank Buckle, a man at least equal in skill and more certain in probity. He rode John Bull to victory in the 1792 Derby and was to have 27 classic winners over the next thirty years. Buckle's reputation, almost uniquely for the times, remained quite unsullied. He was even said on one occasion, at Lewes, to have beaten a horse that he had backed himself when he was offered a late ride in the race. His deceits as a jockey were legitimate ones.

He could not only hold a horse back for a final dash to the finish but could also, for instance, show sham activity, giving the false impression that he was driving his mount hard and making it difficult for rivals to know what pace they had to contend with.[24] Typically, he had been born into racing, or at least into its periphery, his father being a saddler at Newmarket, and had worked his way up as a groom in Lord Grosvenor's stables. Among his particularly notable feats were riding the first Derby/St Leger double on Champion in 1800 and, towards the end of his career in 1823, winning the Derby and the Oaks at the same Epsom meeting. He had, too, some famous defeats. His mount Sancho broke down in a match against Pavilion at Lewes in 1806, a contest which had drawn the Prince of Wales himself from nearby Brighton. At York, in the previous year, Buckle, giving four pounds in weight, had also been beaten in a two-mile match by the dashing Lady Alicia Thornton, riding side-saddle. His victories though were notable and his skill and reliability brought him prosperity, being able, it was said, to make £1,200 a year. With all his virtues, however, he was no pioneer of new sporting habits and attitudes. He bred greyhounds and fighting cocks, and he also rode to hounds, quite probably with his own pack. What this 'ornament to the turf,' as Pierce Egan called him, did exemplify was the fact that honesty could still exist in sport alongside traditional sporting tastes.[25]

Employment in the racing world could not only be virtually life-long but was also relatively accident-free. On the racecourse spectators were more likely to be killed or injured than were jockeys, while the hunting field saw many more casualties than the raceground. Cricketers, too, were fairly safe, the rare roughness from a disgruntled crowd or frustrated opponents excepted.[26] Within actual play there are few reports of serious injury. It was, though, inevitably another story among the professionals of the other major spectator sport. The lives of pugilists are usually better recorded than those of jockeys, who were the adjuncts of horses, or cricketers, who were part of a team. The pugilist, by contrast, was a man on his own and his individual performance was the very substance of the sport – the braver the man, the more punishment he could well have to suffer. Actual deaths, however, were surprisingly rare in the formal prize ring, although they were much more frequent in fights at humbler levels.[27] The most notable victims were Earl, killed in his fight with Tom Tyne before the shocked Prince of Wales at the start of the sport's revival, and Sandy M'Kay some forty years later, marking an important stage in pugilism's decline. The fighters themselves accepted some injuries as part of the job and if death was rare, serious injury was frequent – a defeated man knocked out by a violent stomach blow, 'speechless, with little hope of recovery,' and Black Jemmy 'apparently lifeless from loss of blood.' Possibly luckier than most were the contestants in a 100 guinea fight in 1797 when the stakes were withdrawn after an hour because neither man could see the other for the bruising and swellings on their faces – the commonly used alternative was to lance the swellings.[28]

The odds might be long, but the ring held out hope of rewards well beyond the working man's normal grasp and the best fighters such as Broughton, Mendoza. Jackson, Gully and Cribb all lived out their full span of years. Of these, for his long-term influence on the sport itself, John Jackson was the most remarkable, an exception from the start in not coming from humble origins. His father was a prosperous builder who had, for instance, been responsible for culverting the Fleet Ditch. If the father had finally put an end to the disreputable Hockley Hole chapter in the sporting story, the son was to add lustre to it not just by his active pugilistic career, which was indeed short, but by his beliefs in its worth, his own all-round athletic enthusiasms (he was a good runner and jumper) and his ability to move in all levels of society. His commitment to the sport was such that, for the first two decades of the nineteenth century, he became virtually both the master of ceremonies and arbiter of the ring. He found, too, a fellow proponent of a combat sport with the same underlying belief in its physical and moral benefits. This was Harry Angelo, then running the family's well established and socially exclusive fencing academy in Bond Street. The two co-operated. Jackson took up neighbouring rooms in Bond Street and D'Angelo would persuade his clients to alternate their exercise between the foils and the mufflers.[29] Here Jackson became friend and tutor to many of the nobility, most conspicuously of course Lord Byron, who referred to him in the well known footnote in 'Don Juan' as 'my old friend and corporeal pastor and master.'[30] In spite of such praise, and being styled 'Gentleman' Jackson, he knew his station in life and was prepared to remain honourably in it.[31]

Another ex-champion, John Gully, had no share of such modesty. While still active in the ring he was being criticised for acting above his rank by sitting in the lower circle at Drury Lane. Much later, after the Spring v Langan fight in 1824, their respective stations were reflected in the fact that while Jackson collected a few pounds for the loser from spectators near the stage, Gully was one of the privileged *on* the stage and the main contributor, with £5, to Pierce Egan's collection there.[32] By birth, manners and general acceptability Jackson might seem much better equipped to climb the social ladder, but it was Gully who had the ambition and the drive to force his way into the ranks of gentility. He had progressed rapidly from being effectively a bookmaker's runner for some of the day's most distinguished gamblers in the land to becoming a gambler on his own account and then a racehorse owner himself. He was well fitted to survive in the shady world of the gaming houses, his physique and his known strength and courage being matched by a straightforwardness in attitude which did not brook any vacillating. In all his long and prosperous progress, while he never let an opportunity for profit escape him and was often being viewed with suspicion, he was never actually found cheating, even in an environment where honesty was a rare commodity. By 1815 the *Sporting Magazine*, reporting a reputed win of 1,200 guineas, already noted his conspicuous advance.[33] Much more was to lie ahead for Gully – classic winner, land speculator, mine owner, and eventually Member of Parliament for Pontefract. He was, to the whole nineteenth century, the supreme example of the sporting route to social mobility and he did it without rejecting any of his pugilistic past or his pugilistic friends. One of the closest of these was his fellow west countryman, Tom Cribb, probably the most popular figure ever to appear in the old prize ring, who had retired unbeaten from the ring in 1813 and spent the rest of a long life as the contented host of his Haymarket tavern.[34]

The early deaths of Ben Brain and Henry Pearce seemed to have little connection with their boxing. The other early death was that of the great Jem Belcher, the long term consequence of being accidentally blinded in one eye when playing racquets, an event which, in spite of his attempts still to fight, put an end to his career and reduced him to disillusionment and drink. The highly colourful Daniel Mendoza, technically the most innovative boxer of the day, had an up and down post-ring career, being at one time or other boxing instructor, recruiting sergeant, and innkeeper, leaving his family in penury when he died. There were other pugilists who used their sport as a stepping stone to a successful later career. Richard Humphries became a prosperous coal merchant, operating from the Savoy steps, and Bill Richmond was among the earliest of a string of flourishing tavern keepers, in his case combining his Horse and Dolphin with much of the management of the neighbouring Fives Court. Jack Martin, at the Griffin, vegetarian and teetotaller, set himself up by marrying a wife with £2,500, became also a successful bookmaker and lived to a ripe old age.[35]

Pugilism, uniquely among the major sports, also offered opportunities to some of the least favoured groups including the considerable immigrant population, concentrated in the cities and particularly in London, and barred from many employments. Neither the country's 20,000 Jews nor the slightly fewer Blacks had much prospect of social advancement. The black, Bill Richmond, was a rarity, being both a qualified craftsman and literate. Routes to progress such as apprenticeships were usually closed to them, as they were for the most part to the even more numerous Irish, an equally depressed group, predominantly unskilled and, like the Jews, facing barriers of religion as well as of race. Fighting was such a weekend way of life in some Irish communities that they almost inevitably produced a whole string of candidates for the prize ring, from Peter Corcoran in the 1770s through such as Michael Ryan, O'Donell, Dogherty and Dan Donelly to the excellent John Langan. Among the Jewish community, Philip Juchau had met his end from a fall in a bout fought on paving stones as early as 1765 and a whole series of Jewish boxers followed, the outstanding ones being Daniel Mendoza, of course, and the lightweight Dutch Sam. Jewish boxers could rely on organised support from their own community and often had little difficulty in also finding gentile backing. It was also noted how well prepared Jewish fighters were and how their welfare was taken care of, with a medical man always present. Irish support was always numerous and rowdy, but not much blessed with money and its boxers had to look elsewhere for backers. This was even more the case with black boxers who had, as it were, no constituency of their own to fall back upon.[36] They were less discriminated against than the Jews and an obviously outstanding fighting specimen like Molineux, carefully brought on by the respected Bill Richmond, had little difficulty in finding sponsors. With all others of his race, though, there was, and would continue to be, a problem of finding consistent backing, reducing black boxers to pick-up fights at race meetings or for a hastily subscribed purse after a main bout.

The rewards for any fighter, of any race or background, were always precarious. Pugilists were entitled to a share of the gate money, two thirds to the winner and one third to the loser, unless the articles for the particular fight stipulated some other arrangement. This *could* be profitable,[37] but it was an unreliable source of income. Unless the fight could take place in some sort of enclosure, gate money became virtually impossible to collect. Humphries and Mendoza had agreed to share the gate money from their Hampshire fight in 1788 but in spite of having pugilists guarding the entrance to the paddock where it took place most of the spectators swarmed past them without paying.[38] The pugilist could never look to gate money as a reliable source of income, but a winner could expect to be given a share of the stake money by his backer and it could be very generous – Johnson (who also profited much more from gate receipts than most later boxers) received £1,000 after his victory over Perrins.[39] While direct benefits from fights could therefore be considerable, they were also highly speculative – and in defeat could be non-existent. It is not surprising that pugilists found more additional means of making money from their sport than other professionals. One possible windfall was a benefit night at the Fives Court, where fellow pugilists would give sparring exhibitions, wearing gloves, and the beneficiary would stand at the entrance holding a bucket for the gate money. The proceeds could run to £200 or more, a popular fighter could well hope to enjoy several such, and they did not depend solely upon being a winner. Tours of provincial towns and cities, giving sparring exhibitions (and extending into Scotland and occasionally Ireland by the early nineteenth century) could also be profitable, particularly for someone as unique as Tom Molineux who spent several years on the road. There were even imposters on the circuit. In 1809 one was found at Ipswich – pretending to be Tom Cribb![40] Boxing schools provided another possible source of income. From the earliest days of the sport pioneers like Figg and Broughton had set themselves up primarily as instructors, after the fashion of the fencing professors. Jackson's academy was the most famous, but it was far from being alone or even being the first. Boxing schools were widespread and it did not to demand great ring fame to run them – Black Jemmy (ten years before his bloody fight with Flowers, already mentioned) was giving lessons in pugilism at Maidenhead in 1793, for instance, and Gulliver, who made no mark as a fighter himself, was being noted as 'a teacher of provincial novices' in 1809.[41]

Pugilists formed a close self-help group and were expected to help in the management of fights, which could bring further profit. They took along their own wagons, formed them up in a circle, and charged up to a guinea a head to those who climbed aboard for a grandstand view. Other employment was on offer, even one step below acting as minder for some raffish aristocrat, and that was as a bouncer and general heavy at one of the gaming houses which began to proliferate in London in the early years of the nineteenth century. Their owners generally, one correspondent alleged, 'retain *prize-fighters*, and persons of a desperate description, who threaten assassination to any person who will molest them.'[42] With such calumnies ever nearby, was it all worth it as far as the pugilist was concerned? Most of them would probably have said that it was. There was that chance of glory far beyond anything that their previous way of life could have promised. Even if they achieved no great success, once they were accepted into what was essentially the brotherhood of the prize ring where there was invariably an opportunity for pickings of some sort, even if they were as trivial as old Caleb Baldwin's orange selling at the Fives Court. Certainly against the financial and social successes of the few have to be set the hazards, injuries and tragedies met by the many – Molyneux dying in the guardroom of Galway barracks with just two of his soldier countrymen for company, Tom Hooper dying a diseased alcoholic in the workhouse, Power and Jay prosecuted for high-jacking a stage coach, and George Head dying just six weeks after claiming that he could drink sixteen glasses of gin without disturbing his wits. Then there was the classic example of a champion in decline in Tom Johnson, who had made more money than most from fighting, and took a public house which quickly became a notorious rendezvous for unsavoury characters. He was an unwilling and shifty witness when one was tried and then hanged for robbing two travellers from Newmarket, gave up his tavern, and took to touting his gambling table around racegrounds and fairs. Finding England unprofitable he moved over to Ireland, took a public house there, was soon ejected from it by the magistrates and finished earning a sparse living teaching pugilism and running his gambling game at Cork until he was another to meet an early death, in 1797.[43] Even for the sober, however, life could be far from easy, especially if they lived to any age. With no provision made for the frail and elderly, penury or the workhouse were common endings, both for the man and, even more so, for the widow. Both 'poor Bill Richmond's widow' and the aged Mendoza, too infirm to support his wife, needed the help of sparring benefits at the end.[44] Whether, outside of these three major sports and the fencing academies, there were many other performers able to make a living from their athletic skills is doubtful. There were well-known prize-winners in a number of sports, such as the Drakes and Thompson in Fenland skating, and men with strong regional or local reputations, such as Wall, the Somerset singlestick fighter, or Marks, the Dorsetshire runner, but their opportunities were bound to be both occasional and modest.[45] The billiards vogue in the 1790s saw Mr Andrews, who could, it was said, have made handsome profits from the game had his match-making been as good as his playing, but the 'Mr' smacks of some degree of gentility, and more clearly available for professional hire were Hughes and Evans, 'the two first cue-players in England.'[46] The one other sport which might have earned a living for the best of its performers was pedestrianism. Foster Powell probably supported himself from athletics, and was still racing in the late 1780s at over fifty. He was, for instance, almost certainly the Powell who won a 120 yard race in November that year on Mitcham Common, this time with 100 guineas at stake, a sum equalling those at pugilistic matches.[47]

What any might make from their own betting is purely a matter of guesswork. To judge from the 1799 report of 'a palpable cross' there was money, if only dishonest money in the sport, and a foretaste of the unreliability that was later to mark its history.[48] The possibilities for profit did become increasingly realistic in the surge of interest in pedestrianism sparked off by Allardyce Barclay's 1,000 miles in 1,000 hours in 1808.[49] Well-known competitors such as Curley, 'the Brighton Shepherd,' were almost certainly now full-time professionals. The most noted of them was Abraham Wood, from Lancashire, the paid man whom Barclay had difficulty in making a match with, in an episode which strongly implies that Wood was in a position to put up his own considerable stake. From 1803, when he competed before a huge crowd on Scarborough Sands to beyond 1815, Wood was running and walking in many parts of the country.[50] Like that other up and coming pedestrian, George Wilson, who was to perform at Blackheath, Wood had an eye to the entertainment value of his sport and was ever ready to put on a show, such as racing against the pugilist Jack Carter, then at the height of his fame, and harbouring some wider athletic ambitions. He gave the fighting man 150 yards in a 2 mile race on the Lea Bridge Road – and lost.[51] Whether, in a contest such as this, there was any other source of profit for the competitor beyond the stake money and any side bets is difficult to know. There may, for instance, have been collections made from the crowds who turned up. The question poses itself in pointed fashion over two separate contests between Curley and Cooke, 'the soldier.' Curley won the first at Lords in June, 1807. The venue, and the reported presence of 'sporting amateurs' and some pugilists, all imply some sponsorship, but then, some six months later, there was a re-match which seems to have been significantly different, It took place on Blackheath, where there could be no possibility of charging 'the great concourse' of spectators for admission, and the two umpires were a Mr Giles, 'a respectable fishmonger from Billingsgate' and 'Richmond (sic), the Black.'[52] It suggests that there may already have been that substratum of minor pedestrian activity so prominently advertised in Bell's Life later in the century, involving lowly staked challenges and usually based on local public houses. Curley and Cooke, incidentally, were adjudged to have drawn this second race, and so neither of them lost by it.

The emergence in many activities of the professional player was a significant feature of the Georgian years. From being an occasional and usually a part-time phenomenon, his became a recognisable employment. In one dimension this was an aspect of rising prosperity. More money became available for sport and larger sums began to depend on the outcomes of individual contests (and from the increase in betting more than from the rise in stakes) and so it became more and more desirable to have the best competitor to protect the investment and well worth paying him to do so. For the player the motives to improve his athletic skills became even stronger than they had been in the past. It could mean a good livelihood, travel, and perhaps even national fame. The obverse of this was the loosening of the once inalienable sporting bonds between the athlete and his living place. Fewer and fewer of the best players would see themselves as inextricably tied to their own village, ward or trade teams. Fewer and fewer teams, in any number of sports, would feel bound to confine themselves to their own local inhabitants, though at the moment, in staked cricket matches, it was still common for the 'given men' – the strangers – to be identified and to be the subject of negotiations when the match was being made and the process of dissolving the birth qualification still had a long history before it. Another consequence of the growth of professionalism was its effect on the gentleman competitor. Faced with an increasing number of paid men who had such a vested interest in honing their particular skills he felt a growing need to avoid what he saw as unequal competition – and it was not merely levels of sporting ability that were at issue. There were many sporting illustrations of the gulf that was held to exist, naturally and inevitably, between the classes, between the gentleman and the workman, whose sense of honour and reliability, whose readiness to meet any dues was always thought to be dubious. There was a sharpening awareness of the distinction between the gentleman player and the paid man and the suspicion that contests between them would provide too many reversals of the natural ranking of society. The result was the appearance of much more competition specifically limited to gentlemen and with it came a growing examination, previously hardly necessary, of the nature and definition of amateurism itself.

For that other large and growing body of people caught up in the sporting experience, the spectators, it usually mattered very little whether the performers were amateurs or professionals. Paid or not, the crowds undoubtedly flocked to see them. What is uncertain, in spite of numerous press comments, is the real size of these crowds. The one report that might just provide a nugget of hard information is of the Carlisle Races in October 1814, when 15,000 spectators were reported to have 'paid at the gates.' Was this literally the case or merely casual and careless phrasing by a reporter in a hurry? If it does mean what it actually says it gives a fairly precise idea of the numbers drawn to a popular race meeting.[53] It *could* be so but strong suspicions must remain, especially with such a round figure as 15,000 quoted as the attendance. Sporting crowds, according to contemporary reporters, had the habit of coming only in a few standard sizes –1,000, 5,000, 10,000, 15,000, or rarely, 20,000. It could even be 100,000 at race meetings such as Epsom or Manchester, a figure which is no more than journalists' shorthand for 'very big indeed.'[54]

What does seem reasonable to assert, however, after all the qualifications have been made and caveats entered, that sporting crowds could certainly be comparable in size with those of today, though they usually came together less frequently. London crowd sizes would, for instance, and as a rough approximation, have to be multiplied by ten to give some idea of present day equivalents. But it is not only the size of spectatorship that presents problems. The make-up of sporting crowds, whether by age, gender, or social class, is not a major preoccupation of most reporting and where there is comment there is often also the suspicion that the wide social appeal of an event is being stressed to enhance its respectability. The growth of spectating was undoubtedly a major phenomenon of the period yet much about it remains comparatively elusive. Who were the spectators? Why did they go? Was sport a unifying force, helping to hold the social classes in harmonious mutual enjoyment of the same contests? Did, by contrast, the increasing class separation appearing in the play itself also begin to show in sporting crowds? Did, on another tack, the 'civilising' process in popular attitudes and behaviour often identified over the same period begin to show itself in more restrained spectators? Do the arguments identifying 'sportsmen' as constituting a distinctive and separate social group have their correspondences with the spectatorship – was there, indeed, any such gathering as 'the sporting crowd,' or were the differences in the composition and conduct of the audiences for different sports more important than any common elements they might display?

As to who went to watch sport, the answer is virtually everybody, in one or other of its manifestations, from the prince to the pauper and the pickpocket, and from the duchess to the dairymaid and the fishwife. Crowd sizes alone, whether for the remaining communal football games, horse races or boxing matches, indicate that the greater part of all big gatherings must have come from the labouring classes. Equally, the frequent presence of the aristocracy and gentry at a wide range of sporting events is quite undisputed. What is much more speculative is the extent to which that broad middle range of the population that lay between the two extremes became involved – the growing professional and commercial classes, the business man, the small manufacturer, and even the superior craftsman and wealthier artisan, often driven by his own economic and social ambitions. Doubts, too, must exist over the participation of those from the several grades of society increasingly being drawn to revived ideas of piety and a concomitant respectability. These latter were doubtless under-represented in many sporting crowds, though not only was backsliding a common failing,[55] but some events, like the boat races on the Thames, must have been decorous enough for even the scrupulous.[56] Then again, however rough and ready some London cricket crowds might have been (and, indeed, some too in the industrial midlands) it was a more homely and comfortable affair over much of the countryside, with its special arrangements for lady spectators often particularly stressed.

The sporting event always likely to have the widest appeal was the local race meeting – Newmarket, being no part of this consideration, with its deliberate shunning of crowds. By contrast, 'our races,' as they were often fondly referred to, attracted young and old, men and women, from all sections of the local community and constituted the greatest communal celebration of the year in many country towns. The presence of the gentry was assured by the balls and assemblies, if not by the racing, and the numbers attending these imply a reaching down the social ladder at least into the farming community and local professional families. The widespread vested interest in the meeting's success assured the support of hotel landlords, innkeepers, saddlers, victuallers, stable proprietors, smiths, and a host of others who could look to profit from the hoped for influx of spectators. Few would not be involved, apart from those critics who objected to the drinking, the rowdiness, the gambling, and the bad company attracted by the races. They were a growing number, but their influence was still patchy and clerics were still often giving races their enthusiastic support well into the 1820s. The extent to which the classes mingled, though, was another matter. The likeliest place for this to happen was between the men who crowded into the cockpit for the morning fights there. On the course itself, the gentry usually kept their distance, viewing the races from their carriages – and this was a prime opportunity to show off the splendour of their equipages – or sitting aloof in the newly erected grandstand. The nearest physical contact that common folk might have with their betters was with some blood riding his horse, often recklessly, among the spectators. Indeed, to set against the celebratory tone of much reporting of races and the happy diversity of its crowds has to be a reminder that meetings not only resulted in frequent accidents but also could well fail to live up to expectations.[57]

The least likely event among the major sports to attract all classes has always been held to be the pugilistic contest. Fight crowds did certainly consist predominantly of a mix of the two extremes of wealth and standing, but there are several pointers to the considerable presence of, for instance, the better paid craftsmen. Descriptions of the conveyances used by spectators regularly take in the whole scale of wealth and social position, typically 'barouches, chaises, buggies, carts, horses, and donkeys.'[58] 'Respectable' tradesmen like the Mr Giles who made the pedestrian match with Bill Richmond would certainly be found among the fight crowds. Master butchers from Smithfield, always ready to promote a bull bait or a smock race, would also be there, as would the theatrical fraternity, always on the edges of respectability and close to pugilism, a surgeon or two and some lawyers, as well as members of the Cambridge colleges at many a Newmarket match. If sureties were needed for pugilists before the courts – a role to which nobody expected the real backers to expose themselves – there would be members of the trading classes ready and wealthy enough to support the accused.[59] Moreover, prize-fight crowds ranged from the select who paid their half guinea to see the third Humphries/Mendoza fight to the 'horrible group of blackguards' at a contest in the fields behind Gower Street in

Conveyances of every sort crowd the road after a thwarted fight. It was in a headlong chase such as this that the pugilist Thomas Hickman was killed as he tried to overtake another coach.

1794, while betwixt and between were many such mixed crowds as that at a Dan Dogherty fight in 1808, with plentiful Irish support and also the whole gamut 'from the duke, the marquis, and lord, down to the costermonger and the kids of the metropolis.'[60] Fight crowds tended to be evaluated according to the numbers and ranks of the gentry and aristocratic supporters, listed by name with great regularity. Their presence was important, not just for giving some standing to the event and ensuring that reasonable order would probably be kept, but also as some guarantee of probity in the outcome.[61] Many local fights, of course, those which were rarely reported unless they resulted in death or prosecution, had no upper class involvement and so did others that did reach the press, generally between lesser boxers and for small stakes.'[62]

In the new century the largest crowds were usually found at fights away from the capital, in Hampshire or Sussex (within reach of Brighton), in racing areas around Newmarket and Doncaster, or in the Leicestershire hunting country,[63] and what becomes more and more noticeable is the ease with which cowds of up to 20,000 could gather in distant country areas and usually be well ordered.[64] The ideal outdoor setting was that in which Tom Belcher fought Dogherty in Ireland in April 1813, in what was effectively a natural amphitheatre, allowing a good view to thousands.'[65] Few sites in England, however, enjoyed such happy topography and even the ideal arrangements could still mean discomfort for many, and the fact that the many were prepared to put up with them is one of the strongest evidences of the appeal of the sport. The Molyneux fight with Rimmer afforded a good example of relatively happy ordering, coaches and wagons parked eight deep in an outer ring, with some spectators in the rear standing on top of them. These were set back 25 yards from the inner ring, where the fight took place.[66] Effectively it was largely separation by social class, though it was also a means of giving as many as possible a view of the fight, with the first ring of spectators lying down at the front, the next sitting behind them, the third rank kneeling, and the rest standing. It has sometimes been suggested that the upper orders were prepared to forego ringside seats so as to avoid being spattered by blood, but this had in no way discouraged them from being at the front in the amphitheatre days and their distancing was more attributable to an understandable reluctance to lie in what at best could be damp grass and at worst sheer mud.[67] It was in the frequent turmoil of a major prize-fight that the established social ordering was likely to be at its most fragile – in the travel to the proposed site, the likelihood of having to move on to avoid the law, the hurried setting up of the ring, the tumult of the contest itself, and then the chaotic return journey, often in gathering darkness. For fights well away from London there could be the additional hazard of finding somewhere to sleep. Bedding down twelve to a room meant that company could not be chosen, and the squire and the smith might find themselves sharing the same barn or stable. There would be something of the same mixing too in the pugilistic public houses and at the Fives Court sparring exhibitions, where the high galleries could only segregate the few. There was still much mingling on the floor between a throng of followers from various stations in life and with enough of the monied there to make pickpocketing worthwhile.[68]

Whatever social mix boxing crowds might or might not be seen to encourage they were rarely praised as occasions for the joy and celebration that cricket could provoke – bells ringing for the whole day at Boston or bands playing. As usual, it is difficult to speak with any certainty over actual crowd sizes. The 10,000 crowds claimed for the Artillery Ground in mid-eighteenth century were said soon to have been well bettered at Hambledon but figures are rarely quoted. Instead there are phrases such as the 'incredible concourse of people' at the disputed Leicester v Coventry match in 1787, the 'immense concourse' at the game between one-legged and one-armed pensioners at Greenwich in 1796.[69] This and other novelties of whatever sort – a new location or at an odd time of the year – seem to have been a particular magnet for crowds, for journalists, or for both.[70] On the other hand there are occasional indications of thin attendances. An obvious case had been when Smith had increased his charges at the Artillery Ground in 1744 and provided benches for spectators to ensure better order, catering for just 800 but not reaching anywhere near that number.[71] Spectator interest in the game doubtless varied considerably, and in the make-up of crowds as well as in their size. At the Artillery Ground, White Conduit Fields and Lords the big matches were typical metropolitan sporting events which drew in crowds that were usually equally typical and often very different from those found elsewhere in the country. The urban cricket gathering was overwhelmingly male and, with modest entrance charges, enjoyed no great exclusivity. Spectators at Sheffield v Nottingham matches, for instance, seem not to have been much restrained by the social niceties and the 'large body of colliers' who caused such havoc at Hinckley after the notorious game in 1787 must earlier have been a significant section of the crowd.[72]

It was in the village or country town setting that cricket was most likely to achieve the social mix and harmony for which it was already being celebrated. Prints of games often show knots of spectators around the ground, with marquees for refreshments, and with women and children, often in family groups, prominent among those present. Positive attempts were made in the catering arrangements – as they were in no other major sport – to attract women spectators and these must, from their frequent appearance in advertisements, have had some success. Village matches were by no means always small affairs, but they usually retained that tone and temper which encouraged the fostering of the rural idyll that was coming to surround the game. Grandstands could be erected, bands play, and the attendance be well over a thousand at some country matches, but there is seldom much sign of friction in the crowds.[73] Servants might well be allowed time off to go to cricket matches, as they might also be, rather more reluctantly, for the races – but not for prize-fights! Once there, even if they could not afford the 'very genteel entertainment' on hand or 'the choicest liqours and viands' in the catering pavilions, they could virtually rub harmonious shoulders with the local gentry.[74] It was a style of cricket which had its roots in the south east, in Kent and Sussex, but it was spreading over the country.[75]

Even where the crowds were 'genteel,' however, there could still be occasional problems. The dividing line between players and spectators had nothing immutable about it. At the more important grounds there was likely to be some minor physical barrier to mark the boundary, but players were expected to field the ball wherever it was driven and could (as in baseball) take catches anywhere in the ground. It left only a thin divide between interaction and interference and the 'boundary' was still a matter for local custom and negotiation.[76] Watching cricket could have its dangers. Injuries to both players and spectators from cricket balls were reported from time to time, though when a tide surveyor was hit in the eye by a ball and had to leave the field the *Hampshire Chronicle* noted that 'he was only a spectator, and therefore did not mar the sport.' Other living creatures could share the dangers. Dogs were often threatened with shooting, for instance, and at least one horse caused an accident after being hit by a cricket ball.[77] The reported instances of spectators themselves causing disruptions of games in this period are, however, remarkably few – many less than the disputes between players themselves, often leading to the abandonment of matches. Even so, the aristocratic London players were ambivalent towards the crowds they attracted and periodically sought means of controlling them more effectively, including having Thomas Lord develop his new ground with a 'high batten fence' to keep out 'improper spectators.' Where a playing area was effectively enclosed, admission charges could impose their own restraints on both the numbers and the nature of the spectatorship. High entrance charges had kept a measure of exclusivity at the boxing emporia in their legal days and the example was always likely to be followed with indoor competitions.[78]

At the other extreme were the free ranging sports with their much greater inherent difficulties of crowd control, the one because its illegality denied it any set locations and the other because its crowds were dispersed over such a wide area. As for pugilism, the problems of separating players from spectators tended to increase rather than diminish during these years. In the first half of the period it was usual to fight on a quickly erected wooden stage. However, and most actual championship matches apart, the fashion changed under pressure from sharper policing to fighting on the turf, the understandable preference of the pugilists themselves, for a softer fall. It meant that the 'ring' now had to be created and it was accepted that this was likely business for the whips and clubs of the attendant pugilists. 'Beating out the ring' was the frequent prelude to the fight itself, and this itself could be a hard task. When the Pugilistic Club was set up the engraved whips of the stewards were seen as just as essential equipment as the official posts and ropes.[79]

The crowd problems facing racing meetings came not so much from spectators on foot struggling for a better view as from careless carriage drivers and horsemen. Pairs of riders mounting their own unofficial challenges on the course during meetings caused three deaths within a few weeks in 1805 (and again perhaps another example of the hectic spirit of the times) killing spectators at Manchester and Reading, while at Litchfield it was the rash rider who was himself killed, colliding with a horsewoman. There had earlier been at least one death of a spectator – at Chester in 1798 – by competing horses being driven off the course by the unfair riding of other jockeys, a practice much criticised in the press.[80] One problem was that many courses were still relatively ill-defined, with perhaps only a short roped run-in to the winning post, and the rest marked only by occasional stakes. Palings were still rare, and trespassing over the course could often result as much from ignorance as from ill-will, though some courses – Reading and Lincoln for example – did earn particularly bad reputation for the indiscipline of their crowds, with complaints of accidents year after year.[81]

Racecourse spectators might occasionally take direct action against a jockey after a race but they could do little to interfere with the race itself. Such intervention by the crowd, however, could often be a problem in pugilism, where the very nature of the struggle meant that spectator support, vociferously expressed, could of itself be crucial to the outcome of a fight without any actual physical interference. The outstanding example of this was in the first Cribb and Molyneux fight, where all the support was for the white champion and Egan was, years later, to admit that Molyneux's 'colour alone prevented him from becoming the hero of that fight.'[82] On the other side of the coin the silence that often greets rule-breaking by the home team or the crowd's favourite was already noticeable. In his third fight against Mendoza, Humphries went down several times without receiving a blow, which was specifically forbidden in the fight articles, but this was not objected to 'as his general manners placed him above suspicion.'[83] At humbler levels of the sport, where there was no strong gentry refereeing, the winner could virtually be decided by acclaim from the crowd, as happened in a Hyde Park contest in 1797 when 'friends of Crispin wanted to prove a foul blow, but the majority declared Burke the conqueror.'[84]

Interaction between watchers and players could take the further step and become a forcible attempt to stop the contest. This took place from time to time throughout the period, often by the crowd breaking the ring, which had become so common as to be referred to as 'a stale trick' by 1805. Again it was at this particular time of upheaval, during 1804/5, that crowd pressures were at some of their most vigorous, though by no means always successful. There was, for example, the unbridled prejudice of the spectators when Wood was having the better of the Jew, Pittoon, and the crowd twice broke the ring, but on the second occasion there was another intervention – from the Bow Street Officers, who put an end to the proceedings.[85] Stale trick or not, it was tried yet again within a few months when young Tom Belcher's carefully nurtured career (against a string of fighters expected to give him no trouble) suffered a setback against Bill Ryan. The strong Belcher clan support claimed a foul blow and broke the ring, but again 'the gentleman who held the purse' refused to be intimidated and declared Ryan the winner, underlining the strength and independence that could be shown by the best of the 'amateurs.' It could be otherwise with fights lacking such influence. Willis beat Caleb Harding, for instance, only because his supporters intervened when he was in difficulties – and in a fight that was unusual because while both had pugilistic training one was described as a copper-plate engraver, the other a horse dealer, and both as 'men of property,' further evidence of the need not to draw class lines too sharply in any of the period's sport.[86] It does have to be added that not all fight crowd interference was damaging – spectators did from time to time intervene in the interests of the fighters, even physically forcing a clearly beaten man to withdraw or separating mutually exhausted fighters after a long well-fought battle and insisting on a draw.[87]

While boxing was the sport most likely to have results influenced either directly or indirectly by crowd pressures, the same could happen, or at least be attempted, in other contexts. Races on the River Thames, for example, with the water crowded by boats of both competitors and spectators, offered considerable opportunities for interference, accidental or sometimes deliberate. Among the considerable number of replays of races there is at least one example of spectator intervention when some spectators 'attempted to foul' the Astley Prize Wherry race in 1806 – again at this time of particularly marked crowd exuberance.[88] In cricket matches it was usually the umpires who were subject to crowd pressures. The virtual riot at Hinckley after the notorious Leicester v Coventry match in 1787 came too late to affect the result – it could only express fury at it – but cricket's other noted pitched battle during the period, that at the annual Clapham v Battersea match a year later, does appear to have arisen from a disputed decision.[89] Again the action in horse races was not greatly subject to crowd influences though it does seem that judges could be put under pressure from the welcome given to a new small stand of their own at Doncaster, 'which entirely excludes the Judge from the company.' Not that racing crowds were by any means universally well ordered and peaceable in their general behaviour – this put the continued running of the Derby and the Oaks at Epsom repeatedly under threat because of crowd problems.[90]

As to the spectators themselves, they could be exposed to many mishaps both on racegrounds and at other sporting events. The size and make-up of its crowds made both the races and the travelling particularly dangerous at Epsom,[91] while those racecourses without permanent grandstands almost all suffered the collapse of a rickety temporary stand at one time or another. In 1787 it was Preston, leaving fifty with broken limbs; at Bath in 1793, where it was put down to overcrowding; and at the massively popular Manchester in 1805.[92] Then pickpockets and thieves were everywhere, even among the throng at Newgate hangings when their fellows were supposed to be providing stark moral lessons. They busied themselves at prizefights, where their most outrageous achievement was to pick the pocket of the stakeholder and make off with the winner's intended reward. They robbed at race meetings from one end of the land to the other, from Morpeth in Northumberland (where there were a dozen victims 'around the stand') to Lewes in Sussex, where the pickings were nearly £100 together with a pocket watch belonging to one of the stewards.[93] Newmarket, in spite of the absence of large crowds to mix with and melt into, attracted the London professionals – and the Bow Street runners, who made arrests there from time to time. Fights there could offer the best opportunities of all.[94] There were other frauds awaiting the gullible, including the imposters going round the country posing as boxing heroes, but crowds were far from accepting deceptions passively and there are frequent examples of immediate rough justice. At Burford Races, when rigged gaming tables were discovered, two 'well known black legs' were given a severe ducking and a third was horse-whipped. A pickpocket taking advantage of the bull bait which followed an 1807 prize-fight was thrown into the Thames and, some three years later, when a fight was clearly fixed, the two would-be pugs were chased off under the threat of horse whipping.[95]

The transitional nature of the period's sport is perhaps nowhere better illustrated than in both the motives and methods of those who provided it and the behaviour of the crowds that came to watch. The crowds still hovered between order and disorder, between an acceptance of their separation from the field of play and a readiness to interfere with the play itself. Whether we should expect to see, in the sporting crowds of an essentially warlike period, much sign of that 'gentling of the masses' which has been identified as a feature of longer term social change is itself debatable. What is perhaps significant is the fact that many of the most boisterous crowd scenes tended to come from those critical years of greatest military danger at the start of the nineteenth century when exception and excess marked so much sporting behaviour. Taking the Georgian age as a whole, and subject to some qualifications in its last years, there does appear to have been a diminution of both crowd violence and of spectator interference. It was possible for sporting events to accommodate increasing numbers from a growing population without any great upsurge of disorder. That the balance was tilting towards discipline and control was nowhere better (or more paradoxically!) illustrated than in the behaviour of boxing crowds. Hordes of them on the move through the country as they were banned from one place after another could seem to pose a threat but even boxing crowds, apart from the fact that they were pursuing an activity that was illegal in itself, were usually models of conformity. They rarely disobeyed any specific local ban on a fight, the presence of a single magistrate was often enough to divert several thousands of them, and once settled they usually showed considerable self-management in arranging themselves in moderately good order. There are some signs, too, of spectators moving away, not certainly from boxing itself, but from the more extreme blood sports – their decreasing availability and changing tastes were doubtless interdependent factors here. While cricket did little to take up the slack until towards the end of the period, there is every sign that horse racing was becoming more and more popular, from the increase in the number of horses being raced, the number of meetings, and the sizes quoted for its crowds, and this in itself would move sports spectating a shade further along the road to acceptability.

Notes

1. *SM*, September 1797, p 327
2. *e.g.*, John Sherman, rebuked by Beauclerk for slack fielding, threw the ball back with such force that it broke two fingers. Ford, *Cricket: A Social History*, p 78.
3. F.S. Ashley-Cooper and Lord Harris, *Lords and MCC*, 1914, p 80.
4. At Lords alone he scored eight centuries and in August 1805 alone he scored one century, one not out half century and took twelve wickets. Sir Pelham Warner, *Lords 1787-1945*, 1946, p 245. *SM*, August 1805, pp 283-286. See also Buckley, *Pre-Victorian Cricket*, pp 41, 48, 75, 78.
5. E.D. Cuning, *ed.*, *Squire Osbaldeston: His Autobiography*, 1926, pp 5-13.]
6. See Birley, *Sport and the Making of Britain*, p 161; Bowen, *Cricket: A History*, p 81.
7. Ford, *Cricket: A Social History*, p 78; Warner, *Lords*, p 25. The ban was for throwing a match, but Lambert was not the only suspect.
8. Egan, *Book of Sports*, dedication, pp iii, iv.
9. One critic said that he might just as well be 'using a field-piece.' See Cuning, *ed*, *Osbaldeston*, p 323.
10. *SM*, July 1830, pp 254, August 1830, pp 272 ff; Miles, *Pugilistica*, III, pp 28/9.

11. In a later example Reigate could not afford the fees demanded by the two guest players they were allowed by Brighton. Ford, *Cricket: A Social History*, p 95.

12. Nyren, *Cricketers of my Time*, Lucas, *ed.*, *Hambledon Men*, pp 44-48; Buckley, *Eighteenth Century Cricket and Pre-Victorian Cricket*, passim; Brookes, *English Cricket through the Ages*, pp 57-61.

13. Nyren, *Cricketers of my Time*, Lucas, *ed.*, *Hambledon Men*, pp 44-48.

14. Within the space of two months in 1787 he was playing at Lords, then at Canterbury, back to Hambledon and finally to Lords again. *Times*, 21 August, 12 September 1787; F. Lillywhite, *F.L.'s Cricket Scores and Biographies* of celebrated cricketers, from 1746 ('Haygarth's "Scores and Biographies"'), vol 1, 1862. For an obituary see *Sarah Farley's Bristol Journal*, 9 January 1780; Buckley, *Eighteenth Century Cricket*, p 144.

15. Egan, *Book of Sports*, pp 338/9.

16. Later in life he would sometimes be playing alongside his son, another John. In 1789 against Hampshire the son was top scorer in the first innings and the father in the second. *Morning Post*, 8 August 1789;

17. Aylward, for instance, was one of a number who played into their sixties and Billy Beldham not only played for 35 seasons but also found the time and energy to produce 39 children from his two marriages. Ford, *Cricket: A Social History*, pp 86/7.

18. *e.g.* the Surrey v All England match in 1807 included only four gentlemen in all and there are many cases of professionals scoring the bulk of the runs. *ibid.*, p 76; Buckley, *Pre-Victorian Cricket*, pp 23, 50, 75.

19. Sir John Sinclair, 'On the Training of Jockeys,' *SM*, December 1806, p 124.

20. Tyrrel, *Racecourses*, p 45. See also, *e.g. Sporting Magazine*, Appendix, Racing Calendar 1807.

21. Onslow, *Headquarters*, p 29.

22. Tyrrel, *Racecourses*, p 80.

23. *ibid.*, p 117; *SM*, December 1792, p 153, November 1808, p 52. Contemporary opinion inclined to Chiffney's side but later historians have tended to see the combined evidence from two meetings as pointing to cheating. *SM*, December 1808, pp 99-101.

24. Even criticism for unneccessary use of the whip by Mr Buckle was voiced very gently. *SM*, July 1821, pp 125-7.

25. Tyrrel, *Racecourses*, pp 20, 82, 48, 172; Egan, *Book of Sports*, pp 185-187.

26. The gun battle, with at least two deaths, between disputing players at Tilbury Fort in 1776 was unique and the attack on Leicester players after beating Coventry in 1788 was rare in its viciousness. *London Chronicle*, 31 October 1776; *Aris's Birmingham Gazette*, 13 August, 1787; *Northampton Mercury*, 11 August 1787; *Leicester Journal*, 11 August, 1787.

27. As well as Earl, killed before the Prince of Wales at Brighton, notable ring deaths included Ben Curtis (Molesey Hurst, 1821), John Wilson (Millbank, 1821) and Sandy M'Kay (No Man's Land, 1833). Outside the formal ring two men died in one afternoon at Birmingham in 1787 and at least three in one month twenty years later, at Cambridge, Reading and London. See *Pancratia*, pp 109, 179; *SM*, February 1800, p 254.

28. See *e.g.*, Ford, *Prizefighting*, pp 36-41.

29. Hearl, 'Polite Accomplishments,' McNair and Parry, *Readings in the History of Physical Education*, p 65. The usual reference to the Bond Street premises as 'Jackson's Rooms' is at best a half truth.

30. 'who I trust, still retains the strength and symmetry of his model of a form, together with his good humour, and athletic as well as mental accomplishments.' *Don Juan*, Eleventh Canto, verse xix, n.

31. See *e.g.* Leslie A. Marchand, *ed, Byron's Letters and Journals, Vol 1, In My Hot Youth*, p 171. When asking Jackson to settle a dispute over the purchase of a pony he added that if the man concerned turned out to be gentleman Byron would deal with him himself.

32. Miles, *Pugilistica*, II, p 72. See also Brailsford, *Bareknuckles*, ch 7, 'Mr Jackson and Mr Gully,' pp 67-78.

33. 'elevated so high from the sod of boxing on the turf of Newmarket, as to have become one of the principal betters on the most distinguished racing courses.' *SM*, June 1813, p 141.

34. See Bernard Darwin, *John Gully and His Times*, London, Toronto, Melbourne and Sydney, 1935, including Gully's account of the Cribb/Molineaux contests.

35. Ford, *Prizefighting*, pp 52, 59.

36. The first black fighter was probably Treadaway at the Marylebone Basin in 1791. Brailsford, *Bareknuckles*, p 15; *Pancratia*, p 103.

37. *e.g.* £800 was collected at Johnson's match with Perrins. Miles, *Pugilistica*, I, pp 84, 61.

38. *ibid.*, I, p 87.

39. For an indication of sums involved in pugilism at this stage see Brailsford, *Bareknuckles*, p 27.

40. See Miles, *Pugilistica*, I, p 241; *SM*, January 1809, p 203.

41. Miles, *Pugilistica*, I, p 246; *SM*, February 1809, p 230; April 1793, p 11. See also *Times*, 28 December 1787; Paul Magriel, *The Memoirs of the life of Daniel Mendoza*, London, New York, Toronto and Sydney, 1951, p 55.

42. *SM*, April 1807, p 25.

43. *SM*, April 1796, p 37; *Pancratia*, p 124; Miles, *Pugilistica*, I. p 64.

44. Ford, *Prizefighting*, p 54; *SM*, March 1830, p 352; September 1828, p 374.

45. *Sports History*, 6, 1985, p 23; *SM*, September 1807, p 287; February 1810, p 256.

46. They were backed in the £100 match made between Sir Horace Mann, Major Foley and Mr Edwards in 1804.*SM*, September 1796, pp 298/9; October 1804, p 44. Mr Andrews was described as a 'perfect vacuum' in all other games!

47. *SM*, October 1792, p 15; *Sports History*, 9, 1986, p 10.

48. *SM*, April 1799, p 84.

49. *e.g.* John Jones who had just won a 500 guinea challenge over 30 miles now found himself backed for 1,000 guineas in an 8 mile race at Newmarket. *SM*, June 1809, p 44; July 1809, p 198.

50. *e.g.*, at Brighton in 1806, Newmarket in 1807, London in 1812 and Wakefield in 1813. *SM*, July 1803, p 222; October 1806, p 41; June 1813, p 139.

51. *SM*, December 1812, p 136.

52. *SM*, June 1807, p 147; January 1808, p 210.

53. *SM*, October 1814, p 42.

54. See also *e.g.*, Wesley, *Journal*, 29 April 1739 for presumably reliable crowd figures.

55. See *e.g.* James Wood, *An Address to the Members of the Methodist Societies*

on several interesting Subjects, 1799; Thompson, *The Making of the Working Class*, pp 442-451; *Primitive Methodist Magazine*, I, 1818, p 218.

56. *SM*, July 1814, p 155. See also *e.g.* June 1807, p 107; September 1798, p 316.

57. See for instance the high anticipation and then the abject disappointment surrounding Egham Races in 1787, *SM*, September 1797, pp 317, 317.

58. *SM*, June 1806, p 133. The chaos of travel to fights is illustrated in the etching, 'Returning from the Intended Fight, Oct. 12, 1801,' *SM*, October 1801, facing p 8.

59. *e.g.* Mr Brand, oyster merchant from the Hungerford Market (worth £200 with all debts paid) and Mr Evans, Billingsgate fish merchant and barge owner, stood for Jem Belcher at Bow Streeet in 1802. *Pancratia*, p 148; Miles, *Pugilistica*, I, p 141. The third and possibly less immediately convincing surety came from a Mr Brown, describing himself as a gentleman able to 'live by my fortune.'

60. *Pancratia*, pp 96, 80/1; Miles, *Pugilistica*, I p 84; *SM*, February 1794, p 288; June 1808, p 137.

61. Though see *SM*, August 1807, p 225 for discontent over the verdict in the Belcher v Dutch Sam fight with some claiming that an honourable result was not always assured if influential money was against them.

62. See *SM*, November 1808, p 91 for a well attended fight with no mention of 'amateurs' present and probably organised by the pugilists themselves with Caleb Baldwin's 'famous bull' baited as a conclusion to the 'sport of the day.'

63. *e.g.*, in Leicestershire and Gloucestershire for Molyneux's fights with Cribb and Carter. See *SM*, October 1805, p 38; April 1813, p 24; Miles, *Pugilistica*, I p 243; II, p 164; *Pancratia*, supplement p 10. (The supplement was added to the second edition to cover fights over recent months.)

64. The difficulties of attempting to hold major contests near the capital in later years are well illustrated in the Turner v Martin fight, *SM*, October 1819, pp 6/7.

65. *Pancratia*, supplement, p 17.

66. *SM*, May 1811, p 54; *Pancratia*, p 356.

67. See Miles, *Pugilistica*, I, p 187; *SM*, May 1808, pp 73-76 for the Gregson v Gully fight.

68. Ford, *Prizefighting*, ch 8 'The Fives Court and the Benefits.'

69. *Leicester Journal*, 11 August 1787; *SM*, August 1796, p 280. Note also the large crowds reported in the 1820s.

70. On ice see *London Chronicle*, 6 February 1776; *Bath Chronicle*, 13 January 1795. As a novelty see *Norwich Mercury*, 1 September 1787; Buckley, *Eighteenth Century Cricket*, pp 76/7, 172, 120/1.

71. A pedestrian challenge could sometimes attract more than a cricket match – spectators arriving for the Brighton Shepherd v Cooke pedestrian contest had to wait for the ending of Mellish and Beauclerk's 1,000 guinea cricket match. Buckley, *Eighteenth Century Cricket*, pp 18/19; *SM*, June 1807, pp 147/8.

72. *Aris's Birmingham Gazette*, 13 August 1787.

73. See *e.g. Kentish Gazette*, 5 August 1780 and Buckley, *passim.*, for further examples.

74. Malcolmson, *Popular Recreations*, p 41; *Reading Mercury*, 22 July 1776; *Kentish Gazette*, 4 September 1779.

75. See *e.g.* a Hertfordshire village match from 1802, Carrington Diaries, Hertfordshire CRO, quoted in *Sports History*, 4, 1984, p 2.

76. *Hampshire Telegraph*, 18 September 1815; Buckley, *Pre-Victorian Cricket*, p 73. See the valuable article 'Cricket Boundaries,' *Sports History*, 10, 1987, p 4.

77. *Hampshire Chronicle*, 10 September 1787; Buckley, *Eighteenth Century Cricket*.

78. *Times*, 22 June 1787; *SM*, October 1804, p 44.

79. Ford, *Prizefighting*, pp 104/5. Stages returned for some provincial fights in the 1820s (most notably for Spring v Langham at Worcester) where no interference was assured.

80. *SM*, August 1805, p 314; May 1798, p 93.

81. *SM*, August 1811, p 238; September 1797, p 288.

82. Egan, *Boxiana*, III, p 493. See Brailsford, 'Morals and Maulers,' *Journal of Sport History*, vol 12, no 2, Summer 1985, pp 126 ff.; *Pancratia*, p 246. Coincidentally Cribb, as a young Bristol newcomer, had faced much worse treatment in his own first fight with George Maddox, an old London favourite. *Pancratia*, p 219.

83. *ibid.*, p 98. 126.

84. *ibid.*, p 126.

85. *ibid.*, pp 211, 206-8.

86. *ibid.*, pp 215 (see also Caleb Baldwin v Dutch Sam, p 211): *SM*, April 1805, p 55.

87. See *e.g.* Beckley v Clarke, *SM*, October 1803, p 8; Fuller v Jay, *SM*, November 1812, p 46.

88. *Times*, 21, 27 July 1787; *SM*, August 1809, p 248; June 1806, p 112.

89. *Leicester Journal*, 11 August 1787; *Morning Chronicle*, 17 July 1779; SM, August 1796, p 280.

90. *SM*, February 1806, p 224; June 1806, p 112.

91. *SM*, May 1803, p 68. The boxer Tom Hickman was killed overtaking another carriage on the way back from the Hudson/Shelton fight fight and on the course at Stamford no fewer than four single horse chaises were overturned in a single day. *SM*, December 1822, p 174; July 1810, p 192.

92. *Times*, 13 August 1797; *SM*, October 1793, p 48; June 1805, p 165. Since there was reported to be 'scarcely a family in Bath which had not some relation' injured in the accident,' a very wide social mix among the race crowd is implied.

93. Ford, *Prizefighting*, p 141; *Times*, 27 September 1787; *SM*, August 1798, p 275.

94. *Times*, 14 April 1787. A pocket book containing £3,500 was stolen during the Gully/Gregson fight, a £300 reward was offered, but the thief decided on a larger commission and returned the wallet lighter by £1,200. *SM*, October 1807, p 29.

95. See also Allen Guttmann, 'English Sports Spectators,' *Journal of Sport History*, vol.12, no.2, 1985, pp 103-1

7.
Sporting Women

The commonly accepted view of women's modern sporting role is that it only emerged into real significance on the coat-tails of male athleticism in the later nineteenth century. There was, in fact, during the previous age, frequent and varied female participation in sporting activities, as both spectators and performers. It does have to be admitted at once that some of the period's most notable instances of female sporting prowess were at the extreme of their sex's participation. Lady Alicia Thornton does seem to have been the only horsewoman to make formal matches with male riders. Mary Anne Talbot, who had spent many years in the navy disguised as a man, does seem to have been the only lady to have fought and won against a man in a pugilistic set-to. The expert lady markswoman reported from Oldham in 1813 was unusual, and there was no known English equivalent of Margaret ych Evan of Llanberis, the 'greatest hunter, shooter, and fisher of her time,' who was, even at seventy years of age, such a wrestler that 'few young men dared try a fall with her.'[1] On the other hand there is steady evidence of female participation in a whole variety of sports, from archery to swimming and from cricket to pugilism.

What there was too was diversity. There were certainly many limitations beyond those suffered by men – there was little opportunity for cross-class participation for example – but there remained scope for much individuality and wide differences of opportunity and inclination. Take, for instance, the mid 1790s. Over the space of months, while Jane Austen was setting out to write *Sense and Sensibility* and Joanna Southcott was still waiting to give birth to the Messiah, the boxing champions, Dan Mendoza and Tom Johnson were acting as seconds in a well organised women's boxing match, a woman pedestrian was winning a wager to run a mile in less than 5° minutes, and Lady Lade was planning a five mile curricle race against Mrs Hodges at the Newmarket Spring Meeting.[2] Meanwhile Mrs Concannon was operating her fashionable gaming house where the minimum stake was a fifty guineas, and on Brighton beach 'all the charms of the fair sex' were being 'as openly displayed to the eye of the gazer, as so many trinkets to be thrown for in a raffle-shop.'[3]

If the legal, economic and social restraints on women were formidable, so were the strengths shown by many in challenging them. There were, for instance, the determined few such as the painter, Angelica Kauffmann, who not only became a founder member of the Royal Academy but also struck a marriage bargain to keep control of her own affairs. Among the upper classes, wealth and privilege could give scope for individual sporting enterprise that went well beyond what custom allowed, while working class women, less restrained by convention, often had wider possibilities for play, if much less leisure to make use of them. For all, though, there were barriers which remained insurmountable. The professional world was closed to them. Outside the stage and the circus, the gaming room and the whorehouse, women could not make a living from any recreational pursuits. Otherwise, though, there were few hurdles which could not be jumped, either by the few or the many. It was still a far cry from the Victorian scene of undisturbed and docile feminine domesticity.

Ladies of the upper classes were certainly seldom prepared in their up-bringing for physical pursuits. While the men did at least have the informal play of their turbulent schooldays, the ladies might be thought destined only for 'still scenes of retirement' and were rarely expected to exercise themselves further than their dancing master demanded. Even he had become less important later in the century and any benefits that the minuet might bring were more than likely to be undone by the posture training to which girls were often subjected.[4] By the end of the eighteenth century the long enunciated pleas of Locke and Rousseau for greater freedom and liberality in the education of both sexes were beginning to have some marginal effects, with Erasmus Darwin advocating 'a greater activity to promote health and growth,' and such games as playing at ball and shuttlecock, swinging, dancing, and the like[5] and Mary Wollstonecraft urging that women should develop strength of body as well as of mind – the two sexes should play together as children, and all be given space for 'gymnastic plays in the open air.' In practice, walking became an acceptable exercise for young ladies, gardening began to be considered 'a truly feminine amusement' and some more adventurous schools even offered riding lessons or took up the vogue for sea bathing.[6]

As the period progressed more and more ladies did share in the new trend for activity that had become fashionable with many of their menfolk and were taking up riding, hunting and shooting. Even if they did not become performers themselves, they could share in the growing interest which, on a midsummer dawn in 1805, and for all the men's attempts at secrecy, attracted to Lords a whole string of ladies of quality to see Lord Frederick Beauclerk race against the Honourable Edward Harbord.[7] While they were rarely at the cockpit, and their presence at bull-baits was uncommon,[8] there were in fact no sports at which the attendance of ladies is not noted some-where or at least implied. Some must always have been with their partners in the grandstands of racecourses such as Epsom when prize-fights took place after the day's racing and their deliberate presence is sometimes noted. Some also must have seen football in one of its many styles – Mary Powell, in Wales, is unlikely to have been either the first or the last lady of the eighteenth century to watch a football match, and almost certainly had her English counterparts, even if they have left no account of it.[9]

Given the male domination of society, the woman's involvement in sport was often as an adjunct of her husband. She might, for instance, admire him playing golf on Blackheath in August 1813 when three marquees were set up by the members for their ladies' entertainment by the members, and the band of the East London Militia further enlivened the day. For the majority of ladies hunting would mean a splendid hunt ball and both archery and

Alicia Thornton, the most publicised female performer of the age, praised for both her beauty and her riding skills. It seems that she died soon after her racing feats as Colonel Thornton is reported as marrying again in 1806.

Mrs Thornton

racing had similar social attractions, while the regattas that became frequent in the latter years of the period frequently took on something of the social tone of race meetings, with some local patron providing polite entertainment at the end of the day's competition or even during the racing itself.[10] Again, traditional play, even if it was under pressure, could still provide occasional amusement for ladies and gentlemen alike. The rural sports on Maiden Castle were, after all, still considered to be an appropriate birthday treat for the royal princesses in 1798. The ladies of the family would also be expected to participate in the celebrations at such patronised events as Lord Clanricade's fete in Hampshire in 1774 or the new squire's coming of age in Berkshire in 1809, while the sports associated with the scouring of the Uffington White Horse attracted 'most of the nobility and gentry of this and the neighbouring counties.'[11]

There were finally those two major sports – cricket and horse racing – where the attendance of ladies was positively expected and encouraged. Early prints of cricket matches regularly show mixed groups of spectators around the ground, women and girls as well as men. Special provision was often promised for them, their own tents 'supplied with the choicest liquors and viands' at Reading in 1776 and at Cockerall's New Ground at Warminster, Wiltshire, in 1800 there was to be a large marquee offering 'genteel entertainment for ladies as well as gentlemen.' The widening appeal of cricket to the polite of both sexes was undoubted, with many reports such as that from North Yorkshire in 1808 of the 'numerous ladies and gentlemen' drawn to both of that summer's games between Weatherby and Harewood.[12] It was the race meeting, however, that attracted women of all stations in life, no less than their menfolk, among the 'fair ladies lolling in all the listlessness of luxury in the elegant land-aulet' described in the merry crowd going to Blandford Races, while Nimrod's account of the Woolwich Garrison Races in 1824 was quite side-tracked by the sight of ladies at the ball and by one beauty in particular.[13]

The ladies certainly sought to look their best. Dressmakers would be in attendance and a 'fashionable' hairdresser even, from Weymouth, was advertising his presence in Dorchester on the day of the race ball, 'for the purpose of rendering his Professional Service to such Ladies and Gentlemen as may require his Assistance.' Appearances were also of first importance on the raceground itself where the ladies were expected to be part of the show and bound to be listed later in the local press. To consider the lady spectator's role in horse racing as merely decorative would, however, fall short of the mark. There was the very occasional lady owner acknowledged in her own right – Lady Bamfylde's Fortune Hunter had won a 50 guinea race at Blandford in 1776 and a filly of Lady Mexborough's, for example, won a match at Doncaster in 1797, though these do seem to have been rare instances. At the other extreme of direct involvement were those who found it a means of livelihood, like the lady of the 'bewitching face' presiding over a gambling table, 'elegantly dressed in a riding habit' at Epping, or, tumbling down the ladder of respectability, even the prostitutes attracted by the crowds.[14]

Growing criticisms of the moral tone of race meetings may have had some bearing on a significant change in female involvement in the sport that began in the 1780s and 1790s. This was in the appearance of prizes advertised as being sponsored by ladies and these Ladies Plates steadily became more and more common, a process which, incidentally, and for some reason, was quicker in Scotland than it was south of the border. By 1797 they appeared at Guildford, Lewes, York and Egham, and there was a Ladies' Purse at Chester. The exact message given by their emergence is not easy to read, whether the title was a purely nominal courtesy or whether they did signify a growth of both female interest and independence. The latter becomes increasingly more likely as Linda Colley has now shown that at this time women were also contributing heavily to the state sponsored Voluntary Contribution to the war effort. The Ladies' Plates might also be held to demonstrate that racing was polite and respectable enough to win the support and encouragement of the gentler sex. What they provided in practice was more competition, sometimes as well rewarded as the main races, or additional contests tagged on to the end of a meeting. Whatever the motives at work these prizes do indicate an added importance being granted to women in one of the country's most developed sports.[15]

It was actually on the racecourse that the most highly publicised female sporting performance of the age took place. On 25th August, 1804, at York Races, Mrs Alicia Thornton rode a challenge match over four miles against her brother-in-law, Captain Flint, for a stake of 500 guineas a side. There were over 100,000 spectators on Knavesmire for the race, attracted by the uniqueness of the event, the renowned beauty of Mrs Thornton and the large side bet which her husband (though there might be some suspicions that the 'Mrs' was a courtesy title) had made with her opponent. Colonel Thomas Thornton, bon viveur, athlete, crack shot, racing man, dog and horse breeder and art collector, was as colourful a character as his lady, and was to claim later that the bet was purely nominal, to 'excite the more curious and bring a fuller attendance at the race.' This could well have been so since at the time York was seeking every means to bring back the crowds that had been lost with the ending of the public hangings on the course on the mornings of its races. The advertising certainly succeeded. Alicia Thornton was a well-known beauty, 'an absolute cracker,' in the words of one recent racing historian. She was a striking sight on the course, mounted on her husband's Vinagrillo. Her jacket was leopard coloured, with blue sleeves and cap, with a buff skirt enveloping her side saddle. Flint had stipulated that she should ride on his left, so inhibiting her use of the whip, but for most of the race she managed to nose ahead – her '*close-seated* riding astonished the beholders, and inspired a general confidence in her success.' After three miles, however, her saddle girth slipped and she could not keep up the pace. The disputes that followed her defeat provoked almost as much interest as the race itself. Captain Flint refused a re-run. The Colonel refused to pay the 1,000 guineas side bet. At the next York meeting the Captain horse-whipped him and the Colonel in turn took him to court – and won.[16]

More to the present theme of female sporting accomplishment, Alicia Thornton's riding prompted both admiration and wonder that she could go so well riding side-saddle. At the same time, as well as all the admiration, there was some tongue in cheek comment about the inducement she gave to women to break their chains, emulate their menfolk, become the talk of all Europe, and be 'personated at Bartholomew Fair and Sadler's Wells.' The same correspondent, though, also suggested that riding side-saddle could be abolished as he had 'been assured by an eminent breeches-maker'(!) that 'by means of a simple contrivance, he could remove all objections to a lady's sitting astride,'[17] one of the more intriguing cryptic comments of an age which, for all its coarseness and scurrility, often failed to call a spade a spade and could never even describe a low blow to a pugilist's genitals for what it was.

With all its disadvantage, riding side-saddle did not prevent Mrs Thornton from later beating no less a rider than Frank Buckle, this time in a much less publicised race, and where she did benefit from a considerable weight advantage. In fact, some ladies of the day who rode to hounds did follow the example of Marie Antoinette and rode astride. It was the rare sight of a woman – and such a woman – riding in a formal race that had aroused so much interest, though even this was no complete novelty, particularly it seems in the north-east. Newcastle in 1725 and Ripon in 1734 had both seen individual women's races, that at Ripon for a prize given by Mrs Aislabie, the wife of a prominent citizen, and to the subsequent outrage of the local reporter who described how 'nine of the sex rode astride, dressed in drawers and waistcoats, and jockey caps, their shapes transparent'. It was his opinion that 'the lady benefactress to this indecent diversion should have made the tenth.'[18]

Incidentally, such a large field, by the standards of the day, indicates that the event must have been popular with competitors, and doubtless, to judge from attitudes towards smock races, with many of the male spectators but thereafter ladies' riding skills came to be exercised almost entirely on the hunting field. Here again the style had been set earlier in the century by Princess Amelia, daughter of George II, who was such a devoted follower of staghounds that she would even turn up in church in her riding habit, her dog tucked under her arm. Ladies did become a not uncommon sight on the hunting field, some of them acquiring considerable reputations. The Countess of Derby, for instance, was said in 1814 to have 'become one of the most dashing female riders in the kingdom, while the 'Lady S—' who was said not merely to follow the hounds but actually to go *with* them is readily identifiable as the first Marchioness of Salisbury who was still hunting in her eighties, in her last years strapped on to her horse![19]

Beyond those involving horses, however, the active sporting opportunities open to gentlefolk were limited. Class lines formed firmer barriers for them than they did for men. They could not frequent the pugilistic tavern, mingle with the miscellaneous company on the floor of the Fives Court or make their wagers at Tattersalls. Many ladies, though, would undoubtedly be happy to be quite unenergetic. In Jane Austen's novels they seldom bestir themselves outdoors for anything more vigorous that a gentle walk and there are frequent contemporary references to feminine idleness and frivolity.[20] There is also, of course, the question of definition. Who was to be considered a lady and what sports she might indulge in, was more a matter of impression and convention than of exact delineation. Females, for instance, certainly boxed, but there are no signs at all that gentlewomen ever did, with or without mufflers, or even in mock play. Women played cricket and there are occasional matches involving ladies such as the extrovert Countess of Derby, but competitive female cricket seems to have been between village girls. There was doubtless too some bowls playing for amusement by ladies in the gardens of English manor houses and the new large rectories, as there is known to have been in Scotland, while sailing was acceptable as we know from the experience of the unfortunate Mr Foote's sister whose voluminous dress kept her afloat while he drowned after their boat capsized on the Thames. Rowing, though, except of the most leisurely kind, would hardly be thought suitable. Foot racing, too, was exclusively a lower class sport so far as women were concerned. Where the competitors or winners are known it is, with few exceptions, by their Christian names only, or even by a nickname.[21]

There are areas where class lines may become blurred. Women running gambling tables, fetchingly attired, at sporting gatherings, or those dancing on stilts at Ascot might well be granted that same precarious genteel status nominally afforded to actresses. When Harry Angelo introduced John Jackson and pugilism into his fencing academy he did not recommend fisticuffs to the ladies, but did encourage them to take up swordplay, asserting that the benefits of fencing exercises were as valid for them as for their gentlemen, but apart from the eccentric Duchess of Queensberry those who did take instruction appear to have been actresses. There are indications of gentility about lady ice skaters, who quite often caught attention. There was the alluring 'trio of Graces' on the frozen canal in St James's Park, splendid visions in their scarlet pellises, who 'performed their mazy movements with so much elegance, taste and precision, as to excite universal admiration.'[22] Ladies also took to the water, though to what extent this was as swimmers and not merely as bathers is uncertain. From the mid-eighteenth century bathing facilities such as Mr Perrot's at Norwich were stressing their suitability for ladies as well as gentlemen. The Golden Lion at Lyme Regis, all through the summer of 1804, was advertising 'sands and bathing equal to any on the coast; with good bathing machines and a hot sea bath,' and there certainly were ladies who did more than bathe. One was reported in the following summer to have made an appearance 'at one of our fashionable watering places in the character of a *Naiad*,' and to have won so much admiration for her skill as to become known as 'the *Diving Belle*,' this obviously being another of her talents.[23]

Reports of this sort, concentrating on the athletic abilities of women performers rather than their appearance, are relatively rare. Published accounts are invariably written by men and presumably with a predominantly male readership in mind. The mere sight of the physical outline of anyone with pretensions to ladyhood invited comment, of admiration or distaste, serious or frivolous, real or hypocritical. Even new fashions could excite such responses. In the late 1790s, when they were showing the natural shape of the body, it was said, 'as if there were no covering at all,' and the habit of lifting petticoats when walking revealed much of the shape of the lady's limbs, particularly 'to the footman who walks *after* her in the street.' With so much prurient curiosity in the air, [24] the special sight of a lady suitably attired for skating or swimming could scarcely be expected to pass without comment, but there was one rare sporting activity which left no room for revelation or breaches of decorum, and one that, on its distaff side, was very strictly confined to lady players. This was archery, the first of those polite pursuits which, with croquet, badminton and lawn tennis later, combined increasingly energetic play with the company of the opposite sex, socially at first and then in actual competition. These pursuits were to provide the avenue into the full blown sporting activity which eventually the whole sex would be able to enjoy. Looking back in the early 1830s to the quite sudden revival of archery forty years earlier, Pierce Egan stressed its suitability for women as well as men and although this view was not universally shared, archery clubs did indeed provide for the lady all the social attractions of the race meeting and the hunt with the opportunity for more personal involvement, for exercise and for competition. At the great meeting of archery clubs at Blackheath in 1792 the ladies appear to have been just spectators though they made a great impression.[25] At home in their clubs they shot with their own bows, at their own targets and for their own prizes, and as winners they might sometimes enjoy national publicity. In some clubs such contests could be quite frequent.[26] It was from the start an exclusive upper class sport, aggressively amateur, rejecting any notion of gambling, having its own strict ordering and respectable enough for both clergymen and ladies to indulge in without shame or slur. It was certainly only a very select handful of ladies, but it was pointing one way to their sex's sporting future, however distant that was to be.

While the ladies of the mansion and the country house were setting off on the long road to sporting acceptability their sisters of the streets and fields had their own very different sporting lives, looking both back to inherited communal celebrations and folk play and also forward, into some of the emergent organised sports of the male world. Their role in traditional play was mainly as spectators, but that itself could be important. The athletic performances of young bachelors were of great practical interest to watching maidens. Among the more favoured classes a promising inheritance, a family name and a good income could do much to compensate for any physical shortcomings a male suitor might display. In the country at large, though, a healthy physique and the stamina and courage that a youth might show in the local sports were all-important. The pairing function was also served in the opposite direction by women's foot races, and much was made of both in contemporary comments.[27] The young men would sometimes eye their prospective partners with the anxiety described by John Clare in his poem 'The Village Minstrel,' where his hero agonises

To see his love lag hindmost in the throng,
And of unfairness in her cause complains;
And swears and fights the jarring chaps among,
As in her part he'd die, b'fore his lass should wrong.

Whether Clare's Hodge was successful in his intervention on his sweetheart's behalf we do not know, but what is certain is that the distinction between player and spectator in folk play was far from absolute and there must have been many other interventions, both male and female – the sly trip of the footracer or the footballer, and even the occasional unladylike push at the edge of a scrimmage.[28]

The activities in which women took part tended to be seasonal, still tied to specific occasions in the calendar. May Day was firmly associated with games that brought the two sexes together. Shrovetide and Lenten games played by women included shuttlecock and battledore, marbles and skipping, whip and top, stoolball, trundling hoops and barley break, this latter being a form of outdoor hide and seek, a type of activity more commonly found in May Day sports.[29] Further down the line – and only doubtfully included among 'sports' even by eighteenth century standards – were the various heaving practices still existing in some parts, holding women spreadeagled by the arms and legs and throwing them in the air.[30] Women's play also tended to retain more pronounced and more persistent ritualistic features than those of the men. One such was an exactness over the number of participants, and with an emphasis on multiples of the magic number of three. The rare English instance of a female football match, from Kent in 1747, and apparently traditional, was between two sides of six. There were, too, twelve old ladies playing trapball in Suffolk, but by far the most frequent number stipulations occur in smock races, which are also the most commonly reported female athletic events from the period, catching the attention of poets and painters, reporters and moralists, sponsors and spectators alike.[31]

Of undoubtedly ancient origin, and still retaining strong ritualistic elements, the smock race had also often assumed some of the commercial

The smock race as part of the pastoral idyll.

features of more recent times and was poised interestingly between the old sporting world and the new. Smock racing was widespread, recorded from all over the country. Most races were part of a programme of sporting events at wakes, fetes or fairs. Some were one-off competitions, either traditional to some calendar occasion or mounted as an additional attraction at some other event. There is good mid-eighteenth century evidence of both styles – from celebrations in Kent in the 1740s, for example, and from several cricket matches.[32] Particularly where there was a commercial promoter he was likely to protect himself against loss by adapting the turf practice of stipulating that a minimum number had to start for the prize to be offered. The minimum number was almost invariably the ritualistic three.[33]

The competitors themselves were often defined by status, age, and even by character. There are some examples of married women competing against the unmarried but this was unusual. Where it did happen, in Kent in 1748, three against three, it was not strictly a smock race since the prizes were half a pound of tea and half a pound of sugar to each of the winning party. The runners were usually described as 'maids,' 'maidens,' or just 'young women,' and the common assumption was that they would be unmarried. Age limits would usually be set in any range between 15 and 30.[34] At one early smock race, at a Clapham Common cricket match in 1700, the prize garment, 'a fine Flanders lac'd smock,' had been valued at £4, but few subsequently came anywhere near that value, most being quoted as worth between half a guinea and fifteen shillings. As an additional enticement the smock would sometimes, as at Sandgate and in the New Forest, be described as decorated with blue ribands, ribands alone sometimes figuring as a second prize.[35] Among the least advertised or reported features of the many smock races that took place were the distances run or the names of the winners. Most of the firm evidence on the former comes from earlier in the eighteenth century, where the distances quoted are between 135 and 220 yards and are often stated in the old measure of 'rods' (i.e. 135 yards is 30 rods of 4° yards each.)[36] The impression from on the evidence from somewhat later races, is that distances may well have lengthened – that in the New Forest race in 1822, for instance, was a half mile contest and there are other similar cases. The women racers, too, remain largely anonymous. Only a few are recorded, such as the runners at the Walworth cricket, Folkestone Bess who won at Sandgate in 1799 – and Mary Britt, who was disqualified there![37]

The smock race was clearly of ancient origin and still often retained vestiges of its old communal and even pagan functions, even when it was taken up by a commercial sponsor. Distantly it may well have had significance as a fertility ritual, a means of choosing the Summer Queen who would bring fruitfulness to the land and the beasts of the field. There were such echoes still in the stresses on both nubility and purity in the contestants. Maidenhead was in the habit of advertising its sports with mock-serious announcements, but there could be truth in jest when it required contestants to be 'under 20 years of age, handsome in person, and chaste in principle'.[38] A tradition still has some residual force if it is worth laughing at. Even races that were part of commercially sponsored sports often called for ladies of 'good character' or 'reputed maids,' and there was at least one warning, from Hayes in 1804, that none will be 'permitted to enter the prize lists who may appear to have drank too freely of strong waters.' The morality ban was, indeed, sometimes applied, as the sad example of poor shamed Mary Britt at Sandgate shows and there was also a frequent exclusion of previous winners. This could be no more than a carry over from the practice of the racecourse, barring previous winners, but is likely, from its early appearance, to be a further echo of folk origins and the need to provide a fresh symbolic queen of the summer for each new season. The banning of the impure and the past winners was long enduring, through into the nineteenth century. The smock, too, was always white, the colour of purity and innocence, and if it was decorated with ribbons, these in turn would always be blue, by way of a Christian overlay, blue being the colour associated with the Virgin Mary. Some anthropologists have even seen the smock itself as a symbol of fertility, while the high pole on which it was customarily displayed before the race carried phallic reminders of its maypole predecessors.[39] If many such elements pointed to a distant origin for smock racing, its durability must also have owed much to its communal usefulness in fostering the pairing of the sexes. The linkage was sometimes made symbolically specific, with the men's race in effect twinned with that of the women, the hat that was to be the male prize also being hoisted on its own high pole.[40] Once into the new century, however, the smock race began to lose its popularity. Throughout the period it had been undergoing transitions of one sort or another and any lay or clerical patronage that it had originally enjoyed was early in decline. By the time of the 1814 Peace Games at Sturminster Newton the smock race and other events were subscribed for by 'the respectable inhabitants' and the same celebrations at Soham moved a step further still into the bureaucratic world, being managed by a committee, meeting in the local schoolroom. More significant was their exploitation, by innkeepers such as the landlord of the George Inn with his clear interest in the Hayes Fair, by the recruiting authorities or the master butchers in St James's Market in 1803 and apparently for their own personal delectation.[41] This latter, like many others by this time, was being run in heats, probably, as with horse races, to give the spectators more for their money. Prizes, too, were no longer invariably a smock or confined to one trophy alone. There could be money prizes or other rewards such as cambric for an apron, silk stockings, cooking utensils or even foodstuffs. Nor were they usually confined to just 'damsels of the village,' as they had sometimes been described, and could sometimes attract female runners with wider reputations.[42]

If there were reputations to be made in smock racing there were also reputations to be lost. The competitors had traditionally been lightly clothed and this gave rise to comments that ranged from the pastoral approbation of poets to the voyeuristic observations of a male orientated press and the disgusted protests of moral reformers. There is the rare suggestion of a woman's race actually run 'stark naked' near London in 1748 but this was certainly not a common practice. Even instances of running bare-breasted, as at the Walworth cricket match in the 1740s, were always rare and by later in the century the competitors always seem to have been covered. At the 1809 Maker Games in Cornwall, for instance, the women were 'to run in shifts.' Nevertheless reporters always had their well salted comments to hand – the racers 'exposed with their wonted generosity those beauties which are best imagined than described,' or elsewhere, reference to 'the *naked truth* of the *game*, and so on.[43] Such remarks make it clear that for many the attractions of smock races were far from solely athletic, and this was not lost upon their moralising critics.

The races provided a pointed target in the growing attacks on wakes and fairs for their encouragement of immorality, and, indeed, for their echoes of primitivism at best and paganism at worst. The preacher George Whitfield advised fellow methodists to 'desist from these anti-Christian recreations' and in the well reported court case brought against the organisers of the Plaistow Whitsuntide sports in 1810 one of the prosecution's main thrusts was against the smock race, 'the last of amusements for any man to recommend to the females of his household, if he at all regarded their morals.' They were 'disgraceful exhibitions' and 'the last example I should wish to hold out for the improvement of female delicacy, propriety and decorum.' For all this tirade, though, it eventually emerged that the women had been substantially better covered than in the traditional chemise, that they were, in fact, dressed as they would be 'when engaged in the labours of the field.'[44]

The Plaistow attack might have failed but it was symptomatic of the declining support for smock races among the more sensitive classes and there is other evidence, from comments on the Cotswold Games, that their appeal was narrowing. By 1813 even that ardent (if odd) supporter of old English sports, J. J. Brayfield, quite ignored smock racing in his recommendations for improving the national character and making 'tenants and dependants brave and good subjects.' All he had to offer the women were 'little prizes' for maidens who 'excelled in a jig or a hornpipe.'[45] The history of the smock race in the nineteenth century is, indeed, one of diminution and fairly rapid disappearance, at least in its traditional forms. At Hebden Bridge in Yorkshire the annual men's race ended around 1820 and the women's race was said to have been discontinued some years before. In Northumberland, where they had once been common, there was only one smock race said to be remaining by 1825. It is more than probable that they lost their appeal to the competitors themselves. There were fewer and fewer parts of the country where the rustic idyll they represented came anywhere near to reality.[46] With better communications and more people living in larger communities the old pairing function of events was becoming redundant, while more and more women were achieving the added independence of paid employment, at least one fifth of them in the first half of the nineteenth century. Much of their work was not conducive to the sustaining of pastoral nostalgia and there is little wonder that smock races disappeared particularly early in many industrial areas. A Holland smock, moreover, was hardly the prize for the new modern woman. Where races did survive it was usually with some more substantial reward in view.

Female pedestrianism, as a parallel sport to the men's, belongs essentially to the later nineteenth century. In pre-Victorian days they had made little impact on the sport and evidence of wagers involving women athletes is sparse. The one event to arouse notable public interest was the two mile race along the Mile End Road in 1806, in spite of the fact that it took place at 5 o'clock on a Sunday morning. A forty six year old jewess named Mordecai took on a man over twenty years her junior, one Mark Levy, at five guineas a side. A large crowd turned out and the betting was heavy, at 2 to 1 on the man, but it was the woman who won. In the time-honoured phrase of the age, 'the knowing ones were taken in.'[47] Money, in fact, was just as likely to be at stake in women's competitions as in men's – they were beginning on occasions to row for money prizes in the 1790s, a practice that gathered momentum as the number of regattas multiplied during the next quarter century. During their particular growth in the 1820s ladies were not only decorative spectators but there were regular races for women rowers. Four-oared gigs were the favourite boats. There was a lengthy women's race for a five sovereigns prize at Saltash in 1824 when the seriousness of the event may be gathered from that it was, in well established male fashion, re-rowed after protests. Three years later the women's race at Southampton was reported as 'the best part of the whole regatta' and by the end of the period women's races were taking place at many west country venues including Plymouth, Devonport, Torquay and Poole.[48]

Gambling was also a feature of women's cricket. It was quite a common game in the south-east of the country from the mid-eighteenth century onwards, after the first recorded match in 1745 between eleven maids of Bramley and eleven from the nearby Hampshire village of later fame, Hambledon. Stake money was highly conspicuous in the gentry backed match between eleven women of Surrey and eleven of Hampshire in 1811 and made for 500 guineas a side. There could also be some active upper class participation, but it seems to have been essentially a country game, played by the female counterparts of the men in the local village teams. One 1775 report, in fact, spoke of women jealous of the sporting fame won by the men and wanting to emulate them, seeking their 'share of the public applause,' but in this instance their intended contest with another Kent village was rained off. One women's match during a Lincolnshire feast week in 1792 was described as 'a very curious game of cricket,' though the only curiosity about the game itself seems to have been that it was won by the girls of Rotherby, which was no more than a mere hamlet.[49] Some other games had an air of greater organisation about them, such as that recalled by Pierce Egan from the early 1800s in front of 3,000 spectators, with distinctive uniforms for the players, a harmonious day which concluded with the players taking tea and coffee together in the local hostelry's largest room. Here was the female version of cricket's serene bucolic idyll, though it was not always so innocently welcomed. A particularly outraged press attack on the women who 'so far forget themselves' as to play cricket at Sileby Feast in 1833 may have been prompted as much by the effects of drink on the women as by their actual cricket playing, and in any event could well reflect the tightening restraints on women's activities as the period drew to close.[50]

Similar disapproval was by then widely directed towards female pugilism. How common more or less formal fist fights between women had been since the advent of pugilism itself is not easy to estimate. Little more than a dozen actual contests have come to light after the 1770s but it seems to have been accepted as a relatively normal activity. There was a well-established tradition of combat sports involving women, from the old cudgel or singlestick bouts between husband and wife teams, a feature of Figg's amphitheatre, where fights were also mounted between well-known female fighters such as 'the City Championess' and 'the Hibernian Heroine.' Perhaps the final indication of the 'normality' of female boxing lies in the way it was reported not as unduly sensational, and seldom as a gratuitous opportunity to watch relatively undressed women, but as a sport in which the athletic effort was worth description.[51]

Impromptu fights between women, arising out of quarrels, must have been commonplace but recorded contests invariably show greater or less degree of organisation and formality and are often premeditated, taking place at pre-arranged times, and for wagers. These could range from the 'considerable' sum fought for by 'two Amazonian Milk-women' on a Sunday morning in 1775 to the quart of gin in a battle at Newport Market in 1807. They drew in the crowds – 'a vast concourse' for Mary Ann Fielding against 'a noted Jewess' (implying an existing pugilistic reputation?) in 1795 and four hundred *women* at a fight near Bristol, one of the few reported from outside London, but from an area, of course, with strong boxing traditions. As with male fights, much betting took place and there was the usual support from seconds and bottle holders (sometimes the husbands), again in accordance with the practice of the male prize ring. Women fighters sometimes chose seconds from their own sex and some themselves acted as seconds to their husbands. The most notable seconds in a women's fight were Tom Johnson, for Mary Ann Fielding, and Daniel Mendoza, for the Jewess, in the fight where the latter suffered over seventy knock-downs, but where each was commended for 'exhibiting many manoeuvres relative to the art of boxing.'[52]

The earlier women pugilists seem to have been well covered, typically in a 'close jacket,' short petticoat, Holland drawers, white stockings and pumps. Later, and possibly at least partly in response to a general loosening of dress styles, they seem to have become less reticent. The Chelmsford boxers were reported as 'being stripped, without caps, and their hair closely tied up' before their particular 'desperate conflict,' lasting 45 minutes. The fighters usually 'disencumbered themselves of most of their habiliments and shook hands,' and there is the possibility that a particularly formal bout in June 1807 at West Grinstead – a well-known location for great male fights at the time – was fought bare breasted. Here there was 'a well-kept ring of very large dimensions,' and twenty-four 'sharp' rounds were fought before the younger, 'an active damsel of twenty-four,' beat an older looking woman with a knock-down blow. The 'amateurs' present nonetheless applauded the loser for displaying 'great bottom,' and for her 'style of fighting.' Such a comment, treating female boxing as serious competition, contrasts with the skittish attitude of most male writers towards smock racing. They were 'heroic females,' for instance, who had a '*well-fought*' battle off the New Road, where everything was 'properly arranged' for the bout. Again, by contrast with the smock racers, quite a number of female fighters are known by name, such as the Bristol combatants, Charlotte York and Mary Jones.[53]

Reported fights would still take place spasmodically in the post-war decades – such as that between two women who had cut their hair for the occasion and fought twenty 'desperate' rounds in St George's Fields in 1822 – but women's boxing seems to have been at its most vigorous in the remarkable few years early in the nineteenth century. It had been in August 1804 that Lady Alicia Thornton had set the tone with her match at York Races. In 1805 there had been the highly unusual smock race organised in March by the Smithfield master butchers, in October the aquatic feats and appearance of the 'Diving Belle' were being celebrated and, in December, those of the lady skaters. In September 1806 there had been the rare instance of a woman athlete running against a man and beating him, and then, in 1807, there were the fights at East Grinstead and the Newport Market.[54] This amount of female sporting activity, both in its extent and its originality, goes well beyond anything so far found in any other short span of years.

What did lie behind what was undoubtedly a burst of women's sporting activity during these years? In April 1803, the *Sporting Magazine* had published an old letter from the late Duke of Dorset in which he praised the cricket match played by the athletic Countess of Derby and other ladies:

> Let your sex go on, and assert their right to every pursuit that does not debase the mind. Go on, and attach yourself to the athletic, and, by that, convince ... all Europe how worthy you are of being considered the wives of plain, generous, and native Englishmen.[55]

It was a message that was in tune with the needs of the time, a call which women were responding to in other directions in support of the war effort. The encouragement which it gave – and there would have been few to take offence at the national and gender chauvinism of its final note – could hardly fail to carry some weight. Equally, a single expressed opinion, however impeccable its source, could never account for what took place. That these were hectic, dangerous and fluctuating years in the country at large has already been noted, together with the various other sporting changes and excitements which particularly marked them. The sporting world as a whole seemed to rise to a new fever pitch of activity in 1807 with 'the spirit of pugilism now prevalent among the lower class of females,' the gambling houses rampant, the largest cock-fighting tournament ever held, the leading amateur athlete of the day racing against the leading professional, Gully fighting a great battle against Gregson and the Sportsman's Gallery opening in Bloomsbury. It was a mood which could well run across both sexes and all classes, but it seems to have been a mood which also passed quite speedily. There was perhaps some significance in the fact that the only hint of women's play in the *Sporting Magazine*'s first issue of 1808 was that Mrs Howe was playing chess daily with His Majesty.[56]

The part played by women in the sporting upheaval of these particular years certainly merits further examination.[57] So far as the broader view of female sport in the Georgian era is concerned there is a general impression of expansion and of relatively widespread female participation, both as spectators and performers. Certainly there was that variety in women's sporting opportunities which adds a note of caution to generalisations – differences between the social classes, differences of place and between town and country. The more privileged women folk were certainly having more sporting possibilities opened to them. The loss of their role as patroness of the local annual feast or other customary celebration was balanced by a new importance as sponsors on the raceground. They were also enjoying some limited extensions of their active sporting opportunities as gentlemen moved more and more of their own sports into the protective and selective ambience of the sporting club, so making some of them – and archery is the prime example – more accessible also to their ladies. If ladies of the period chose to become wedded to the virtues of domesticity they did so still from choice more than from any inflexible demands of society.

The sports of women of the labouring classes were both more diverse and also changing more rapidly. Even in rural England there were growing economic and cultural differences between those counties where landowners had to compete with nearby industry to retain labour, and those where, by contrast, more intensive farming was producing labour surpluses. Traditional women's competitions could appear increasingly irrelevant in one setting or a nostalgic reminder of more secure times in another. The same nostalgia could take traditional female play into towns, where it might appear in altered forms, or where, on the other hand, women were more likely to be drawn at least to the edges of some of the rougher sports. There were already at one extreme the pipe smoking pit-bank girls of the Black Country, calling for their pints, swearing and gaming alongside the men, and growing numbers like them. On the other hand, and poised between the two extremes were the women in the households of craftsmen, small farmers, better off artisans, tradesmen and the like, below the sporting ranks of the gentlefolk but cut off by social preference or religious principle from the pursuits of their somewhat less well off sisters. There are already signs of these restraints becoming more extensive – the nonconformist pressures against communal play in the interests of the fireside and the family, a growth in prudery which frowned on any display of the female form, the social requirements for respectability over one ever widening section of the population and the economic forces soon to be depressing the rest. For the most part, though, women's sport did survive and even enjoy modest prosperity to the end of the wartime period, even if there were the later signs that it would change more profoundly and, if anything, less positively even than that of the men.

Notes

1. *SM*, August 1804, p 227; May 1804, p 107; April 1813, p 17; April 1799, p 8.
2. *SM*, July 1795, p 224; August 1795, p 280; December 1794, p 164. The race was doubtless prevented by Lady Lade's pregnancy – see July 1795, p. 168.
3. *SM*, January 1796, p 215; October 1795, p 51.
4. For example see the regimes that the writer of children's books Mary Sherwood and the mathematician Mary Somerville were subjected to. F. J. Harvey Darton, *The Life of Mrs Sherwood*, 1910, p 34; Martha Somerville, *Personal Recollections of Mary Somerville*, 1873, p 22.
5. See *e.g.* Maria Gisborne, *An Enquiry into the Duties of the Female Sex*, 1797, p 76 and *passim*.
6. D. Gardiner, *English Girlhood at School*, 1929, pp 354, 343; Rev. John Bennett, *Letters to a Young Lady*, 1795, 2 vols., II, p 10; Mary Wollstonecraft, *A Vindication of the Rights of Women with Strictures on Political and Moral Subjects*, 1790, pp 34, 81, 251. A school at Dunster advertised itself as only half a mile from the sea-shore, 'where are several bathing machines kept.' *Sherborne Mercury*, 13 February 1809.
7. *SM*, June 1805, p 167. The spectators included the Duchesses of Devonshire and St Albans and Ladies Castlereagh, Charlemont and Heathcote.
8. Though Queen Anne was a bull-baiting enthusiast and there are mentions of dogs being tossed into ladies' laps by the goaded bull. L. Thomas, *Prying among private papers: Chiefly in the Seventeenth and Eighteenth Centuries*, New York, 1905, p 93; C. Hole, *English Sports and Pastimes*, 1949, p 28; W.

Howitt, *The Rural Life of England*, 1838, p 268; Boulton, *Amusements of Old London*, I, p 8

9. Young, *British Football*, p 45. See *e.g. SM*, May 1823, p 102.

10. *SM*, August 1813, p 240. A 'splendid breakfast' was served to 150 guests by Sir Charles Morgan, Bart., during a race between Brixham fishing smacks, September 1809, p 260, and for extravagant archery and hunting entertainment see February 1811, p 226, August 1799, p 229. For entertainment at regattas see August 1809, p 217 (Windermere); *Sherborne and Yeovil Mercury*, 21 September 1795; 4 August 1800 (Fowey.)

11. *Annual Register 1798*; *Hampshire Chronicle*, 18 July 1744; *SM*, July 1809, p 196; *Reading Mercury*, 1780, quoted in Goulstone, *Summer Solstice Games*, p 93.

12. *Reading Mercury*, 22 July 1776; *Bath Chronicle*, 22 July 1800; *SM*, September 1808, p 283. For examples of cricket grandstands see *Kentish Weekly Post*, 13, 27 July 1773; *Public Advertiser*, 10 September 1773;

13. *SM*, November 1831; June 1824, p 186. See also G. E. Lanning, 'Horse Racing in Dorset,' Langford, ed., *Dorset Year Book 1988*, pp 12-18.

14. *Dorchester County Chronicle*, 15 September 1836; *Racing Calendar 1797*, p 104; *SM*, April 1795, p 38. Similarly alluring ladies were frequent at meetings, *e.g.* at Worcester. *Aris's Birmingham Gazette*, 24 August 1829.

15. *Racing Calendar* 1797, pp 73, 86 and *passim*; Colley, *Britons*, p 261.

16. *SM*, November 1805, p 57; Tyrrel, *Racecourses*, pp 80/81; *SM*, August 1804, p 227; November 1805, pp 57/8; March 1806, p 298.

17. 'It is difficult to say whether her horse-manship, her dress, or her beauty were most admired, the tout-ensemble was unique.' Egan, *Book of Sports*, p 131; SM, August 1804, pp 281/2.

18. Tyrrel, *Racecourses*, pp 82, 70. See also *Newcastle Courant*, 28 August 1725;

19. Fulford, *George the Fourth*, p 14; *SM*, November 1814, p 94; December 1799, p 153; John Timpson, *Timpson's English Eccentrics*, Norwich 1991, p 146.

20. See *e.g. Times*, 2 July 1787.

21. Strutt, *Sports and Pastimes*, p 103; Robert Scott Fittis, *Sports and Pastimes of Scotland*, Paisley, 1891, pp 200/1; Goulstone, *Summer Solstice Games*, p 28.

22. Laird, *Royal Ascot*, p 44; Hearl, 'Polite Accomplishments,' McNair and Parry, *eds.*, *Readings in the History of Physical Education*, p 61; *SM*, December 1805, p 159; P. H. Dorrell, 'Early Nineteenth Century Skating in the Fens,' *Sports History*, 6. 1985, p 24, where they were 'in plaid vests and drawers trimmed with sable, and a cap of the same materials, surmounted by a plume of black feathers.'

23. *Norwich Mercury*, 10 May 1746; *Western Flying Post*, 9 July 1804 and subsequent insertions; *SM*, October 1805, p 48.

24. *SM*, October 1798, pp 3/4.

25. Egan, *Book of Sports*, pp 243/4. See also *SM*, April 1793, p 59; May 1793, p 70. For objections to female archery (they would be better 'playing on the harp, or dancing a minuet') see December 1819, p 110.

26. See *e.g. SM*, August 1815, p 200 (the Misses Boultbee and Phillimore taking the ladies' prizes at the Woodmen of Arden's summer meeting); June 1794, p 206.

27. Parkyns, *The Wrestler*, p 20. See Malcolmson, *Popular Recreations*, ch. 4, 'Social Contexts,' pp 53-55 and *passim*.

28. Theo Arthur, 'The Derby Game,' William Andrew, *ed.*, *Bygone Derbyshire*, Derby, Hull and London, 1892, p 219.

29. Wright, *Calendar Customs*, I, pp 28, 36; Dyer, *British Popular Customs*, p 86. See also e.g. William Smith. *Morley: Ancient and Modern*, 1866, p 142.

30. See Fittis, *Sports and Pastimes of Scotland*, p 164; Hone, *Every-Day Book*, 1826, pp 260, 223-225; Wright, *Calendar Customs*, I, pp 34/5, 107/8; William Howitt, *The Rural Life of England*, pp 180/1; Brand, *Popular Antiquities*, pp 97/8.

31. *Sports History,*.7, 1985, p 9; *Kentish Post*, 22 July 1747. See Goulstone, *Summer Solstice Games*, p 54.

32. Much detail on women's racing is in Goulstone, *Summer Solstice Games*, ch 3, 'Smock Racing,' pp 32 ff. Surprisingly it has only three very brief passing references from Malcolmson. The best known of those at cricket matches is that between 'The Little Bit of Blue (the handsome Broom Girl)' and Black Bess of the Mint at Walworth Common. *Penny London Morning Advertiser*, 11 June 1744.

33. e.g, at Thrale, Berkshire. *Reading Mercury*, 4 July 1757.

34. *Kentish Post*, 23 July 1745 (and just, quite incidentally, as Charles Edward Stuart was dropping anchor off Erisca); Boulton, *Amusements of Old London*, II, p 235; Goulstone, *Summer Solstice Games*, p 17

35. *e.g.*, at Theale half a guinea and at Sandwich 16s.0d. in 1750 but down to 15s.0d. three years later. See *Reading Mercury*, 4 July 1757; *Kentish Post*, 20 July 1750, 4 July 1753; Goulstone, *Summer Solstice Games*; *BLL*, 13 March 1822.

36. See advertisements and press reports in Goulstone, *Summer Solstice Games*, pp 16, 23, 32, 53 and *passim.*, and *e.g.*, *Kentish Post*, 8 June 1726, 20 July 1746.

37. *SM*, April 1813, p 20; *BLL*, 31 March 1822; *SM*, April 1799, p 25.

38. *Kentish Post*, 21 June 1750; 4 July 1753; *Sports History*, 7, 1985, p 12.

39. *Kentish Notebook*, 1889, in *Sports History*, 4, 1984, p 19; 7, 1986, p 12. See *e.g.*, J. G. Frazer, *The Golden Bough*, 1935/6 edition, pp 56/7. Mary Britt's disqualification may well have been over doubts as to her maidenly status. *SM*, April 1799, p 25.

40. Goulstone, *Summer Solstice Games*, p 35 and passim.

41. Brown, *ed.*, *Dorset Folklore* by William Barnes, p 8; *Sports History*, 9, 1986, p 5; 4, 1984, p 19; Boulton, *Amusements of Old London*, II, pp 235/6; *SM*, March 1805, p 304

42. *Reading Mercury*, 12 June 1775; Goulstone, *Summer Solstice Games*, p 32 and passim. A coming of age celebration in Somerset sought to attract 'the most light-heeled damsels' from that and 'the three neighbouring counties.' *SM*, May 1811, p 99.

43. Goulstone, *Summer Solstice Games*, pp 22, 70; *Sherborne Mercury*, 8 June 1809; *SM*, April 1813, p 20 (where another Tothill Fields smock race is also reported): March 1805, p 346.

44. Christopher Whitfield, *Robert Dover and the Cotswold Games: Annalia Dubrensia*, London, 1962, pp 68/9; *SM*, July 1810, pp 167, 192; August 1810, pp 209-14; September 1810, p 263; October 1810, p 18.

45. Whitfield, *Cotswold Games*, p 69; *SM*, April 1813, pp 29/30.

46. Goulstone, *Summer Solstice Games*, pp 34, 22; Brand, *Popular Antiquities*, p 234. Not even milkmaids lived a life of rural innocence and their unseemly

behaviour in London parks was being complained of from the 1760's onwards. Dorothy George, 'London and the Life of the Town,' A. S. Turbeville, *ed.*, *Johnson's England*, 2 vols., Oxford 1933, I, p 183.

47. *SM*, September 1806, p 269. For earlier female pedestrians see *SM*, October 1792, p 13; August 1795, p 280.

48. *SM*, September 1828, p 386; M. Wright, 'Women's Rowing Matches in 19th Century Regattas,' *Sports History*, 4, pp 14-16.

49. See Netta Rheinberg, 'Women's Cricket,' Swanton, *ed.*, *World of Cricket*, p 1132; *Morning Chronicle*, 7 July 1775; *SM*, December 1792, p 170.

50. Egan, *Book of Sports*, pp 346/7; *Nottingham Courier*, 4 October 1833.

51. See Boulton, *Amusements of Old London*, I, pp 30/1; II, pp 234/5.

52. Whitaker, *Eighteenth Century Sunday*, p 144; *SM*, October 1807, p 42; July 1795, p 225; *Pancratia*, p 113; *SM*, August 1793, p 316.

53. *SM*, June 1807, pp 149/50; *Pancratia*, p 120; *SM*, July 1813, p 195. See also February 1807, p 251.

54. *SM*, April 1822, p 53; February 1807, p 251.

55. *SM*, April 1803, pp 13/14.

56. *SM*, January 1808, p 205.

57. Possibly on the lines of Dennis Brailsford, '1787: An Eighteenth Century Sporting Year,' *Research Quarterly for Exercise and Sport*, vol 55, no.3, 1984, though this itself is now in need of considerable infilling and updating in the light of more recent research.

8.
The Clubs and the Rules

This was the age when sport first became a matter of institutions and systems almost as much as of people. Those who made up the sporting world, the patrons, promoters, players and spectators, were all in their different ways seeking more regular and reliable play and seeking a continuity which could depend upon something more secure than custom and oral tradition. How and how far they escaped from the limits of the past varied from one sport to another but in all clearer statements of rules emerged and formal associations were established. Nor was it mere coincidence that the two should appear together. Each needed the other to give cohesion to increasingly complex activities which had outgrown informal and unwritten practices. It was from the clubs that, in large measure, the promulgation and interpretation of the rules for play derived. They had been comparative rarities before the last quarter of the eighteenth century, with the Jockey Club, Hambledon and the White Conduit Club as the most notable national examples and cricket the only sport to have any number of local clubs and societies. By 1820, by contrast, hunting, coursing, sailing and archery were all centred around associations of one sort or another, and in several instances one club, such as the Jockey Club or the MCC, was being increasingly acknowledged as the leading authority in its sport.

The fact that one of the earliest activities to attract a substantial following was a team game gave much initial impetus to the club system. Players needed to come together and some mutual organisation could smooth their arrangements. They would first assure themselves of the rules of play, practise, play among themselves, then issue challenges, and play matches.[2] They adopted means of identification which might at first be no more than coloured ribbons, but soon become more and more elaborate. They became a badge of membership and often the sign of another feature of the sporting club – its tendency to social exclusivity. While there was no inevitability about this process clubs did both reflect and often reinforce the steady hardening of existing divisions and distinctions between people both inside and outside sport.

The Jockey Club had been aristocratic from the start, even if its membership was an aristocracy of wealth as well as of breeding – at the turn of the century some half of its members with listed colours had titles. After the death in 1727 of the rough-shod and autocratic Tregonwell Frampton, clothed in his splendidly titled authority as Keeper of the Running Horses for the crown,[1] the absence of royal interest in the sport from the first two Georges gave the racing nobility their opportunity to take up the reins themselves and gradually build up their own organisation. By the 1770s, with Sir Charles Bunbury now at the helm, they had pronounced on the weighing in of riders, the overnight declaration of intent when a horse was entered for two races, and the growing complexity of weight for age allowances designed to give closer competition. A comprehensive resolution of 1770 set out what amounted to a whole scheme of management for Newmarket. Three stewards from among the members were given wide executive powers, including that of determining, along with a referee appointed by each party, any disputes.[2] From then onwards the Jockey Club steadily extended its authority, and never more decisively than when it warned off the Prince of Wales's jockey. Its widening influence on racing as a whole – which, it never seems to have sought with any vigour – was encouraged by the participation of members in local meetings, the publication of its orders and decisions and by the growing readiness of disputants from other courses to refer to it as a final court of appeal.

The Jockey Club was to provide the first institutional model for a national sports organising body, even if it did so unintentionally. The club system, though, was rarely reproduced in horse racing at the local level where meetings were usually run by a race committee which might be little more than an *ad hoc* arrangement with a membership (and indeed often an existence) that was transient. Some hunt clubs, tending to have greater permanence, did begin to mount their own races but the only conspicuous actual *race* club was the Bibury Club, and that confined its races to invited members of the Jockey Club.[3] Cricket, by contrast, depended on local clubs to bring players together and to keep them together, and not just for a one-off annual event but for a series of matches. Like horse racing it did exist on two levels, the national and the local, but the two were never as distinct from one another as they were in the early days of the turf. The Hambledon Club, in particular, was a remarkable coalition between national and local interests in the game.

By the 1770s cricket teams usually had some more or less formal organisation and a regular meeting place, nearly always a tavern. The association could be close and public houses would sometimes even give the teams their names. The Cambridge Town team was evidently drawn from the best players in its tavern clubs.[4] The fact of a common meeting place for cricket clubs does not, of itself, provide much indication as to their make-up, given the tavern's capacity to cater across the social classes. From the financial information from some early clubs the picture that emerges is one of considerable diversity, with entrance fees ranging from one shilling to £1, costs from one penny a game to a £2 annual subscription and an annual dinner costing anything between one shilling and £4.[5] However the overall impression given by advertisements for players is that town clubs in particular sought to recruit from at least the middling classes – it was 'a select party of gentlemen' at Newcastle, 'the young gentlemen' of Pontefract playing those of Wakefield, and there were '11 gentlemen of Bath' in a match in 1798.[6] The evidence though is conflicting. The professionals who were brought into the bigger matches had learned their cricket almost invariably in village teams where the costs cannot have been too demanding, even though many came from the somewhat better paid craftsman class. Again, as the game spread into the manufacturing areas, it was the elite industrial worker who tended to play – miners in the West Midlands, lacemakers in Nottingham, cutlers in Sheffield, and so on.[7]

The evolution of any national authority for cricket was even less clear-cut than for horse racing. The game did though from the first have laws, which imply, consciously or not, universal application and not just rules designed originally solely for one venue. Moreover, through the experience of the Hambledon Club alone the game also inherited several significant features for the future of sport, and stretching far beyond cricket. In the first place the club owed its foundation largely to a group of old boys from a single school, Westminster, who came together sharing a common earlier sporting experience. This was also to be a telling route in the diffusion of several sports, particularly football, in the next century. As the original Hambledon membership increased it also widened its social range – more than half were commoners without titles of any sort.[8] It also firmly established the role of the paid players. The membership itself had its exclusivity marked by full dress uniforms of sky-blue coats, black velvet collars, and buttons inscribed 'C.C.' The professionals were more simply dressed, but on the field competition was equal.[9] Indeed, the most innovative playing feature of the club was the attention given to improving performance, through care-fully organised practices, where batsmen were limited to thirty runs each. This brought a raising of standards, keeping the Hambledon men together in the likelihood that they would find better sport within the club than outside it. Not that it could always be as clear-cut as that, however, as some active Hambledon members also continued to make matches on their own account away from the club itself.[10] It was the type of interaction between the club and the personal sponsor that was to continue into the next century even as the club more and more displaced the individual promoter.

The decline of Hambledon in the later 1780s is perhaps easier to account for than its earlier success, though it does have intriguing aspects. The circumstances that could attract both wealthy patrons and large crowds to a remote corner of Hampshire were bound to be transient. Patrons grew older. Local talent became scarce and so did local interest as players were recruited from more distant parts. There were other possibilities. The club was certainly raffish in tone, when its members were in their cups, and – with Tom Paine at a meeting in 1796 – had possibly become radical in its politics.[11] By then such politics were out of favour and cricketing interest had moved firmly to the London clubs, to the White Conduit and its successor in 1787, the Marylebone Cricket Club, rapidly being known as MCC. There was considerable continuity in membership through all three clubs and although one newspaper notice might have implied great exclusivity (noting that the White Conduit field was available for hire as 'the Noblemen's time' for the season was over[12]) a list of members, in fact, shows no great exclusivity. What is quite likely is that a handful of the old aristocratic patrons continued to book the ground for MCC matches – they certainly arranged many of its earlier contests and it was two of their number, Lord Winchelsea and the Duke of Richmond, who took the lead in persuading Thomas Lord to move to a new ground in Marylebone, providing the basis for the change of name of the club.[13]

The MCC came closer to being cricketing equivalent of the Jockey Club as the period ended. By the start of the nineteenth century many of the big London matches involved the club and it was at least tacitly being accepted as the game's law-making body. Soon it would be deciding on disputes, though cricket's arguments were always likely to be of a different order and call for more urgent decisions than those in horse racing or, for that matter, in pugilism, where they were generally by way of post-mortems on completed past events. Whether a man was out or not at cricket had to be determined at once for the game to proceed.[14] It was unlikely, in any event, that the cricketers would look to the Jockey Club for their model as there was – surprisingly in such a multi-sport age – very little overlap between the two sports. Few of the well-known cricketers were even subscribers to the *Racing Calendar*. Among the exceptions were Lord Winchelsea, as prominent on the turf as he was on the cricket field[15] and Harry Mellish, who, in spite of holding the record for the quickest gambling away of a vast inheritance and being no cricketer of any mark himself, did have the distinction of beating Beauclerk, the prime match-maker, when their two teams met at Lords for the 1,000 guineas a side match in 1807.[16] By contrast, many of pugilism's most prominent supporters were also involved in horse racing and virtually everybody of note mentioned among big fight spectators was a subscriber to the *Racing Calendar*.[17] Given the common interest it is not surprising that boxing's influential men should look to the turf for their model as a means of controlling and organising their sport.

The timing of the foundation of the Pugilistic Club, announced in 1813, owed, however, as much to the special circumstances of the day as to the general vogue for new clubs and societies. Boxing found itself suddenly in an unaccustomed position. In April, Tom Cribb announced his retirement after his long reign as champion and there was neither some obvious successor in waiting (such as John Gully had been) or two clear contenders to settle the issue between them (such as Humphries and Mendoza). Within weeks of Cribb's announcement came the report that 'A pugilistic amateur Club of seventy members, at around five guineas each, has been formed, to reward pugilists, defray subscription purposes, &c.' There was no mention of the championship, but the members must have seen themselves as having a decisive say in who should fight for the title. The avowed aims were to create 'a regular fund for the support of gymnastic exercises' (hence the frequent early references to it as the 'Gymnastic' Club), to provide purses, and to arrange and control fights. The club certainly did all these things from the start but its lack of either a more assertive agenda or a readiness to act promptly beyond these limited aims soon revealed its weakness.[18] Socially at least it was off to a good start, with nearly fifty members at the first annual dinner. Sir Henry Smith was in the chair and Lord Yarmouth spoke 'at some length on the national utility of the pugilistic art.' Soon, through its influential contacts, it was setting up safe sites near the capital, such as

Coursing among the sports elite at Swaffham. The next pair of grey-hounds to compete are being held back by an attendant.

Molesey Hurst, Bushey Wood and Bushey Park. By having its own stakes (marked, like the whips, with the club's insignia) and its own ropes, the club also regularised ring sizes and generally brought added uniformity to the sport.[19] It had, though, to depend considerably on the cooperation of the boxers themselves and in spite of the presence and authority of Jackson himself as secretary and master of ceremonies at its fights this was not always forthcoming. For all its members' fine uniforms – blue and buff coats, yellow waistcoats, and buttons engraved 'P.C.', an echo of Hambledon's 'C.C.' and the blue ribbons in the hats of the pugilists paid to keep order at its fights – it was tentative in its initial approaches to disputed results though it did for a few years have some impact as a promoter and organiser. It rarely exercised decisive authority. By 1820 only seven turned up for the annual dinner and the Pugilistic Club was formally dissolved in December 1825 after a fight riddled with more than the usual range of deviousness. An attempt at revival through the Fair Play Club in 1828 was virtually still-born when the proposed Ward v Byrne fight ended in total fiasco a few months later.[20]

Other sports to develop clubs with some claim to national standing were the Cumberland Society which, on the Thames at least, was clearly accepted as the court of appeal over disputes in prize races,[21] and in coursing the Swaffham Society, founded by the Earl of Orford in 1776, which, after its rules were quoted in full in the first issue of the Sporting Magazine became the model for the many other coursing clubs which followed rapidly upon it.[22] The presence, however, of a leading club enjoying national prestige left the autonomy of local associations quite intact. Only the Pugilistic Club had some positive notion of influencing the whole of its sport – and that failed.

It was in the local clubs that practice was regularised and skills improved. Hunt clubs speeded up the breeding of specialised fox hounds and new sports like sailing went ahead at pace as the specialised societies competed against each other, demanding increasing competence from their members. These were typical in calling for considerable physical effort while also inevitably limiting their membership by the experience their activities involved. The rapid growth of rowing and sailing regattas in the later years of the period was often centred on a local sailing club,[23] and although many of these early regattas were much more open than they later became – with races for working boats or women rowers, for instance – the clubs' main competitions were for members in their own boats, and ownership was apparently a condition of club membership. Even more expensive, considering the uniform, equipment, and horses involved were the driving clubs such as the 'Barouche,' the 'Four-in-hand,' the 'Benson,' led by Sir Henry Payton and the 'Whip Club,' led by Charles Buxton, the 'leader of the Charioteers,' and including such all-round sporting enthusiasts as Lord Saye and Sele.[24]

The club, however, did have an inbuilt tendency to go beyond what its sport required, adding its own demands, and making club membership also an assertion of class solidarity. Exclusion became as important to its members as inclusion, with sometimes strict limitations on numbers, often expensive uniforms and subscriptions which could be prohibitive. Even the relatively modest three guineas a year for the Hambledon Club or the Toxophilite Society put them well beyond the reach of even the prosperous craftsman, let alone the ten guineas a year called for by some hunt clubs.[25] Uniforms, already an essential in many sporting clubs, became particularly fashion conscious during the crisis years of the Napoleonic War when Volunteer Corps vied with each other in the production of elaborate military dress. The hunt clubs in turn, as Linda Colley has pointed out, assumed 'a dashing close-to-the-body costume that quite obviously mimicked military uniform,'[26] while other sporting clubs went far beyond the utilitarian in their choice. The MCC members, for instance, had sky-blue coats with silk buttons, nankeen waistcoats and breeches, with drab beaver hats, green on the inside, while even a local cricket club like Richmond was demanding a narrow gold-laced hat to go with the white jacket and drawers of its members. It was though quite usual to have to lay out £10 on a volunteer uniform and if games playing received rather less high a priority than home defence during the critical invasion-fearing years, these were the same people, bringing something of the same attitudes to both.[27]

The tendency to exclusivity in sporting clubs was not just to keep the lower orders themselves at arm's length, natural as this would have seemed, but also to separate their particular activities from plebeian sport, with its persisting reputation for roughness, disorder and disrepute. Their sporting activities were to be seen as decorous and even estimable. They sought either to distance themselves from gambling or at least to make it safe and reliable. Barclay's unease over making a match directly with a professional pedestrian reflects the doubts over whether a member of the lower classes

Women archers featured more in illustrations than any other sportswoman. Here the formidable first Marchioness of Salisbury, noted too for her passion for hunting, is seen in action at Hatfield House.

could be expected to subscribe to gambling's code of honour. One immediate effect was to sharpen up the already existing distinctions between the amateur and the professional sportsman. Competition between members of different classes became rarer and rarer away from the cricket field, and even there the professional was severely circumscribed in everything other than the actual exercise of his playing skills. Pedestrian challenges across the social classes became such rarities as Beauclerk's race against a fishmonger and Mr Williams' contest against Cooke the soldier.[28] In the age's most widespread sport, horse racing, the line between the gentleman and the rest and between the amateur and the professional was being drawn more firmly. Paid jockeys and gentlemen riders still frequently competed in the same event, but races confined to gentlemen became more common, with hunts often leading the way in promoting closed races limited to their own members.[29] Defining races bluntly as 'for horses Rode by Gentlemen' could, though, readily give rise to difficulties of interpretation as exemplified in a Yorkshire court case in 1803 when a farmer successfully claimed the prize denied to him originally because he seemed to fall short of the requirements for gentility![30]

A sign of some of the extremes to which exclusivity and elitism might be taken was there already in the composition of some of the archery clubs where social imperatives were always likely to take precedence over athletic interests. The original Toxophilite Society, while by no means open to all, was not only relatively modest in its financial demands but had the sport itself high on its agenda. Elsewhere clubs could be at least as celebrated for their sumptuous balls and grand dinners as for their shooting. The other characteristics of the archery clubs were their distinctive uniforms and the pseudo-military appearance of some of their proceedings, exemplified in that great meeting of archery clubs at Blackheath in May 1793. Six beautiful marquees were erected, with banners flying, and the flavour of the event was set by the extensive 'General Orders' for the day which had the shooters forming up in line and marching to the beat of a drum. Perhaps inevitably, in the reporting manners of the day, 'the beauties in the circle of carriages which surrounded the enclosure upon the Heath, out-numbered and outshone those of any assembly we ever saw,'[31]

It was in one of the archery clubs that the high water mark of elitism was eventually reached. The Royal Foresters, originally founded during the first fitful revival of the sport under Charles II, were relaunched in 1812. For membership, not only was gentility and 'respectability of character' demanded, but candidates had to give proof that they were gentlemen, on their father's side, for three generations at least, verify this on oath, and produce a certificate signed by 'a beneficed clergyman, a barrister-at-law, or a field or flag officer.'[32] There was to be no room for the newly rich here, no space for those who had had to buy their own furniture. It was a sign both of high snobbery and the difficulty of maintaining it, of distinguishing between inherited wealth based on land (and hence natural gentility) and acquired prosperity based on successful venturing. To be sure of the credentials of the visibly successful became increasingly difficult – by no means all the obviously prosperous folk had such well known pasts as the failed butcher turned pugilist, John Gully, or the two former fishmongers, Tattersall and Crockford. [33] There was, of course, another side to the coin – to gain entry to one of the new sporting clubs was a sign of social acceptance for the ambitious. For limited groups of the newly wealthy, sport had already become a means of climbing the class ladder.

Not all the clubs, however, had quite such serious intent. They included such oddities as the oarsmen's 'Funny Society' announced in June 1808, but sadly without any prospectus as to its intended activities and the 'New Jockey Club', seemingly an early excursion into steeple-chasing and originating at Oxford, 'where rational amusements consist in violent and dangerous exercises, such as riding helter skelter over hedge and ditch as fast as possible, towards the nearest steeple from the place of starting.'[34] The sporting club as an institution also achieved one of the final accolades by becoming the subject of parody. In the heavy humour of the day, the *Sporting Magazine*, in 1801, published the rules of a pretended 'Crudiverous Club,' to consist of 'twenty-four Members and their Bottle-holders.' Among its rules, these are typical: 'No member to bring more than one bull-dog into the Club-room at the same time,' and 'Gentlemens' bludgeons to be of the weight, length and standard of the Club.' However, actuality itself could scarcely be improved upon. Only a few months earlier there had been set up a 'Kicking Club' by twelve members who met in a tavern in St James's Street and whose diversion consisted of emerging, in fours, at around midnight, each member then having to kick every man he met. Not surprisingly this proved to be one of the least enduring of the day's societies. Their fellow citizens singularly failed to share in the members' amusement, one of the wealthiest of the kickers was thrown into a horsepond, another spent a night in the cells, and the other ten were all beaten up![35]

The advent of the sporting club meant that the idea of regular, frequent, and predictable play was able to take firm hold. A sustained programme of competition *between* clubs was still some way off, inhibited both by the absence of any regular set occasions for play and also by the continuing complexities of making matches involving stake money, though a set pattern of meetings was often established *within* clubs, from the Cutter Club races every Sunday on the Thames, cricketers like those at Birmingham's Washwood Heath and the Toxophilites who met twice a week.[36] The occasional publication of scores from internal competitions – the Married v Single, A to M against N to Z, Smokers v Non-smokers and so on – can suggest a healthy measure of well organised play within these limits. There was, too, a steady increase in inter-club events, a steady increase in the overall sums involved in sporting challenges and an increasing complexity in the competitions themselves, all of which threw an ever greater weight on the rules ,of play and on the means of arbitration when these rules were in question. From the middle of the eighteenth century there were moves towards greater formality and precision in playing arrangements. In tune with the contemporary interests in law, exemplified for example in the welcome given to Blackstone's *Commentaries on the Laws of England* in 1769, it was natural enough for contracts to be agreed on matches of all sorts, from matrimony to sport, both of which might be held to combine a demanding urge with a financial bargain. It was largely out of such compacts that sporting rules emerged and developed, the children of a sometimes uneasy but generally workable alliance between the gambling impulse and the law of contract.

These two constituents were not, however, the acknowledged sole begetters of sporting rules. Several pursuits looked to some real or reputed historical authority for their original regulations – coursing, to the sixteenth century Duke of Norfolk and bowls would claim that its rules were decided by the triumvirate of Charles II and the Dukes of York and Buckingham in 1670.[37] Where money was at stake the details were often, by the middle of the eighteenth century set out in relatively formal Articles of Agreement and these had a strong tendency to become so consistently similar and repetitive that the essential elements in them were often incorporated into later versions of the central rules – cricket already provided a classic example of this process and pugilism was to do so several decades later in the Revised Rules of the London Prize Ring. By then, if such articles were still drawn up their significance was usually reduced to providing little more than details regarding the stakes.

Running through all match making was the gambling code itself, and much of the fairness demanded of sporting contests depended heavily on the honesty of the gambling. There were advantages in the apparent strictness of the betting code at a time when many of the rules of sports and games themselves were still only emerging. Gaming rules might be unwritten, but their requirements were common knowledge. Gambling debts were the first call on a gentleman's purse, before anything that he might owe to his tailor, his grocer or his victualler, and failure to meet them meant social ostracism. At another social level there was the basket in the cockpit in which to hoist the welsher to the ceiling and the horse-whipping or the nearest pond for the racecourse cheat. Once committed to a bet, there was no going back. The rule was 'play or pay' and failure to compete meant forfeit.[38] For a backer to demand the return of his stake money from him before a fight was seen as giving John Jackson an unimpeachable reason for withdrawing from his role as unofficial organiser of the prize-ring.[39] The gambling rules of the day were, in fact, stricter than they later became, still carrying about them some lingering traces of the ethics of chivalry and embodying concepts of honour which went well beyond what was expected in the market place or on the stock exchange. Backing a man or a team was still seen as something more than a mere financial transaction. The sporting contestant, whether horse, pedestrian, or pugilist, was still notionally his backer's representative, his residual champion, carrying his colours. Any dilution of this allegiance could readily been seen as dishonourable. This was pointedly illustrated when all bets on the intended Gully v Pearce fight in 1805 were called off after one enterprising gamester first bet heavily on Pearce when the odds on him were long, and then equally heavily on Gully when Pearce became the favourite, so that he could not fail to win. Fortunes might be made in commerce by such successful insuring of an investment, but not in the betting room.[40]

Within this broad and fluctuating framework of theory and practice, of law, custom, inherited modes of play and contrived conditions, sports worked out their own individual codes of rules. As the first major sport to be formalised, horse racing's regulations were relatively sophisticated. Its first set rules were designed originally for Newmarket alone, but in their fullest form, in the Articles for King's Plates, they would be applied on at least the twenty or more courses where these plates were competed for. They went into considerable detail. Horses were not to be more than six years old, they must keep to the course, and jockeys were not to 'cross, jostle, or strike or use any other foul play.' Contraventions of the rules would result in life-long bans on both rider and owner.[41] While neither the Current Rules and Orders of the Jockey Club nor the General Rules for Racing published annually in the *Racing Calendar* mention the King's Plate regulations, they represented the bench mark against which all racing codes would be judged, leaving the other published rules to concentrate almost wholly on the terms and conditions for staking and betting, the basic reason, after all, for the setting down of rules in the first place. Racing's regulations were not significantly elaborated in the second half of the period. What did occur was their gradually wider and wider acceptance on all the courses in the country.

Cricket's rules, by contrast, underwent considerable change, bringing it close to the modern game by the 1830s. The first known regulations for the game, found in the Articles of Agreement for a match between the 2nd Duke of Richmond and Mr Broderick in 1727, were doubtless largely a recognition of existing standard practice. They were still skeletal, concerned with umpires, choice of pitch, and method of scoring runs. As with most early sporting rules the terms of wagers and the means of arbitration were of first importance. Cricket's gambling regulations, in fact, were to remain in force until the 1870s and the first known *Laws* – with their inbuilt claim to universality – gave them much prominence. These laws of 1744, though, show that the game had already taken on many of its permanent features. They dealt with the length of the pitch, the size of wickets, the weight of the ball, and the still familiar forms of dismissal – bowling, caught, stumped, run out and obstructing the field.[42] The next revision of the laws, agreed at the Star and Garter Inn, Pall Mall, in 1774, by 'a Committee of Noblemen and Gentlemen of Kent, Hampshire, Surrey, Sussex, Middlesex and London,' reflecting the game's power base, made relatively minor changes, the most important being the addition of leg before wicket to the methods of dismissal.[43] The final and decisive alteration to the style of play came in the revision of 1828 which, after at least two years in which the game had both prospered and faced frequent disputes over bowling methods, allowed round-arm deliveries but with no 'part of the hand or arm above the ELBOW at the time of delivery,' and full overarm bowling would not be long delayed.[44]

Cricket's rules were unusual in their early assumption that they would have wide application. Pugilism's first rules, like the turf's, had just a single venue in mind, being 'produced by Mr Broughton, for the better regulation of the Amphi-theatre, and approved by the gentlemen, and agreed by the pugilists, August 18th, 1743.' The rules were simple, forcibly stated, and easily understood. Again they were much concerned with fight organisation, decision making and arbitration, and designed to make the gaming more reliable. In fact, the only regulation governing the actual fighting was in Rule VII:

> That no person is to hit his adversary when down or seize him by the hair,
> the breeches, or any part below the waist; a man on his knees to be reckoned
> down.

An alternative version substitutes the word 'ham' for 'hair' and may have greater validity since, for instance, many early illustrations show the fighters with virtually shaven heads.[45] Broughton's code remained the staple of boxing until replaced in 1853 by the much expanded Revised Rules of the London Prize Ring, though it always needed supplementing for fights of any consequence, and particularly so after the amphitheatre was closed and they moved into the open. Articles of Agreement were again the means for defining such arrangements as the size of the stake money, the date of the contest and the intended venue, often expressed as 'within x miles of London.' The deficiencies of the code, so far as the actual fighting practices went, soon became apparent. In particular, they made no reference to falling without receiving a blow and so bringing the round to an end, which could reduce fights to farce. Articles began to specify that this falling without a blow would constitute foul play, and well before the end of the period this seems to have been accepted without specific statement.[46]

As distinct from the regulations in these newly organised sports, the rules inherited from earlier centuries for bowls, coursing, and cocking make surprisingly little reference to gambling. With cocking and coursing there is certainly a good deal of detail as to how the contest is to be conducted and adjudicated, but even this is lacking in the rules for bowls ascribed to Charles II and his two dukes, though it was known to have been a great gambling game even in their day. The only reference to gaming was in the rule that 'Bowlers nor bettors shall not do anything to prejudice or favour a bowl by wind, hat, foot or otherwise, and if done, the cast shall be lost.' The rules of bowls were certainly widely accepted and players from different parts of the country had no difficulty in making matches against each other.[47] Both coursing and cocking were apparently simple happenings in which one animal sought to kill another. The complexity of the inherited rules in both constituted typical attempts to ritualise and sanitise what was essentially a crude and primitive amusement. In coursing, as well as defining the roles of the 'fewter,' the man who released the greyhounds, and the 'hare finder,' responsible for the prey, the rules were also concerned with the method of scoring matches, with an attempt to stress style and skill in the dog's performance, to encourage as much refinement as the nature of the sport allowed. The prize did not necessarily go to the greyhound that made the kill.[48] Cocking likewise had complicated rules defining both the responsibilities of the handlers and the limitations placed on their interference with the birds. The *Racing Calendar* in the 1770s would print model articles for a cock match, leaving blank spaces for entering the time, place, number of cocks to be fought and particulars of the stakes. These referred also to following 'the usual rules of cock-fighting as it is practised in London and Newmarket,' which included a count to ten in several circumstances which might interrupt the fighting, the count which was to carry over from the cockpit to the prize-ring.[49]

The newer sports of the eighteenth century quickly acquired their own rules. In rowing these were minimal, confined to interference with competitors either from rival scullers or from spectators' boats, but they were enough to have the long-standing Doggett's Coat and Badge race re-rowed on a number of occasions. In 1809, it was because of the first contest 'having been declared foul.' Sailing matches could, from the start of the sport, give rise to more diverse problems and by the late 1780s the Cumberland Club was being looked upon as the source of its rules, pronouncing on such issues as to whether using an oar to punt a boat in shallows was legal.[50] Regional sports had developed their own formalities. Singlestick play, for instance, followed the tendency of brutal sports to achieve such nicety as they could muster by insisting on skill rather than crude force. The object was not to floor the opponent but to draw blood with as light a blow as possible to vulnerable parts of the face and head. The rules set the size of the stage at a minimum of 16 feet square, and the length of the sticks at 3ft 2ins. A 'head' was scored when a blow produced a one inch run of blood above the chin, but there could be no score if an opponent's stick was broken or knocked from his hand.[51]

Local rules – or the absence of much regulation of any sort – existed in some sports. Man-to-man fighting in Lancashire owed nothing to

Broughton's code, with the struggle really beginning rather than ending when a man was brought to ground, a tradition which made the London ring initially deeply suspicious of any fighter coming from that part of the country. Local rules, too, governed the playing of the one widespread game which had so far achieved no national form. This was, of course, football, which may appear either to have no rules at all or to follow a wide range of different practices in various parts of the country from the minimal exhortations of the Haxey Hood game allowing a man to be knocked down but not hurt to relatively elaborate versions in both East Anglia and parts of the West Country, contests between teams of equal numbers, with restricted playing areas, and various conventions regarding tackling and scoring.[52]

Rules alone though were not enough of themselves to ensure good order in a game. They could minimise disputes but there had to be means of arbitration for the controversies that were bound to occur. The civil courts were there, as a last resort, and they were resorted to with some frequency – over a bet on a football match in 1795, a billiards fracas in 1804, an accusation of running in a walking match in 1806, and earlier an action by bell-ringers to secure the prize they had won.[53] The reason for this recourse to law was, of course, the virtual absence of any final authority within the sports themselves. The regulatory bodies for individual sports, if they existed at all, were still young, uncertain of their powers, and few were even beginning to recognise themselves as such by the end of the period.

Internal methods of arbitration were, not surprisingly, again most developed in horse racing. As the longest established, highest capitalised and most heavily wagered sport, it was here that there was the most pressing need to have sure means of settling differences. The system was still not fully rounded by the end of the period, but had made great steps forward with the Jockey Club largely accepted as the appropriate court of appeal for all disputes from all courses. The extension in the early nineteenth century of the Jockey Club's authority arose from a number of sources. Newmarket owners running their horses on provincial courses had come to expect the same rules to apply there and an expanded sporting press made the Club's rules more widely known. Public knowledge of the rules was a prime incentive to their application.[54] Stewards at country meetings, whose major qualification was their ability and willingness to provide a substantial prize did not necessarily have any very wide experience of the sport and must have appreciated having a court of appeal available to complainants. Matters had certainly moved forward from the 1730s when local disputes might be settled by a majority vote among the subscribers present. As judges the stewards could well come under pressure from the crowds – even at Doncaster the new building arrangements were commended for isolating them from the spectators [55] – and there was much to be said for having a second and final opinion. Some decisions that judges were faced with were certainly taxing and some could hardly be legislated for or pronounced upon, defying even the wisdom of the Jockey Club, but more and more disputes were being submitted to Newmarket and from Irish as well as English meetings. There were, though, still uncertainties about its competence and its parameters were defining themselves, after the fashion of the Common Law, on a case by case basis. It declined, for instance, to make judgements if it did not have all the material information about the case and sent one appeal back to Lewes on this account. Solomon like, the stewards there divided the winnings equally.[56]

The Jockey Club drew much of its authority over the sport merely by indicating that if asked to adjudicate it would do so only if its own rules were followed.[57] Its prime concern was with the best interests of Newmarket owners wherever they were racing, and it did not deliberately seek to extend its authority. Indeed, the ambitions of others for its competence were the more extensive – or the more erratic. It was reported after the Barclay/Wood race, from which Wood had to withdraw with an injury, that the Jockey Club had 'not yet pronounced' on whether bets should be paid but with the implication that it might well do so. The wagers were in fact settled, but there is no evidence that this was at the Club's behest or that it had any intention of going beyond its own sport. When *Pancratia*, just as it was going to press, reported the disputed fight between Hall and Donnelly, it did state that 'The result must be left to the Jockey Club' but given the date (1814) this could equally be intended to refer to the 'Pugilistic Club.'[58]

The emphases in cricket were slightly different. From the mid-eighteenth century its laws were clearly meant to be self sufficient and their interpretation on the field vested firmly in the hands of the umpires, the 'sole judges of all outs and ins, of all fair and unfair play.' Although from its foundation in 1787 the Marylebone Cricket Club became the leading authority on the game, day to day interpretations and judgements lay with the umpires and there is little early evidence of the MCC's being referred to as a final court of appeal. There was a rare instance of a resort to the 'Cricket Society' after one of the troubled Leicester v Coventry matches in 1788. The issue at stake was whether the batsman, having originally blocked a ball, could then use his bat again to prevent it from rolling on his stumps. The match was resumed a month later, before any reply had been received, but after the Leicester players began to get on top the Coventry team left the field, with the match unfinished,[59] just one outstanding example of the numerous disputes over umpires' decisions. As the game became more complex so the role of the umpire could become even more thankless. The failure of umpires to agree was not uncommon. Typically, and in another match involving the trouble prone Leicester club, this time against Nottingham in 1781,

> 'the Nottingham umpire declared the man out, the Leicester umpire declared him in, the law was appealed to, notwithstanding which the Nottingham umpire persisted in his declaration; both umpires then called play, and at length the Nottingham club refused to bowl ... thus ended the match.'[60]

It was a not uncommon conclusion. Bias could lie at the heart of some disputes, unconscious doubtless in some cases, but in others apparently deliberate. Ignorance of the laws was also often alleged. The infamous affray at Hinkley in 1787 arose, it was alleged, from faulty decisions from an umpire 'unacquainted with the game,' though this was admittedly from the *Leicester Journal*, itself possibly not an unbiased source![61]

A number of causes were to lead to the virtual elimination of disputes between umpires. One was the ruling by the MCC in 1816, Lord Frederick Beauclerk informing the Oakham and Melton Clubs that there need be no reference to the uninvolved umpire in declaring whether a man was out. There was too a wider and surer knowledge of the laws and a greater neutrality in the umpires themselves. The umpire had often originally been regarded as a member of the team and the 1727 Articles in fact say as much – 'that twelve gamesters shall play on each side.'[62] Until at least to the turn of the century the umpire could still appear to be effectively manager of his team, selecting players, deciding when a game should be given up as lost, or writing to the local press as spokesman for the club.[63] Mr Banbury, the Coventry umpire in the match with Leicester in 1788, was landlord of the Golden Cap Inn, fielded his own team on the nearby Gosford Green, and carried home the ball and stakes in triumph.[64] At the other extreme there could be umpires who were presumably very disengaged from the proceedings, such as the two gentlemen from Kent and Middlesex who stood at a village game at Wincanton in 1772, to all round satisfaction of both players and spectators. Similar impartiality began to be sought in highly staked matches by having reserve professionals stand as umpires.'[65] This was the ideal mode of arbitration, but at the other extreme there could still be passions which yielded to no rational judgement and which, in 1809, after a disagreement in a single wicket match, led to the duel between Ensign Mahon and Assistant Surgeon Louis O'Hara and the death of the latter.[66]

In pugilism the rules for arbitration were as forthright as those in the laws of cricket. Broughton's Rule 6 stated that, 'to prevent disputes in every main battle,' each fighter should have a gentleman to act as umpire and if the two could not agree they should choose a third as referee. Even more so than in horse racing and cricket, these were counsels of perfection. They were applied with consistency only to highly staked contests and even there were far from solving all the problems. In lesser fights the judging could be very informal.[67] In disagreements over big fights there could be same ambiguity about the umpire's role as in cricket. In a sense, each represented his own man. When Perrins came from Birmingham to face Johnson, Mr Meadows came too as his umpire and there were other occasions where the umpire's affiliations are quite apparent. The neat model of the rules, echoing the courtroom with its two advocates and a judge, was seldom realised if there were serious disputes. The decisive nature of the contest itself and its frequently incontrovertible end did, of course, prevent much possible contention and umpires, if they could not always be objective, had to be flexible. They were undoubtedly helped in this also, for some twenty of the sport's best years, by John Jackson's presence at the ringside as interpreter of the sport's rules, and his absence could be noted with regret.[68]

Difficulties none the less remained if serious difference arose. An outstanding example of this occurred in the fight between Tom Belcher and Dutch Sam on 28 July 1807 when Sam landed a blow on Belcher's face as he was falling. Jackson said that a man was not 'down' until his hands reached the ground, which was not the case here. Even so, the umpires would not agree and the referee, Lord Say and Sele, declined to pronounce. It was then put to Lord Archibald Hamilton and eventually it was agreed that the only solution which would satisfy would be to put the boxers to 'a new trial' to settle the issue themselves in the ring. Hotly disputed fights, in fact, seldom yielded to the simple clear-cut scheme for arbitration laid down in the rules. The umpires in the Watson v Hooper fight in 1790 did eventually call on the referee, but only after 'continual altercations' between the two sides, with Watson 'seven times generally accused of striking unfair blows before Hooper was declared the winner.'[69] The absence from the sport of any court of appeal beyond the loose informal band of gentleman enthusiasts, invariably referred to as the 'amateurs,' was not remedied either by the foundation in 1814 of the Pugilistic Club or that of the Fair Play Club in 1828, the one being too slow to take action and the other being overwhelmed almost at once by blatantly fraudulent contests.[70] In spite, however, of such failures, and however uneven and uncertain it was, there was a general strengthening of both the rule making process and the means of arbitration as sport developed during the Georgian years. Even at its humblest levels the need for assurance over methods of refereeing was making itself felt. A village innkeeper on the Great West Road, whose written poster for his rustic Whitsun revels was mocked by the *Sporting Magazine*, nevertheless asserted that all disputes were 'to be determined by the umpires.'[71] In most sports the rules had become more comprehensive and increasingly discriminating between good and bad practice, aids at once to both sharper competition and greater fairness. In horse racing, cricket, sailing, coursing, and – spasmodically – in pugilism there were central organisations which exercised some greater or less measure of influence over the sport as a whole, making always for more consistent competition and giving increasing scope for growth.

The changes, though, were not all positive. In the post-war period in particular there were, in several directions, threats to such fair play as had been established over the previous hundred years. This reminder, though of growing hazards is not to belittle the efforts of those sporting lawmakers and arbitrators who had enabled sport to reach the stage of development which it had come to enjoy by the second decade of the nineteenth century. Their efforts, and those of the many others who, as organisers, players and spectators, had participated in the growth of old and new competitive pursuits had, particularly during the middle years of the Georgian period, been the moving spirits behind the significant changes in sporting styles, organisation and reliability. Already, however, in looking predominantly at those middle years, there have been frequent indications of problems to come and it is these as well as the opportunities for the future that, in summing up, will be part of the legacy that Georgian sport would leave behind.

Notes

1. See *SM*, January 1798, pp 224-6, in an article which establishes its tone from the very first words – 'In the year 1727, there lived a wretch named Tregonwell Frampton ....'

2. See *e.g. Racing Calendar 1773*, pp xxviii-xliv. The club also published its first list of owners' colours in 1762 (headed by the Duke of Cumberland) and this was updated annually.

3. For hunt clubs mounting race meetings see *SM*, October 1805, p 44 (Newcastle); April 1810, p 19 ('Essex Fox-Hunting Races'); and *e.g.*, April 1799, p 61, and June 1801, p 163 for the Bibury Club.

4. *Sports History*, 7, 1985, p 13; 9, 1986, p 19; Ford, *Cricket: A Social History*, p 109; Buckley, *Eighteenth Century Cricket*, p 123.

5. The two extremes quoted are the York and Princess Plains (later West Kent) clubs.

6. Ford, *Cricket: A Social History*, p 71; Buckley, *Eighteenth Century Cricket*, pp 102, 186.

7. It was suggested that cricket flourished earlier than football in nineteenth century Liverpool because it attracted those in skilled trades who won their free Saturday afternoon well before the unskilled workers. Roy Rees, 'The organisation of sport in nineteenth century Liverpool,' Roland Renson, Pierre Paul de Nayer, Michel Ostyn, *eds.*, *The History, the Evolution and Diffusion of Sports and Games in Different Cultures*, Brussels, 1976, pp 237-247.

8. See *e.g.* Nyren, *Cricketers of My Time*, passim.; Holt, *Sport and the British*, p 26.

9. Ford, Cricket: *A Social History*, pp 52-62.

10. The 3rd Duke of Dorset played also for 'Kent,' 'England' and his own team. The 4th Earl of Tankerville's county side went under the name of Surrey. *ibid.* See also *e.g.*, Buckley, *passim.*

11. Bowen, *Cricket: A History*, pp 63/4.

12. *Morning Post*, 6 August 1785.

13. Ford, *Cricket: A Social History*, pp 62/3.

14. See *e.g. SM*, November 1810, p 91; *Maidstone Journal*, 9 August 1791; Buckley, *Eighteenth Century Cricket*, pp 154/5.

15. According to one unflattering report he gave over 'every spare hour to cocking, milling, or some other gentlemanly amusement.' Ford, *Cricket: A Social History*, pp 62/3.

16. *SM*, June 1807, p 148.

17. See *Racing Calendar 1797*, pp xxliii/xxliv; vii-x.

18. *SM*, April 1813, p 7; June 1813, p 142; *Pancratia*, supplement p 28. The foundation of the Pugilistic Club is often wrongly ascribed to 1814.

19. See *e.g.* Ford, *Prizefighting*, ch 5, 'Development and Promotion,' though Ford's estimate of the effects of the club is probably too optimistic.

20. *SM*, June 1820, p 150; December 1825, p 110; October 1828, p 446; November 1828, p 79; February 1829, p 368; April 1829, pp 426/427.

21. *Times*, 20, 21, 27 July 1787.

22. *SM*, October 1792, p 19. For the rules of coursing in full see Egan, *Book of Sports*, p 391.

23. *e.g.* the Bristol Sailing Society, Windermere Sailing Club, and Erith Sailing Society. *SM*, August 1796, p 269; August 1809, p 217; May 1815, p 89.

24. *SM*, February 1811, p 253; March 1809, p 276. See also *e.g.*, *SM*, July 1808, pp 191/2.

25. Guy Paget, *History of the Althrop and Pytchley Hunt*, 1938, pp 72-93. The Pytchley was limited to 40 members and the Swaffham Coursing Society to 26 (i.e. the number of letters in the alphabet!) Fines were often imposed for not wearing club uniforms appropriately.

26. Colley, *Britons*, p 172.

27. Before hunts largely settled on scarlet coats and white cord breeches the Tarporley, for example, had blue frock coats, scarlet capes, waistcoat and buckskin breeches. *SM*, May 1798, p 73; Henricks, *Disputed Pleasures*, p 139, Colley, *Britons*, p 268.

28. *SM*, October 1807, p 6; September 1797, p 304; September 1808, p 286.

29. *Racing Calendar 1797*, pp 10, 82.

30. *SM*, August 1803, pp 267/8.

31. *SM*, January 1794, p 206. Egan, *Book of Sports*, p 242n. For one club's social round see William Beckford, 'Society of the Woodmen of the Ancient Forest of Arden,' *Archer's Register*, 1879, pp 24-39.

32. C. J. Longman and H. Walrond, *Archery*, New York, 1894, p 210; Henricks, *Disputed Pleasures*, p 141.

33. A similar certificate, here signed by the commanding officer, was needed for entry to the Yeomanry Stakes at Dorchester, confirming that the horse concerned had been owned for at least six months 'and ridded (sic) during the whole of each day's exercise.' (*Dorset County Chronicle*, 15 September 1835).

34. *SM*, June 1808, p 147; August 1795, p 286.

35. *SM*, December 1801, pp 115/6; July 1801, p 189.

36. See George, *London Life in the Eighteenth Century*, p 273; *SM*, January 1794, p 206; *Sports History*, 7, 1985, p 13.

37. Egan, *Book of Sports*, p 387; Haynes, *Story of Bowls*, pp 59-61. The Prince of Wales in this period also decided shooting distances for the clubs he patronised. Elmer, *Archery*, in Henricks, *Disputed Pleasures*, p 141.

38. With the exception, later in the period, of bets on the Derby and St Leger with their massive numbers of early acceptances and later non-runners.

39. *SM*, November 1822, p 101.

40. *Pancratia*, p 237. There was also unease over owners running more than one horse in a race, but it was sometimes a virtual necessity when fields were small. There were more legitimate suspicions of 'sham' matches where the two owners knew that one horse was the better runner and both bet on it, 'for the joint account.' (*SM*, June 1799, p 134. For a clear illustration of the extent of later 'falling off' in this respect see *e.g.* Salisbury, *SM*, September 1842, p 359.

41. In *e.g. Racing Calendar 1773*, p xxx.

42. Ford, *Cricket: A Social History*, pp 16/17; Brookes, *English Cricket through the Ages*, p 44.

43. Ford, *Cricket: A Social History*, pp 19, 99/100.

44. *SM*, June 1828, p 176.

45. *Pancratia*, pp 42/3. The alternative version (Miles, *Pugilistica*, I, p 25) has some support from the fight where Jackson held Mendoza by the hair and pummelled him, and to little complaint. *Pancratia*, p 119; Miles, *Pugilistica*, I, p 95.

46. For falling without a blow see e.g. Johnson v Ward, 1787. *Pancratia*, pp 71/2.

47. Brailsford, *Sport and Society*, p 212; Haynes, *Story of Bowls*, pp 59-61. One 'great match for fifty guineas took place at York between bowlers from Derbyshire and Birmingham. *SM*, June 1806, p 111.

48. Egan, *Book of Sports*, pp 386-8

49. *Racing Calendar 1773*, pp xx, xxiv; *Racing Calendar 1797*, p 188. The model articles continued to be published in the Calendar into the nineteenth century. Similar 'Articles for a Dog match,' relating to a fight on 17 May 1891, were reproduced in the *Black Country Bugle*, no.116, November 1981.

50. *SM*, August 1809, p 248; *Times*, 12, 27 July 1787.

51. The rules for singlesticks are in the *Sporting Magazine*, December 1809, pp 97/98. For further details see also Barnes' account in Brown, *ed*, *Dorset Folk Lore by William Barnes*, p 11.

52. See Carew, *Survey of Cornwall*, I, p 73; Strutt, *Sports and Pastimes*, pp 92/3; Young, *British Football*, pp 38,63; Malcolmson, *Popular Recreations*, pp 35/6, 113.

53. *SM*, April 1795, p 8; January 1804, pp 200/201; September 1806, p 276/277; *Sherborne Mercury*, 5 April 1737.

54. For publication of the Rules and Orders of the Jockey Club see *SM*, December 1792, pp 145 ff.

55. *Sherborne Mercury*, 31 May 1737; *SM*, February 1806, p 224.

56. *SM*, August 1808, p 241. For an Irish appeal see December 1792, p 179. Another referred case, for example, concerned two horses accidentally brought down near the winning post by a servant trying to clear the course. *Racing Calendar 1797*, p 59.

57. J. Mortimer, *The Jockey Club*, 1958, pp 59/60.

58. *SM*, December 1807, p 103; *Pancratia*, supplement p 22.

59. Ford, *Cricket: A Social History*, p 17; *Leicester Journal*, 24 October, 1 November 1788; *Coventry Mercury*, 29 September, 13, 27 October 1788; Buckley. *Eighteenth Century Cricket*, pp 132-134. The 1788 case was complex, also involving the replacement of one umpire by another – who reinstated a man who had already been given out!

60. *Leicester Journal*, 22 September 1781; Buckley, *Eighteenth Century Cricket*, pp 93, 135. Umpiring was described as an 'unpleasant task' when Lord Winchelsea once took it on as he felt it was too cold to play. *Maidstone Journal*, 26 May 1799. See also 'Cricket Umpires,' *Sports History*, 9, 1986, pp 2/3.

61. *Leicester Journal*, 11 August 1787; Buckley, *Eighteenth Century Cricket*, pp 84, 119/120. For a warning to beware of a team's biased umpire see *Ipswich Journal*, 8 August 1778.

62. For parallel instances see ''Eleven and Twelve in Cricket' and 'Five and Seven in Bell-ringing,' Goulstone, *Summer Solstice Games*, pp 65-67; *Northampton Mercury*, 24 June 1776; *Reading Mercury*, 22 May 1789.

63. *Leicester Journal*, 19 October 1982; Buckley, *Eighteenth Century Cricket*, p 9; Goulstone, *Summer Solstice Games*, p 65

64. *Coventry Mercury*, 1 November 1816 (n.b. another late season match.)

65. *Bath Chronicle*, 20 August 1772; *York Herald*, 17 September 1814; Buckley, *Pre-Victorian Cricket*, pp 79, 70; *Eighteenth Century Cricket*, pp 58/9; *Sports History*, 9, 1986, pp 2/3.

66. *Bury and Norwich Post*, 21 June 1809.

67. It could be done, for instance, by any gentleman happening to be present or just by crowd opinion. See *Pancratia*, pp 43, 115, 126.

68. *ibid.*, pp 91, 86/7; Miles, *Pugilistica*, I pp 62/3. See also *SM*, August 1823, p 270 – 'the absence of a man of influence is greatly felt.'

69. *Pancratia*, pp 293/4, 94, 104, 106.

70. *Pancratia*, supplement, pp 28, 32, 37; *SM*, December 1814, pp 159/160; Brailsford, *Bareknuckles*, pp 89, 98.

71. *SM*, July 1795, p 223.

TRANSITIONS

9.

Blood Sports and Bloodstock

Where then did sport stand after the guns had fallen silent and the country was facing the equal difficulties of peace? As the Georgian age shaded towards the Victorian the years of excitement slipped into the past, those energetic years that had demonstrated the essential continuity of the country's sporting life and the inventiveness of its sportsmen and women, their zest for innovation in devising new means of competitive amusement and new means of organising and regulating their play. The impact of changing attitudes had shown itself in several directions – in an increasing diminution of many of the older communal recreations, in the rising importance of economic interventions in the sporting world, and in a sharpening class segregation in play, some of it incidental, a product of the inherent nature of the competition itself, but more and more of it deliberate and contrived as class consciousness became increasingly sensitive and social discriminations more searching. The continuing force of these stresses in the new circumstances was far from certain and the coming changes were as likely to produce greater divergence as greater similarity between one type of sport and another. As with all other human activities sport, after the end of the Napoleonic Wars, would have to exist alongside high prices, popular unrest and, for a decade or more, vigorous repression, to exist in cities which had outgrown such local government as existed or in a countryside often depressed by poverty. Sport, which had itself often been looked upon as an activity needing reformation, would then, in turn, have to face the consequences of active new social and political concerns. Before the age was out the great Reform Act of 1832 would signal the shift of political power from the aristocracy to the middle classes, long suspicious of so much in popular sport and recreation.

In looking at the fortunes in this new setting of the established sports inherited from the past, the animal sports present an obvious starting point since they were to be the first of the age's recreational pursuits to be re-shaped by statute. Earlier, in the eighteenth century, they had been noted as ranging from the most crude and boorish to the most sophisticated and systematised. The effects of the past hundred years had been to pull these two aspects of animal sport even further apart. Horse racing had its failings but generally went from strength to strength. On the other hand, and certainly in terms of expressed public opinion if less so in terms of popular support, there was an important shift away from blood sports, though the movement was (and still is) selective. At the outer edges of acceptance, even in the latter part of the eighteenth century, was cock-throwing and it needed very little shift in opinion to deny any future to this old Shrovetide amusement. Most local bans against it were effective by the new century but its remnants still lingered on in places.[1] Warwickshire justices were still taking action in

1814 and in the 1820s the Mayor of Warwick was warning against a revival of 'so disgraceful a practice' which was thought to have been abandoned, a first hint of that regression in behaviour which characterised the 1820s in several of its sporting aspects. At the same time William Hone was claiming that cock-throwing was 'still conspicuous in several parts of the kingdom' and, on the authority of William Barnes, asserting that 'in some of the villages of Dorsetshire and Wiltshire, the boys, at Shrovetide, still kept up a custom called *Lent-Crocking.*' The old practice was also said to have persisted until mid-century in parts of Buckinghamshire.[2]

The other animal sport to come under heavy pressure was bull running. In the overall sporting scene this was a minor annual activity confined to very few locations, but the contrasting histories of the two bull runs which the later eighteenth century had inherited from the past are instructive. The complexities of the factors that could operate upon all animal sports are well illustrated in their differing fates, that at Tutbury, on the Staffordshire/Derbyshire border being suppressed in 1788, and the Stamford event resistant to repeated attacks in the 1790s and surviving until just after the 1835 Cruelty to Animals act. Certainly on the undemanding scale of contemporary cruelty, this Stamford run did not rank among the worst. It made November 13th a boisterous, noisy day, attracting large crowds to the town, but it was usually good humoured, the men being armed with nothing more than sticks to goad the animal. The gentlefolk of the town and the more restrained among its citizenry would view the day's events benevolently from their upstairs windows and the whole tone of the day – for all but the bull – was one of festivity.[3] By contrast, the Tutbury run had degenerated. The town lay just inside the Staffordshire boundary and the intensity of county rivalries guaranteed an invasion of Derbyshire men striving to drive the bull into their own county, with the locals fighting to prevent them. The result was 'a calamitous catalogue of bones being broken, skulls fractured, and lives lost.' The Duke of Devonshire, who currently held Tutbury Castle, was 'pleased to abolish' the custom in 1778, and did so with little sign of effective opposition. The probability is that the annual invasion was unwelcome to at least as many as supported it.[4]

The situation at Stamford held many differences. The town was prosperous and self-assured, one of the most important staging posts on the Great North Road. It was also a flourishing sporting centre, with its races, its cricket, its hunting men and its thriving local wakes, celebrated by the poet John Clare as 'a round of festivity.' The inhabitants could feel confident in their resistance when proceedings were first begun against the run in 1788, a move unlikely to have been the result of local pressure but rather a typical response to George III's recent proclamation against vice and immorality. The result of this first suppression attempt is best described as a draw – there was a minor chase of one bull through one part of the town while the authorities had been diverted by another elsewhere. The late 1780s were not the 1770s. There was a more assertive sporting spirit in the air. Nor, perhaps, was the local grandee, Lord Exeter, either as powerful or as committed as his fellow peer and the next year brought a clear victory for the merrymakers, even the dragoons brought in to keep order joining the chase themselves. The authorities ceased to struggle, waiting for the event to whither on the vine but what, after another half century, finally brought it to a halt was not so much any moral change of heart as the reaction of ratepayers to the high cost of policing it.[5]

If bull running was a story of both suppression and survival so was bull baiting, and on a vastly more extensive scale. It was under increasingly heavy pressure in the last years of the old century and needed strong local support or the force of tradition in order to continue. It had the former in Birmingham and the Black Country and the latter to maintain such conspicuous annual events as the Wokingham bait. Increasingly the provision of animals for baiting was in the hands of innkeepers, or other small-scale local entrepreneurs, and baits were still also common accompaniments to pugilism at its rougher end. Any assumption, however, that baiting was exclusively an amusement of the lowest orders still has to be questioned. Just as the ladies and gentlemen, tradesmen and aldermen, dressed their windows for the Stamford bull run, so bull baiting could appear in such relatively respectable settings as the Totnes Race meeting, where it continued into the 1820s.[6] In the Black Country towns of Tipton, Bilston and Oldbury there were, if anything, more bulls being baited in the 1820s than in recent past years[7] and there are frequent reports in the *Sporting Magazine* indicating the continued frequency of bull baiting – at Madely Wake, Shropshire and at Rochdale (where a bridge collapsed with nine deaths) in 1820, at Durdham Downs, Bristol (where it was followed by 'the usual quota of bouts of fisticuffs') in 1822 and a particular offensive bait at Hounslow in 1825, coinciding incidentally with the first meeting of the 'Society for Protection of Animals.'[8] Such reports, however, are, by the 1820s unfailingly critical and prosecutions (as in Shropshire in 1820 and at Chester in 1822) are reported with approval in the sporting press.[9]

The possibilities of refining and developing such a sport as bull baiting were always going to be limited, but there was some attempt to make it more orderly, even trying to introduce some notion of fairness. In a 'fair' match, dogs were set to the bull singly. Count was kept of the number of dogs employed. There were pauses between sets of attacks by the dogs, and if the bull was brought to the ground, seized by the nose, for example, there would be cries of 'Wind! Wind!' to try to pull off the dog and give breathing space to the bull. Nor was the outcome by any means always predetermined. Any bull that overcame the dogs (which not infrequently happened) was much admired, though his fate was usually to be taken back to provide more sport on another day. Where protests were likely to be at their most vocal and to come even from the usually tolerant was when the baiting was thought to be unfair, with the bull physically maimed, for instance, to hamper its movement, or held on too short a tether to allow it to manoeuvre.[10]

Early attempts to ban bull baiting through parliamentary action may have failed, but local suppression steadily hedged the practice into narrower and narrower confines. Even actual bans might be unnecessary – in January 1815 there was a successful prosecution at the Hampshire Quarter Sessions following a bait at Cowes, Isle of Wight, finding the perpetrators guilty of committing a nuisance. It would take another quarter of a century to see the end of bull baiting, but its demise could be foretold, and as a result not only of a new view of what constituted 'sport.'[11] In spite of the 1820s tendency to excess in some of its cruder sporting pleasures most of the more extraordinary exploitations seem to have ceased. No more is heard of odd fights such as that between a dog and a monkey with a stick, a 'long main o stags' promised for a sensation seeking York racecourse in 1806 or an oxen race planned for the Edinburgh meeting.[12] Such horrors as eating a large live cat for a wager seem to have been consigned to the past,[13] and bear baiting had become a comparative rarity, partly owing to the cost of bears. Travelling showmen preferred to have them dance rather than fight. Badger baiting, as a regular and extensive public spectacle, also probably disappeared in the capital, along with bear baiting, after the closing down of Black Boy Alley, but its continued existence up and down the country cannot be doubted. It could (as Malcolmson noted) be carried out much more secretively than bull-baiting, usually before small crowds and without attracting a great deal of attention.[14]

More significant than these in the overall sporting scene were the animal fighting sports. Their advocates could claim that it was in the nature of the animals concerned to fight each other and that the contestants could be fairly matched. Certainly, for all the evils inherent in the fighting sports, they did play an incidental part in the movement of sport itself towards more equitable competition. Cocks were precisely paired by weight in all the more heavily staked cock fights, and much more so than were human beings in their combat sports. Gamecocks were also trained for their task more thoroughly and single-mindedly than were any human contestants – perhaps, a cynic might say, because they, along with horses, had in total much more money staked on them than did human competitors. This was certainly a strong incentive to refining and balancing the sport as precisely as possible, as well as making for sharper competition. Surviving or not, a significant part of the legacy that cocking had already put in place was its model of county matches and there continued to be more county contests in the cockpit than there were on the cricket field.

Dog fighting never approached the sophistication of cocking. It must have been common, however, even as a relatively organised sport, when a dog could change hands which had already fought a hundred and more 'battles.' Fighting was not only frequent but also unlikely to be hindered, an accepted form of amusement – a regular part, for instance, of the Easter festivities at Tothill Fields. It was mainly enjoyed by the lower orders, but also attracted some of that sporting band of 'amateurs' whose tastes were nothing if not catholic. In fact, and in defiance of any notion of a consistently steady improvement in sporting manners, bloody contests involving dogs

The age could take its amusement from animals in many forms and a sporting journal saw little amiss in illustrating them, as here in The Fight reported from Worcester between the Dog and Monkey and The Squirrel Hunt .

became more common than before in the 1820s, underlining again the press report in 1822 of 'the great increase, within the last four or five years of the SAVAGE and BARBAROUS SPORTS.' Dog fights were frequently reported in the sporting press at stakes anywhere between £10 and £500 and were still in 1835 being noted as part of the 'pernicious activity' of the bulk of Birmingham's population.[15] It is likely that some of the more highly staked dog fights were subject to articles of agreement as to their conditions, though there is no direct evidence from the period. Such agreements though were essential to formal cock matches. Between wealthy individuals there could be up to 1,000 guineas staked on the contest as a whole and up to 50 guineas for each individual fight, as well as £20,000 or more placed in side bets on the result.[16] The stakes for county matches were certainly usually more modest, between 100 and 500 guineas, but this still called for a careful agreement over the terms of the encounter and a probable resort to the model articles for cock matches published annually in the *Racing Calendar* .

Cock fighting had strong claims to being the period's most widespread sport, both socially and geographically. The annual open contests for high stakes were mounted at the Cockpit Royal where, according to Pierce Egan, the season began just after Shrovetide.[17] There would be energetic preparation of the performers, and not just here,[18] but also for the rougher style of cocking described in the song 'Wednesbury Cocking,' where a dispute between rival Black Country colliers and nailers led to a fight in which the two birds were trampled to death. Between the two extremes were contests of all shades of social and economic standing. While county matches were those most reported, there were other geographically based contests such as the Gentlemen of Islington against those of Hackney for 50 guineas, Brentford versus Kew and Richmond, and what was described as an annual match between Barnet and St Albans as well as matches made by individuals. There were, too, the Long Mains and Welsh Mains which called for so many combatants that they must have attracted entries from a wide range of owners. The 288 cocks that fought in seven days at Usher and Ward's Pit at Newcastle (and claimed as a world record) must have included quite a few pitmens' birds, for instance, especially given their known enthusiasm for the sport. Another style of cocking took place at some customary celebrations, such as at Sandgate in April 1799, and for prizes such as bacon, a fat hog, or a fat bullock.[19]

The cockpit crowd continued to show an unusual degree of social mixing, Pierce Egan's descriptions still echoing those of von Uffenbach from a hundred years earlier – 'The noble lord and the *needy* commoner, are both at home after they have paid their *tip* for admission.' The 'tip', though, must have deterred some. It was five shillings at the Cockpit Royal, but Egan still has little truck with Cheney's old 'Rules and Orders,' with their demand for social stratification of the crowd. 'Etiquette,' Egan responds, 'has nothing to do with a Cockpit; and a master of ceremonies would have a troublesome time of it to keep anything like order.' The spectators are too much interested in the fighting to 'consider who they may chance to "*rub against.*"'[20] This enthusiasm for cocking showed few signs of abatement. It may have lost some of its upper class support from the 1820s, but from the evidence of, for example, race meetings, this may well have been exaggerated.[21] Certainly there were local suppressions, such as that at Nottingham, and the Preston Cockpit was rented out as a moral lecture hall in 1830 but in that same year, at the races, there were well staked cocking matches at, for instance, Chester, Manchester, Stafford, Newton and Buxton[22] and a year later a new pit was being opened on London's Millbank.[23] Moreover the 1835 Act was not effectively applied to cockfighting until The Royal Society for Cruelty to Animals began to bring actions in the late 1830s. Among many examples of continuing matches after the passage of the act were those between The Gentlemen of Devon and their Cornish counterparts in 1836 and that between the Gentlemen of Nottinghamshire and those of Yorkshire as late as 1840 and there are many similar reports.[24] It seems indeed safe to say that there was no popular will in favour of banning cock-fighting – and actual anger among the lower classses when the suppression was not applied also to what was seen as the upper class sport of fox-hunting. There was a growing realisation that the new middle class masters in the reformed parliament would be likely have their own views, as yet not fully rounded, on the proper nature of the people's recreation.

It is easy to forget that, no matter what its final fate, given the widespread popularity of cock-fighting, the people who supported it and were steeped in its habits and practices, were the same people who were involved, and would become involved, in sports which had a longer term future than that held by the cockpit. Cocking matches, for instance, had proved easy to express in terms of well-known local rivalries – Lancashire v Yorkshire, Nottinghamshire v Yorkshire, Northumberland v Durham, Oxfordshire v Berkshire, Norfolk v Cambridgeshire, Cheshire v Staffordshire and so on. There was also, though, a cocking fixture list of county matches more geographically ambitious than that yet found in cricket – Yorkshire playing Northamptonshire, for instance, Cheshire against Leicestershire, Middlesex against Lincolnshire and Leicestershire, and Lancashire v Nottinghamshire, which had become virtually an annual event at Manchester Races in the later years of the period.[25] While the identification of these as 'County' teams was, of course, in one sense spurious, bringing together as they did only a few directly interested parties, the resort to county affiliations was to be not only the basis of first class cricket, but also to the organisation of much future competition in England. Athletics, hockey and football would be among the many other sports that would adopt the county format as they devised their pattern of management, and would continue to do so for long after the counties had ceased to enjoy their past virtual monopoly of local government power, some, like Middlesex and Yorkshire, only surviving as sporting entities.

For the fox hunter it was not the county that mattered so much as the 'country,' the expanse over which his particular pack of hounds ranged. Faced by few effective critics, hunting, chasing and shooting, could all grow and prosper and among them no sport developed as fast and as widely as fox hunting during the late eighteenth and early nineteenth centuries. Techniques became more sophisticated, hounds were bred and managed to become faster and more ordered, the number of organised hunts grew to well over two hundred by 1815, and there were few parts of the country where the fox was not hunted. The absence or scarcity of foxes in any particular district was no impediment. Kennelled foxes were always available and, far from justifying hunting as a means of controlling the animal, active steps were taken to foster its breeding.[26] Hunting the hare on horseback was virtually a forgotten sport by 1800 although hares were hunted enthusiastically on foot and there continued to be even more packs of harriers than foxhounds. This was a sport for both remote rural areas such as Dorset, where Mr Yeatman's Beagles could have a 20 mile chase around Hazlebury Bryan (with, unsurprisingly, only one gentleman still with the huntsman at the death), and also for the city fringes where such as the Putney Harriers would pursue their prey over Wimbledon Common. Others preferred more wholesale methods – Lord Craven was said, 'in the course of a few days' to have killed 'no less than *sixteen hundred hares* on his estate at Ashdown Park. Disbelief over the figure has to be tempered by other reports of mass slaughters of wild life at this time and immediately after.[27]

Stag hunting was effectively moribund. Stag hounds were now kept largely for decorative purposes, only three packs remaining in the early nineteenth century, and all reduced to chasing carted deer. It had in fact become more of a ritualistic outing than a true hunting sport by the 1820s. The traditional Epping Easter Hunt, where the same stag was 'hunted ' for four successive years at the start of the new century, was only a few paces nearer to farce than the aristocratic sport which it aped.[28] Fox hunting itself had, by contrast, become a much more serious affair over the years. An advertisement in the national press seeking a furnished lodge with stables 'in a good Sporting Country' was no longer the novelty that it had been in 1787. It had to be near a good stage coach route and doubtless the advertiser was looking to the Great North Road and to what had become the prime hunting shires of Leicestershire, Rutland and Northamptonshire, where the sport was at its most vigorous – and most expensive.[29] The annual cost of managing a hunt anywhere in the country by the 1830s could run to £2,000, and in these prime hunting shires it could go much higher. There remained individuals wealthy enough to carry such burdens – Squire Osbaldeston among the most prominent of them so long as his fortune lasted – but the new mode was for gentlemen to combine in subscription packs, which, like the Pytchley, usually limited themselves to a set number of members.[30] Hunting styles also altered. In earlier times there had been dawn starts, following the scent of well fed and sluggish foxes as they made their way back home. Now earths were stopped during the night, the fox was left in the open and by the time the hunt set out in late morning it had become lively and prepared to run for miles. The hunters matched the new speed of the chase by having their horses hacked to the meeting point by servants to keep them fresh, and even by having several horses available at locations where they were likely to change rides. There was, too, increasing ritualisation – the distribution of the fox's brush, head and paws to the most successful riders, and the blooding of the young, smearing their faces with the dead creature's gore. Far from seeking to keep down the fox population, the hunting squires made it virtually a protected species. Many hunts, though, still placed little reliance on nature to provide them with their prey and released kennelled animals or 'bag foxes' to ensure a chase.[31]

The hunts went from strength to strength. In 1834, for instance, *Bell's Life* would regularly be notifying 60 or more meetings in the forthcoming week and the only flies in the traditional sportsman's ointment were the abolition of the property qualifications in the Game Laws in 1831 and the coming of the railways, the one seen as a parliamentary sop to its middle class constituency and the other taking unsuitable would-be hunting men like Surtees' Mr Jorrocks into the countryside. The other chasing sport, coursing, also expanded considerably and became more sophisticated through the period, though hardly now retaining all of its old social tone. Surtees again looked down on it as a 'smaller grade of gambling'[32] and there was certainly much informal coursing wherever hares were to be found. Under its formal rules it was the practice to concentrate on the skills of the chasing dogs and sometimes to award the match to the more agile greyhound if its manoeuvres happened to drive the hare into the path of a clumsier rival, enabling that dog to make the kill. Fairness as between the two competing greyhounds was also improved by the invention of the double spring clip, which ensured that both were released at the same moment, though the result could still be a matter of personal judgement.[33]

It might be – and was – argued that both coursing and hunting constituted civilised forms of sport, an advance on the crudities of animal baiting and giving the prey some chance of escape, which many hares did in fact manage to take. On the other hand both the foxes and the hares were often domestically reared animals, with little practice in making long runs and no knowledge of the countryside into which they were released, doubtless a

Hawking had spasmodic publicity. It was thought a novelty in 1815 though this print is from over twenty years earlier. The ambitious prey appears to be a heron!

reason for complaints from several coursing meetings that the hares were too feeble to test the dogs.[34] Meanwhile the slaughter of other creatures went on apace, made all the more effective by improvements in the design and manufacture of guns. Apart from Lord Craven's massacre of hares on his estate and Osbaldeston's hundred pheasants a day, squirrels were shot at, the skilled lady marksman from Oldham could outdo her brother in bringing down skylarks and sparrows were netted while roosting – one description of this particular amusement was accompanied by a recipe for sparrow pie![35] A group of city sportsmen in London seem to have provoked some hilarity when they acquired from a nearby farmer rights to shoot thrushes and sparrows on his land whereas the shooting on the Sussex coast of wild swans was reported with enthusiasm and the bringing down near Bishops Stortford of an eagle was met with the bland comment that they were very rare so far to the south![36] By contrast with all this miscellaneous mayhem, hawking, newly revived by Lord Rivers and other gentlemen and demonstrated by them at Newmarket in 1815, could appear as a sport of considerable refinement.[37]

The transition to the next age had meant the early abolition of one animal sport. It saw also the movement of another from the light into gathering gloom and doubt, from progress and innovation to moral stagnation. This was the fate of horse racing and one which it was to share with at least two other spectator sports, pugilism and pedestrianism, whose reputations were fading fast by the 1820s. Along with cricket, horse racing was the sport which, during the latter part of the eighteenth century and the early years of the nineteenth, took the most decisive steps towards its modern form. It made general overall progress in virtually every direction – more horses being bred and raced, more race meetings, better prizes and better standards of both organisation and racing. There may have been the odd difficult years when its future, in face of other distractions, had seemed less than certain, but if there were occasions when journalists sounded less than optimistic about the health of racing these turned out to be false alarms.[38] By 1800 the St Leger and the Derby were clearly beginning to set new standards and raise new expectations in the sport, with consequences which were to go well beyond racing itself – stressing speed over staying power, initiating the all-important shift away from strength, stamina and endurance in favour of quickness and skill, a movement that was to be the main stylistic characteristic of the next phase of many competitive sports. It was progress that had not been inspired by some one grand design but had arisen out of a variety of different motives. There was, for example a growing minority interest in younger horses, whose races had to be shorter but produced much more exciting finishes than the usual marathon heats which so often left one horse plodding home alone with the rest almost out of sight. They had, too, the economic advantage of promising an earlier possible return on the capital outlay the horse represented. Local pressures were also at work producing the first classic races not, as might have been anticipated at Newmarket, where owners remained obsessed by their highly staked two-horse matches, but at Doncaster and Epsom, early signs of the general provincialisation of sport that was to be another feature of the next one hundred years.

The first of the classic races had its origins in Colonel Anthony St Leger's enthusiasm for races confined to three year olds. He arranged an unnamed sweepstake for them at Doncaster in 1776. It was run for the first time as the 'St Leger' in 1778.[39] The introduction of the race coincided with the transfer of the meeting to its permanent future site on the Town Moor. In 1803 the King's Plate from the defunct Burford meeting was transferred there and by the time the royal princes favoured the course with a visit in 1806 they were able to enjoy the architect John Carr's new grandstand, celebrated as 'a most beautiful edifice.'[40] For the first thirty years of the nineteenth century Doncaster was the most consistently successful of all the country's race meetings and was regularly being compared with New-market, almost always to the latter's disadvantage. There was 'little worth reporting' of Newmarket's first October meeting in 1826, while Doncaster flourished. Newmarket was 'never suffering as now' a year later when Doncaster was 'swallowing up' all the autumn interest and both of the 1828 spring meetings were said to be poorly supported. Not that Doncaster could ever be without its problems at a time when difficulties of every sort began to riddle the racing scene. The decision by the Doncaster Corporation to widen the start area of the course did something to diminish the numerous false starts which had bedevilled the St Leger in recent years, most of them contrived in attempts to tire fancied horses. There were increasing betting problems – the chase to betting shops in distant towns when the St Leger favourite pulled up in training in 1819, the purchasing of a heavily backed horse in order not to run it and leave the race open to another at longer odds and then, in 1829, such an invasion of roughnecks and cheats that they had to be chased out of town.[42] It reduced to rosy memory the 1823 comment, when all bets had been paid up there, that there was 'never a sounder or more responsible set of betters.' Perhaps the final accolade, though, did come in the same year when a company was formed to build a stand at Epsom – like Doncaster's.[43]

The classic card was completed when Newmarket at last realised that it was being left behind and set up the Two Thousand Guineas over the Rowley Mile in 1809, following it with the One Thousand Guineas for fillies in 1814.[44] The best horses were still being almost exclusively bred and housed there and 41 of the winners of the Derby in the first 45 years of its running were trained on the Heath, but other courses were both increasing their prize money and showing a concern for both runners and spectators that was foreign to racing's headquarters. By the mid-1820s even the pre-eminence of its horses was being called into question[45] and Newmarket continued to decline into the thirties, when one new reason was given as the demands of parliament at the time of the Reform Bills,[46] though the underlying cause lay in the higher prize money that drew owners away to other courses.

Epsom, once leading racing men had led a successful campaign against attempts to enclose the downs in 1813, survived the difficult years ahead reasonably well. It could not avoid its bad patches – there was a particularly poor meeting in 1826 when the 'badness of the times' had greatly reduced the crowds[47] – but it had, of course, from the turn of the century, its own two classic races as the centrepieces of its programmes. They largely owed their existence to General Burgoyne, best known for surrendering his army to the colonists at Yorktown in the American War of Independence, and subsequently managing the family racehorses of his relation, the Earl of Derby. It was Burgoyne's idea to set up a race similar to St Leger's – a former comrade in arms – but to confine it to three-year-old fillies. It was first run at Epsom in May 1799, and named after the house where it had been conceived, namely The Oaks. The idea of the Derby followed directly from the fillies' race and when a name for it was discussed over dinner the honour went to Lord Derby himself. The Derby's greatest days were still to come later in the century as progressively greater numbers began to flock across the downs to the Epsom meeting, making it, of all the country's races, the one that best combined mass fairground festivity with quality competition. For the time being it had to face most of the problems that were weakening the turf everywhere in the last years of the age – many false starts in the 1828 Oaks, for instance, and betting irregularities, ignoring the exception of the Derby, along with the St Leger, from the 'Play or Pay' rule.[48] It was though ideally placed to provide the amusement craved for by London's rapidly expanding population, and even if the racing was not always of the best or most reliable Epsom could always benefit from the zest for enjoyment, the passionate urge among urban workers in particular to exploit every rare chance of holidaying, and which could also bring success elsewhere, even to city meetings that offered racing of no special distinction. The massive six-figure crowds reported from Manchester, where the racing itself was relatively unspectacular, were further ample indication of this. York's loss of its public hangings and the effect of this on attendances also emphasises the fact that the day's racing was by no means the only attraction which could draw crowds to the raceground. It was said in 1806, when Doncaster was becoming all the rage, that the York meeting, once the north's major racing event, enjoyed less 'company' than in the past and thereafter, in spite of some good years, it continued to fall gradually behind its Yorkshire neighbour.[49]

Fashion could be decisive for those meetings which depended on the presence of the quality rather than of the masses, witness the complete falling away of spectators at the Goodwood meeting in 1807 when the Duke of Richmond himself was absent, whereas the year before it had been 'attended by an immense number of nobility and gentry,' nearby Chichester had been 'full of company,' the theatre, on two nights, 'had a very crowded and brilliant audience,' and the 'elegant supper' and ball at the Town Hall on the Thursday night had included 'some of the handsomest ladies in the kingdom.'[50] It was to recover somewhat, at the expense of Brighton, but Ascot, which was used to attracting custom from right across the social divides, continued to enjoy an erratic history. It had reached one of its many peaks in the early 1790s when the Prince of Wales saw his Baronet, at 20 to 1, win the Oatlands Stakes, then the richest race in the land with 2,950 guineas for the winner. Then two years later it was said to have 'not only eclipsed but totally suppressed several surrounding races' but such was the behaviour of the crowd that the Oatlands was moved to Newmarket in the following year and Ascot had a run of poor meetings. By 1798 it was 'but a poor epitome of its former greatness.'[51] In spite of the continuing poverty of its fields it had, from 1822, Nash's excellent brick and stone grandstand and the continued support of George IV for whom, by 1826, its meeting constituted one of his few remaining public appearances. By then the long-standing pattern of its royal week was already recognisable. The sovereign was usually present on the opening Tuesday, Wednesday from 1807 was Gold Cup day, Thursday drew the largest crowds and was becoming known as Ladies' Day, while Friday was essentially a tailing off day, before small crowds.[52]

Only a handful of meetings had some sense of security over even their permanence, let alone enjoying a relatively assured pattern of events. Many were still quite tenuous affairs, the most solidly based usually enjoying the backing of the local corporation or of some powerful local dynasty. Race committees could come and go, and so could their meetings. They were dependent on local enthusiasm and energy and already likely to be facing the threat that was to put a permanent close to many in the coming decades, namely the opposition of local evangelicals, often backed by the equal opposition of employers. For example, Maidenhead, where Methodism was strong, for all its successes in the early 1790s, only survived in 1801 'after a severe contest between a few spirited gentlemen in the neighbourhood, and the rigid and reformed religionists of the town.' In many places there were not enough of the 'spirited gentlemen' to maintain the races, for whatever reason. Bath lost its meeting for fifteen of its most fashionable years at the turn of the century, while even Brighton lapsed as the Prince of Wales lost interest.[53] The *Sporting Magazine* of July 1798 remarked on the transient nature of the sport locally and produced a list of 47 meetings which had disappeared in the past fifty years. This process continued, but at least it was matched by new meetings and the revivals – Monmouth after 33 years, Barnet after 10 and, within weeks of Bath's renewal, Egremont in Cumberland after 'a great number of years.'[54] Even where there was continuity the course itself often changed, a matter of little difficulty in most places, where there were no permanent buildings. Leicester, for instance, moved to at least its third location in 1806.[55] This sense of impermanence continued. The attacks of reforming clerics and their followers grew stronger and more widespread. Major meetings like Cheltenham had to withstand pressure – and face the burning down of its grandstand, from unidentified causes – none of which though was to prevent it from going from strength to strength in the late 1830s. The change in fortune of a meeting could be quite abrupt. At Southampton, for instance, there were 30,000 reported at each day of its races in 1822 yet only two years later it was said that these races would be the last unless they improved both the standard of the racing and the state of the course.[56]

With all its comings and goings and its increasing failings horse racing was still the one really national spectator sport, with meetings taking place in every quarter of the land, many of them now long erased from the turf's memory. To make a fairly random selection across the country, there were in the early nineteenth century races at Morpeth, Penrith, Nantwich, Grimsby, Burton-on-Trent, Walsall, Bromsgrove, Beccles, Chippenham, Tavistock and Totnes. Set against what had usually been run of the mill meetings such as these were those considered important enough to have the King's Plates bestowed upon them. In the 1815 season these were Newmarket (as unique here as elsewhere with no fewer than three plates), Salisbury, Ipswich, Guildford, Nottingham, Winchester, Lincoln, York, Richmond (Yorkshire), Lewes, Canterbury, Lichfield, Newcastle on Tyne, Doncaster, Carlisle, Chelmsford, Ascot and Warwick.[57] At the other end of the market were meetings which by one means or other apparently slipped past the legal restrictions meant to impose limits on racing. There are many examples of legitimate meetings offering their necessary £50 purse but with a require- ment, unlikely to be fulfilled, for a minimum number of entrants. Then in Dorset alone in the 1830s there were at least two events – at Sherborne and Sturminster Newton – which were described as 'Diversions' but were in effect horse races in all but name but with no prize of £50 value. Prosecutions of such events seem to have been very rarely undertaken and one reported over racing at Bagslake Common near Rochdale in 1821 seems to have been on the grounds of public nuisance and failed on a technicality.[58]

With all its vagaries and uncertainties both the timing and the styles of racing saw gradual progress. Dilatory time-keeping began to be tackled and would need to be remedied as communications improved. More courses experimented, not usually very profitably, with a second meeting in the year. The change that was to prove decisive, however, and to shape the whole future of flat racing, was the movement towards shorter races for younger horses, a change that went forward alongside the notable advance in the quality of the bloodstock itself. Post to post competition spread only relatively slowly. By 1838 major meetings such as York had largely given up racing in heats but these continued to occupy at least half the cards at country meetings such as, for instance, Blandford and Hereford.[59] The change was not particularly helped from Newmarket, where meetings were still dominated by two-horse matches but the new direction for horse racing had been well set by the 1830s and this in spite of complaints from traditionalists that breeding for speed alone and running young horses 'of little bone' limited ownership and produced weight limits that virtually barred gentry riders.[60] It must have been the pace of the new breed of racehorses which had already so impressed de la Rochefoucauld in 1784, with his astonished comment that

> when you are close to them you can hardly follow them with the eye – they travel more swiftly than a flash of lightning. The jockeys are obliged to keep their heads low in order to breathe. Their passage through the air is so swift that otherwise they would be choked.[61]

He must have been watching some of the progeny of Eclipse. By a happy coincidence for the turf, and in one of those cases where it is not easy to distinguish cause from effect, the interest in races for three-year-olds coincided with the appearance in numbers of horses sired by that superlative racer. Trained and raced by Dennis O'Kelly, Eclipse won all his eleven races in 1769 and 1770, as well as walking over in seven others where no competition could be found to face him. As a stallion he then revolutionised the breed, injecting into it a new speed through his distinguished line. As a sire he directly produced winners of over 850 races, worth over £150,000 in stake money, and one of his progeny, Hambletonian, a grandson, not only won the St Leger and the Doncaster Cup on successive days in 1795, following it up in the next year by winning the Cup again and beating that year's Leger winner in the process, but also took part in one of the most celebrated matches of the age. He ran against Diamond for a stake of 3,000 guineas (with £10,000 said to be 'depending') at Newmarket in 1799, giving three pounds in weight and still won at 5 to 4 on.[62]

The sums involved here reflect the sport's gradual commercialisation, with its dependence on specialist riders, its high stud fees and above all the rising prices of horses themselves. There were repeated complaints at the cost of stallions' services from the 1790s onwards – one owner it was said had none at less than £20 – and this, it was claimed, would drive the farmer and the small man out of racing altogether,[60] but there were soon numbers of stallions (lists of them in the Sporting Magazines of June and July 1820, for instance) whose offspring's winnings had run to five figures. The dramatic inflation, though, came in the prices of provenly successful horses. Eclipse had been bought originally for 1,500 guineas (though O'Kelly was said to have refused Lord Grosvenor's offer of 11,000 guineas later) while by 1813, 6,000 guineas were being turned down for the St Leger winner, Altisidora.[63] The trade in bloodstock had itself begun both to flourish and become international – Drummer was sold and sent to India in 1814, Diomed went to the United States, and by 1830 horses were being sold to Australia.[64] As the sums involved in racing grew ever larger, however, the corruption to which the sport was always exposed grew steadily more conspicuous. *The Times*, never more than lukewarm towards horse racing in the 1790s (though it was the one piece of 'Sporting Intelligence' which it regularly reported), was predicting its demise with some regularity. After its pessimism about betting in 1787 it was back on the same theme in 1793, following a disastrous Ascot and a Newmarket meeting which had been the 'most thinly attended of any within the annals of the turf.' Certainly, some of the scandals, deceptions and actual crime that were to dog horse racing for most of the next half century had already begun to make an appearance. There was the poisoning of the water troughs, first at Doncaster and then at Newmarket, not done as protests against the sports of the privileged but to thin out the competition and for which the tout Daniel Dawson was hanged at Cambridge in 1812 before a crowd of 12,000, far greater than any ever to grace the Heath's racing.[65] Most of the deceptions were still mild, compared with what was to come but of Lord Egremont's five Derby winners in the first years of the nineteenth century two at least were actually four-year-olds, although it is accepted that the deception was the trainer's and not his lordship's. Not that all owners were so scrupulous. The 1814 St Leger favourite, Belville, was bought by 'a couple of _____' (sic) to prevent it winning as they would have lost 'vastly.' They pretended it had gone lame, but the dishonesty was immediately transparent. The 1840s were to see the nadir of the turf's reputation but already by the end of this period there was deceit, deception, bribery, corruption and violence enough. The odd blatantly crossed race could be dealt with summarily by having the offending jockey 'soundly horsewhipped' as at Tunbridge in 1824 and, *in extremis*, a band of roughs could be physically driven off as at Doncaster.[66]

The major problem lay almost certainly in the withdrawal of the more scrupulous traditional owners either from the sport itself or, more often, from the close attention that they had often given to its affairs in the past. A changing moral climate, a growth in respectability, increasing criticism of gambling sports and gatherings such as race meetings, were all having their effects. Owners could begin to feel it necessary to appear involved in more serious matters. By the 1830s Newmarket, in silent acknowledgement of Sabbatarian criticism, had ceased to gallop horses on Sundays before a week's racing as in the past and even Doncaster could suffer from attacks by its stricter citizens – though in 1832 it was cholera they were using as an excuse. It was, of course, the time when Lord Melbourne remarked how religious everyone was becoming but it meant that the turf was more and more at the mercy of those whom by the movement towards the new morality had left behind.[67]

Yet for all the evils that were increasingly besetting it the turf had made great strides in the previous hundred years. By the time the Georgian age gave way to the Victorian the great classic races were firmly established and the Derby and the St Leger were beginning to be recognised as events of some national importance – even at what was described as a poor Epsom meeting in 1837 the Derby was worth £3450 and 10,000 official racecards were sold on Derby day.[68] The sport was organised by a Jockey Club which, without being deliberately entrepreneurial, was gradually being accepted as racing's overall authority and this meant that there was already a structure with the potential eventually to correct the sport's worst ills. It was a sport which now had its fixed points on the sporting calendar with renowned meetings, however well or ill they might be faring at any given moment, at Newmarket, Epsom, Doncaster, Ascot and Goodwood, as well as the looser regularity of regional circuits taking in the county meetings. Its venues varied in their degree of development, some with fine permanent grandstands, others with temporary and rickety scaffolding, but the courses were generally up to the task they had to fulfil. It was still a popular sport, drawing increasingly larger crowds. It was also, within a cautious conservatism, prepared to innovate, to begin to change the emphasis in racing styles and even, at its fringes, prepared to experiment with alternatives to simple flat racing. At the same time the sport had become more thoroughly professional and had seen the full appearance of the paid specialist jockey. It still remained, though, a sport based on the aristocracy and the landed classes, and their code of honour was still thought to hold good within it, even if there were clear signs that this hold was, in fact, loosening. Questions about the sport's reliability could already be asked on the basis of its current experience. Would its old morality be sustainable in the freer enterprising society which was now emerging and permeating every area of life where there was money to be made? The great might grow even wealthier, but could their repute, and that of their recreations, increase in proportion? Increasingly exposed on the one hand to those whose prime interest was profit rather than sport, and on the other to critics both religious and social, the one competitive sport over which they appeared to hold the most unquestioned sway could already be sensed to be under considerable threat.

Notes

1. *SM*, June 1795, pp 157/8; March 1795, p 331. At the end of the century both Strutt and the *Monthly Magazine* regarded it as nearly extinct. Malcolmson,

Popular Recreations, p 121.

2. Hone, *Every-Day Book*, quoted in Malcomson, *ibid.*; Brown, *ed.*, *Dorset Folklore by Wiliam Barnes*, pp 11/12. The mayoral warning from Warwick is particularly interesting, coming as it did from a town that was at that very time housing two major prize-fights in front of its racecourse grandstand and actually mustering 25 of its constables to keep order at one of them! See Brailsford, *Bareknuckles*, pp 87, 90.

3. From Malcolmson's description in *Popular Recreations*, p 47, n.55, based largely on local press accounts.

4. *SM*, October 1795, pp 260-262.

5. See Malcomson, *Popular Recreations*, pp 126-135.

6. *SM*, June 1821, p 144.

7. *Aris's Birmingham Gazette*, 4 August 1823, 9 August 1824, 13 August 1828; *Birmingham Journal*, 10 March 1856. Baiting in the Birmingham area is particularly well covered in Reid, 'Beasts and brutes,' Holt, *Sport and the Working Class*, pp 13-17. For the Wokingham bait see *SM*, December 1808, p 120 and for the traditional Bachelors' Acre bait at Windsor, October 1806, p 43, December 1806, p 160.

8. *SM*, August 1820, p 244; November 1820, p 56; March 1820, p 271; July 1825, pp 291, 296. In 1822 there were reported to be 6 to 10 places in London where weekly baits were held. *SM*, April 1822, p 38.

9. *SM*, August 1820, p 244; September 1822, p 313. See also the Lincoln November 5th bait, November 1819, p 89.

10. For admired bulls see *SM*, March 1805, p 350; November 1808, p 91; October 1806, p 43 and for 'unfair' baits see e.g. December 1801, pp 132/4; November 1820, p 66.

11. *SM*, August 1813, p 213; January 1815, p 206. See also August 1820, p 244 for a Shropshire case.

12. *SM*, May 1799, p 103; April 1806, p 46; *Times*, 1 May 1787. The dog, incidentally, was the 10 to 1 favourite but the monkey leapt onto its back and nearly beat it to death before being pulled off.

13. *SM*, March 1794, p 326, among a list of extraordinary wagers. The bet was for £5 to eat the largest black Tom in the neighbourhood. He bit off the head first and ate the poor beast in fifteen minutes without apparent ill effects.

14. *SM*, April 1803, p 56; April 1805, p 19; Malcolmson, *Popular Recreations*, p 135. See also obituary of J. J. Brayfield, *SM*, March 1821, p 283.

15. *SM*, October 1803, p 43; August 1795, p 233; April 1813, p 21; October 1824, p 57; January 1825, p 308; *BLL*, 25 May 1828; Hutton, *History of Birmingham*, pp 199-200.

16. e.g., *SM*, June 1796, p 167; May 1793, p 124.

17. The old Cockpit Royal in St James's was demolished in 1810 and replaced by that in Tufton Street, *SM*, October 1810, p 43; Boulton, *Amusements of Old London*, p 177.

18. See e.g., *SM*, December 1805, pp 140/1

19. See e.g., *SM*, May 1805, p 105; June 1808, p 189; February 1794, p 237; May 1796, p 105; July 1813, p 156; April 1807, p 3; April 1799, p 25; Egan, 'The Cockpit,' *Book of Sports*, pp 145-155.

20. Egan, *Book of Sports*, p 154. Malcolmson, *Popular Recreations*, pp 49/50;

Cheney's Rules and Orders are quoted in Longrigg, *English Squire and his Sport*, p 174.

21. e.g., by Malcolmson, *Popular Recreations*, p 135.

22. Church, *Victorian Nottingham*, p 15; Harrison, *Drink and the Victorians*, p 117; *SM*, June 1830, p 135; July, p 253; August, p 320.

23. *SM*, June 1831, p 143. A new pit was also opened at York in 1829. *SM*, July 1829, p 164.

24. *BLL*, 7 February, 24 April 1836; 13 January, 9 August 1840.

25. *SM*, June 1808, pp 145, 189; June 1813, p 105; June 1814, p 136; June 1815, p 135. See also previous cocking references.

26. See 'The Early History of Fox Hunting,' *Edinburgh Review*, no 93, January 1901, p 74; Egan, *Book of Sports*, pp 210 ff.; *SM*, April 1826, pp 363/4.

27. Munsche, *Gentlemen and Poachers*, p 33; *SM*, January 1810, p 194; January 1806, p 168; December 1804, p 164.

28. *SM*, September 1803, pp 289-300; April 1805, p 55. The only occasion on which the Royal Staghounds had a real chase appears to have been in pursuit of a wounded stag, May 1814, p 59.

29. *Times*, 23 February 1787.

30. Colonel Cooke's *Observations on Fox-hunting*, quoted in Egan, *Book of Sports*, p 217n., calculated that it cost £2,235 a year to run a pack of hounds, which Egan himself regarded as a considerable under-estimate.

31. *SM*, May 1810, p 83. For long chases after kennelled foxes see *e.g. SM*, November 1808, p 69; April 1809, p 7.

32. *BLL*, 12 January 1834; Birley, *Sport and the Making of Britain*, p 183. See also R. S. Surtees, *Mr Sponge's Sporting Tour*, (1853) for another hunting undesirable.

33. Munsche, *Gentlemen and Poachers*, p 33; Egan, *Book of Sports*, p 391. There were now numerous coursing societies and coursing meetings – see *e.g., SM*, February 1802, pp 242, ff.; December 1809, pp 112 ff.; December 1812, pp 103 ff.

34. At Malton in November 1790, while the company was 'very numerous during the whole week,' the hares 'generally ran but indifferently,' though doubtless not intentionally. At Amesbury four years later the sport was poor because the hares were too feeble to test the dogs – on the other hand those 'on other parts of the Wiltshire Downs' were reported to 'possess their usual excellence.' (*SM*, November 1799, p 62; October 1803, p 47.)

35. *SM*, April 1813, pp 3, 17.

36. *SM*, December 1792, p 189; February 1815, p 356; March 1804, p 303.

37. *SM*, May 1815, p 88.

38. The *Racing Calendar* regularly produced statistics of the horses that had been raced in past years which demonstrate the progress made. See *e.g.* 1888 Calendar, p 731. For gloomy reports see *e.g. Times*, 16 April 1787; *SM*, October 1793.

39. Tyrrel, *Racecourses*, pp 48-50 and passim.; See also J. S. Fletcher, *History of the St Leger Stakes*, 1902.

40. Tyrrel, *Racecourses*, pp 44, 48. See also *SM*, November 1795, pp 89/90; February 1806, p 224.

41. *SM*, November 1826, pp 3, 45; November 1827, p 2 ff; November 1828, p 2.

42. *SM*, September, p 183, November, pp 19, 57, December, pp 115-116, 1819. Among other later scandals was the doping of the odds-on Leger favourite, Plenipotentiary, in 1844, Tyrrel, *Racecourses*, p 53.

43. *SM*, September 1823, pp 303-304; January 1829, p 241.

44. Tyrrel, *Racecourses*, pp 118 ff and passim.; Onslow, *Headquarters*, pp 47/8 and *passim.*

45. It was claimed that even the best Newmarket horses could not now be certain of winning provincial races while third class ones could in the past. *SM*, September 1824, p 341. The one major stud not at Newmarket was the Dennis O'Kelly's based on his Eclipse progeny at Epsom. See Tyrrel, *Racecourses*, pp 119, 115.

46. *SM*, May 1831, p 66. There was also an early example of parliamentary pairing when Lord Chesterfield and the Duke of Portland decided, as confirmed political opponents, to go Newmarket together rather than to a House of Lords vote, June 1832, p 130. See also 'Review of the 1831 Racing Season,' February 1832, p 253.

47. *SM*, May 1813, p 91; June 1826, p 66.

48. Tyrrel, *Racecourses*, pp 176-180; *SM*, June 1828, p 78; February 1829, pp 269-270.

49. *SM*, June 1805, p 165; August 1806, p 208; September 1806, p. 168.

50. *SM*, May 1807, p 98; May 1806, p 58.

51. Tyrrel, *Racecourses*, p 146; *SM*, May 1793, p 109; June 1796, p 160; June 1798, p 154.

52. *SM*, June 1822, p 135; Fulford, *George IV*, p 255; Laird, *Royal Ascot*, 1976, p 28.

53. *SM*, October 1801, p 51; March 1811, p 303; July 1811, p 191; July 1815, p 187.

54. *SM*, July 1798, p 199; October 1810, p 41; August 1809, p 242.

55. Tyrrel, *Racecourses*, p 110.

56. Aylwin Sampson, *Courses of Action: The Homes of Horse Racing*, 1984, p 49; SM, August 1822, p 26; August 1824, p 277.

57. *SM*, April 1815 and *passim.*; *Racing Calendar*, *passim.*

58. *Dorchester County Chronicle*, 20 August, 22 September 1835; *SM*, September 1821, p 256.

59. *SM: Racing Calendar 1838*, pp 7, 6, 11.

60. 'A Lover of the Turf,' *SM*, June 1797, pp 129/130. See also November 1819, p 63.

61. Quoted in T. H. White, *The Age of Scandal*, 1950; 1962 edition, p 21.

62. Tyrrel, *Racecourses*, pp 115, 117, 48; *SM*, February 1799, p 275; March 1799, p 309. See also November 1819, p 63.

63. *SM*, April 1795, p 6; July 1795, p 222; February 1815, p 352.

64. *SM*, May 1814, p 86; March 1830, p 348.

65. *Times*, 2 July 1793; *SM*, May 1811, p 97; Tyrrel, *Racecourses*, p 50.

66. Tyrrel, *Racecourses*, p 180; *SM*, October 1814, p 39; September 1824, p 352. What was possibly the peak of turf corruption would eventually come in the 1844 Derby when not only were there two four-year-olds among the starters but another horse ran under a false name, the favourite lost its chance by foul riding and another fancied horse was held back by its jockey, who had bet on another runner. (Vamplew, *The Turf*, p 83).

67. *SM*, May 1829, p 3; May 1831, p 34; October 1832, p 4901. In 1832 so many were going to church on Sunday morning 'as if Newmarket had not been a

sporting town,' May 1832, p 2.
68. *SM*, June 1837, p 131.

10.
Heroes and Enigmas

Eclipse and Hambletonian were doughty all-conquering creatures whose fame was known wherever there were enthusiams for horse racing, but horses were only the start of it. This age created the sporting hero, larger than life and nationally known – and it was to be almost exclusively a male creation for the next hundred years. Previously anything approaching national fame had come to a very few sportsmen such as Jem Broughton but by 1800 there were cricketers well enough admired to be sure of drawing in the crowds, professional jockeys famed enough to attract high fees, pedestrians and pugilists whose names and feats were widely celebrated. Many have already been mentioned in some general context or other – their origins and status, their dependence or otherwise on patrons, their capacity to profit financially from their sport, and the like – but their overall achievements deserve more personal notice. They were the outstanding individual performers around whom the progress of Georgian sport was so largely built.

Pedestrians tended to be among those who, by picking their events and challenges with care, could enjoy a long competitive life. Foster Powell, born at Horsforth, near Leeds, in 1736 appeared early in the present story and enjoyed frequent and varied success until past his fiftieth year. In November 1773, for instance, for a 100 guinea wager, he covered the 400 miles London to York and back in six days, a time brought down in turn by three other performers to 5 days 14° hours by the 1780s. This feat and to a lesser extent the shorter return London to Canterbury trip which he completed within 24 hours in 1787 were the regular bases of long-distance challenges at this time, giving way later to events performed on a single site. Well into the veteran stage, Powell was beaten by Andrew Smith, 'a famous runner of that time,' in a one mile match on Barham Downs, but he was also credited with a possible four minute mile on Molesey Hurst.[1] In the last decades of the old century pedestrianism was sharing in the current widespread revival of sporting enthusiasms and contests were frequent, among them a 120 yard sprint on Mitcham Common between Gunnell and Powell (though described as 'a plater from Birmingham' and questionably Foster Powell.)[2] The seriousness of the competition meant that there was still a demand for the services for some of the sport's older celebrities such as Jack (or John) Smith, who had won cups at the Artillery Ground in the 1760s and now enjoyed a considerable reputation as a coach and most notably as one of Allardyce Barclay's first mentors, training him for his winning challenge (for £5,000 from the ever-ready Mr Fletcher) to cover 90 miles in 21 hours in 1801.[3]

More and more well known performers made their appearance in the new century, the most widely famed of them the Lancastrian, Abraham Wood, who had already been drawing in the crowds for several years before coming to particular notice in 1806, running at Brighton. For two busy seasons this became something of an athletic centre with, for instance, Henry Mellish and Mr Crampton distinguishing themselves in leaping and jumping. Wood himself raced all over the country, already effectively a full-time professional, ready to take all opportunities offered for – so far as is known – legitimate profit. He was attracting large crowds (a 'vast concourse' of several thousands at Wakefield in 1813) through to the end of the period and beyond.[4] As was the case with the boxers there were many good pedestrians competing at the time. Curley, 'the Brighton Shepherd,' had the two well reported races with Cooke, 'the soldier,' in 1807 and (the one involving the pugilist Bill Richmond) 1808. There was John Jones, who appeared from Wales in June 1809, made an instant impact and attracted such out of the ordinary stake money – £500 in his successful race against the Lancastrian William Williams over 30 miles 'on the Hereford Road,' followed within weeks by a match against Edwards over 8 miles at Newmarket for no less than 1,000 guineas.[5] There was Robert Ellerby, 'the celebrated Yorkshire runner,' taking on a wager to go 100 miles in 18 hours at York Races in 1814, as well as the unfortunate George Wilson with his frustrated Blackheath marathon challenge in September 1815.[6] By then there was Joseph Beal, as near to being a formal professional champion as the sport had yet possessed. He began, at the age of 19, by beating Abraham Wood over 4 miles on York Racecourse in 1811. He then defeated Isaac Hunsworth of Bolton over 2 miles in what seemed an unchallengeable time of 9 minutes 48 seconds, repeating the victory some months later. He was early praised as 'the best runner now in England,' so much so that at the ripe age of 21 he retired, having won all his races and having no rival in sight.[7] However, he was competing again three years later, beating the Lancashire runner, Brierley. Beal's first defeat came unexpectedly in 1820 in a two mile race with John Halton ('the knowing ones were completely taken in.') Beal beat Ashton on Pontefract Racecourse in 1821 but retired for good after losing to him in a four mile race on Doncaster Racecourse in the following year.[8]

In the early nineteenth century the paid men were having to share the limelight with an amateur whose general fame outdid their own. This was, of course, Allardyce Barclay. He started young in August 1796, at the age of seventeen, making and winning a wager to walk six miles in an hour, 'fair heel and toe,' and followed it up with one or more challenges annually over the next few years. In November 1801 he made a wager of 5,000 guineas to walk ninety miles in 21° hours, almost by way of rehearsal and preparation for the great marathon feat that was to come later. He accomplished it with some ease on the York to Hull Road, starting near midnight and walking through the night. For some years he then spent much of his energies on his Scottish estates but did continue to race, over shorter distances, beating Captain Marston, for example, over 1 mile for 100 guineas at Eastbourne 'before some hundreds of spectators' in 1804 and Mr Colburn over just 440 yards at Lords in 1806.[9] The great match itself, the pedestrian event of the age, came a few months later. Captain Barclay made a wager of 1,000 guineas with Mr Webster to go a thousand miles in a thousand successive hours, at the rate of one mile in every hour. He started at Newmarket at midnight on Thursday 1 June 1809. After the first week the crowds began to gather and Barclay had more and more need of his minder, the pugilist John Gully, to keep his path clear. By the last night of the challenge there was not a bed to be had for miles around, the huge throng of spectators included at least two dukes, three earls and any number of lesser nobility and gentry, while it was reckoned that £100,000 had been bet on the outcome.[10]

Barclay's feat marked an important staging post in the history of athletics in considerably raising the threshold of possible performance, by giving a target for achievement which caught imaginations not only by its high demands but also by its rounded mathematical simplicity. It had been thought by 'the best judges' as 'beyond the powers of human nature,' but was, in fact, to be bettered several times within a few years.[11] It also turned attention to training methods. Barclay had been coached by both Jack Smith (whose methods were described in the *Sporting Magazine* of December 1798) and the old pugilist, Will Ward, and he then in turn became a trainer himself, subjecting Tom Cribb to the rigorous regime which brought him victory over an out of condition Tom Molyneux in their second fight. His career as a trainer did though end sadly, many years later, when his man, Sandy M'Kay was fatally knocked out by Byrne in 1830. Nor was he unfailingly successful as a performer and there was, of course, the anti-climax of his encounter with Abraham Wood, which had appeared to promise so much.[12]

That was an honest enough contest but the suspicions around it not only reflected an acute class consciousness but also an awareness of how susceptible this sport in particular was to sharp practice. There was clear evidence of this in 1819 in a match between Hardy and Davis where Hardy, before the race, was given 25 guineas and a bottle to drink by an apothecary. He took both, threw the bottle away and won the race. The apothecary was said to have lost £500 as a result, giving rise to the comment that 'so numerous are the frauds committed in these matches, that they have created a general distrust.[13] The distrust continued to grow. From the mid-1820s the *Sporting Magazine* became less and less interested in the doings of the pedestrians and it was left largely to the less demanding pages of *Bell's Life* to report most of the achievements of Shepherd, the final professional pedestrian of note in the period. He was a distance runner who made his name in 10 mile races in the late 1820s and subsequently also took up both longer and shorter challenges with success.[14] Even that journal was noting the sport's corruption by the end of the period and in almost identical words, yet such was the demand for sporting entertainment, particularly in the industrial areas where most events now took place, that even a corrupt sport was better than no sport at all. So much so that 62 races or challenges were noted in *Bell's* first 'Chronology of Pedestrianism,' for 1838, a far from exhaustive list not even including all the contests reported in the newspaper itself.[15]

It was again, though, a sport which had made great progress before it was, in one sense at least, undermined by its own success. At all levels the prize money could fully bear comparison with, for example, what was available in boxing. Even in the earliest days there had been challenges for 100 guineas for a return walk to Land's End and for 200 guineas at the Artillery Ground in the 1750s. By comparison, Humphries' much anticipated first fight with Mendoza had been for 200 guineas, the same stake for which Cribb fought Belcher in 1807. By this time pedestrian contests could attract at least as much, though certainly the 1,000 guineas said to be staked on Jones and Edwards was exceptional.[16] One important pioneering feature of pedestrianism was the opportunity it offered for statistical comparisons, the first sport to do so if the complex but distant scoring system of the medieval tournament is discounted and cricket is regarded as still evolving. Marathon events became more comparable by moving away from point to point challenges, with their varying terrains, gradients and surfaces, to the use of measured courses. There were many fewer place to place events after the turn of the century. The favourite venue for long distance events became the raceground where times could become comparable. Ipswich, York, Goodwood, Epsom, Brighton and Newmarket were among those which saw long distance challenges between 1804 and 1815, and later Doncaster became particularly favoured while the movement towards even more specialised running areas gathered pace rapidly – there was 'Hounslow inclosure-ground' in 1818, the 'extensive inclosure' at Kilmersdon, near Bath, in 1821, and in 1825 the 'prepared ground' near Daventry, the 2 mile circle at Ashted Park and Sheffield's famous Hyde Park Ground by the mid 1830s and the first real running track laid out at Lords in 1837.[17]

The times quoted for longer distance events were, in their nature, less at the mercy of erratic time-keeping than the shorter distances. Though still susceptible to mis-reporting they usually seem feasible – 25 miles in 3 hours or 20 miles in 2 hours 15 minutes (the latter by Abraham Wood) compare for instance with later modern timings.[18] So far as the much longer walks are concerned, they became tests of general fitness and endurance rather than specifically athletic ability – the comparison with horse racing in heats is irresistible for the stress on stamina above skill – though it has to be acknowledged some of the distance specialists, and notably of course Allardyce Barclay, would also tackle short distances successfully. It was in these shorter races and challenges that the timing becomes less reliable. There was the initial problem of having numerous different distances to contend with, though the mile was the exception, the one landmark with an overall attraction, and even at this early stage seen as having four minutes as its target time. Foster Powell's naked trial run in 1787 was said to have taken him within three seconds of it, and Curley, the Brighton Shepherd was actually claimed to have achieved it on Clapham Common in 1807, but what he did in fact run were four separate quarter mile stints at under a minute each over the space of some three hours! The ambitious certainly thought that the target was a realistic one. Mr Joliffe, having run the mile in five minutes in 1805, then 'engaged to run the same distance in four minutes and to leap a given height at stated intervals.' It has to be assumed that this bold attempt to create simultaneously both a new flat record and a new steeplechasing event came to nought. The professionals were more cautious. Joseph Beal, for instance, knew that his comfortable four mile time was 21 minutes and he based his challenges around that.[19]

Over the sprints there were the dual problems of diverse distances and unreliable time keeping. While watches were capable of fine timing there has to be doubts about the exactness of some claims. Even a 10 mile challenge in November 1799 was said to have failed only by 1 minute and half a second! Among the many distances raced were 100 yards, 120, 140, 150, 200, 220, 240, and so on, though times were seldom quoted for them.[20] If there was any tendency towards uniformity it was in a slight favouring of 120 and 200 yard races, but more research would be needed to confirm this. Overall, the trend to diversity, to the invention of new challenges, was stronger than any urge to establish competitive standards, at least outside the long distance events. Diversity, moreover, was far from stopping merely at alternative distances. Pedestrians were nothing if not innovative. They played their full part in the search for new competitive amusement that characterised the age, the provision of novel excitements for backers, participants and spectators. Much of the growing novelty, however, began to take pedestrianism down pathways which were more akin to circus performance than athletic contest. Odd wagers had begun to crop up before the turn of the century – a gentleman hopping 120 yards in five minutes for £500 in 1792 and Will Hopcraft, a known Birmingham pedestrian, apparently failing in a puzzling contest at Lords to pick up 100 stones 'each a yard distant' in 44 minutes four years later. They multiplied after 1800 and, as a final example of idiosyncrasy, a £500 wager involving one gentleman going from London to Dover and back while the other (and eventual loser) made a million dots with pen and ink on writing paper.[21] There were, however, occasional novelties which held promise for the future, notably in the appearance of some field events (as with Mellish and Crampton at Brighton) and, as well as the usual one-off contest, the mounting of actual athletics meetings with a programme of different events, a pattern known at Belsize Park in the earlier eighteenth century, but since rarely found outside rustic celebrations. With the start of an annual sports day at the Royal Military College, Sandhurst, in 1812 and Mason's Necton Games in 1817 the way opened for the mounting of athletic competition on a more organised and regular basis.[22] The various communal celebrations that involved athletic competition of one sort or another – 'Rustic Sports' as they were commonly described – did continue through the period but their role in the development of modern athletic forms was limited and, if anything diminishing. There was indeed some occasional criticism of the lack of real athletic exertions in these sports, a sense of decline from some more vigorous age, real or imagined. There was Brayfield's complaint over the 'new divertisements' that some sponsors were promoting, pointing particularly to running races 'tied up in sacks, instead of shewing the activity of their feet.' He was echoing the spirit behind the programme for model sports projected in 1811, which was remarkably original and far-sighted, not only including running events both for juniors of 16 and under and for men, but also proposing rewards for achieving set standards as well as for winning. The boys would run half a mile. Those who did it in 2° minutes would receive a guinea, while any who managed it within two minutes would have 2 guineas. For the men, running a mile in 5° minutes qualified for 2 guineas, while a time of five minutes earned no less than 3 guineas. The liberality did not extend to providing athletic competition for women but, remarkably, in order to foster the skills of the young, it was proposed to award a guinea to the parents of performers who achieved the faster times.[23]

There is no indication that such urgings to rational recreation in the form of athletics had much practical effect. The tendency was towards the exotic and the humorous on the one hand and the increasingly heavily wagered on the other. And as more money became involved in the sport, so it became more prone to both dispute and sharp practice. There was the occasional 'palpable cross' (as when a 5 to 1 favourite lost a race) but most stratagems were more indirect – false starts in sprints to tire rivals (as on the racecourse) or interference of many sorts with performers, from putting small pebbles in a walker's socks to actual doping.[24] The turf, even with a body of such influence as the Jockey Club, found great difficulty in keeping the cheats at bay. Pedestrianism was, if anything, heading for even greater problems. Its undoubted expansion was already beginning to make it more and more vulnerable. As a sport lacking either settled forms or regular locations, and usually dependent on the honesty of just one or two individuals, it defied all possibility of finding the means to exercise control over its proceedings.

The close affinity between pedestrianism and pugilism has already been noted. They were both individual man-to-man contests. They even had a considerable overlap in clientele, both in backers and even among performers, with many pugilists, from John Jackson to Jack Carter, taking to athletics as a supplementary sport. Both shared the same looseness of organisation without any sign of overall control and while pugilism might have the advantage from its more consistent and coherent gentry support, it did have to face the added hindrance of illegality. Even more thoroughly than pedestrianism it made its Georgian journey from darkness into light and then back into the gloom again.

Once the ring began to attract its influential support in the later 1780s up to the retirement of Tom Spring in 1824 the bareknuckle sport enjoyed the most flourishing – and least tarnished – years of its history. What the sport uniquely enjoyed was the notion of the *champion*, giving it a singular mark of overall supremacy, and one that could usually be determined through a clear process of challenge and response. From Tom Johnson's unquestioned assumption of the title in 1788 to Tom Cribb's retirement in 1813, its ownership was never in dispute for long, except in the ring itself. This application to a competitive sport of the concept of a *champion* simply as the best performer, with its other past medieval associations virtually stripped away, was a decisive step in the whole movement towards more organised and clearly measurable play. The appearance of champions in one activity after another has since been a constant feature of sporting history and they multiply still by the year, and in almost any geographical ambit from, say, the school to the world. Even at this time, with Tom Cribb challenged by an American black in Tom Molyneux, there was a first suspicion that a championship could possibly extend beyond an individual country, though it was to take another fifty years, and the confrontation of Tom Sayers by the American, Heenan, to firmly establish the idea of a *world* championship.

Tom Johnson who, with no apparent need for the frauds and subterfuges of the recent past, carried all before him between 1783 and 1791 when, by now in his forties, he was beaten by the Bristol collier, Ben Bryan (or Brain), known, more from the attractions of alliteration than his physical size, as 'Big Ben.' Two other luminaries of the sport were already waiting in the wings, fighting for the right to challenge Johnson when Bryan stepped in. They were the Jew, Daniel Mendoza, and Richard Humphries, dubbed the 'gentleman boxer' from the new and somewhat more polished manners he brought to the ring. After three hard fights it was Mendoza who emerged on top and when Bryan died without defending his title in 1794 he was acknowledged as champion. He in his turn was beaten the next year, perhaps not wholly fairly, by that other 'gentleman' of the ring, John Jackson, who was to play such an integral role in the sport's later history as its general factotum, tightening its organisation and also, through his connections with fencing, enlarging its horizons. By the time Jackson retired in 1800, again never having defended his title, Jem Belcher had emerged as his acknowledged successor. Regarded by many as the finest of all the bareknuckle fighters, Belcher was effectively beaten not in the ring but at the racquets court in St Martin's Lane, where an accidental fierce blow from a ball cost him the sight of one eye. Sadly, because he was obviously handicapped, he continued to fight and lost his title to Henry Pierce – 'Hen. Pierce,' and so inevitably 'The Game Chicken' – who in turn retired from ill-health three years later. Again there was an heir apparent in John Gully, who had bravely and narrowly lost to Pierce and who himself retired after a matter of months to begin another and even more fruitful career. This left Tom Cribb, probably the age's most popular boxer, and the undisputed champion from 1809 to 1813, when he began his long and contented life as an innkeeper in London's Haymarket. With his departure the championship was in limbo, his benign shadow still dominating the boxing scene.[25] There were aspirants to the title such as the northerner, Jack Carter, the boxer with pedestrian ambitions (and an excellent clog dancer into the bargain) and Dan Donnelly, the Irish Champion, who made a successful foray into England, but no fighter was to emerge convincingly until Tom Spring came up from Herefordshire in 1817.[26]

Spring's arrival lifted the sport from the slough of distrust into which it had been falling. By 1821 he had beaten all possible claimants to the title – Painter, Carter, Ben Burns and Tom Oliver – and clearly stood head and shoulders among his contemporaries though he still had to defeat Bill Neat to be indisputably acknowledged as the champion.[27] His two great defences of his crown were both against the strong and brave Irishman, Jack Langan, in what were the final great contests of bareknuckle fighting's golden age. Already with most other fights there were doubts about their honesty – Martin v Ben Burns in 1824 was described as 'another example of the degraded state to which the ring is reduced.' The championship itself could appear to be contaminated when Jem Ward, whose first fight had been the most palpable cross imaginable, was allowed to take the title. The machinations which followed, the absence of any reliably straightforward contests, were all the more frustrating as Ward was an exceptionally skilled and careful fighter, relying much on his footwork and ringcraft.[28]

Even in the sport's best years there had been occasional suspicions of fight fixing but they had always been the exceptions rather than the rule. The younger Belcher, Tom, had his early ring career as carefully nurtured by the family as any modern prospect by his manager, fighting a whole string of intendedly easy opponents on which to build a reputation. It had included a match against Bill Ryan in 1805 which appeared not to be going according to the script when, after 25 rounds, Ryan unexpectedly gave in, 'not without a suspicion of CROSS PLAY.'[29] There had been the odd dubious match between minor pugilists, and there was Carter, for instance, unaccountably falling, apparently unconscious, from his second's knee during a break between rounds, after being clearly on top through the whole of his 100 guinea fight with Tom Molyneux – it could not escape notice that the two of them were frequent companions on sparring tours.[30] There was, too, the question of whether Dutch Sam had thrown his fight with Knowlesworthy, where the purse was from the untainted source of the Pugilistic Club but it was claimed that £100,000 at least had been lost on the fight over different parts of the kingdom.[31] Nevertheless, it had always been the numerous honest encounters that had won most attention, the sequence of champions, the best known men of their times, catching their country's imagination, cheered by the populace and feted by the sporting aristocracy as no other sportsmen were, the great exemplars over a relatively few brief years of what was bound to be an eventually doomed sport.

With its noted figureheads to look up to and try to emulate it is not surprising that, with all its cruelties and hazards, pugilism flourished at all levels. The number of fights and fighting men multiplied. Organised fights grew in number and frequency with, for instance, at least seven in London alone in the one month of April 1805, as well as the 'monthly exercise of pugilistic science' at the Fives Court,[32] and if, as has been suggested, these were particularly extravagant sporting times, the same intense activity was seen in later and less excitable years such as 1810, with fights located in Nottinghamshire, Wiltshire, Coventry, Kent and Sussex and for stakes ranging between 200 guineas and £20. This is indicative not only of the popularity of the sport but also of its geographical reach and the extension of this reach began to markedly accelerate in the last few pre-Victorian years. By the later 1830s, in fact, over a third of the fights were taking place in the growing industrial areas and a single weekly issue of *Bell's Life* could be notifying contests to come in Birmingham, Bradford, Belper, Sheffield and Walsall.[33] Some parts of the country had always been noted for producing pugilists. Lancashire had Carter and Gregson and Birmingham had Jacombs, Perrins, Stanyard and Fewtrell, while the most famous of them all, Bristol, claimed not only a string of champions in Brain, Belcher, Pearce, Gully and Cribb, but also had numerous other well-known performers, including Will Warr, Bob Watson and George Nicholls. What lay behind Bristol's pre-eminence as a pugilistic nursery can only be guessed at. It was a prosperous and presumably a well fed city, disposed to produce young men healthier than the average whose stamina was developed by life in a city of steep hills. It had too its own flourishing and vigorous pugilistic tradition on Clifton Downs and at Bath's nearby Lansdown Fair, and there were always Bristolians in the wings, waiting the chance to make their way to London.[34] The frequency of local fist-fighting, often at humble levels, can be judged from the regular press accounts of resultant deaths, but there were many long term fighters, like the country tinker, Sylvester, who was said to have won fifty battles before he was beaten near Newbury. The heroes of the ring came in all sizes. Fighting fame could vary in its extent and could be very local. There was the man in a 20 guinea fight in Hampshire who was described as 'the terror of his village.' On the other hand individual cities would produce champions who enjoyed quite widespread regional reputations. There was James Stringfellow, 'many years the champion of Nottingham,' and 'Docky' More, the 'hero of Sheffield,' that city's champion and an early conquest of Bill Richmond's.[35] Local fighting was of course a very variable activity, ranging from the apparently quite formal to a simple settling of disputes. One of the oddest of these to be reported was a fight at Islington between a costermonger and Hodge, 'the noted dog-finder'(?), over the best means of dressing a pennyworth of sprats, an indication of the extent to which pugilism had penetrated into the popular culture, as did too that battle between Trigg, a carpenter, and Hawkins, 'a countryman,' as a result of a dispute concerning 'a black-eyed damsel.' Although the differences flared up on the Saturday night, the bout was properly deferred until Tuesday – the fighting day.[36]

Pugilism's most famous exponents brought added style to their sport. Johnson initiated the cautious approach, prepared to hold back and then, on the offensive, to concentrate on weak spots in his opponent's defence. Daniel Mendoza added speed to the manoeuvring, was noted for the 'astonishing quickness' of his blows and was said to hit more often and defend better than any man so far in the ring. Richard Humphries also offered style, one that was characterised by elegance and good bearing, 'a manly fighter,' who 'displays more grace in his various attitudes than any pugilist of the modern school.' Between them, Mendoza and Humphries gave new dimensions to the sport, raising expectations that a bout would involve more than mere mindless slogging. Jem Belcher followed, refining ring practice further, by his rapid foot movement, his deftness and his power in his punching, and then Tom Cribb became the first great counter-puncher, prepared to give way and invite attack in order to find an opening for his own blows.[37]

The heightened sense of style was not confined to the mode of fighting alone. It followed the common pathway taken by sports as they developed their own distinctiveness by elaborating procedures and creating rituals. Pugilists became conscious of their public image and attuned their manners and dress to new expectations. A whole sequence of practices accrued to the fight itself, rituals which transformed the contest into a theatrical performance, with its preludes and epilogues, the fight itself at its most dramatic heart. On entering the ring their dress was distinctive, their colours – always yellow with the many Bristolians – proudly displayed on scarves around their necks. The scarves were tied to the post in the fighter's corner and it became the victor's right to take up those of a defeated opponent and wear them with his own. Other ring practices firmly established themselves – the hat thrown into the ring by way of challenge and the sponge or towel thrown in as a sign of surrender, all practices which have left their permanent marks on the language.[38] It was as much theatre as sport, with the triumphant hero borne proudly away in his backer's fine coach at the end of the performance and the defeated, if he was fortunate in his friends, being nursed back into consciousness. If not, he might well play to the full the tragic role that act five of the drama could call for.

After nearly forty years of popularity and growth, however, pugilism could no longer give any impression of robust health after the mid-1820s. Like pedestrianism and, to a somewhat lesser extent, the turf, the ring was losing too many of those patrons who had combined both wealth and honesty. It had never found effective means of accommodating itself with integrity to circumstances where its financing had become the overriding consideration, where the money was unquestionably being given the priority over the sport. There was now much more acrimony and haggling over stake money than there was actual fisticuffs. In their fight near Doncaster in October 1831 there was uproar when Sampson was felled by Brown, the ring was broken, Brown was struck by spectators and hit with a stake and the referee fled to Doncaster. The stakeholder[39] condemned the violence to Brown, the clear winner, but on his return to Doncaster declared for Sampson. It was at last all too much for the *Sporting Magazine*. 'Comment is uncalled for: but if a final "knock-down blow" were wanted for the Ring, nothing could have been more effectual than the issue of this, "the last fight on the list!"'[40]

It was effectively the end of pugilism's prospects of ever becoming an acceptable sport in its current form, prospects which were never bright once the moral tide began to turn, given bareknuckle fighting's unavoidable brutalities. What was not quenched, though, was the demand for sporting entertainment from the working masses, still severly restricted in their opportunities. If they could not be engrossed by honest competition they were prepared, as with the pedestrian, to make do with what was on offer and far from seeing a reduction in fights at the end of the Georgian period there was undeniably a steady increase. If the spectators were denied quality they could at least have quantity. In 1843, for example, *Bell's Life* not only published a list of the year's 122 fights but also acknowledged that 'many minor fights took place' of which it had no record.[41] It was another of the sports that had to await both a further extension of the new respectability and the advent of new forms of recreation.

While there were these doubts about the future of both pugilism and pedestrianism both had shared until the last years or so of the period in the general sporting progress. Amid this progress, however, there remain some doubts and puzzles and, paradoxically, they centre primarily on the two sports that were to become the national summer and winter games by the end of the Victorian age. Cricket's enigma is a relatively minor one, football's quite wholesale. In cricket it is a matter of trying to estimate the extent to which the earlier years of the nineteenth century shared in the general advance of the game, still almost as much of a mystery as it was when Eric Parker called it 'The Dark Chapter' and Rowland Bowen considered it likely that the game was in something of a slump between 1799 and 1824, though he granted that 'for many years little is known of what was going on.'[42] While this is an exaggeration, and there is a good deal of information about individual matches, the difficulty lies in drawing the evidence together towards some coherent conclusions. However, this is only a trivial problem compared with that facing the football historian. Even the always enthusiastic and optimistic Percy Young had to entitle his chapter on this period 'The Struggle for Survival' and reluctantly to echo Strutt's opinion that the game had 'fallen into disrepute' and was 'little practised,'[43] while subsequent chroniclers of the game have usually thought it safer to evade the problems presented by this period in its history.

As has been seen, cricket had already become a complex and sophisticated game, quite identifiable with its modern form. Its language had become largely familiar – 'fielding' was a recognised activity and fielding positions, such as 'slip,' 'second slip,' 'short slip,' and 'point,' were being identified and named.[44] Two decisive steps which would promote the future growth of the game had also been taken. Round arm bowling had begun to release it from the limits imposed by the old underarm method and another potential for progress lay in the dawning concept of play without stake money, a notion that had always been hard for the eighteenth century mind to grasp. Cricket, though, was involved with money in the acceptable sense. It was the only sport apart from horse racing which had, on any scale, become business as well as play. It not only had its professional players and its gate money from spectators, but also its manufacturers, its traders in equipment and dress, and its commercial promoters. Batmakers had been advertising their wares since the 1770s and specialist balls of different makes ('Budd's Patronised Game Balls and Clout's best Game Balls' for instance) were being advertised for sale,[45] if not as yet from specialist suppliers. In August 1784 when the Digby family at Sherborne Castle bought two bats (one at 4s. 9d. and the other at 5s .0d.) and ten balls (at 6s. 6d.) they did so from what appears to have been the local hardware shop, while a Nottingham advertisement from 1817 for bats and balls came from Mr Corbett, Perfumer, etc., of Bridlesmith Gate.[46] Publicans again profited from the game from many angles – as hosts for club meetings, as caterers, as equipment suppliers, sometimes as proprietors of cricket grounds and indeed as groundsmen as well.[47]

The question is whether this progress took place with equal consistency through the period. There were the well-known early alarms – in 1767 that it might be displaced by golf, and over its 'degeneration' in 1774[48] – but these did not point to any serious hiatus in the game's development. There was indeed some strengthening and broadening of the game in its upper reaches as the century drew to a close and lesser contests were also on the increase, so much so that the *Sporting Magazine* in 1794 had to apologise for not having enough space to publish details of all the games that were being reported to its offices. The highly staked matches began to thin out after 1800 although they did not disappear altogether and for some years wartime pressures were doubtless responsible for a certain falling away. The proportion of games involving military teams over the next few years certainly increased, but the extent of wartime disturbance in those areas where village cricket had its deepest roots is difficult to assess. John Goulstone, questioning Bowen's pessimistic view of the 1800s, has pointed out that there was no decline in the number of games reported in its heart-land of Kent during this decade, remaining at about 30 except in 1803 and 1804 when invasion was at its most threatening. The number slumped to 7 in 1803 and of the 18 matches in the next year four had a military flavour about them.[49]

Fluctuations in the game's popularity may well sometimes have been as much a matter of place as of time. It would be making modern assumptions to expect a steady continuity in sporting experience at this time. Local race meetings came and went with great frequency and it would be unreasonable to expect any other sport to have a universally uninterrupted local history. There are many instances of cricket being first on the wane and then appar-ently picking up again.[50] The game was clearly widely *known*, and some clubs could exist for many years before competing outside their own membership, an outstanding if explicable example being the Cornish Cricket Club established at Truro in 1813, almost certainly having a continuous history from the number of later references, but not playing inter-club matches before 1830.[51] Such gradations from informal play, through internal games, to set matches against others make for difficulties in defining the true geographical spread of the game. There is the Dorset example from 1738 to indicate that it seems to have had a developed form of cricket very early and yet in 1822 the *Sporting Magazine* was saying that previously it 'had been but little in practice' there.[52]

Among several factors which infer, but far from prove, that cricket's otherwise steady progress did undergo something of a pause at least around the first decade of the nineteenth century is the reduction in the number of games reported in the national press, reflecting if nothing else a decline in reader interest. It is known too that the game did lapse in some places. At Brighton its falling away might well be put down to the absence of the Prince, but elsewhere reasons for decline have to be guessed at. Some of the most persuasive pointers to possible losses of the game come, in fact, from references to later revivals. At Saffron Walden it was reported in 1811 that 'the practice of this manly game' had been restored to its former excellence, and, once the wars ended, came reports of its now thriving state in Norwich and Salisbury, of new full size stumps in use in Essex, revival at Lichfield, and a new enthusiasm for higher standards of play by the employment of skilled coaches.[53] For all the problems that the game might have experienced in the immediately preceding years, cricket entered the Victorian age still in good standing and in better health than any other popular sport. It remained the 'true English game' and its myth was still only slightly tinged by the virtually unavoidable deviousness and deceit which was tainting other major sports. It certainly had its sharp practice, some of it within the laws – the bowler tossing the ball up into the sun to dazzle the batsman, the choice of wickets to suit the side's own bowlers, and so on. There was Beauclerk's scheming match making, always likely to be countered by the devices of the professionals, and there was certainly aggressive behaviour on the field, the sort of sledging of a young batsman described by Mary Mitford, and doubtless examples of what much later was described in the scorebook as 'frightened out'! However, in spite of Pyecroft's accusation that gentlemen players would often throw games there was probably less corruption than in the old Hambledon games when the 'blacklegs' used to congregate round the paid men at the Green Man during London matches, hoping to buy the result they wanted. It remained the 'delightful and manly exercise' that the *Sporting Magazine* had described it as in 1727, and still 'considerably on the increase.'[54]

It was not in the nature of football to be open to such corruption. Local rivalries were its usual motive force. There is little evidence of playing for stakes or of betting on games. A rare exception came in 1795 when the King's Bench heard an appeal from an assize court decision on the payment of stake money.[55] The virtual absence of any pecuniary involvement may well help to account for the slimness of the contemporary record. With 'game' and 'gaming' still tending to be seen as synonymous, neither the editor of the *Sporting Magazine* nor Pierce Egan in his *Book of Sports*, for example, saw football as of much importance. The one made many more references to bell ringing than to football and Egan did not give the game a mention at all. What is beyond speculation is that the game continued to be well known, and comments on it assume this common knowledge. Among the 'Miseries of Human Life' listed by a correspondent in 1806 are, as well as being bowled first ball at cricket, playing football on 'sloppy' ground, where the ball becomes 'muddy, sappy, and rotten.' Then there was a later complaint about being called indoors to meet company when 'pasted with mire from head to foot,' from footballing. and then 'to be suddenly called off by a party of ladies, who hurry you away without even allowing you a moment to wash you hands, still less to change your stockings.'[56] Such sidelong glimpses suggest that it was commonly played, though much of the direct evidence continues to be of a game for boys and youths. That old rough London sporting ground, Tothill Fields, had ten acres (!) marked out for the Westminster scholars in 1810, schoolboys at Hitchin had their own ground until 1819, French and English boys played at Stoneyhurst during the war years, and football was well established at schools such as Rugby where William Webb Ellis made his mythical name.[57]

This boyhood play was unlikely to attract much attention. Much more comment, most of it critical, was provoked by the annual mass contests which still took place up and down the country. Malcolmson identified sixteen of them at Shrovetide alone and while dating is sometimes uncertain quite a number still flourished at the end of the period. Their prospects, however, in urban settings at least, were precarious. One of most fully reported – and largely by way of attempts to stop it – was the Derby game between the parishes of St Peters and All Saints. It was a handling, not a kicking game, the ball carrier being propelled by the crowd. The ball was thrown up in the market place and the goals were each just over a mile distant, one a garden gate and the other a water wheel, which could only be reached through the mill-stream that was often shoulder high at Shrovetide. The bells of the winning parish were rung as soon as the ball had been goaled, by which time there would have been twenty to thirty fights but, it was claimed, no long-standing emnity.[58] Annual contests also existed in some smaller communities – between villages such as Halloton against Melbourne in Leicestershire, between two ends of the town as at Bromfield in Cumberland or just between two streets as at Helston in Cornwall. In other places the competition was more broadly based, typically town against country, for example at Bury, Beverley, Keighley, and Sedgefield in Cumberland, where the game was reported in the press in 1802.[59] After the attempts at suppression in the 1740s and 1750s there were some thirty years of relative tolerance and it was not until the 1790s, as suspicions of all mobs became heightened, that further attacks were launched. It was, however, a fitful business. There seems to have been no widespread support for suppression, with even the militia failing to help the Kingston magistrates in their attempt to prevent the local Shrove Tuesday game in 1799. From the evidence of later prohibitions alone it is clear that many of the mass games were still taking place as the period came to end, among them those at Nuneaton, Workington, Alnwick, Ashbourne and Twickenham.[60]

Whatever the distant ritualistic origins of these contests, well before the late eighteenth century they had come to serve other purposes, working off old grudges, asserting communal unity and establishing individual status. Their public prominence has almost certainly distorted the overall pre-Victorian picture of football as a whole. There is appreciable evidence that the game was commonly played in forms far removed from the simple folk struggle, indications of matches that were more formal, deliberately arranged, with small and equal teams, and taking place on defined and marked out playing areas. Recalling his youth from earlier in the period, 'Huntingdeniensis,' the would-be poet responsible for 'The Football Match' in 1807, described how 'the ground is mark'd, the goals prepared,' for what turns out to be both a kicking and carrying game, with even some heading:

Ralpho's lofty forehead stopp'd its force,
And by the contact, chang'd its furious course,
He rubb'd the place, and smiling at the pain,
Resum'd his wonted hardiness again.

With the ball at one point described as the 'stiffen'd globe'Ralpho's discomfiture is understandable – our own at the execrable verse is only made endurable by the usefulness of its content![61] Information on specific matches, however, is thin throughout the period. In the 1770s there were contests advertised in East Anglia and reports of games being played as far apart as Lancashire, Hertfordshire and Devon, but the line between the more contained and regulated contest and the wide-ranging free-for-all is sometimes blurred. At Hitchin, for example, which had the marked field where scholars, and possibly others, played the game, the match between the town and Gosmore in 1772 still had the old unordered flavour about it, with the ball going into a pond, being forced along several streets, and finally goaled in the church porch.[62] Most matches reported from later in the period tend to have a northern emphasis including a 'severe contest' lasting six hours between the Lincolnshire villages of Osbournby and Billingborough, the three day six-a-side match (!) between Sheffield and Norton in 1793, and the game played on Kennington Common between immigrants from Cumberland and Westmoreland. These could exhibit a degree of organisation with, for instance, teams wearing some distinguishing mark – Billingborough had blue ribands while the Norton players wore green and their opponents red.[63]

The current health of the regional variations of the game, hurling in the far west country and camping in East Anglia and the Home Counties, is not easy to determine. References to hurling are still as likely as not to be to Strutt's game 'played by parties of Irishmen' who 'used a kind of bat to take up the ball and strike it from them.' Hurling in the West country fashion was, though, certainly being noted as a popular feature of such local celebrations as the Tavistock Revels in the 1770s and a reminiscence from 1823 describing camping implies that it was being played in recent years.[64] What did persist, and persist widely, was the informal playing of the game that lay somewhere between the mass struggle and the organised and arranged small side contest. More or less impromptu play must have been common, as it was on Sundays in Keighley, giving offence to sabbatarians. It was popular in Lancashire mill towns and 'a game which the common people of Yorkshire are particularly partial to, the tips of their shoes being heavily shod with iron.'[65] It was the sort of game which Dr Butler of Shrewsbury School saw as only fit for butcher boys, and it was the frequent and casual street play of this sort that was often being seen as more of a nuisance than the occasional mass game. In 1790 the Lancashire Quarter Sessions backed up the Bolton magistrates in their action against football play in the market place that spilled over into neighbouring streets, and steps were being taken against street football either as a public nuisance or a breach of the peace – at Hull in 1818, for instance – long before it was specifically banned under the 1835 Highways Act.[66]

It all amounts to further indications of the flourishing state of football, even if its liveliness existed for the most part beneath the recognised surface of early nineteenth century sport. It might well not figure in the recommendations of those who sought to rationalise the diversions of the people, nor in the enterprises promoted by commercially alert innkeepers. It had neither the orderliness and decorum sought by the one, nor the means of keeping a thirsty crowd together sought by the other, and its public status was doubtful in the eyes of both. Yet it was there. It was clearly being played widely, and was being enjoyed both by the upper classes in their schooldays and by some of them afterwards, as well as by iron-shod factory hands. The roots of the game were very much alive. Football only needed its codification, those 'smaller numbers' and restraining rules which Richard Mulcaster had looked to a couple of centuries earlier, and also its approved times and places, for it to emerge into the world of organised play. It would, nonetheless, have taken great prescience in 1815 to predict that this would become the major winter game, watched weekly by great crowds, by the end of the century.

Notes

1. *SM*, October 1793, pp 13-15.
2. *Times*, 1 November 1787. See also 29 March, 22, 30 June, 9, 26 October and 'Athletics Notices from The Times,' *Sports History*, 9, 1986, pp 9/10. I am also indebted to John Goulstone in correspondence for several athletic references.
3. *SM*, October 1792, pp 14/15; Miles, *Pugilistica*, I, p 436.

4. *SM*, October 1806, p 41; April 1806, p 239; June 1813, p 139. For other of Wood's races see *e.g.*, October 1807, p 4; April 1809, p 43; December 1812, p 138.

5. *SM*, June 1807, p 147; January 1808, p 210; June 1809, p 144; July 1809, p 198.

6. *SM*, July 1814, p 182; September 1815, pp 244-6. See also *SM*, April 1822, p 51.

7. *SM*, September 1811, p 290; *Sports History*, 8, 1986, 'Joseph Beal, the First Runner in England,' pp 25/6.

8. *SM*, February 1820, p 247; March 1820, p 300; *Sports History*, 8, 1986, pp 25/6.

9. *SM*, September 1804, p 313; August 1806, p 242. See also Miles, *Pugilistica*, I, pp 435-439.

10. *SM*, June 1809, p 108; July 1809, p 198; Miles, *Pugilistica*, I, pp 438/9.

11. See *SM*, October 1808, p 41; September 1809, p 285. The 'Barclay Match' was, for example, achieved again in Sheffield by John Wright in 1822. (*SM*, May 1822, p 103)

12. *SM*, October 1808, p 41; August 1806, p 242; September 1804, p 313; June 1830, pp 254-256; October 1807, p 4.

13. *SM*, February 1819, p 216.

14. 'John Shepherd, "The Yorkshire Phenomenon,"' *Sports History*, 9, 1985, pp 7-9. See also e.g., *BLL*, 1, 15 June 1828.

15. 'scarcely does a race come off where there is not the most barefaced attempts at "foul play" resorted to,' *BLL*, 1 January 1837; 30 December 1838.

16. *SM*, March 1793, p 53; November 1804, p 98; May 1806, p 90; June 1805, p 167; February 1808, p 264; March 1808, p 322; May 1809, p 94; August 1806, p 242-243.

17. *SM*, October 1818, p 32; July 21, p 198; February 1825, p 377; BLL, 17 April 1836.

18. *SM*, October 1795, p 23; October 1806, p 43.

19. *Sports History*, 7, 1985, p 9; *SM*, October 1807, p 43; March 1806, p 119; *Sports History*, 8, 1986, p 25.

20. *SM*, November 1799, p 94 and *passim*.

21. *SM*, May 1796, p 80; March 1796, p 337; December 1801, p 153; May 1815, p 90

22. Melvyn Watman, *History of British Athletics*, 1968, p 17.

23. *SM*, April 1813, pp 29/30; January 1811, pp 141/2.

24. *SM*, April 1799, p 84; February 1807, p 251; September 1815, pp 244-246; Wilson, *A Sketch of the Life of George Wilson; Sports History*, 5, 1984, pp 10-14.

25. For fuller details of the sequence of champions see *Pancratia*; Miles, *Pugilistica*, I; Fred Henning, *Fights for the Championship*, 1902; Brailsford, *Bareknuckles*.

26. Miles, *Pugilistica*, II, pp 174, 138-154; Egan, *Boxiana*, III, pp 77-79.

27. A previous fight between Neat and Thomas Hickman ('The Gas Man' from his Black Country origins) had been billed somewhat extravagantly as 'for the championship.'

28. *SM*. October 1824, pp 61-63 and, on the lamentable state of pugilism, November 1826, p 56.

29. *Pancratia*, p 230; *SM*, June 1805, p 150.

30. *SM*, April 1813, pp 24/5. In another bout Dixon and Brennan had agreed not to hurt each other and share a 20 guinea purse but the crowd was not taken in and

they were driven off under threat of horse whipping, April 1810, p 30.

31. Miles, *Pugilistica*, I, pp 457-460; *SM*, December 1814, pp 159/160.

32. *SM*, April 1805, pp 50-56. See also June 1806, p 146.

33. *Pancratia*, pp 332-334; *SM*, January 180, pp 192-194; March 1810, p 30; April 1810, pp 30, 35; *BLL*, 8 March 1838.

34. See *SM*, January 1808, p 207; January 1813, p 206.

35. *SM*, February 1807, p 251; January 1809, p 204; April 1810, p 45; Miles, *Pugilistica*, I, pp 288/9.

36. *SM*, July 1795, p 163; March 1796, p 289; October 1804, p 44.

37. *Pancratia*, p 72; *SM*, April 1793, p 11; Ford, *Prizefighting*, pp 121/122.

38. See e.g., Ford, *Prizefighting*, pp 108/9.

39. John Beardsworth, highly successful but none too scrupulous owner of a Birmingham carriage business, of whom a much too flattering account appears in Egan's *Book of Sports*, pp 113-120.

40. Miles, *Pugilistica*, II, pp 450-452; *SM*, October 1831, p 468.

41. BLL, 7 January 1844.

42. Eric Parker, *The History of Cricket*, undated, p 84; Bowen, *Cricket: A History*, pp 79/80.

43. Young, *British Football*, p 61; Strutt, *Sports and Pastimes*, pp 93/4.

44. *Sports History*, 3, 1983, p 4; 8, 1985, pp 8-10.

45. *e.g.* bats by William Staples at Sevenoaks, *Kentish Gazette*, 11 May 1774; 'Budd's Patronised Game Balls and Clout's Best Game Balls,' by James White at Brighton, *Sussex Weekly Advertiser*, 12 June 1809; Buckley, *Eighteenth Century Cricket*, p 64; *Pre-Victorian Cricket*, p 90.

46. *Nottingham Journal*, 21 June 1817; Buckley, *Pre-Victorian Cricket*, p 53. I am indebted to Ann Smith, working on the Digby archives, for the Sherborne reference.

47. The demand for cricket equipment could come from a wide age-range – see Kenneth Bourne, *Palmerston: The Early Years 1784-1841*, 1982, p 7.

48. Buckley, *Eighteenth Century Cricket*, pp 46, 67/68.

49. *SM*, September 1793, p 237; June 1810, p 132; July 1811, p 138. I am indebted to John Goulstone in correspondence for this information on Kent cricket.

50. *e.g.* Birmingham which had a cricket society in 1760 and revivals in 1803 and 1805, all associated with different locations. Buckley, *Eighteenth Century Cricket*, p 38; *Pre-Victorian Cricket*, pp 42, 44.

51. Buckley, *Eighteenth Century Cricket*, p 66.

52. *Sherborne Mercury*, 9 May 1738; *SM*, August 1822, p 265.

53. *SM*, June 1811, p 145; July 1819, p 197; Buckley, *Pre-Victorian Cricket*, p 91. The Grantham Club players were trained by 'Nottingham professors' and Leicester by 'Mr Howard of the Marylebone Club,' pp. 107, 127.

54. Ford, *Cricket: A Social History*, pp 34, 78, 102; *SM*, June 1827, p 114.

55. It was alleged that the stakes had been paid over though the terms of the wager had not been met, *SM*, April 1795, p 8.

56. *SM*, October 1806, p 19; August 1807, p 223.

57. Young, *British Football*, pp 63/5; Gourlay, *History of Sherborne School*, p 302.

58. *SM*, June 1830, p 224; Malcolmson, *Popular Recreations*, p 36 and passim; Young, *British Football*, pp 4/5.

59. Wright, *British Calendar Customs*, I, pp 118, 27; III, p 245; J. Nicholson, *Folk Lore of East Yorkshire*, 1890, pp 34 ff.; *Sports History*, 7, 1985, pp 5-7; Malcolmson, *Popular Recreations*, p 37; *SM*, March 1802, p 348.

60. Malcolmson, *Popular Recreations*, pp 138-145.

61. *SM*, December 1807, pp 153-155.

62. Malcolmson, *Popular Recreations*, p 38; Young, *British Football*, pp 56/7.

63. *SM*, August 1795, p 276; May 1796, p 105. See also Young, *British Football*, pp 57-61; *SM*, June 1809, p 33.

64. Strutt, *Sports and Pastimes*, pp 92/3; Malcolmson, *Popular Recreations*, pp 113, 35/6. The cautions over the similarities between Major Moor's account of hurling and the original have to be born in mind.

65. Whitaker, *Eighteenth Century Sunday*, p 140; Young, *British Football*, p 58.

66. Young, *British Football*, p 180; Malcolmson, *Popular Recreations*, pp 138-145.

11.

A Taste for Diversions

In an age of expansion, experiment and novelty it is little wonder that sport and recreation should take on these same characteristics. There was a ready response to the thirst for entertainment, for excitement, for spectacle, and for new competitive activity. It was another aspect of that 'craving for extraordinary incident, which the rapid communication of intelligence hourly gratifies,' lamented by William Wordsworth as blunting the sensibilities.[1] Its sporting consequences though were far from damaging and it is fitting to round off this exploration of the Georgians at play with a reminder of the many new sports which they contrived. Among the most notable – and among the most innocent – were the water sports. The possibilities for play offered by the country's rivers and its surrounding seas were exploited as never before and competitive activities which had previously, if they existed at all, been limited or occasional, rapidly took on the forms which they were to carry into the modern sporting world.

Competitive swimming was the least of them in its development. In any organised form remained something of a rarity until the very end of the period when the National Swimming Society was inaugurated and formal championship races began.[2] On the broader front there was a growing acceptance across the social classes of physical immersion in what had often previously been regarded as a dangerous element. By the end of the eighteenth century faith was growing in the health-giving qualities of sea water bathing, a practice given much impetus by what were seen as beneficial visits to Weymouth by the ailing George III. Sea dipping became so highly esteemed indeed that one Wiltshire parson saw an annual trip to the coast for this purpose as total justification to his bishop for temporary absence from his parish.[3] The extent to which the popularity of bathing extended to *swimming* is less clear. Strutt had his usual doubts. After describing swimming as 'an exercise of great antiquity; and, no doubt familiar to the inhabitants of this country at all times,' he is 'sorry to add' that it is now 'by no means so generally practised with us in the present day as it used to be in former times.' There seems to be little evidence to support this, at least so far as London was concerned. Swimming in the Thames was certainly popular, and even in the park lakes, to judge from protests over the nudity there and the swimmers' liking for Sundays. Many learned to swim in childhood, from Samuel Johnson (whose skill in the water was later commended by his Brighton 'dipper') to Palmerston, who could swim before he went up to Harrow at the age of 12. Strutt's dismissal of it as 'boys' amusement' hardly squares with either the known accomplishments of such as Benjamin Franklin who swam from Lambeth to London Bridge or Lord Byron who went three miles with the tide from Lambeth in 1807 or with the reputation of some lady swimmers such as the 'Diving Belle' reported with such enthusiasm two years earlier.[4] Some of the artificial swimming baths, moreover, like Peerless Pool in London (at 60 yards by 30) and the Ladywell Pool in Birmingham were designed and advertised specifically as *swimming* baths and although municipal baths, from the late 1820s onwards, were built for hygienic rather than recreational reasons, they would do much to foster the gradual growth of swimming as a competitive sport.[5] Before that time reports of races or wagers are rare. There was a race between two brothers from London Bridge to Kew in 1793, this possibly catching the eye because it was for a 'considerable wager' and the swimmers drank several glasses of wine in the water while on their way. It did perhaps take exceptional circumstances for swimming contests to be reported, none more so than the race between two watermen towing their wherries by the teeth and against the tide. The competitors were said to have 'displayed wonderful strength in the art of swimming,' and, presumably, very healthy teeth. This race took place, incidentally, on Monday 9th July 1810, a day when there was also an important rowing race on the Thames, though whether there was any deliberate connection between the two happenings is not clear.[6] There appears to have been no swimming – at least none that was planned – at any other of the many boating events and regattas.

If swimming was rarely considered in competitive terms skating, by contrast, and in spite of its inevitably much more occasional nature, made striking progress. It showed a remarkable capacity to make rapid use of its opportunities for competition and even to make important innovations. Purely as a recreation, skating retained its popularity, creating scenes such as those which had given offence to Sabbatarians in the middle of the century. Sunday remained a favourite skating day when the ice allowed it – and sometimes when it didn't. Its strength on the Serpentine was dubious on Sunday 13th January 1805, but gradually more and more skaters ventured out. There were some fifty on the ice in the afternoon when it broke. Two youths were trapped under the ice, one was rescued but the other died. Such occasional tragedies proved no deterrent. In the next winter the frost was hard enough to allow for reportedly excellent skating on both the Serpentine and the St James's Park canal and not only did the three strikingly attired ladies attract attention but so also did a group of guards officers who 'evinced a consummate proficiency in the art.'[7] They may well have been profiting from the guidance given by a fellow soldier, Robert Jones, Lieutenant of Artillery, in his *Treatise on Skating*, published in 1772 and dedicated to Lord Spencer Hamilton, said to be an expert on the ice. Figure skating was certainly developing recognised manoeuvres by this time – the Edinburgh Skating Club, with at least half a century's history behind it, had a demanding entrance test which included a figure similar to a figure of eight and also a jump over two top hats on the ice.[8]

More surprising, given the natural limitations on its performance, was the growth of speed skating as a competitive sport with its well known players, its crowds, wagers, betting, and various types of contest. It was obviously wholly dependent on hard winters to provide sufficient time both for the ice to harden and matches to be arranged. It was, equally obviously, likely to be a very localised sport, at least in any sustained form, centred on the long levels of the Fen country. Among the period's severe winters were those of 1798/9, 1802/3, 1809/10 and 1810/11, the last two, coming in succession, apparently giving particular continuity and impetus to the sport.

The Drakes of Chatteris and Thompson of Wimblington have already been noted as performers who could make appreciable part-time profits from competitive skating and there were other celebrities, such as Green from March who, in 1811, was offering to compete against any man in England apart from Thompson, who, for his part, made no exceptions and stated that 'he would not refuse to run against any man in England.' Crowds came to watch. There was 'a numerous concourse of people' at Wisbech for a contest for a 20 stone hog in 1799, 5,000 or more for a 100 guinea match in 1803 and similar crowds attracted to events in 1910/11, all in the Fens.[9] Contests tended to take on a greater variety of forms than in any other sport, possibly a consequence of skating's spasmodic nature and the need to set up such competition as could be mounted at short notice, giving little opportunity for one settled pattern to emerge. There were, for instance, team matches – 3 of Chatteris against 3 of March in 1803 and what seems to have been a similar but two-man match, Chatteris (the two Drake brothers) against Earith in 1810. There were individual matches, with two miles as a favourite distance, and while wagers against the clock, so common in pedestrianism, seem to have been a rarity, it is highly likely that such marathon efforts as that of Francis Drake (presumably another of the family) in going from Whittlesea Mere to Mildenhall in Suffolk were taken on for a wager of some sort. What became a popular form of competition, however, was the knock-out between eight skaters. This in itself was a remarkable innovation. Skaters might always refer in their challenges to 'running' against rivals but they took this mode of competition not from pedestrianism but from cock-fighting. If league competition had its first roots in the racecourse practice of running in heats, the knock-out cup competition, with its gradual elimination of contestants, derived from the Welsh main of the cockpit. The usual description of such tournaments referred to eight skaters and seven matches, making its shape quite clear, and it is interesting to speculate on why this particular sport should resort to this scheme, novel so far as human competition was concerned. The hurried circumstances under which skating competitions had to be arranged might well provide most of the answer. The knock-out left no scope for haggling over the conditions of play – these were the same for all – and there would be no crowd disappointments such as Thompson caused by refusing to skate a match in 1811 because the course was less than the 1° miles stipulated. So popular had skating become in all its various forms that in just two successive days in January 1811 there were not only two such knock-out events, one on the Old Bedford River and another at County Wash, but also matches at Wisbech, March, Benwick, Ramsey and Nordelph, where there were no fewer than three. All in all, what had earlier in the period been little more than occasional recreation, was, by the end of it, a definable sport capable of mounting matches and challenges of up to 100 guineas.[10]

The aquatic sports of rowing and sailing made, if anything, even more spectacular progress. Not only did the long established rowing competition among professional watermen become more intense but the sport began to be taken up also by the gentleman amateurs, another reflection of their increased zest for physical activity. A new impetus to professional rowing came from the establishment of the two annual contests for prizes given by the proprietors of the Vauxhall Gardens and Astley's Equestrian Amphitheatre respectively. They appeared for the first time in the later 1780s, further significant expressions of the sporting renaissance beginning in those years. The attraction of the races, with a new wherry as the prize, was immediate, to would-be competitors and spectators alike. 200 watermen entered for the first race and lots had to be drawn to select the seven pairs who would actually row.[11] Such was the excitement and success of the Vauxhall initiative that one of the day's great entertainment rivals, Astley's Royal Amphitheatre, launched another race three years later. The arrangements varied over the years. Astley's race in 1801, for instance, was notified as for 'water-men below the bridge only,' and the competition would sometimes have what appear to have been preliminary rounds. Strutt, in one of his rare references to any sporting innovations of his own day, wrote that two or three 'heats or trials' were held to choose rowers for the prize wherries.[12] Matches made for wagers also became more frequent. In some months, such as October 1805, there would be several such contests to report, while the occasional unusual competition attracted special attention. There had, for instance, been a marathon event in the previous February when a group of army officers sponsored a race between London and Gravesend watermen from Rotherhithe, down the estuary, round the Nore and back, involving eight hours continuous rowing. There was heavy betting and the Gravesend men won, doubtless better used to coping with the choppy winter waters of what was, at its extremity, virtually the open sea.[13]

What is often unclear from reports, however, is whether contests were for professionals or for amateurs and this doubt could exist also among the growing number of regattas. That at Twickenham in 1798 was specifically mounted to encourage local watermen. Professional and amateur rowing races did often coexist, and professional sailors also competed in regattas. Brixham fishing smacks competing off Tenby in 1809 were certainly being sailed by fishermen but whether the same applied to the cutters that competed off Bradwell in Essex for a prize silver cup in 1787 can only be guessed at. Trade is implied in the statement that they came from several different ports, but cutters were as popular for pleasure as for work, and there was the nature of the prize to be taken into account – watermen usually putting money above silverware.[14]

Cutters had long been the favourite boats of London apprentices and continued to be so well into the nineteenth century.[15] Racing between boats was inevitable and it seems likely that known rowing clubs at the end of the eighteenth century like the Star, Arrow, and Shark, were either Cutter Clubs

A view of two of the newer sports, steeplechasing and sailing, from Pierce Egan's Book of Sports *at the end of the period.*

or their immediate descendants. The social make-up of competitive rowing on the Thames at this time is accordingly difficult to determine and the transition of the sport from an apprentice jaunt to a gentleman's club-based pursuit needs further research. Whether, for instance, the two six-oared boats that raced from Westminster Bridge to Kew for a wager of twenty guineas on a December Sunday in 1803 were rowed by gentlemen or apprentices is not known, and there are other similar cases. Here the size of the wager might suggest the former, but the day pointed to apprentice oarsmen. What is certain is that rowing races were taking place which were specifically described as between gentlemen. By then a number of them would have been introduced to the sport during their time at school or university. Rowing and punting were established at Eton by the 1790s, when T. F. Dibden also listed rowing among the main amusements at Oxford, although it only showed signs of some permanent organisation emerging there in 1815 when eights had appeared and Brasenose was quoted as Head of the River, followed by Jesus in second place.[16]

It is clear too that from around 1805 there is a new pattern of racing on the Thames. The old course to Kew is deserted, races tend to become shorter, and gentlemen oarsmen begin to be precisely specified. There were even precocious attempts to achieve equality of opportunity between the gentlemen who raced for a silver cup in 1807 in boats owned and manned by them – they all rowed in boats other than their own, 'as a fairer point.' It provided 'a pretty aquatic spectacle' for the great numbers on the river who came to watch.[17] The other 'pretty aquatic spectacle' to appear in the period was the regatta. There are various claimants to the first such event – Walton on Thames (1758) and Ranelagh Gardens (1773) for example[18] – though they remained relatively rare and occasional until the turn of the century, when they begin to appear in some numbers. The great decades for the founding of regattas were to be the 1820s and 1830s, when initially they would typically include not only both rowing and sailing events but also races for both amateurs and professionals. At first their form was indeterminate, and likely to include contests for professional watermen as at Twickenham and matches as well as races. By 1801 the regatta at St Paul's, Deptford, was already being described as 'annual,' though this term, in the optimistic usage of the day, could again imply an intention as much as a previous history.[19] Within a few years regattas were beginning to appear on other waters than the Thames and to quite clearly combine both rowing and sailing. The 'water frolic' at Yarmouth in 1810 included both and that on Lake Windermere involved both gentry and professionals with a sailing match for 50 guineas and a race between Bowness fishing boats. In typical transitional fashion, and as a further reminder of the continuing strength of the old, it also picked up activities from earlier communal recreation, the races on the lake being followed by wrestling, leaping and running on land.[20] The growth of regattas accelerated rapidly in the 1820s and by the end of the decade in the south west alone they were regular features at Plymouth, Dartmouth, Dawlish, Teignmouth, Cowes, Southampton and Weymouth.[21]

Organised sailing races on the Thames had been well established since the 1780s. One of the earliest full reports is of a contest for a cup given by the Duke of Cumberland ('value £20') on 17 June 1776. Ten boats sailed a course from Blackfriars Bridge through Fulham Bridge and back, the first five all finishing within a minute of each other. The club bearing the duke's name was already in existence and when the proprietors of the Vauxhall Gardens announced their sailing race for gentlemen it was to be subject to that club's rules.[22] With Astley's offering a similar prize a few years later there were two competitions of substance for gentlemen to sail for, as well as occasional races and matches and also, as sailing societies expanded, their own internal club contests. There were also one-off events such as that for the 'beautiful' £50 cup given by the Contractors of the Lottery in 1807 and some long distance challenge matches.[23] It is again, though, not always made clear whether contests were for 'gentlemen's pleasure boats' or for working craft, though the internal competitions being increasingly mounted by sailing clubs for their own members – such as the Erith Sailing Society's annual plate – were clearly amateur events. The impression, too, is that competitive sailing spread more quickly around the country than did rowing, though again more local research is needed to confirm this. Certainly by the early years of the nineteenth century there were already popular venues away from London such as Southampton Water where there was, for example, the race from Cowes round the Needles buoy and back in 1799 and that for cutters sponsored by Mr Rose in August 1804. Among other known sites of racing in the first decade of the new century were Bristol, Yarmouth, and the Essex coast. There were doubtless more and the number was to grow rapidly within a few years.[24]

During the period itself, though, it was London that saw most of the boating action. No new sporting activities added more to the popular entertainment of the capital than those on the Thames, still the city's great highway. The activities on the river regularly attracted large crowds. There were said to be 10,000 for a waterman's race in September 1797, frequent references to the banks being 'lined with spectators' and numerous boats crowding the river itself for closer views of the proceedings.[25] Little wonder that sponsors found them a lucrative attraction even if money probably played a lesser part in them than in most other sports. Gambling is seldom mentioned – one of the few references to heavy betting is on the match between the Fox and Westmoreland Societies in July 1810[26] – but local support for watermen could sometimes become so fierce that attempts were made to interfere physically with the action. There could, of course, be much at stake, and not just the prize and the honour. The 1801 Doggett's winner, Curtin, it was reported, also 'obtains an exception from pressing during life,' no mean reward given the current state of His Majesty's ships and their constant greed for new crews.

There could too be other disappointments beyond fouled races. The wind might fall calm, the powerful Thames tides could ebb and flow at inconvenient times, or it might rain. On this occasion in 1801, for instance, there had to be a re-row since the original race had not begun until there was slack water, at about 8.00 p.m., after which the boats 'got foul' just above Westminster Bridge, by which time it was nearly dark and so young Curtin had to wait a further fortnight before securing his victory.[27] All in all, though, a new branch of sporting activity had made its successful entry and its growth would continue apace. Eventually the waterman's trade would itself virtually disappear as more bridges were built and modes of transport changed, but before then the water sports themselves would be tightly appropriated by new generations of class conscious sportsmen and become the vehicle for the most extreme of the definitions of professionalism.

The aquatic sports were no means the only channel for new sporting habits and enthusiasms. Bowling and the several small ball games enjoyed varying degrees of prosperity and progress. Those based on the age-old amusement of hitting a ball against a wall made the most decisive advances, becoming formalised into fives and, as a new game, into rackets. Meanwhile, tennis continued as a subdued minority sport, limited in its traditional mode by the relative rarity of specialised courts, bowls continued its long transmutation from high profile Restoration rowdiness to Victorian gentility, and skittles became the game of the tavern or its back garden. Golf in England remained confined to the band of enthusiasts picking their way round the picnic parties on Blackheath, and occasionally entertaining their own ladies there, with most Englishmen inclined to agree with the young Palmerston who took up the game while studying in Edinburgh, there not being enough to 'muster up' for cricket – he found it 'a poor game compared to cricket, but better than nothing.'[28]

Fives was in a state of transition. By the 1830s it was to become a highly popular spectator sport over a broad area of the south west, from Warwickshire down through into Dorset. It had also its developed London version based on the Fives Court in St Martin's Lane and other well established London venues such as the Rosemary Branch and Copenhagen House. The St Martin's Fives Court played such a central part in the history of pugilism that its original and continuing use for the ball game tends to be pushed into the background, though it had housed fives playing for nearly half a century before the pugilists saw it as a convenient place to hire for their exhibitions – their stage there was always a temporary affair, erected and dismantled again as it was needed. The court continued to house fives playing until its demolition in 1826, to make room for Trafalgar Square, and when the best players such as John Cavanagh were appearing the proprietor could fill his galleries at half a crown a head, much the same as it would cost to watch an evening's sparring.

At his death in 1819 the *Sporting Magazine* described Cavanagh as 'a fine, sensible, manly player.' He was instrumental in improving the skill levels of the game. He was much praised by Pierce Egan for his play, quickly spotting an opponent's weaknesses, deceptive in striking the ball, disguising his gentle shots, and tenacious in defence if he fell behind. Egan also praised the game itself as 'the finest exercise for the body, and the best relaxation for the mind,' and even taking into account his irresistible tendency to exaggerate – he praised rackets in virtually identical terms – fives was clearly a well-developed sport in the capital by the end of the period.[29] Egan's experience of it does not appear to have gone beyond London, or he may have felt that elsewhere the game was still too crude and unorganised to merit comment, an opinion that would at best be only partially true. The long standing playing of the game in Somerset churchyards, making use of the smooth hamstone walls at the base of the church tower, still continued but the constant struggles with parsons and churchwardens, combined with the possibilities for profit, prompted the erection of some of the most imposing early sporting structures in the country. It seems certain that most of the half dozen or so specially built fives walls, largely in the south-east of the county, were in use well before 1800, their design reflecting the local ancestry of the game, imitating as they do the church walls for which they substituted. The Fleur de Lys at Stoke-sub-Hamden has the most imposing example. The house, formerly the vicarage, had become an inn in the middle of the eighteenth century and it is probable that its fives wall, a huge buttressed structure at the end of its garden, was constructed at that time. Written records appear to be non-existent and all that can be said with certainty is that fives was flourishing in the area and that local innkeepers were actively promoting it as a profitable spectator sport – on or off the premises.[30] There are few other signs that the game was developing to this extent. At Richmond, in Yorkshire, it was quoted, along with cricket and football, as a favourite Easter activity,[31] but such comments are rare. It may well be that fives, in its varying stages of formality, was, like football, so taken for granted that it usually passed unrecorded. Like football, but in much more minor key, it did have those popular roots from which it would grow into one of the spectator sports of the Victorian era.

The opportunistic spirit and innovative drive that vitalised the sporting life of the age is well exemplified in the rise of rackets. At the start of this period, to judge from a 1788 illustration, it seems to have been occasionally played in tennis courts, using one wall with a chalked target area. Its emergence from Fives as a game in its own right was gradual. Bat-Fives, using a wooden bat approximating in size and shape to a tennis racquet, and adopted by some of the public schools, provided the intermediate stage, until the bat was superseded by an actual racquet. This ancestry is underlined by the

Typical of some half dozen similar fives walls in south Somerset, this at Shepton Beauchamp, built c. 1800, stood in what was the yard of the New Inn but is now private houses.

continuing use of the term 'Fives' to describe the game until well into the 1780s. Its surprising nurseries were the King's Bench and Fleet Prisons, where there were both suitable walls and gentlemen debtors with any amount of time and energy to spare. The King's Bench even had its acknowledged racquet master with his own hut in the courtyard, one Hoskins, a prisoner there for no less than 38 years. In the prisons there were others who came to live by the game, and there were spectators from both within and without to applaud their play. Indeed, the scene at the King's Bench became one of '*gaiety* and *dash*' according to Egan, with prisoners visited by 'some of the most elegant (*sic*) dressed females in the kingdom.' The game grew in popularity outside the prisons and the Fives Court in St Martin's Lane was yet again a ready made venue. It was here that Jem Belcher lost an eye playing racquets in 1803, effectively ending his boxing career. He was just one of the many pugilists to take up the sport and it was, for instance, as a racquets player that John Gully, in the King's Bench for debt, first attracted attention, before he put on the mufflers to spar with his visiting fellow Bristolian, the boxing champion, Henry Pierce.[32]

Early records of the game are, however, scanty. The names of a few notable players from the period are recorded – Lewis, Mackey and Smith, for instance, whose trials of skill attracted 'visitors of the most elegant description' to the King's Bench, while Cavanagh showed the same skill with both racquets and fives. There appear to have been few specialised racquets courts even in London. Egan mentions only three in the late 1820s and there is little sign at that stage of the game's adoption in any formal sense elsewhere in the country.[33] It remained a minority activity as did tennis itself, with its highly specialised and expensive court as well as costly balls and racquets. There was an outdoor form of the game though how systematised it was is hard to say. An intriguing comment in the *Sporting Magazine* in September 1793 suggests that it was developed enough to become a possible rival to cricket but neither style of the game aroused much interest. There were few courts left for play, the most notable being the Royal Tennis Court in Haymarket, where the Duke of Cumberland had promoted boxing matches in the 1760s and where there are some later faint signs of revival – it was here that Mr Cox, the proprietor, played a match against M. Marquise of Paris in 1815, presaging Waterloo a month later with a victory over the Frenchman. It was the first of several such Anglo/French encounters that were to follow in the sport during the next few years.[34]

Bowling, in its various forms, was another of those several popular sports that were undoubtedly played far more than they were recorded. If there is a predominant theme to be found in its history during this period it is one of ever sharper distinction between the bowling green and the skittle alley. Strutt noted of bowling that it was 'a very popular amusement' during his early life, acknowledged that greens were still to be found in 'most country towns of any note' but that only a few remained 'in the vicinity of the metropolis,' and concluded that 'none of them are so generally frequented as they were accustomed to be formerly.' As is often the case, Strutt's verdict seems somewhat questionable. There are numerous provincial indications of a thriving sport from the opening of a new bowling green in Plymouth in 1767 to the frequent sale notices later for inns which make a point of their possession of a green.[35] Nottingham's bowling greens increased in number, including a new one in the Park, opened in 1807. At Lancaster there were two, one on the banks of the River Lune and the other in the Castle Grounds for the use of the prison warders, while greens were once commonly attached to Birmingham inns, to judge from a sale notice for the Bowling Green Tavern, Holloway Head, in 1848 which spoke of the house having the only one still remaining in the centre of the city.[36]

The pressure on space in the centre of a city like Birmingham had been growing through the eighteenth century. It had gradually been whittling away, for instance, at the two acre croft that had once been attached to King Edward's School where eventually the railway would take over the site to house New Street station. Moreover, it was not only in the towns and cities that recreation spaces underwent change of use. Wordsworth recalled a small lakeside inn of his youth where he had played on the 'smooth platform' of a small bowling green 'through half an afternoon,' only to find later that it was gone, displaced by 'the Hall.'[37] The general absence, though, of much comment on bowls as a game almost certainly arises, as Malcolmson noted, from the fact that it usually took place at casual social gatherings. Although their names are lost, there must have been many bowlers who achieved the local fame of the 'well-known' Mr Yates whose death at the age of 89 was reported in 1794 and who had for over fifty years been a celebrated player on different greens around Bridgnorth. The nature of the game played by Mr Yates and other 'green' bowlers seems to have been a near ancestor of the modern game. On the other hand, those 'bowling' competitions taking place at wakes and revels were almost certainly some form of ninepins. Such contests were diminishing, and apparently more quickly even than the festivals to which they belonged. The clearest indication of the nature of the play involved comes from the advertisement for the Stonehenge Sports of 1781, where he 'that gets the most pins in three bowls' is to have the prize hat of £1 value – provided, that is, that enough contestants enter to cover its cost![38] Aiming at pins, though, was increasingly being seen as an alley game, and tending to be mentioned mainly in connection with the unproductive amusements of the idling working classes. It was, according to the *Sporting Magazine* in 1801, 'a favourite amusement' and so well known that a statement of its rules was unnecessary. It was a comment which could well apply to other widespread but little recorded play – such as football.[39]

Bowling was one old sport which continued to evolve during these years. Another was wrestling, which briefly enjoyed a national vogue as the chief combat sport for a few years in the later 1820s. It might for several generations appear to have lost out to the starker drama of the prize ring and to have been squeezed back into its celtic fringes, but it continued to flourish there unabated. Its highly publicised national revival came when the doubts and deceits of pugilism had finally become too obvious for even the most patient and forgiving to endure. In the late 1820s it would be wrestling bouts that were as likely to be set up as fist fights in Tom Cribb's tavern, and such wrestling venues as the Golden Eagle in Mile End Road, Chelsea's Wellington Ground, the Eyre Arms in St John's Wood or – most of all – the Eagle in the City Road became for several years the focus for the capital's leading combat sport.

Wrestling does, in fact, present the interesting example of a sport in transition at this time. The annual wakes and festivals in which it often played a prominent part were in steady decline but as its role here diminished it began to emerge in its own right, even if this emergence was predominantly as a regional sport. Mention of it as part of folk events becomes more occasional through the second half of the eighteenth century. Among the few later instances are those from Wiltshire – at the Stonehenge Sports in 1781, for a pair of buckskin breeches – and from Dorset, where it formed part of the royal birthday entertainment at Maiden Castle in 1798.[40] Wrestling also became less common at fairs. It was still surviving at the Chesham July Fair in Buckinghamshire in 1761 and a match is recorded at Thornborough

Fair in the same county in 1777 though there is little sign of wrestling later in this context. Even more pronounced was the diminution of gentry sponsorship, which had once been fairly frequent, with examples from 1737, 1740, 1751 and 1773.[41]

This did not, though, signal a permanent decline in wrestling, certainly in the main areas of its original popularity. By the new century it was moving firmly into the sphere of spectator sport as a competitive activity in its own right. The transition is well illustrated at Carlisle, where wrestling still persisted as part of the traditional Ascension Day celebrations in 1814, but it was, by then, also appearing as a major set piece, with large scale competition, at the town's race meeting, where it was at least as important to most of the spectators as the horse racing. In the same year the town also saw a contest, 'for a large purse,' between East and West Cumberland. In the south west there were also free standing wrestling competitions – at Falmouth there was 'one of the greatest ever known in Cornwall' in 1808 and there were competitions at, for example, both Saltash and Exeter in 1811, the latter a very substantial meeting with 41 matches fought among 12 players. Events such as these confirm the strong regional roots of the sport, and regional wrestling was still going from strength to strength. It was attracting crowds of over 10,000 in the west by the 1820s, when it was described as Devon's 'chief pastime,' and there had emerged two rivals for its championship in that county's Polkinhorne and Cornwall's Cann, whose competition aroused national interest.[42] It was only then that the sport made its wider impact. The Good Friday wrestling in London that is well reported through into the early years of the nineteenth century, was essentially an overspill from the north west, organised by the 'Society of Cumberland and Westmoreland Youths,' migrants to the capital from those parts. According to Egan, 'scarcely anything was heard of the sport during the remainder of the year, except in a private match or two.' It was as such private matches came to prominence and those in the prize ring lost all reliability, when wrestling had its heroes and boxing had none, that it became a nationally recognised spectator sport, its emergence from the fete and the fair accomplished. Egan was to report on its popularity 'amongst the admirers of athletic sports in the Metropolis,' so much so that proprietors of cricket-grounds, bowling greens and the like were presenting numerous silver cups to attract wrestling competitions.[43]

The search for sporting novelty and experiment also saw horse racing explore two new forms, one of which was never to strike deep roots in Britain, however much it flourished elsewhere, while the other was to have a very active future. These were trotting and steeplechasing. Trotting matches began to be reported from time to time in the new century – one at Manchester, for instance, in 1806, over 5 miles, for 200 guineas, and on which there was 'great bettings.' Similar highly staked matches became quite frequent[44] – but it is not always clear what style of contest they involved. There was both trotting in harness, pulling a light gig, and trotting with a rider. The former was generally preferred, but there were protests that it involved cruelty to the horse if races were of any length.[45] A similar craze, or rather the reappearance of a mid-eighteenth century fashion, when gentry had disturbed the Sunday peace on the roads with coaching races, was the interest in coach driving as a skill – and as a means of boisterous competition. The fashions for both tandem driving and trotting were also productive of many accidents and collisions and looking through the *Sporting Magazine* for 1827 produces a feeling of readiness for some new form of transport to meet the zest for speed![46]

Steeplechasing was still regarded as a curiosity. It had a dual ancestry, deriving from cross country matches on the one hand and hunt races on the other. There were isolated examples of the former from at least the mid-eighteenth century when Mr O'Callaghan challenged Mr Edmund Blake to a 4° mile match between their respective parish churches in 1752. The first true jump race, as against a match, may well have been that in Leicestershire in 1792 between three riders for 300 guineas stake money.[47] The other parent of modern jump racing was the hunt. While races for hunters became common both at established meetings and at those specifically mounted by the hunts themselves, they still seem to have been overwhelmingly contests over the flat. The remarkable exception is the reported construction of a hurdle course at Bedford in 1810, with eight fences, each 4 feet 6 inches high. As this is still the minimum height for a steeplechase fence it seems reasonable to regard this as one of true ancestors of jump racing.[48] Where cross-country races did occur they continued to be reported as strange events. In January 1804 it was 'steeple-hunting,' described as 'a curious horse race,' or, in the next year, as an 'Extraordinary Steeple-race' in East Anglia, involving three riders, 'a match which had excited much interest in the sporting world, and which among that community is denominated a Steeple-Race.'[49] They would soon be much more frequently noted – in successive months in 1820, for instance – and by February 1829 William Lyon of the Waterloo Hotel had built his grandstand at Aintree and within months was attracting 30,000 to his first races there.[50]

There is again one sport which was both well reported and also acknowledged as being unique to Britain. This was bell ringing. The enthusiasms aroused in 1660 when the church bells could be rung for pleasure and not just as a call to worship had never diminished and competitive bell ringing had flourished from the early in the eighteenth century. Malcolmson noted it at various fairs in Suffolk, Hertfordshire and Northamptonshire in the middle years of the century and a team of Sherborne ringers had actually gone successfully to Taunton assizes to claim the 'Six Prize-Shirts' they had won in a match at Mudford but had not received.[51] Such competition was frequent and flourishing, occurring for example in 1775 at Maldon in Essex, and at Bray and Hurst in Berkshire. Other Berkshire contests followed – at Swallowfield and Hurst again in 1780, and at Binfield in 1784 – and doubtless more local research will reveal many others elsewhere, such as the Whit Monday ringing at Stanmore in Middlesex in 1787. The contests had taken on a standardised form by this time, the prize going 'to the company that rings the best round peal, to continue fifteen minutes.' The prizes –

often hats – were relatively expensive in total as compared, for instance, with what was usually on offer for competitions at wakes and revels. They would have cost Thomas Matthews of the Six Bells Inn, the sponsor of the Bray contest almost £3, while at Hurst there were not only the 'six very good hats' for the winners, but also six pairs of gloves for those second and 'six handsome ribbands for the third best peal.'[52] The problems involved in judging unmeasurable mixes of the athletic and the aesthetic cannot have changed much over the years, whether the activity is coursing or ice dancing, and in bell ringing it was further complicated by having judges who could hardly avoid being to some extent advocates for their own men. It became recognised as an unsatisfactory means of reaching fair decisions and neutral umpires began to make an appearance. They seem to have been first mentioned in that advertisement for the 1789 contest at Warfield stipulating that there would be 'proper umpires' engaged, 'unconnected with any of the ringers,' though how widely and how quickly this new practice was taken up is uncertain. What is certain is that bell ringing contests remained popular, with what seems to have been a particular burst of activity (or at least of its reporting) in 1807, when there were competitions as far apart as London and Yorkshire.[53]

As well as competitions concerned with the quality of ringing there also began to be attempts to set records for quantity, for speed and stamina. It was a sport that came into particular vogue in the 1790s, another early aspect of that growing tendency to look to the statistical and the record. Grandsire triples and bob majors became as much the currency of sport as miles and runs. At Horsham in November 1794 a complete peal of 5040 grandsire triples was rung in 3 hours 3 minutes, only to be just bettered three years later by the Union Society of Newcastle and Gateshead (in 3 hours 1 minute) celebrating their new peal of bells at All Saints Church. There had earlier been, for example, much activity at St John's Church, Bromsgrove, where a team of ringers took 4 hours 15 minutes to ring a complete peal of Bob Majors – it was their second attempt on the same day, a rope having broken in the morning. They fared much better later in the year with a well publicised time of 3 hours 28 minutes.[54]

Bell ringing was one of the period's sports which appeared to be fading in the later years and which would enjoy only a subdued future, though the array of winning certificates on display in some bell towers even today indicates its continuing attraction to enthusiasts. It does offer a prime example of the fact that exactly the same physical action may or may not be classed as 'sport,' according to the context in which it occurs and the intent behind it. Ringing the bells to call the faithful to worship is one thing, ringing them in competition, whether against others or against the clock is another. So it is with various styles of killing wild creatures. Done in a group, and usually accompanied by a certain amount of ritual, it is likely to be accepted as a sport. Done by an individual it may be for the pot or for pleasure, or indeed for both. In shooting, for example, a whole complex of factors was operating. Improvements in technology have, over the centuries, always been widening the possibilities for the creation of new sports and improvements in the old. Surprisingly for an age of great technical innovation there are few instances of this having effects on sport during the period. The manufacture of small balls doubtless improved, but it awaited the arrival of rubber for its great stride forward, and skates probably benefited from the advances in metal working. One of the few examples of significant progress came, perhaps inevitably in such a military age, in the design and manufacture of guns. There were great improvements in the effectiveness of shotguns in the two decades following the introduction of Nock's patent breaching mechanism in 1787, culminating in the invention of a repeater rifle in the United States as the period drew to a close.[55]

Such developments were followed with interest, giving impetus to competitive shooting as well as further encouraging the propensity to slaughter virtually anything in the wild that moved and every bird that flew – herons, swans, larks, and even that eagle near Bishop's Stortford. The pheasant, as a poor low flyer, became a favourite target and, armed also with their new guns, more and more of the better off could feel themselves to be quite accomplished marksmen. They had their eccentrics. There were those city sportsmen who preserved their thrushes and sparrows on the suburban farm up the City Road. Better equipment, though, meant a new opportunity for competition and there were now many more shooting contests. The usual targets were released pigeons, suitably restricted to make them easier to hit. Among the recorded competitions were a match between eleven marksmen at North Cray, Kent, in 1801, where much betting was reported, and one on Ripley Common, Surrey, in 1809, remarkable because it was seen as a county contest between Bedfordshire and Buckinghamshire, involving three 'noted shooters' from each county and with 200 guineas at stake.[56] Shooting at fixed targets also came into vogue. Wagers over aiming at an orange with a pistol over 12 paces held perhaps an unsubtle warning to would-be duellists whose frequent appearance was a reminder that the human species itself was not immune to death by gunshot, a fate met, of course, by two of the age's most rakish sportsmen, Barrymore from a careless accident and Camelford from a careless challenge. The demands of wartime and the existence of so many men under arms was an encouragement to rifle shooting and there were numerous competitions for the military. In 1801, for instance, when guns were at the forefront of the country's attention, the proprietors of pleasure gardens were showing their loyalty by awarding silver cups for shooting matches, 'for the volunteer corps of the metropolis' at Ranelagh, and for 'Gentlemen Volunteers' at Bermondsey Spa, while news was being spread of a new mode of shooting game with 'air-rifles.' Nor were contests confined to the soldiery. There are signs of an established sport in the report of a match at Manchester in 1806, shooting at targets at 100 yards and for a wager of 200 guineas a side. Not only was there the common report of much betting, but the winner, Ainsworth, 'offered to shoot with any man in England for 1000 guineas.'[57]

The rearing and shooting of game birds became both sport and business on a substantial scale. From the start of this period there were large sums being spent on the rearing and protection of birds – £200 a year at Longleat and over £350 at Goodwood. The protection of these and lesser investments had been the motive for establishing the Game Association but as an effective national body it was confined to the 1750s and 1760s, when county associations began to replace it. Already large moorland areas in the north were being leased out for shooting and by the 1790s the battue system was being widely adopted, having the birds driven to where the guns lay in wait for them. The huge bags that resulted from a combination of this practice and the improvements in guns were frowned upon by purists like Colonel Peter Hawker who published his *Instructions to Young Sportsmen* in 1814, but this did nothing to deter shots like Osbaldeston from boasting of their hundred birds in a day.[58]

Fishing, on the other hand, had little of the competitive about it. It was still pursued for the pot or for individual pleasure and aroused little comment in any sporting context. Strutt was silent, noting only that he had nothing to add to what was already known of the pursuit. Commonplace as it was, the angler would find himself competing only with the fish, the gamekeeper, or – since it was a favourite Sunday recreation – Sabbatarian zealots. The only fisherman to find fame in the *Sporting Magazine* was John Kirby, the Keeper of Newgate, described in his obituary as 'a celebrated angler,' with much detail about his funeral but nothing else about his fishing. There were a few rare examples of otherwise respectable folk who seem to have made a sport out of poaching fish as well as fowl – the Ashley family of Tysoe in Warwickshire, for instance – but most illegal fishing was done for hunger or for profit. It was hunger, too, which could tempt fishermen such as the pastoral poet John Cunningham to a Durham river bank on a Sunday afternoon and to respond to the remonstrances of the portly cleric who came across him there with the comment that, from his appearance, if the reverend's dinner was likewise 'at the bottom of the river long with mine, you would angle for it, though it were a fast-day, and your Saviour stood by to rebuke you.'[59]

The line between 'sport' and other pursuits is hard to draw today. Its central territories may be easily recognisable but its boundaries are never irrevocably fixed. In the years around 1800 definition is all the harder. Sports and pastimes, games and gaming, amusements and pleasures, playing and entertainment, all merged into each other even more imperceptibly than they do now. The most profitable final view of the sport of this period may well be to see it in these terms, as just one aspect – an important and growing one – of an equally thriving, expanding, and totally diverse range of activities which were (the few professional sportsmen apart) distinct from daily labours and conducive to a myriad of satisfactions, some old and many new.

There could even be times when the work itself became a game. When 170 new gas lamps were installed to light the Halifax streets in 1807 there was a £50 wager that one man could not light them all within an hour. He did so in 45 minutes. Competition could often be related to work, but put into a sporting context – Essex ploughboys striving to turn the straightest furrow to win the prize pair of breeches in 1788, or the farmers and land-owners of the Bath and West Society already holding their annual shows and being well reported in the press.[60] Then there were the gooseberry shows in the north, with the three usual classes at Chester in 1796 – yellow, green, and white – and even more purely for pleasure, the numerous floral societies. Nottingham's 'Ancient Society of Flowerists' had been holding its annual shows since 1761 and some gardening societies had already become specialised. Bromsgrove, for example, was mounting its 'respectable florist meeting' in 1787 for 'auriculas and polyanthuses.'[61] Birmingham had its music festivals from 1768 and sport itself had its own art centre with the opening in 1807 of the Sportsman's Gallery, reflecting their fishing interest some years later in a painting by a certain John Constable, *Landscape. Boys Fishing*:

> The scenery is gay, true to nature, and pleasing to the eyes. The serious attention of the boys in preparing the fatal bait to delude the timid, but greedy inhabitants of the chrystal pond is hitted (sic) at with great skill by the painter.[62]

Animals could be a source of many new pleasures. It had become the age of the fancier. At the annual dinners of the Canary-Bird Society birds would be changing hands at up to 39 guineas each while pigeon racing was becoming a popular competitive sport. As well as flying them in straight races there were individual wagers every bit as idiosyncratic as those contrived by the pedestrians – to fly 40 miles in 12 hours, for instance, in 8 different five-mile trips from different parts of London.[63]

There were numerous and ever varying entertainments. The Astleys had brought a new dimension to the circus, with horses that could, for instance, dance minuets and hornpipes according to Horace Walpole.[64] Nor were the pleasures confined to London – the eighteenth century had been a great age of provincial theatre expansion while racecourse crowds in Yorkshire could watch with wonder as Mr Sadler's balloon soared above them. There could be the commoner sight of militia drilling, which could lure Sunday crowds away from the preacher or the macabre attraction of the public hangings, meant to be dire warnings of the price of crime, but treated as entertainment in much the fashion of horror movies. The Newgate fare in 1787 consisted of 12 in February, 15 in April and 10 in November, and new gallows were erected in 1805, 'the appearance of which are favourably spoken of.'[65] Many of the day's sights and pursuits were, however, happy ones, some shared across the board. There were the well known characters of the day who would look to sport for their relaxation – many to horse racing, Hazlitt to fives, Cruickshank to rowing and both of them to boxing, Byron as pan-athlete, and the stars of the theatre, multi-sided sportsmen and women, and when it was Kean who presented the cup to Tom Cribb on his retirement it was the champion of one stage acknowledging the champion of another.

And on a final quietly competitive note there was Mrs Howe's regular chess games with George III, never for more than a guinea a game, the only visitor with the privilege of using the same door to the palace as that used by the royal family itself.[66]

This very diversity that had elaborated the period's sporting and recreational experience is the feature that emerges most forcibly from examination of the evidence on the ground and some revaluation of its sporting significance is called for. Certainly some important accepted stresses have been wholly justified by this survey – the undoubted development, increasing sophistication and commercial orientation of the major sports of horse racing, cricket and pugilism, together with the growth of such relatively novel pursuits as fox-hunting, archery, rowing and sailing. These have regularly and rightly been at least noted by previous writers. On the other hand, what has consistently been understated – and indeed often entirely ignored – is the persistence of forms of play inherited from the past, of traditional recreational habits, and the frequent nostalgia for them where they had disappeared. Alongside fascination with the new, sporting enthusiasms were often directed with at least equal warmth to inherited pursuits which may have had little future but which enjoyed a vital present. Much of this old recreation still persisted and more of it was remembered. Parish wakes could still attract merrymakers from a wide local catchment area. Some had been wholly or partly taken over by commercial sponsors, some undergoing varying degrees of change by the addition of newer forms of competition and entertainment but still recognisably tied (even if it was sometimes artificially) to a past recreational scheme. There were still enough vigorous examples of local wakes in the 1830s to present problems of Sabbath breaking to the young and equally vigorous Lord's Day Observance Society. On the national scale, seasonal feasts and celebrations remained widespread, particularly at Easter and, above all, at Whitsuntide, all occasions for recreations which, with or without more modern flavourings, drew their inspiration predominantly from old communal practice. Moreover, as with precocious usage of the term 'annual' often to express a hope for the future rather than a description from the past, so there is evidence from time to time of the deliberate creation of the 'traditional' by an enterprising promoter – witness the 'country wake' at Mill Hill and the various 'Rural Sports' mounted by innkeepers. Theme park Britain has a long history and these were among the several evidences of the pastoral longings which were readily aroused in the expanding towns and cities. In town and country alike, though, there was great and certainly under-reported vitality in some of those sports which had few articulate defenders in their own day and proved too unattractive to be graced with chronicles of any significance from the first generation of sports historians, whose motives were invariably to elevate the status of their own particular pursuit. Yet it was the baiting sports, dog fighting, and, most of all, cock-fighting, that had their wide followings over these years. Unlike the newer organised sports these would be available virtually everywhere and often with considerable frequency. There is every likelihood, to put it at its lowest, that these older pursuits were enjoyed by more of the population than those drawn to the organised sport that has always caught most of the attention.

Other factors, and not merely the appeal of novelty, have worked to strengthen the emphasis on the more 'modern' elements in the sporting experience of the age. Some of the original blame does, as was suggested at the outset, lie with the otherwise totally worthy Joseph Strutt. If not always by specific denigration – and there was a good measure of that – by his tone and his omissions he was regularly implying that there was little worth much consideration in the inherited popular recreation that he recognised as still persisting. It was a bad start and since his day it has had few historians to come to the rescue though there can now be every expectation that the historical interest in popular culture will also bring its benefits to popular recreation. So far, the concentration has tended to be on suppressions rather than continuations. By contrast, other sports, those with future respectability, have had their profiles enhanced by their own historians. Their stories have been quite well publicised, if sometimes only sketchily detailed, but there has been little reliable, datable, or comprehensive recording of traditional recreational events. Even among the organised sports it has been those with a continuing history, those whose basic practices have proved morally acceptable to succeeding generations, that have been most fully celebrated. Although telling their story does not require their defence, there has still been no noteworthy history of cock-fighting, let alone of dog fighting or bull-baiting. It is not only in political history that the winners compile the records.

The absence of serious enquiry into the animal sports not only leaves gaps in our factual knowledge of events and practices but also, and perhaps more importantly, it diminishes our understanding of the way the contemporary mind operated in its sporting contexts. The all-pervading nature of the animal sports, the virtual impossibility, even for those who later came to oppose them, of growing up in these times without gaining extensive knowledge of their practices, made them an inescapable element in the playing experience of all, from future cricketers and boxers to bell ringers and ice skaters. So much that became common elsewhere, and in more admissible settings, derived originally from the animal sports – the count of ten, the ring that could still be so-called after it became a square, the knock-out competition, the matching of competitors by weight, the three day county match, for instance, and even their sheer frequency – that some sensitivity towards them is essential if a full appreciation of the more enduring play forms is to be achieved.

What also proves to be more complex than might have been expected is the influence of economic change. Commercialisation has tended to be seen as the enemy of traditional folk recreation, undermining its simple innocence and spontaneity, but the reality was, in fact, often quite different. If a sponsor – more likely than not an innkeeper – could find an existing feast or other long-established local celebration that he could latch on to and effectively take over then this was a much quicker and more convenient road to profit than setting up some wholly new and speculative venture of his own. He might spice up the proceedings with jingling matches, sack races or donkey races – but all in all he was as likely to be a preserver of past pleasures as their destroyer, as numerous newspaper advertisements demonstrate. On the other hand, the commercial promoter was more likely than most to have his antennae sensitised to changes in popular taste and be the readier to cater for what was already being recognised by others as well as Wordsworth as a new thirst for sensation, speed, excitement and spectacle. The new mood began to show itself in all the major sports, in different forms and in different intensities but none the less moving in a common direction. There were increasing numbers of shorter races for the younger, faster horses. The better boxers were nimbler on their feet, they were likely to be matched more evenly and more adept in their showmanship although in their sport it would take many decades to find an alternative means of finding a result other than by slow attrition and total surrender. Cricket, by contrast, had made great steps forward in its skills of both attack and defence while the new water sports all tended to go straight into direct and conclusive contests without the cumbersome heats that had usually marked earlier competition. Another beneficiary from the sporting mood of the later eighteenth century was the female sex. It is clear that women of the comfortable classes could if they wished – and many of them did – take some part in a range of sports from hunting to archery as well as having an involvement in their local races. Smock races, the continuing folk games and sports and, for the belligerent, the occasional pugilistic contest, all point also to continuing opportunities for the less privileged.

The example of women's sports activity, however, serves as a reminder that sporting development neither runs in some golden line of continual 'progress' nor indeed, where it does change, does so at some inevitable and consistent pace. The next fifty years or so of female sport were to be a period of restriction rather than expansion and other elements in the country's sporting life show similar unevenness. The changes it underwent during two short phases, in those highlit years around 1790 and the early 1800s respectively, in many respects outweigh in importance and innovativeness all that happened in the rest of the period. What produces these bursts of sporting activity – and indeed the extent to which they may appear in other forms in other periods is an interesting study of itself. A possible parallel, for example, might lie in the sudden wholesale collapse of all restraints on Sunday sport in the early 1980s. Without any change in the law relating to Sunday play there was the first Sunday Football League match (in 'normal' times, as distinct from during a fuel crisis) in February 1981, the first F.A. Cup tie a few weeks later, the first Sunday play in a Test Match in the summer and Sunday play at Wimbledon in the following year.[67] Just as in the earlier case in the late 1780s here again it was almost as if great change was just waiting to happen, like a bud unfolding, as soon as the season was right. In the second bout though, in the early 1800s, it was all much more complex and ambiguous, involving some changes that were out of the sporting mainstream, tangential activities that could seem to be daring reactions to desperate national circumstances, an indication, if any were needed, of the strength from time to time of political impacts on sport. Throughout the period, and for most of it in less dramatic but deeper seated fashion, the political climate was moulding attitudes to play and the long critical war years in particular had their clearly identifiable influences, from the status they gave to the fighting and hunting sports to the intensely nationalistic protectiveness afforded to what could be perceived as a manly game such as cricket.

Closing comments on the Georgian age as it drew to a close – in the ring, on the turf and the track, and perhaps even on the cricket field – had to be tinged with doubt. The advances made in sporting practice had been remarkable. In sporting theory, in the mental and moral climate of play, they were less notable and what had happened was in some respects to prove a false dawn of modernity. The creative years had put many of the external features for future growth in place, but at heart sport still half belonged to an unreconstructed older world. That world was changing. It was about to change more rapidly still, to become more astringent, to expect greater constraints, greater seriousness. Morally it would be more demanding. The restrictive ethics of the middle class would increasingly squeeze those tendencies to amorality that had pervaded both the aristocratic and plebeian ends of society, those two poles from which sport's greatest encouragement came. All this was happening at the very moment when sport itself was losing the moral structure on which it had largely depended for its good order and for what might give some species of respectability, namely its gambling code. English sport was still to go through several of its most difficult decades before its own ethical standards could manage to live alongside those accepted by society at large. That it depended so heavily on gambling was bad enough, but for the betting itself to become unreliable and more and more a source of criminality and corruption consigned most sport to the realms of the totally unacceptable in the minds of a growing majority.

There would need a whole complex of new circumstances for sport to be saved. Among them were to be the discovery of leisure by the rising middle and professional classes and their search for acceptable forms of play. With it was the gradual breaking of what had seemed an ineradicable link between contest and stake money and the ending of gambling's central role in sport. Finally, this had to be cemented into the later Victorian and Edwardian scheme of things by a particular school system which had discovered in play a selectively available route to all the virtues, private and civic alike.

For the time being, as the period neared its end in 1829 two contrasting experiences illustrate, as perhaps no others could, the Janus-like posture in which sport found itself, both looking back to an old culture and forward to a new one. On the one hand there was the decade's most unlikely hero in Billy the Dog whose speciality it was to kill a very large number of rats in a very few minutes. For month after month, over more than five years in the 1820s, his feats were celebrated in the pages of both the *Sporting Magazine* and *Bell's Life*. He was backed for £100 to kill 100 rats in eight minutes at the Westminster Pit in October 1823 and then bringing his time down to 6 minutes 13 seconds two months later. He was fighting a match against 'the Berkshire Rat-killer the next year as to who could kill 50 rats in the shortest time and he won easily. Several years later his appearance was being advertised 'for the satisfaction of several persons of distinction' to perform 'his wonderful feat.' It mattered little that the rats were probably doped, the excitement, the gore and the gamble on whether he would succeed in meeting the particular night's challenge could fill any London cockpit. And death was not the end of his fame. Stuffed, Billy the Dog was to ornament the bar at Tom Cribb's Union Arms for many a year, a reminder of the past, of days that were fading.[68] But there was another totally different event, one that looked forward to a wholly different world of sport. A race was arranged in 1829 between oarsmen from Oxford and Cambridge Universities. It was to be rowed for pleasure, for the satisfaction of competing. It had no dependence at all on stake money, the crews, many with distinguished careers in the church ahead of them, stressing their complete financial detachment from the outcome. The appeal of this first University Boat Race to spectators was immediate, drawing as many as 20,000 to Henley,[69] attracted by a contest between crews that would, as far as could be judged, be evenly matched and in competition which promised to be completely fair and open. It provided a signpost to the directions in which sport as a whole would have to travel to win its future.

Notes

1. See preface to *Lyrical Ballads*, 2nd edition, 1801.
2. Charles Lewis and Harold Kenworthy were early winners in NSS races and the first individual swimmers to find fame. *Sports History*, 9, 1986, p 16; 2, 1982, p 17
3. Ransome, *Wiltshire Returns*, p 584
4. Strutt, *Sports and Pastimes*, pp 73, 203; Whitaker, *Eighteenth Century Sunday*, pp 125, 131 and *passim*.; Bourne, *Palmerston*, p 7; Boulton, *Amusements of Old London*, II, p 239; *SM*, October 1805, p 48.
5. *Aris's Birmingham Gazette*, 4 June 1787 and frequently repeated; Birley, *Sport and the Making of Britain*, p 308.
6. *SM*, August 1793, p 316; July 1810, p 156. The race was in coxed four-oared wherries between the Fox and Westmoreland Boat Societies, but it is not clear whether there was any deliberate connection between the two events.
7. *SM*, January 1805, p 322; December 1805, p 156.
8. J Charles Cox, *ed.*, in Strutt, *Sports and Pastimes*, 1903 edition, p 76; Nigel

Brown, *Ice-Skating: A History*, 1959, p 3.

9. *SM*, February 1799, p 275; February 11, p 239. P. H. Dorrell, 'Early 19th Century Skating in the Fens,' *Sports History*, no.6, 1985, pp 23/4.

10. *Sports History*, 6, 1985, pp 23/4.

11. *Times*, 2,6 July 1787.

12. Strutt, *Sports and Pastimes*, p 78. Astley's 1811 race consisted of three separate stages, with breaks between them, *SM*, June 1811, p 141.

13. *SM*, September 1796, p 324; October 1805, p 47; February 1804, p 262.

14. *SM*, September 1809, p 260; *Times*, 19 September 1787.

15. *Report of the Police of the Metropolis 1816*, p 213. See also George, *London Life in the Eighteenth Century*, p 272; Whitaker, *Eighteenth Century Sunday*, pp 152, 163.

16. Cleaver, *History of Rowing*, p 70; Christopher Dodd, *The Oxford and Cambridge Boat Race*, 1983, p 38.

17. *SM*, November 1804, p 99; September 1809, p 260; June 1807, p 107. For earlier races with an 'apprentice' flavour see e.g. September 1796, p 324; October 1799, p 4.

18. Cleaver, *History of Rowing*, p 70; Holt, *Sport and the British*, p 22.

19. *SM*, September 1801, p 325. The Blackwall Regatta a month later included matches as well as races, October 1801, p 31.

20. *SM*, July 1810, p 156; August 1807, p 244; August 1809, p 217.

21. *SM*, September 1825, p 371; September 1827, pp 389-390; November 1828, p 65.

22. *Town and Country Magazine*, June 1776; Egan, *Book of Sports*, pp 355/6; *Times*, 12, 19, 20, 21, 27 July, 1787.

23. *SM*, July 1807, p 160. See also August 1797, p 278.

24. *SM*, May 1815, p 89; August 1804, p 266.

25. Strutt, *Sports and Pastimes*, pp 78/9; *SM*, September 1797, p 328. See also, e.g., October 1801, p 36; June 1807, p 107.

26. *SM*, July 1810, p 156.

27. *SM*, August 1801, pp 231, 258.

28. Bourne, *Palmerston*, p 15.

29. *SM*, February 1819, p 210; Egan, *Book of Sports*, pp 229/230.

30. See *Somerset and Dorset Notes and Queries*, 17, 1923, pp 75-77; Graham White, *Fives: an Old West Country Game*, South Petherton, 1980; Brailsford, *British Sport*, pp 68/9.

31. Clarkson, *History of Richmond*, p 294. At Birmingham the astringent Hutton ranked fives with 'quoits, skittles and ale,' *History of Birmingham*, p 130.

32. Julian Marshall, *Tennis, Racquets, Fives*, 1890, pp 43/4; Egan, *Book of Sports*, p 288; *SM*, July 1803, p 224; Brailsford, *Bareknuckles*, pp 36,75.

33. Egan, *Book of Sports*, pp 225-230.

34. *SM*, September 1793; Strutt, *Sports and Pastimes*, p 89; *Pancratia*, p 51; *SM*, May 1815, p 88.

35. Strutt, *Sports and Pastimes*, p 218; *Western Flying Post*, 4 May 1767. See also e.g. *Sherborne and Yeovil Mercury*, 19 February 1816.

36. Church, *Victorian Nottingham*, p 15; M. A. Speak, 'Social Stratification and Participation in Sport in Mid-Victorian England,' Mangan, *ed.*, *Pleasure, Profit and Proselytism*, p 52; *Birmingham Journal*, 5 February 1848.

37. Brailsford, *Sport and Society*, p 229; Wordsworth, *The Prelude*. Book 2.

38. *SM*, November 1794, p 108; *Salisbury Journal*, 2 July 1781. See also *Reading Mercury*, 12 June 1775; Goulstone, *Summer Solstice Games*, pp 54, 17, 83.

39. *SM*, June 1801, p 137. It was reported to be a common Birmingham pursuit, Hutton, *History of Birmingham*, p 130; Langford, *Century of Birmingham Life*, I, pp 257/8.

40. Goulstone, *Summer Solstice Games*, pp 16, 83, 89.

41. Malcolmson, *Popular Recreations*, pp 21, 57, 73. The lone example of tavern sponsorship found was the 1740 match at Highworth, Wiltshire.

42. *SM*, May 1814, p 94; October 1814, p 42; June 1808, p 143; September 1811, p 29; August 1811, p 241. It was very heavily reported for a few years in the 1820s, see e.g. January 1824, p 190; November 26, p 55; May 1827, p 59; July 1827, p 243; September 27, p 393. For Cann v Polkinghorne see also *DNB*.

43. Egan, *Book of Sports*, pp 321, 326.

44. *SM*, July 1806, p 198; June 1808, pp 103, 114/5. See also February 1811, p 252 – Hampton Court to Kingston for 50 guineas – and, for example, July 1819, p 195; August 1819, p 247; February 1820, p 247; March 1821, p 240; January 1822, p 192 and passim.

45. *e.g.* complaints of cruelty at 14 miles in an hour, *SM*, July 1820, p 172.

46. See *e.g.*, *SM*, March 1809, p 276 and, among many later examples, March 1821, pp 280/1; November 1821, p 86; January 1822, p 192, April 1822, p.49.

47. Ayres and Newbon, *Over the Sticks*, pp 11/12.

48. *ibid*, p 13.

49. *SM*, January 1804, p 170; December 1805, p 111.

50. *SM*, November 1820, p 89; December 1820, p 109; Reg Green, *A Race Apart: The History of the Grand National*, 1988, pp 9-10.

51. Malcolmson, *Popular Recreations*, p 24; *Sherborne Mercury*, 5 April 1737.

52. *Reading Mercury*, 15 May 1775, 22 May, 10 July 1780; 3 May 1784; 7 May 1787; *Chelmsford Chronicle*, 19 May 1775; *Reading Mercury*, 23 June 1755; Goulstone, *Summer Solstice Games*, pp 66/7 and for further references see p 108, n23.

53. *Reading Mercury*, 23 May 1789; *SM*, May 1807, p 90.

54. *SM*, November 1794, p 105; October 1797, p 48; *Aris's Birmingham Gazette*, 22 January 1787.

55. Hopkins, *The Long Affray*, pp 69/70; *SM*, June 1813, p 141.

56. *SM*, April 1801, p 216; December 1809, p 140.

57. *SM*, August 1801, p 259; September 1801, p 320; November 1801, p 84; June 1806, p 111. There was also a match between the Nottinghamshire Militia and the Honorable Artillery Company on that multi-sport venue, Stamford Racecourse, August 1811, p 241.

58. Munsche, *Gentlemen and Poachers*, pp 36, 44/45, 57-59; Birley, *Sport and the Making of Britain*, p 175.

59. Hopkins, *Long Affray*, pp 24/5; *SM*, February 1819, p 187n.

60. *SM*, June 1807, p 107. Parson Woodforde's *Diary*, Whit Monday, 1788; *SM*, December 1797, p 153.

61. *SM*, August 1796, p 274; Church, *Victorian Nottingham*, p 17; *Aris's Birmingham Gazette*, 23 April 1787.

62. *SM*, November 1807, p 60; May 1813, p 81.

63. *SM*, November 1806, p 95; May 1793, p 121; October 1795, p 22.

64. See *Letters of Horace Walpole*, *ed.*, Mrs Paget-Toynbee, Oxford 1903, pp xiii,

54-55.

65. *SM*, August 1814, p 227; September 1814, p 275; *Times*, 15 February, 27 April, 2 November 1787; *SM*, January 18095, p 224.

66. *SM*, January 1808, p 205.

67. For L.D.O.S interventions see Dennis Brailsford, 'The Lord's Day Observance Society and Sunday Sport 1813-1914, *The Sports Historian*, 16, May 1996, pp 140-155.

68. *SM*, October 1823, p 45; December 1823, p 165; March 1824, p 351; June 1825, p 186; *BLL*, 25 May 1828.

69. Cleaver, *History of Rowing*, p 53; Dennis Brailsford, 'Oxford and Cambridge: A Theme in the Early Growth of Modern Sport,' Sandra Kereliuk, *ed.*, *The University's Role in the Development of Modern Sport: Past, Present, and Future*, Edmonton, Canada, 1983, pp 42-45. See also H. M. Abrahams and J. B. Kerr, *Oxford versus Cambridge*, 1931.

SELECT BIBLIOGRAPHY

Journals consulted included the *Racing Calendar* (in particular for 1773 and 1797); *Sporting Magazine* and *Gentleman's Magazine*. Newspapers included *The Times, Bell's Life* in London, *Observer, Aris's Birmingham Gazette, Warwickshire Advertiser, Sherborne Mercury, Western Flying Post, Salisbury Journal* and *Dorchester County Chronicle*, and valuable press references also derive from Buckley, Goulstone and Malcolmson.

Contemporary Sources

Addison, Joseph, *The Spectator.1711-1714*.

Alken, Henry, *The National Sports of Great Britain*, 1821.

Armstrong, John, *The Art of Preserving Health*, 1744.

Assheton, Nicholas, *The Journal of Nicholas Assheton of Downham*, Chetham Society, 1848.

Bailey, N, *An Universal Etymological English Dictionary*, 2nd ed., 1724.

Bamford, Samuel, *The Autobiography of Samuel Bamford*, Vol.1, Early Days, ed. W.H.Chaloner, 1967.

Barnes, William, *Some Dorset Folklore by William Barnes*, ed. Theo Brown, St Peter Port, Channel Islands, 1969.

Barry, Edward, *A Letter on the Practice of Boxing, Addressed to the King, Lords, and Commons*, 1789.

Baxter, Richard, *A Christian Directory*, 2nd.ed., 1678.

Beckford, Peter, *Thoughts upon Hare and Fox Hunting*, 1781.
    The Minutes of the First Independent Church (now Bunyan Meeting) at Bedford 1656-1756, ed. H. G. Tibbutt, Bedfordshire Historical Society Publications, vol.55, 1976.

Blundell, Nicholas, *The Great Diurnal of Nicholas Blundell of Little Crosby, Lancashire*, ed.J. J. Bagley, Record Society of Lancashire and Cheshire, 2 vols 1968-1970.

Bourne, Henry, *Antiquitates Vulgares; or, the Antiquities of the Common People*, Newcastle, 1825.

Brand, John, *Observations on Popular Antiquities*, Newcastle, 1777; 1813 London ed.

Brown, A. F. J., *English History from Essex Sources 1750-1900*, Essex Record Office Publications, no 18, 1952.

Buckley, George B., *Fresh Light on Eighteenth Century Cricket*, Birmingham, n.d.
    Fresh Light on Pre-Victorian Cricket, Birmingham, 1937.

Burne, Charlotte S., *Shropshire Folk-lore: A Sheaf of Gleanings*, 1833.

Burton, Robert, *The Anatomy of Melancholy*, 1621.

Byrom, John, *The Private Journal and Literary Remains of John Byrom*, Chetham Society, 1854.

Byron, Lord, *Byron's Letters and Journals, Vol.1, In My Hot Youth*, ed. Leslie A. Marchand. Don Juan, 1819

Carew, Richard, *A Survey of Cornwall*, 1602.

Chafin, William, *Anecdotes and History of Cranborne Chase*, 1818, Wimborne 1991 edn., ed. Desmond Hawkins.

Chesterfield, 4th Earl of, *Letters to His Son and Others*, 1929 edn., ed.R.K.Boot.

Clare, John, *The Village Minstrel*, 1821
    Selected Poems and Prose, ed Eric Robinson and Geoffrey Summerfield, 1966.

Clarkson, Christopher, *The History and Antiquities of Richmond in the County of York*, 2nd edn., Richmond, 1821.

Clayton, John, *Friendly Advice to the Poor*, Manchester, 1755.

Clegg, James, *The Diary of James Clegg of Chapel en le Frith 1708-1755*, ed., Vanessa S.Doe, Derbyshire Record Society, 1978-1981.

Close, Francis, *The Evil Consequences of Attending the Race Course Exposed*, 2nd edn., Cheltenham, 1827.

Cone, Carl B., ed. *Hounds in the Morning: Sundry Sports of Merry England*, Lexington, 1981. (Extracts from the *Sporting Magazine*.)

Cope, George, *The Origin, Excellence, and Perversion of Wakes or Parish Feasts*, Hereford, 1816.

Cullen, William, *First Lines in the Practice of Physic*, 1776; Edinburgh, 1796 edn.

Darwin, Erasmus, *A Plan for the Conduct of Female Education in Boarding Schools*, 1797.

Defoe, Daniel, *A Tour Through the Whole Island of Great Britain*, 1724-1726.

Denson, John, *A Peasant's Voice to Landowners*, Cambridge, 1830.
    Miscellaneous Antiquities of Dorking, ed. J.L.Andr,, Surrey Archaeological Collections, vol.14, 1899.

Douch, Henry, *Hints Respecting the Public Police*, 1786.

Drakard, John, *The History of Stamford*, Stamford, 1822.

Eden, F.M., *The State of the Poor*, 1797.

Egan, Pierce, *Boxiana: or, Sketches of Modern Pugilism*, 1815-1829; 1821 edn., 3 vols.
    Pierce Egan's Book of Sports and Mirror of Life, 1832.

Ferguson, R.S., ed., *Kendal Book of Record 1575*, Kendal, 1892.

Fielding, Henry, *A Proposal for Making an Effectual Provision for the Poor.* 1753.

Gisborne, Maria, *An Enquiry into the Duties of the Female Sex*, 1797.

Godfrey, John, *A Treatise upon the Useful Science of Defence*, 1747.

Goulding, R.W., *Louth Old Corporation Records*, Louth, 1891.

Gray, Thomas, *Poems, Letters and Essays*, 1912 edn.

Hone, William, *The Every-Day Book*, 2 vols., 1825-1827.
    The Table Book, 2 vols., 1827-1828
    The Year Book 1832.

Howitt, William. *The Rural Life of England.*, 2 vols, 1838: 2nd ed. 1 vol., 1840.

Hutchinson, William, *A View of Northumberland*, 2 vols., Newcastle, 1778.
    A History of the County of Cumberland, 2 vols., Carlisle, 1794.

Hutton, William, *The History of Birmingham*, 1789.

Isham, Thomas, *The Journal of Thomas Isham, of Lamport, in the County of Northampton*, 1671-1673, ed. Walter Rye, Norwich, 1875.

James I, *Declaration of Sports*, in L.A.Govett, *The King's Book of Sports*, 1890.

Jenyns, Soame, *Disquisitions on Several Subjects*, 1782.
  Kendal Book of Record 1575, ed. R.S. Ferguson, Cumberland and Westmoreland Antiquarian and Archaeological Society, Kendal, 1892.
Langford, J.A., *A Century of Birmingham Life: a chronicle of local events, 1741-1841*, 2 vols., 1868.
Latimer, John, *The Annals of Bristol in the Seventeenth Century*, Bristol, 1900.
Law, William, *A Serious Call to a Devout and Holy Life*, in *Works*, 9 vols., 1762; Brockenhurst, Hampshire edn. 1893.
Lawrence, John, *A Philosophical and Practical Treatise on Horses, and on the Moral Duties of Man Towards the Brute Creation*, 2 vols., 1796-1798.
Lillywhite, F., *F.L.'s Cricket Scores and Biographies of celebrated cricketers, from* 1746, 1862.
Litt, W., *Wrestliana; or, An Historical Account of Ancient and Modern Wrestling*, Whitehaven, 1823.
Locke, John, 'Some Thoughts Concerning Education,' in H.R.Penniman, ed., *On Politics and Education*, Toronto, New York and London, 1947. Lord's Day Observance Society, Quarterly Publications, 1846-1848.
Lucas, Theophilus, *Memoirs of the Loves, Intrigues, and Comical Adventures of the most Famous Gamesters and Celebrated Sharpers in the Reigns of Charles II, James II, William III and Queen Anne*, 1714.
Marat, W., *The History of Lincolnshire*, 3 vols., Boston, 1814.
Mendoza, Daniel, *The Memoirs of the life of Daniel Mendoza*, ed., Paul Magriel, London, New York, Toronto and Sydney, 1951, p 55.
Misson, Henri, *M.Misson's Memoirs and Observations in His Travels over England, with some Account of Scotland and Ireland*, ed. John Ozell, 1719.
Mitford, Mary Russell, *Our Village: Sketches of Rural Character and Scenery*, 5 vols., 1824-1832.
More, Hannah, *Strictures on Female Education*, p 1779.
Mosley, Sir Oswald, *History of the Castle, Priory, and Town of Tutbury*, 1832.
Mulcaster, Richard, *Positions*, 1581; ed.R.H.Quick, 1888.
Nichols, J., *The History and Antiquities of the County of Leicestershire*, 2 vols., 1798.
Nichols, J.B., *Anecdotes of William Hogarth*, 1833. *Notinghamshire: Extracts from the County Records of the Eighteenth Century*, ed. K.T.Meady, Nottingham, 1947.
Nyren, John, *The Cricketers of my Time*, 1833; in E.V.Lucas, ed. *The Hambledon Men*, 1907.
Oliver, George, *The History and Antiquities of the Town and Minster of Beverley, in the County of York*, Beverley, 1829.
Osborne, Dorothy, *Letters of Dorothy Osborne to Sir William Temple*, ed.E. A. Parry, 1914.
Osbaldeston, George, *Squire Osbaldeston: His Autobiography*, ed.E. D. Cuning, 1926.
Owen, William, *An Authentic Account of the Fairs in England and Wales*, 1756 and later editions. *Pancratia; or, A History of Pugilism*, by 'J.B.', 1811; 2nd edn, 1815.
Parkyns, Sir Thomas, *The Inn-Play: or, Cornish-Hugg Wrestler*, 3rd ed., 1727.
Pepys, Samuel, *The Diary of Samuel Pepys*, ed. Henry B.Wheatley, 8 vols., 1904/5.

Pope, Alexander, *Essay on Man*, 1733.

Primatt, Humphry, *A Dissertation on the Duty of Mercy and Sin of Cruelty to Brute Animals*, 1776. Racing Calendar.

Richards, John, 'Extracts from the Diary of John Richards, Esq., of Warmwell, in Dorsetshire, 1679-1702,' *Retrospective Review*, I, 1835.

Saussure, C‚sar de, *A Foreign View of England in the Reigns of George I and George II: The Letters of Monsieur C‚sar de Saussure to his Family*, ed. Madame van Muyden, 1902.

   The Servants Calling; With some Advice to the Apprentice, 1725.

Shaw, Stebbing, *The History and Antiquities of Staffordshire*, 2 vols., 1798-1801.

   Shropshire Records: A full List and Partial Abstract of the Contents of the Quarter Sessions Rolls: 1690-1800, ed. Lancelot J.Lee, Shropshire County Council, n.d. 'Society for the Suppression of Vice, Proceedings,' *Edinburgh Review*, January 1809.

Somerville, William, *The Chace*, 1735.

   Hobbinol, or the Rural Games, 1740.

Spershott, James, *The Memoirs of James Spershott*, ed.F.W.Steer, Chichester Papers, no.30, 1962.

Stott, Joseph, *A Sequel to the Friendly Advice to the Poor of the Town of Manchester*, Manchester, 1756.

'An Archdiaconal Visitation of Stow,' ed. Joan Varley, *Reports and Papers of the Lincoln Architectural and Archaeological Society*, New Series, II, 1948.

Strutt, Joseph, *The Sports and Pastimes of the People of England*, 1801; reprint of J.Charles Fox 1903 edn., Bath 1969.

Troughton, Thomas, *The History of Liverpool*, 1810.

Tucker, Josiah, *An Earnest and Affectionate Address to the Common People of England, Concerning their Usual Recreations on Shrove Tuesday*, n.d. (mid-eighteenth century).

Uffenbach, Zacharias Conrad von, *London in 1710. From the Travels of Zacharias Conrad von Uffenbach*, ed. and translation W. H. Quarrell and Margaret Mare, 1939.

Walpole, Horace, *Memoirs of George II*, in *Works*, 1798. Letters of Horace Walpole, ed. Mrs Paget-Toynbee, Oxford, 1903.

Wedgwood, Josiah, *Letters of Josiah Wedgwood 1762-1780*, 2 vols.,

Wesley, John, *Journal of John Wesley*, ed N. Curnock, 8 vols., 1909.

Willis, Browne, *The History and Antiquities of the Town, Hundred, and Deanery of Buckingham*, 1755.

Willmott, B.M., *An English Community: Batheaston with S.Catherine*, Bath, 1969.

Wilson, George, *Memoirs of the Life and Exploits of George Wilson, the Celebrated Pedestrian*, 1815; also in *Sporting Magazine*, September 1815. *Wiltshire Quarter Sessions and Assizes 1736*, ed J.P.M.Fowle, Devizes, 1955. *Wiltshire Returns to the Bishop's Visitation Queries 1783*, Mary Ransome, ed., Wiltshire Record Society, XXVII, 1971, p 248.

Wollstonecraft, Mary, *A Vindication of the Rights of Women with Strictures on Political and Moral Subjects*, 1790.

Wood, James, *An Address to the Members of the Methodist Societies, on Several Interesting Subjects*, 1799.

Wood, John, *A Description of Bath*, 1765; Bath 1969 edn.

Woodforde, James, *The Diary of a Country Parson: The Reverend James Woodforde*, ed.John Beresford, 5 vols., Oxford, 1924-1931.

Wordsworth, William, *Preface to the Lyrical Ballads*, 1800 edn. The Prelude.

Young, George, *A History of Whitby*, 2 vols., Whitby, 1815.

Secondary Sources

Andrew, William, ed., *Bygone Derbyshire*, Derby, Hull and London, 1892.

Armitage, J, *The History of Ball Games* (in *Rackets, Squash Rackets, Tennis, Fives and Badminton*, ed. Lord Aberdare, Lonsdale Library, vxi, n.d.)

Ashley-Cooper, F.S., and Lord Harris, *Lords and MCC*, 1914.

Birley, Derek, *Sport and the Making of Britain*, Manchester and New York, 1991.

Boulton, W.B., *The Amusements of Old London*, 2 vols., 1890.

Bowen, Rowland, *Cricket: A History of its Growth and Development throughout the World*, 1970.

Brailsford, Dennis, *Sport and Society: Elizabeth to Anne*, London and Toronto, 1969. *Bareknuckles: A Social History of Prize-Fighting*, Cambridge, 1988. *Sport, Time and Society: The British at Play*, London and New York, 1991. *British Sport: A Social History*, 1992; 2nd edn., Cambridge, 1997.

Briggs, Asa, *The Age or Improvement 1783-1867*, London and New York, 1959; 1979 edn.

Brown, Ford K. *Fathers of the Victorians: The Age of Wilberforce*, Cambridge, 1961.

Brown, Nigel, *Ice Skating*: A History, 1959.

Browning, Robert, *A History of Golf: The Royal and Ancient Game*, 1955.

Burnett, John, *Sporting Scotland*, Edinburgh, 1995.

Burrows, G.T., *All About Bowls*, n.d.

Church, Roy A., *Economic and Social Change in a Midland Town: Victorian Nottingham 1815-1900*, 1966.

Clarke, John, and Critcher, Charles, *The Devil Makes Work: Leisure in Capitalist Britain,* Urbana, IL, 1985.

Clay, William K., *A History of the Parish of Waterbeach in the County of Cambridge*, Cambridge Antiquarian Society, 1861.
A History of the Parish of Milton in the County of Cambridge, Cambridge Antiquarian Society, 1869.

Clarke, Peter, *The English Alehouse: A Social History 1200-1830*, London and New York, 1983.

Cleaver, Hylton, *A History of Rowing*, 1957.

Clifford James, *The Young Samuel Johnson*, 1955.

Colley, Linda, *Britons: Forging the Nation 1707-1737*, New Haven, Connecticut, 1992.

Cousins, Geoffrey, *Golf in Britain: A Social History from the beginnings to the present day*, 1975.

Cox, Robert, *The Literature of the Sabbath Question*, 2 vols., Edinburgh, 1865.

Cumins, John, *The Hound and The Hawk, The Art of Medieval Hunting*, NewYork, 1988.

Cunningham, Hugh, *Leisure in the Industrial Revolution*, 1980.

Darton, F.J.Harvey, *The Life of Mrs Sherwood*, 1910.

Darwin, Bernard, *British Sports and Games*, 1940. et al.,
  A History of Golf in Britain, 1952.

Deuchar, Stephen, *Sporting Art in England*, New Haven, Connecticut, and London, 1988.

Dodd, Christopher, *The Oxford and Cambridge Boat Race*, 1983.

Dunning, Eric and Sheard, Kenneth, *Barbarians, Gentlemen and Players: A Sociological Study of the Development of Rugby Football*, Oxford, 1979.

Eliot, Elizabeth, *Portrait of a Sport: A History of Steeplechasing*, 1957.

Fittis, Robert Scott, *Sports and Pastimes of Scotland*, Paisley, 1891.

Ford, John, Prizefighting: *The Age of Regency Boximania*, Newton Abbot, 1971
  Cricket: A Social History 1700-1835, Newton Abbot, 1972.

Fulford, Roger, *George the Fourth*, 1935.

Gardiner, *English Girlhood at School*, 1929.

George, M.Dorothy, *London Life in the Eighteenth Century*, 1925; 1966 edn.

Golby, J.M. and A.W.Purdue, *The Civilisation of the Crowd: Popular Culture in England 1750-1900*, 1984.

Gourlay, A.B., *A History of Sherborne School*, Winchester, 1951.

Green, Reg., *A Race Apart: The History of the Grand National*, 1988.

Guttmann, Allen, *Sports Spectators*, New York, 1986.
  Women's Sports: A History, New York, 1992.

Hammond, J.L. and Hammond, Barbara, *The Town Labourer (1760-1832)*, 2 vols, 1917; 1949 edn.

Haynes, Alfred H., *The Story of Bowls*, 1972.

Harrison, Brian, *Drink and the Victorians: The Temperance Question in England 1815-1872*, 1971.

Harrison, Mark, *Crowds and History: Mass Phenomena in English Towns 1700-1833*, Cambridge, 1988.

Hendricks, Thomas S., *Disputed Pleasures: Sport and Society in Preindustrial England*, New York, 1991.

Hill, Christopher, *Society and Puritanism in Pre-Revolutionary England*, 1964.

Hole, *Christina, English Sports and Pastimes*, 1949.

Holt, Richard, *Sport and the British: A Modern History*, Oxford, 1989.

Hopkins, Harry, *The Long Affray: The Poaching Wars in Britain 1716-1814*, 1985.

Hunter, Sir Robert, *The Preservation of Open Spaces, and of Footpaths and other Rights of Way*, 1902.

Hutchins, J., *The History and Antiquities of the County of Dorset*, Westminster, 1868.

Jaeger, Muriel, *Before Victoria: Changing Standards and Behaviour 1787-1837*, 1967.

James, E.O., *Seasonal Feasts and Festivals*, 1961.

Laird, Dorothy, *Royal Ascot*, 1976.

Longman, C.J. and Walrond, H., *Archery*, New York, 1894.

Longrigg, Roger, *The English Squire and his Sport*, 1977.

Lyte, N.C.Maxwell, *A History of Eton College*, 1440-1875, 1875.

Malcolmson, Robert W., *Popular Recreations in English Society*, Cambridge, 1973.

Marples, Morris, *A History of Football*, 1954.

Marshall, Julian, *The Annals of Tennis*, 1878. *Tennis, Racquets, Fives*, 1890.

McKendrick, Neil, Brewer John and Plumb, J.H., *The Birth of a Consumer Society: The Commercialisation of Eighteenth Century England*, 1982.

Miles, Henry Downes, *Pugilistica: The History of British Boxing*, 3 vols., Edinburgh, 1906.

Mingay, G.E., *English Landed Society in the Eighteenth Century*, London and Toronto, 1963.

Mortimer, Raymond, *The Jockey Club*, 1958.

Munsche,P.B., *Gentlemen and Poachers: the English Game Laws 1671-1831*, Cambridge, 1981.

Murray, Geoffrey, *The Gentle Art of Walking*, 1939.

Murray, William J., *The World's Game: A History of Soccer*, Urbana, IL, 1996.

Onslow, Richard, *Headquarters: A History of Newmarket and its Racing*, Cambridge, 1983.

Paget, Guy, *The History of the Althrop and Pytchley Hunt*, 1938.

Parker, Eric, *The History of Cricket*, n.d. (Lonsdale Library, vol.xxx)

Perkin, Harold, *The Origins of Modern English Society 1780-1880*, London and Toronto, 1969.

Pimlott, J.A.R., *The Englishman's Holiday: A Social History*, 1947.

Plumb, J.H.,*The First Four Georges*, 1956.
The Commercialisation of Leisure in Eighteenth-century England, Reading, 1973.

Porter, Enid, *Cambridgeshire Customs and Folklore*, 1969.

Reid, J.C., *Bucks and Bruisers: Pierce Egan and Regency England*, 1971.

Rosenfeld, Sybil, *The Theatre of the London Fairs in the 18th Century*, Cambridge, 1960.

Smith, William, Morley: *Ancient and Modern*, 1866.

Stephen, Leslie, *History of English Thought in the Eighteenth Century*, 2nd edn., 1881.

Swanton, E.W., ed., *The World of Cricket*, p 1966.

Thompson, E.P., *The Making of the Working Class*, Harmondsworth edn., 1968.

Timpson, John, *Timpson's English Eccentrics*, Norwich, 1991.

Trevelyan, G.M., *English Social History*, 2nd edn., 1945.

Tuer, A.W., *Luxurious Bathing*, 1880.

Tyrrel, John, *Racecourses on the Flat*, Marlborough, 1989.

Vamplew, Wray, *"The Turf": A Social and Economic History of Horse Racing*, 1976
Pay up and Play the Game, Cambridge, 1988.

Walvin, James, *The People's Game: A Social History of British Football*, 1975.

Warner, Sir Pelham, *Lords 1787-1945*, 1946.

Weinstock, M.B., *Old Dorset*, Newton Abbot, 1967.

Whellan, William, *The History and Topographyof the Counties of Cumberland and Westmoreland*, Pontefract, 1860.

Whitaker, W.B., *The Eighteenth Century English Sunday*, 1940.

White, Graham, *Fives: an Old West Country Game*, South Petherton, 1980.
Whistler, Laurence, *The English Festivals*, 1848.
Whitfield, Christopher, *Robert Dover and the Cotswold Games: Annalia Dubrensia*, 1962.
Wigglesworth, Neil, *A Social History of English Rowing*, 1992.
Wigley, John, *The Rise and Fall of the Victorian Sunday*, Manchester, 1980.
Willey, Basil, *The Eighteenth Century Background*, 1934.
Wright, A.R., *British Calendar Customs*, 3 vols., 1936-1940.
Wymer, Norman, *Sport in England: A History of Two Thousand Years of Games and Pastimes*, 1949.

Essays and Articles

Birley, Derek, 'Bonaparte and the Squire: Chauvinism, Virility and Sport in the Period of the French Wars,' J.A.Mangan, ed., *Pleasure, Profit and Proselytism: British Culture and Sport at Home and Abroad 1700-1814*, 1988.
Brailsford, Dennis, 'Religion and Sport in Eighteenth Century England: "For the Preventing or Punishing of Vice, Profaneness and Immorality,"' *British Journal of Sports History*, vol.1, no.2, September, 1984.
Dorrell, P.H., 'Early Nineteenth Century Skating in the Fens,' *Sports History*, 6, 1985.
Hearl, Trevor, 'Polite Accomplishments: A Forgotten Heritage in British Physical Education,' McNair, David, and Parry, Nicholas A., *Readings in the History of Physical Education*, Hamburg, 1981.
Judd, Mark, 'The oddest combination of town and country: popular culture and the London Fairs 1800-60,' Walton, John K. and Walvin, James, *Leisure in Britain 1730-1939*, Manchester, 1983.
Poole, Robert, 'Oldham Wakes,' Walton and Walvin, *op. cit.*
Reid, Douglas A., 'The Decline of Saint Monday 1766-1876,' *Past and Present*, 71, 1976. 'Beasts and brutes: popular blood sports c.1770-1860,' Richard Holt, ed., *Sport and the Working Class in Modern Britain*, Manchester and New York, 1990.
Speak, M.A., 'Social Stratification and Participation in Sport in Mid-Victorian England,' Mangan, ed., *op. cit.*
Thompson, E.P., 'Time, Work-Discipline and Industrial Capitalism,' *Past and Present*, 38, 1967.
Tranter, N.L., 'The Patronage of Organised Sport in Central Scotland 1820-1900,' *Journal of Sport History*, vol.16, no.3, winter 1989.
Vamplew, Wray, 'Sport and Industrialisation: An Economic Interpretation of the Changes in Popular Sport in Nineteenth Century England,' Mangan, ed., *op. cit.*
Wigley, E.A., 'A Simple Model of London's Importance in Changing English Society and Economy 1650-1750,' *Past and Present*, 37, July 1967.

Index